T5-CWM-008

The Philosophy of

JONATHAN EDWARDS

The Philosophy of

JONATHAN EDWARDS

From His Private Notebooks

Edited by

HARVEY G. TOWNSEND

GREENWOOD PRESS, PUBLISHERS
WESTPORT, CONNECTICUT

Library of Congress Cataloging in Publication Data

Edwards, Jonathan, 1703-1758.
The philosophy of Jonathan Edwards from his private notebooks.

Reprint of the 1955 ed., issued in series: University of Oregon monographs. Studies in philosophy, no. 2.
Includes bibliographical references.
1. Philosophy. I. Title. II. Series: Oregon. University. University of Oregon monographs. Studies in philosophy, no. 2.
B870.A5 1972 191 72-7503
ISBN 0-8371-6511-3

UNIVERSITY OF OREGON
MONOGRAPHS

Studies in Philosophy

No. 2. September 1955

Originally published in 1955 by the University of Oregon, Eugene

Reprinted with the permission of the University of Oregon

Reprinted by Greenwood Press,
a division of Williamhouse-Regency Inc.

First Greenwood Reprinting 1972
Second Greenwood Reprinting 1974

Library of Congress Catalog Card Number 72-7503

ISBN 0-8371-6511-3

Printed in the United States of America

Table of Contents

Introduction

In the heritage of American thought the work of Jonathan Edwards will always have a large place. In judging the historical importand of any system of thought, nothing can be more irrelevant than the observation that it is no longer in style. The importance of Edwards in the history of American philosophy is to be measured rather by the manifest influence he has had and even more by the range, depth, and security of his hold on the philosophical ideas and methods of his own time. When judged by either of these tests, Edwards is found to be a great American philosopher.

It is no part of the present purpose to trace the influence of Edwards on American culture. None of my readers are likely to doubt that it was very great. What is not commonly known and accepted, however, is that Edwards was an eminent philosopher in terms of the standards of eighteenth-century thought. Considering his isolation, and the consequent poverty of opportunity, he had an astonishing acquaintance with current thought. His home preparation for college in the family of a clergyman and his college training in preparation for leadership in the New England church conspired to furnish him with a solid background of classical learning. But it was the peculiar bent of his mind that subordinated this cultural background to an interest in the science and philosophy of his own day—the first half of the eighteenth century.

When he entered Yale College in 1716 at the age of thirteen, the two great names of the English intellectual world were probably Locke and Newton. He became acquainted with them at once, and they so fired his imagination that he may reasonably be said to have learned his philosophy from Locke and his science from Newton. Many years after college, according to his first biographer, Samuel Hopkins, "Taking that book [Locke's *Essay*] into his hand, upon some occasion, not long before his death, he said to some of his select friends who were then with him. That he was beyond expression entertain'd and pleas'd with it, when he read it in his youth at college; that he was as much engaged, and had more satisfaction and pleasure in studying it, than the most greedy miser in gathering up handfulls of silver and gold from some new discovered treasure."[1] Locke's *Essay* had been known to the

[1] *The Life of the late Reverend, Learned and Pious Mr. Jonathan Edwards, etc.*, 1765, p. 4.

learned world for a quarter of a century, but even so it is remarkable that a thirteen- or fourteen-year-old boy in a provincial colonial college should find it and make it the cornerstone of his intellectual life. It is reasonable to suppose that he turned over the pages again and again, noting the topics, method, and style and almost unconsciously becoming interested in whatever had interested Locke. He probably learned for the first time the names of some of the authors to whom Locke refers. And he must have discussed Locke's ideas eagerly with any who could share them. But more than all else he pondered alone over the vast intellectual world here first opened to his eager young mind.

Everything in the philosophy of Edwards resembling the thought of Bishop Berkeley can be accounted for without the supposition that he was acquainted with Berkeley's writing, by the simple hypothesis that he was led to his conclusions by reading and reflecting upon Locke as a passionate young Christian would reflect. There is no reason to believe that he knew anything of Berkeley's philosophy until long after he had read Locke;[2] but it is certain that he did have some acquaintance with English Platonists—More, Cudworth, John Smith, Norris, and probably others—directly or indirectly. He might have found out something of Arthur Collier's *Clavis Universalis,*[3] but whether he did or not the theological lore with which he was acquainted from his childhood and in which he lived and breathed during his whole life was fit soil in which the seeds of Locke yielded a harvest of Platonic or Neoplatonic idealism.

As a matter of fact there would have been less speculation on Edwards' debt to Berkeley if a more-adequate statement of his views had been generally available. For it is only in two or three isolated passages that the philosophy of Edwards resembles that of Berkeley, or at least that of Berkeley's *Principles.* There is indeed a family resemblance between Edwards and the Berkeley of the *Siris;* but such a resemblance would hardly have suggested to anyone that Berkeley was the source of Edwards' idealism. The *Siris* was not published until 1744, which was nearly a generation after Edwards had formulated his views. The resemblance would more probably have suggested a common ancestry; for it is in the *Siris* that Berkeley most nearly

[2] In this connection it ought to be remembered not only that the Jeremiah Dummer collection of books, which was the Yale Library when Edwards was a student there, contained no Berkeley title, but also that the books given by Berkeley to Yale in 1733 included "of Berkeley's own works only *Alciphron.*" See A. C. Fraser, "The Life and Letters of Berkeley," in *The Works of George Berkeley, D.D.*, 1871, vol. 4, p. 194, n. 3.

[3] See John H. McCracken, "The Sources of Jonathan Edwards's Idealism," *Philosophical Review,* vol. 11, 1902, pp. 26-42.

approaches the Platonic tradition of idealism and it is unmistakably to that tradition that Edwards belongs.

In order to account for the Platonism of Edwards it is not even necessary to suppose that he had any extensive firsthand knowledge of Plato's works.[4] He often quotes Plato and refers to him and his doctrines with approval; but an examination of such passages shows quite clearly that his knowledge of Plato was fragmentary and usually indirect. He came by his Platonism through the long line of Christian scholars from St. Augustine to the Cambridge Platonists. His debt to them and to Locke makes it entirely unnecessary to suppose that he owed much to Bishop Berkeley.

A second major influence in the formation of the philosophy of Edwards has been too commonly neglected. I refer to works in natural science and specifically to those of Sir Isaac Newton.[5] When Edwards entered Yale in 1716 he had access to one of the few copies of the *Principia* then in America.[6] It was one of the first two or three to come to America. It was a copy of the second edition and came to the Yale Library as a gift from the author within a year of its publication in 1713.[7] While it is not recorded that Edwards was delighted with the *Principia* as he had been with the *Essay,* there is unmistakable evidence that it greatly influenced him. Indeed, it is probable that he was acquainted with Newton before he discovered Locke. For his first attempt at philosophical writing was the little essay *Of Being* and the following speculations on space, gravitation, and atom.[8] Writing in his diary on February 12, 1725, Edwards says, "The very thing I now want, to give me a clearer and more immediate view of the perfections and glory of God, is as clear a knowledge of the manner of God's exerting Himself, with respect to spirits and mind, as I have, of His operations concerning matter and bodies."[9] The statement plainly

[4] In the Dummer catalogue we find *Platonis opera omnia Graece et Latine, fol.* In the absence of certain identification, it is possible, even probable, that the edition was the famous one by H. Stephanus, in three volumes, published in 1578. It is not certain that Edwards had access to this work, however, since 260 of the books of this collection were lost in the transfer of the college from Saybrook to New Haven. See F. B. Dexter, *Documentary History of Yale University,* 1916, p. 160; see also *Papers in Honor of Andrew Keogh,* 1938, p. 480.

[5] See J. H. Tufts, "Edwards and Newton," *Philosophical Review,* vol. 49, 1940, pp. 609ff.

[6] James Logan had a copy of the *Principia* in Pennsylvania in 1708. See Frederick E. Brash, "James Logan, a Colonial Mathematical Scholar, and the First Copy of Newton's *Principia* to Arrive in the Colony," *Proceedings of the American Philosophical Society,* vol. 86, 1943, pp. 3ff.

[7] Frederick E. Brash, "Newton's First Disciple in America," in *Sir Isaac Newton, 1727-1927, a Bi-Centenary Evaluation of his Work,* 1928, p. 315; see also *Papers in Honor of Andrew Keogh,* 1938, p. 464.

[8] Below, pp. 1-20.

enough records the order in which these two aspects of philosophy appeared in his experience. He did not thereafter lose interest in either of them, although his interest in "spirits and mind" came to be paramount. It is to his early interest in "matter and bodies" that we must trace one of the fundamental beliefs which he held throughout his life —that the physical world is the direct expression of God's being and nature, and therefore that physical science is the source of man's natural knowledge of God.

It is remarkable that Newton should have found so zealous a disciple in a far-away frontier school at a time when he was getting scant hearing in the great universities of his own country. Cajori quotes Hodlay as saying that "Rohault was still the Cambridge textbook in 1730, three years after the death of Newton and forty-three years after the appearance of Newton's *Principia*."[10] Making allowance for the fact that a textbook in use does not prove that another book setting forth a rival theory was unknown or unappreciated, it is nevertheless noteworthy that during Newton's lifetime Edwards was poring over the *Principia* in Yale College. Perhaps it was the simplicity and lack of intellectual sophistication at Yale which opened the door to Newton. The notorious rivalries and jealousies connected with Newton's work when it appeared in Europe were remote indeed from New Haven. There were probably no confirmed Cartesians there to defend the theory of vortices and no partisans of Leibnitz to defend his claim to the invention of the calculus. To the young Edwards it was enough that here was a book of transcending interest to satisfy his hunger for a knowledge of God's world.

We may reasonably suppose that it was the third part of Newton's book, "The System of the World," which caught and held the attention of Edwards. Indeed it was that part which interested the majority of readers. The records show that many saw in Newton's system of the world alarming atheistical and antireligious implications. Not so, Edwards. By temperament and early training he was already a rationalist. It seems to have been natural to his mind to suppose that the world is a completely rational system, plan, scheme, purpose. Whatever else he may have found in Newton, he must have found confirmation and strengthening of his natural inclination.

Rationalism is not the whole of Edward's philosophy but it is the

---

[9] *The Works of President Edwards with a Memoir of his Life,* 10 vols., 1829-1830, edited by Sereno E. Dwight, vol. 1, p. 105. Unless otherwise indicated, all references hereafter to the works of Edwards are to the Dwight edition.

[10] *Sir Isaac Newton's Mathematical Principles of Natural Philosophy and his System of the World,* with an historical and explanatory appendix by Florian Cajori, 1934, p. 631.

basis of it. The absolute reign of universal law was the presupposition of all his speculations and the object of his most ecstatic religious devotions. It was the relentless logic of Edwards to include man and all his works within the universal order. Such thorough-going rationalism is at least one of the primary sources of the distinctive problems of philosophy; for philosophy is more than being a man—it is an attempt to understand him. Edwards' attempt to understand man resulted in making man a subordinate part of the rational order. The exaltation of God, His infinite majesty, wisdom, and power, are in dramatic contrast with man's littleness, ignorance, and folly. Men are caught in the web of time, bound by the laws of their finitude. This extreme rationalism was met, both within the church and outside of it, by a strong revulsion of feeling. After Edwards the main tendency of American philosophy exalted man rather than God. The world was represented as plastic, disordered, unfinished, a challenge to Yankee shrewdness, ingenuity, and clever devising.

Which of these rival hypotheses is true does not depend upon which is ascendant in any time or place, if the rise and fall of theories is itself a part of rational order. At least Edwards would have supposed so. For, though he would hardly have subscribed to an economic determination of history, he certainly had no doubt that it was fully determined by divine decree.

Such a theory of human life is unlikely to be popular in any age; but it was especially unpalatable to the 'romantic' temper of the great American adventure. The spirit of that adventure was freedom. To men flying from the restraints of church and state, a rationalistic philosophy seemed new bondage. There is a latent suspicion in the mind that the reign of universal law precludes the attainment of man's dearest desires. If all things, including man himself, are bound by laws (whether of kings, of nature, or of God makes no difference), how can we hope to transform the world into the pattern of our dreams?

A philosophy like that of Edwards may seem to depress the spirit and weaken the resolution. It enjoins humility and resignation; it requires us to purge our minds of vanity and ignorance, and offers as a reward only submission. It is a grim view of human life, frought with labor, discipline, and tragedy. Its truth alone could commend it. But such was the philosophy of Edwards, and it was the supposed truth of it which commended it to him. The contemplation of the tragic character of life, however, did not in fact lead him to despair; for, like Spinoza, he found a promise of salvation in the knowledge of a joyful participation in the rational order.

Anyone who examines the literature of American philosophy will discover that there is a tantalizing lack of printed source materials for the philosophy of Edwards. There is no lack of words and pages of words but there is a lack of a cohesive body of his philosophical doctrines. The standard editions of his works were prepared in the spirit of that tradition of ecclesiastical controversy in which Edwards had, indeed, lived and died but which has very little interest to present-day students of philosophy. In these editions the philosophical doctrines are overshadowed by the great bulk of other material. The result is that interest in Edwards has mainly taken the form of exhibiting him in popular literature as a stock example of puritanical religiosity. Perhaps nine people out of ten who know anything about him at all think that he was a benighted Malvolio who preached hell fire and the damnation of infants. To such he is a straw man, a kind of personal devil. A recent biography by Miss Winslow is bound to secure for Edwards, the man, something like justice in popular knowledge and esteem.[11] But there is also need of a condensed and faithful report of Edwards, the thinker. The present volume is a contribution to that end.

Edwards has often been praised for his relentless logic. But few have been able to say what his views of logic were. What was his theory of knowledge—was it Lockean or Kantian, both or neither? We have often been reminded of his pantheism, but we have lacked available materials for a sober estimate of it. We have been told that Edwards agreed with Bishop Berkeley, but no one could say with confidence how his theory resembles Berkeley's and in what respects the two differ.

The most-complete and definitive edition of the works of Edwards appeared in 1829-30 in ten volumes edited by Sereno E. Dwight. And the most-important thing about this edition for the student of philosophy is that it included some previously unpublished material from manuscripts. In the first volume Dwight not only presented a careful and extensive biography of the man but nearly one hundred pages from a youthful manuscript *The Mind* and other material which the editor called *Notes on Natural Science*.[12] This publication made many aware for the first time of the voluminous manuscripts left by Edwards.[13] These manuscripts were subsequently described in some detail, and various excerpts have been published in widely separated times and places.

---

[11] *Jonathan Edwards, 1703-1758,* by Ora Elizabeth Winslow, 1940.

[12] Vol. 1, pp. 664-761.

[13] The bulk of the materials are in the Yale Library. A good description of them, "On the Manuscripts of Jonathan Edwards," by Franklin B. Dexter may be found in *Massachusetts Historical Society Proceedings,* 2nd series, vol. 15, 1902, pp. 1-16. A briefer listing of the manuscripts, both at Yale and elsewhere, is given by Miss Winslow, *op. cit.*, pp. 373ff.

But even before the Dwight publication some attempt had been made to print the unpublished writings of Edwards. Two works of the greatest philosophical importance appeared in 1765: *A Dissertation on the End for which God created the World* and *A Dissertation on the Nature of True Virtue.* Later, in 1793 and 1796, two volumes were edited and published by John Erskine in Edinburgh, Scotland. These volumes were drawn from the manuscript known as the *Miscellanies.*[14] They did not, however, add much to our knowledge of the philosophy of Edwards but merely continued the tradition of theological controversy. They are not generally accessible and are, moreover, textually unreliable. About the middle of the nineteenth century a new and complete edition of the works of Edwards was projected,[15] but because of misunderstandings and other difficulties was never carried through to publication.

The present volume is intended to make available, mainly from unpublished material, a coherent body of the philosophical opinions of

---

[14] *Miscellaneous Observations on Important Theological Subjects* and *Remarks on Important Theological Controversies.* These two volumes are indeed taken from the manuscript but the editor destroyed all the marks by which the extracts could be traced to their original. He took great liberties with the text, disregarded all chronological order, patched together widely separated excerpts, and added whatever connections or conjunctions seemed appropriate to him. The first volume is printed as three parts of unequal length; the second volume is divided into seven chapters. When Dwight republished this material in his edition of 1829 he took further liberties with the text of Erskine's books. He omitted the quotations made by Edwards and printed by Erskine, and divided the first volume into chapters; but more important than all else he further revised the text to bring it into conformity with his notion of style. He defended his policy in the following words, "especially from a due regard to the author's reputation which is deservedly high—it is obviously necessary, that a selection more choice and scrupulous be now made." Vol. 7, p. 198.

[15] The history of this episode in the annals of the Edwards manuscripts is not fully recorded; but we do know that a plan for a complete edition of his works was made by his heirs who had the manuscripts at that time, and that the transactions involved the irresponsible actions of the astonishing Alexander B. Grosart. He took some of the manuscripts with him to Scotland. He never rendered a satisfactory accounting for some of them, and it may be that the priceless document called *The Mind* was lost at that time. He published a volume, *Selections from the Unpublished Writings of Jonathan Edwards,* Edinburgh, 1865. It is rare. *A Catalogue of an Exhibition held in the Day Missions Library Illustrating Congregationalism before 1800,* New Haven, 1915 p. 28, says that the principal source of the Grosart volume is Edwards' interleaved Bible, the manuscript of which is at Yale. It was during this period that the impression gained currency that Edwards had expressed some esoteric theological heresies in his private papers. As far as can be judged by extant manuscripts, the impression has no foundation. His doctrine of the Trinity, for example, is neither historically strange nor biographically astonishing. See George P. Fisher, *An Unpublished Essay of Edwards on the Trinity,* 1903, Preface.

Edwards to supplement the works already accessible in the standard editions.

The documents from which I have compiled the text are three: (1) the manuscript which was published by Dwight in 1829 under the title, *Notes on Natural Science;*[16] (2) Dwight's printed text of the work entitled *The Mind;*[17] (3) the manuscript known as the *Miscellanies.* Each of these requires some comment.

(1) The manuscript of the *Notes on Natural Science* is in the Andover Newton Theological Library at Newton Centre, Massachusetts. It has been described more than once; I have found it to be approximately as it is described by Dwight[18] and Smyth.[19] It bears no title, the one by which it is known apparently having been given to it by Dwight.[20]

It is not, in my opinion, a single manuscript but a composite of three, loosely related. The evidence for this opinion is diffuse and perhaps not conclusive. As a whole the manuscript consists of thirty-two pages on folded foolscap, sewed together in three distinct parts. The handwriting strongly suggests that the three parts belong to the same youthful period of Edward's life, but they have little internal connection with one another and it seems doubtful that the author considered them as a unit.

The first part consists of four pages on two half sheets of foolscap, tied together with a coarse thread. It contains a brief essay titled *Of Being,* together with what probably is a footnote—"Of the Prejudices of Imagination"— and seven supplementary notes. The handwriting is very small but very legible. I take this to be the work of the young Edwards and probably his first attempt at philosophical writing. Numerous references are found elsewhere in his manuscripts, particularly in *The Mind* and the *Miscellanies,* to a demonstration of the necessity and character of being. These references point unmistakably to this essay, *Of Being,* as the point of departure of his philosophical journey.[21]

The second part consists of sixteen pages on four folded sheets of foolscap—three of them infolded in the fourth and stitched together with thread in such a way as to make a thin book. On four of the first six pages there is a demonstration of the atomic properties of matter.

---

[16] Vol. 1, pp. 702-761. In Edwards' idiom it would have been "natural philosophy" rather than "natural science."

[17] Vol. 1, pp. 664-702.

[18] Vol. 1, pp. 41-43.

[19] Egbert C. Smyth, "Some Early Writings of Jonathan Edwards," *Proceedings of the American Antiquarian Society,* n.s., vol. 10, 1895, pp. 218ff.

[20] Vol. 1, p. 41.

[21] This theory is also supported by a study of the handwriting, spelling, and style by Ebgert C. Smyth in the article cited in n. 19.

Pages 4 and 6 are blank. The remainder of the thin book contains two independent lists of topics and propositions on which Edwards apparently proposed to write as opportunity offered.[22] Most of the topics have only indirect philosophical importance, however interesting they may be in themselves.[23] I have therefore included only the first four pages, in which the author discusses atoms. Although there is no direct reference in these four pages to the essay *Of Being,* the subject matter is so congruent as to make it likely that they followed, at least psychologically, the writing of the first essay.

The third part of the document consists of twelve pages, i.e., three sheets of folded foolscap with two infolded in the third. It contains miscellaneous items on topics in natural science. Some of the items are numbered, though certainly not in Edwards' handwriting. There are several characteristics of this part of the document which set it off from the others. First of all, it is markedly ununified. The topics have no cross-references and usually no connection even of subject matter.

A second distinguishing characteristic of the third part is that at some time a vertical line has been drawn through the middle of many of the items. Some of these marks were afterwards erased. But both the lines and the erasures are such as to make it certain that the marks were not in ink. These facts are hard to explain. If the author had crossed these items out, for whatever reason, he would almost certainly have used pen and ink as he does elsewhere.[24] Moreover, his characteristic method of crossing out what he had written was either by a

[22] These may be found in Dwight, vol. 1, pp. 715-761. He has, however, confused and misrepresented the numbering of the items. There are in fact two series numbered in Edwards' own hand. One of these begins on page 7 (somebody has numbered it "11" on the assumption that it is a part of a single work) and continues on pages 9, 10, 12, 13, 14, 15, 16. It contains 65 items. At the head of this series is written, "Things to be considered . . . [below] an[d] written fully about." (The manuscript has a shorthand symbol for "below.") The second series, beginning on page 8 and continuing on page 11, consists of 28 numbers. Dwight transposes the two, designating the second series as first and adding numbers 29, 30, and 31, the text of which he takes from the third part of the document, where the numbering is not that of Edwards. He then designates the first series as second and adds all numbers higher than 65. The higher numbers were taken from part three and were not numbered by Edwards.

[23] A few of them refer directly to the preceding propositions and corollaries on the nature of atoms. Wherever that is the case, I have presented the relevant material in footnotes in the appropriate places in connection with the text.

[24] It is highly improbable that he had any other writing material, though he might have used charcoal or other crude instrument. Lead pencils were not in commercial production until after Edwards' death. However, George Berkeley left a manuscript of "A Tour in Italy, 1717-1718" written partly in pencil. See T. E. Jessop, *A Bibliography of George Berkeley,* 1934, p. 87, MS. 4.

great cross from corner to corner or by a stroke of the pen horizontally through each line of text. I am convinced that the crossing out of these items was done by someone else.[25]

A third distinguishing characteristic of the third part of the *Notes on Natural Science* is the presence of shorthand. There are three shorthand memoranda.[26] They have been deciphered by William P. Upham.[27] The memoranda have no significance beyond showing that Edwards was perhaps considering the publication of a work on natural science. Too much mystery has sometimes been attached to his use of shorthand. Some have imagined that he held esoteric or even heretical doctrines which he concealed in 'private characters.' There is not the slightest evidence to support such a theory. A far more-probable one is that the use of shorthand represents a youthful enthusiasm which waned during his mature life. In the list of topics "to be considered below and written fully about" in part two of *Notes on Natural Science,* no. 43 has an undecipherable place name written in shorthand. It reads "43. To observe about all stones being broken pieces of stones, and instances seen in journeys to . . . , Connecticut."[28] The place names, both town (undecipherable) and state, are in shorthand. Except for a few similar memoranda in his sermons, I have found no instances of shorthand in his manuscripts other than those mentioned by Upham. It is especially significant that there seems to be no use of shorthand in the *Miscellanies,* where we might expect to find it. It is not improbable that by the time Edwards began the writing of the *Miscellanies*[29] he had lost his interest in shorthand and dropped it,

[25] All of the manuscripts which I have examined have been corrupted by readers and editors. If it is not always possible to be quite sure that a corruption is present, there are at least three circumstances which, when present, leave little doubt. They are: (1) where the handwriting is not that of Edwards; (2) where his quaint eighteenth-century style has been changed to make it conform to later or more polite grammar; and (3) where a lead pencil has been used. I suppose that the corruptions are the work of various persons at various times. But there is good reason to think that many of them were the work of Dwight or his assistants in the first half of the last century. It is probable that, in this particular manuscript, Dwight gave numbers to unnumbered items, numbered the pages on the assumption that it was a single unified document, made the vertical marks, and undertook to improve the style.

[26] Not two as stated by Smyth, *op. cit.,* p. 219.

[27] "On the Shorthand Notes of Jonathan Edwards," *Massachusetts Historical Society Proceedings,* 2nd series, vol. 15, 1902, pp. 514ff. This valuable paper throws much light on Edwards' use of shorthand.

[28] Dwight leaves out the latter part of this sentence.

[29] Keith Rinehart, in an unpublished thesis (*A Comparison of the Writings of Jonathan Edwards Concerning God's End in Creation as Found in his Early Unpublished "Miscellanies" and in a Dissertation Posthumously Published,* University of Oregon, has shown conclusively that the *Miscellanies* was begun about 1722.

except for place names and other frequently recurrent words or phrases, such as "⊙" for world.

Even if the preceding observations on the nature of this manuscript do not fully prove that it is a composite of fragments rather than a single unified document, one fact is clear and sufficient for the present purpose—that part one and a portion of part two as described above are of great philosophical importance, whereas the remainder is interesting chiefly on other grounds. The justication for republishing even a portion of a document already in print is that the selected parts are vital elements in Edwards' philosophy. Moreover, even if Dwight's edition of it were easily accessible, the liberties which he took with the text make it desirable that an accurate text of the more-philosophical portion be made available.

(2) The second source for the text below is the Dwight edition of the famous and extremely important work, *The Mind.*[30] If the lost manuscript should ever be recovered, it is unlikely that substantial changes in the interpretation of Edwards would be necessary. For whatever faults Dwight may have had as an editor, a proclivity to misinterpretation was not one of them. He may have 'improved' the style but probably presented the meaning accurately, except that his punctuation may sometimes have obscured it. It is evident that he rearranged the items to satisfy his conception of unity; but he seems to have kept the original numbers and thus enabled the reader to reconstruct the order of the manuscript.

The compelling reason for republishing *The Mind* is that it is indispensable in the interpretation of Edwards' philosophy. My secondary purposes are, first, to rearrange the items as nearly as possible in their original order and, second, to repunctuate the whole document in the interest of lucidity and force. In the absence of the manuscript we must assume that the numbers printed by Dwight are Edwards' numbers, even though there is reason to suspect that they are not entirely reliable.[31]

---

[30] Vol. 1, pp. 664-702; see also vol. 1, ch. 3.

[31] One reason for questioning their reliability is the fact that, as printed, there are two 21s, two 25s, and two 65s, and that 33, 44, 46, 50, and 52 are missing. It is possible that the original showed the same discrepancies, though in the *Miscellanies* and elsewhere Edwards shows a meticulous regard for systematic accuracy in numbering. It is not impossible that *The Mind* is an exception in this respect; for we know that the author worked over the material with a view to its expansion and publication. The internal evidence for this appears in the text below, but there is collateral evidence in a manuscript at Yale which is generally taken to be an index to *The Mind*. It seems to refer to the topics of *The Mind* but gives them an order quite different from that which we have. The only item in the index which I can positively identify with one in the text is no. 71, which is there listed as "p. 1." This index may, however, represent the author's effort to systematize and expand the notes into a treatise.

As for the punctuation, it is to be recorded that throughout the unpublished manuscripts of Edwards there is no reliable punctuation to be found. He wrote for his own eye rather than as one who attempts to convey precise meaning to another. When he is at his worst, sentence structure is almost nonexistent, the phrases and clauses streaming along for half a page after a verb before a substantive. His structure is often ungrammatical, and meanings have to be discovered by laborious analysis. Any editor, therefore, must supply the punctuation. The standard can be only clarity and force.

Punctuation is subject to fashion and the current fashion is bound to be reflected in the work of an editor. Dwight, when faced with the necessity of punctuating the document, added commas, colons, and semicolons profusely, leaving the long sentences. The result is often obscurity and a sense of confusion for the modern reader. I have used fewer commas and more periods, on the theory that the resulting clarity is a sufficient justification. The student may refer to Dwight's edition of the work for comparison.

It is to be regretted that the manuscript of *The Mind* is lost, not because it might have helped with punctuation but because it would have enabled us to restore the actual words of Edwards. We might also have made useful observations of the numbering of items and any physical signs of use or abuse of the manuscript. Dwight consciously and openly undertook to improve Edwards' style by making it more elegant. In doing so he may not have changed the meaning, but he has quite often detracted from the force and vigor of Edwards' native style. There are numerous illustrations of this in the *Notes on Natural Science,* where it is possible to compare the print with the manuscript. Thus he prints "It is" for " 'Tis," "the other" for "t'other;" he changes verbs to conform with subjects in number and tense; and otherwise gives a false impression of the actual style of Edwards. He omits some phrases or notes such as the one mentioned by Upham,[32] "like the Earl of Shaftesbury." He adds numbers to unnumbered items and rearranges them to conform to his conception of relevancy. If Dwight has done these things in the case of *Notes on Natural Science,* it is presumable that he has done similar things with *The Mind*. It is therefore a pity that the manuscript of this all-important work is not available. Lacking it I have followed the text of Dwight except for punctuation.

(3) The third document is the *Miscellanies*. This is a vast store of items or entries varying in length from a single sentence, or even a phrase, to extended treatises which if printed would make small

[32] *Op. cit.*, p. 516, n. 2.

books.[33] The greater number of these items concern church doctrinal matters and theological disputes. There are also frequent quotations from books or magazines which Edwards was reading. The whole manuscript is contained in eight volumes and is accompanied by a ninth volume which is the author's careful and elaborate index of the other eight. Unlike the other two sources for the present text, this document covers all the periods of the author's life from about 1722 to the very end. It is, in effect, a commonplace book. It was, like the other two in this respect, not written for publication but for the sake of study and meditation. The author drew upon it in preparing sermons and publications, often lifting from it phrases, illustrations, and whole passages. But as it stands it is a private notebook and must be thought of as a mere record of miscellaneous observations put down from time to time as they occurred to him.

The *Miscellanies* is remarkable for its almost complete objectivity. There is nothing in it to suggest a diary, and whatever biographical value it has is purely inferential and subordinate to its overt interest in ideas, theories, and reflections on the nature of things. It is impossible to date any portion of it by finding references to events known to have been of vital importance to Edwards. No echoes have been discovered, for example, of the tumultuous events of his trial and dismissal from the church in Northampton. There may have been periods in which he wrote nothing in this manuscript; but there is every reason to think that he had it constantly at hand and that his attention to it was sustained and continuous. If such was the case it is remarkable, and to many temperaments incredible, that when writing in the privacy of his own study he did not allude to the stirring events and personal anguish or joy of the day's experiences.

It is reasonable to suppose that the *Miscellanies* was begun after his student days at Yale when he first faced the problems of professional work. In it he could formulate and clarify his ideas. From it he could appropriate and compound material for sermons. It begins with items designated by the letters of the alphabet, omitting *j* and *v*. He evidently did not anticipate the hundreds of items which would one day appear. The single alphabet is then followed by the double, i.e., *aa, bb,* etc. He then begins with a number series and continues it to the end with a few additions or interpolations, as *27a.*

33 In addition to Erskine's two volumes of selections, some additional material from the *Miscellanies* has been published: "Miscellaneous Observations," Dwight's edition of the *Works,* vol. 8, pp. 485-603; "Types of the Messiah," *Works,* vol. 9, pp. 2-110; minor fragments, as in *Two Hundredth Anniversary of of the Birth of Jonathan Edwards,* Andover, 1904, Appendix I. Including selections in the present volume, it may be estimated that approximately three-fourths of the manuscript has been published in more-or-less adequate texts.

The index was probably begun after a considerable amount of the text had accumulated and only when he found the need of it. But it was thereafter continued *pari passu* with the writing. It has proven to be of great assistance in the study of the manuscript. It has also served as the structural feature of the text printed below. Preliminary study of the *Miscellanies* satisfied me that, while there was philosophical wheat to be found, there was a much greater bulk of philosophical chaff. For the purposes in mind there could be no point in publishing the entire document. I therefore set about constructing a body of philosophical material drawn from the whole. The index proved to be the perfect instrument for accomplishing the purpose. Here was Edwards' own classification of topics, his own explicit judgment of what entries belonged together. Moreover, in the index, the entries were all neatly arranged in serial order so that, if any growth or change had occurred during his life, the examination of the successive writings would uncover the fact. Since an item was frequently entered under two or more headings, the reader of the document could readily explore the interrelation of ideas and topics. It therefore came about that the author supplied the editor with a guide to his philosophical writings in the *Miscellanies.*

Using this principle of selection, I assembled a large body of the text and put it into typewritten form. Of this vast compilation a further selection was imperative. The principles of selection employed at this stage were relevancy and purity. Relevancy means relevant to the exhibition of Edwards' philosophy. If a passage referred to in the index proved to be mainly an exegesis of some scriptural text or a quotation from some book or magazine, I rejected it. The principle of purity means that I selected only those items which were relatively free from extraneous matter. If an item was so involved in theological idiom that the philosophical idea was obscured or minute, I rejected it. The result is a body of philosophical writing arranged alphabetically by topics and chronologically within each topic. Thus the index has enabled me to bring together, for example, all that Edwards wrote in the *Miscellanies* on the "Being of God," from the beginning to the end and in the order in which he wrote it. It is doubtless possible that some important statement by Edwards on any given topic has been left out, but it is not probable. Every attempt has been made to present his topics in their fullest form, omitting only redundancy and irrelevance. Whenever portions of any single topic have been omitted, the fact is indicated.

The three documents from which this volume is made up have certain natural relations to each other. In the first place they are all 'private notebooks.' The author did not intend to publish them. In the case of the first two, it is true that he considered expanding them into books for publication; but he certainly did not suppose that they would be made public in their present form. In the case of the *Miscellanies* there is no unity of subject matter, except that which is due to the fact that the author wrote day after day whatever seemed to him to be worthy of thoughtful reflection and expression. If the first two documents had never been made public, Edwards as a thinker might have lapsed into an obscurity which he does not deserve, simply because his published titles bear to the modern mind the *odium theologicum*. Had he lived in other circumstances or had he been in a secular profession, what were his private papers might have been his public ones. He was more churchman than philosopher, but his private papers show that under other stars he might have been more philosopher than churchman. He must have found scant occasion to share his abtruse philosophical doctrines with the good neighbors of his parish; and even his colleagues, whom he met at infrequent intervals, would usually have found his mind beyond their depth. He had to commit his thoughts to paper and turn them over in his own mind.

Secondly, the three documents, at least roughly, followed one another chronologically in the order named. The first two have become fixed in our minds as two separate works of the youthful Edwards. This fixed idea is the result of Dwight's editorial work upon them. The idea is probably not essentially misleading, because at some time or other Edwards looked upon them as separate, as is made certain by the outline of topics for a work on "The Mind" which Dwight prints[34] at the beginning of *The Mind*. Dwight there records the fact that the outline appears at the end of the manuscript. "The preceeding articles," he say, "were set down from time to time at the close of the work, in two series; the first ending with no. 26."[35] In that outline an introductory section is to deal with the following topics: "Concerning the two worlds—the external and the internal: the external, the subject of natural philosophy; the internal, our own minds. How the knowledge of the latter is, in many respects, the most important. Of what great use the true knowledge of this is; and of what dangerous consequence errors here are, more than in the other." This is ample evidence that Edwards at some time or other distinguished between the *Notes on Natural Science* and *The Mind,* but it tells nothing of the order in which they were written and is not to be taken to mean that he made the distinction while he was writing the various parts of the notes. It is far more probable that the distinction was an afterthought

[34] Vol. 1, pp 664-668. See also below, pp. 69-73.
[35] Vol. 1, p. 668.

and represents a period in his life when he re-examined his earliest writings and contemplated putting them in order for publication. This theory is strengthened when we observe that, in the work on natural science also, there is an homologous detached list of "things to be considered below and written fully about." It is a fair supposition that both these lists were drawn up at the time when Edwards was reconsidering his early writings with a view to their expansion and publication.

In short, I suppose that what we know as two works were originally one series of memoranda which Edwards wrote while he was absorbed in the study of Locke and Newton during his early college years, probably between 1717 and 1720. These early writings were the expression of a radical idealism, which he considered at the time and later to be original and sufficiently startling to need considerable defense against misunderstanding.[36]

It seems likely that so the matter stood when he first took up the burdens of his professional life and began writing the *Miscellanies.* From this point onwards philosophy was crowded into second place though by no means forgotten. It became marginal as far as his writing was concerned and occupied a margin of his time; but it was fundamental in his experience and thought, as is shown by his sermons and by many parts of the *Miscellanies.* When destiny had placed him in the wilderness of Stockbridge as a missionary to the Indians and when the mastery of his profession had given him greater repose, he wrote his major published philosophical works: *A Careful and Strict Inquiry into the Modern Prevailing Notions of that Freedom of Will, which is Supposed to be Essential to Moral Agency, Vertue and Vice, Reward and Punishment, Praise and Blame* (1754); *A Dissertation Concerning the End for which God Created the World;* and *A Dissertation Concerning the Nature of True Virtue.* The reader of these books may now observe that the author took extracts from the *Miscellanies* to construct them. But their subject matter is by no means the only important philosophical material in the *Miscellanies.* There is much that reverts to his early idealism and gives body to the mere sketch found in the *Notes on Natural Science* and *The Mind.* Moreover, the *Miscellanies* often presents a freshness of expression and meaning which illuminates his published books.

In bringing these three documents together an attempt is made to display the whole character of Edwards' philosophical opinion. Although the greater part of the text is here published for the first time, there is a lesser part which could be found already in print. It did not

36 See Upham, *op. cit.*, p. 520.

seem wise to adhere rigidly to an original plan of publishing new material only, because I soon discovered that the result would be but to add another fragment to the already long list of fragments of the philosophy of Edwards. Admittedly, anything short of a complete, definitive, and final edition of his works, published and unpublished, is in a sense a fragment. It is unlikely that such an edition will ever be justified; for there is much in Edwards of which adequate report has already been made in his published works. What is needed and what is here supplied is a gathering together, mainly from primary sources, of his more strictly philosophical writing. A student will, however, still need to study the familiar published works of Edwards and particularly the three mentioned above.

In editing the documents presented here some working rules had to be adopted regarding punctuation, capitalization, spelling, and references. Of the first enough has been said already. Edwards was not consistent in his use of capitals. He begins sentences without capitals, uses them mysteriously and promiscuously for nouns, adjectives, adverbs, prepositions. Sometimes he may have used them for emphasis and again probably for no better reason than that his hand made them there. It is particularly noticeable that names for the Deity are not regularly capitalized. It seemed advisable to disregard his capitalization entirely and to follow the usual present-day conventions. Spelling presented greater difficulty. His spelling is inconsistent but often interesting for its quaint flavor. I wish I might have retained it as a means of conveying to the reader the feeling for the man and his times, but other considerations led me to conform the text to the rules of modern print. Throughout his writing, and conspicuously in the *Miscellanies,* he uses several arbitrary signs—"S" for Scripture, "X" for Christ, "⊙" for world, and the like. I have converted these signs into words. In references to the works of Edwards I have used the Dwight edition (1829-30) because it is the most complete. But whereever possible I have used chapter, section, or paragraph numbers in order that the references may be found by those who lack access to the Dwight edition.

I hope that the common and deserved reputation which Edwards has as a stylist, and which has led many anthologists to include selections from his writings in their specimens of English prose, will not be lessened by the publication of this text. These manuscripts were not intended for publication and there are many faults of style which the author would doubtless have corrected. Yet under the circumstances I have chosen to leave them, because my correction would falsify the record of informal writing in his private papers. Perhaps the fault most to be regretted is the author's carelessness in using plural verbs with singular subjects, and the reverse. The meaning, however, is not obscured by such faults; and, notwithstanding them, many passages may be found to illustrate the strength, balance, and force of good eighteenth-century prose.

I am under great debt to many who have helped me in various ways to bring this work to completion. To the Yale University Library and its staff I am particularly indebted for the opportunity to work with the manuscripts there and for their unfailing courtesy in lending assistance. The same is true in the case of the Andover Newton Theological Library. Mr. Richard D. Pierce of that library was especially helpful, both in person and by correspondence. In a different but indispensible way I have been greatly helped by various students at the University of Oregon who came to me under the provisions of the National Youth Administration. My thanks are especially due to Mr. Benson Mates and Mr. Keith Rinehart for intelligent and faithful assistance in making transcriptions.

Finally, to the State Board of Higher Education in Oregon I owe thanks for grants in aid of research, without which the necessary expenses of the undertaking could not have been met.

H.G.T.

The manuscript of this book was completed at the time of Dr. Townsend's death on December 19, 1948. Some editorial problems which arose after his death are partly responsible for the delay in publication. The work as it now appears is substantially the book he planned. The principal lack is an index, for which Dr. Townsend left only fragments and an outline of form. An attempt was made to complete the index on the basis of his notes, but the results were not satisfactory. It has, therefore, been decided to omit the index to avoid further delay in publication. Since the first two parts are relatively short and the selections from the *Miscellanies* are topically arranged, it is believed that readers of the book will not be seriously handicapped.—GEORGE N. BELKNAP.

Of Being[1]

That there should absolutely be nothing at all is utterly impossible. The mind can never, let it stretch its conceptions never so much, bring itself to conceive of a state of perfect nothing. It puts the mind into mere convulsion and confusion to endeavor to think of such a state. And it contradicts the very nature of the soul to think that it should be. And it is the greatest contradiction and the aggregate of all contradictions to say that there should not be. 'Tis true we can't so distinctly show the contradiction by words, because we cannot talk about it without speaking horrid nonsense and contradicting ourselves at every word, and because 'nothing' is that whereby we distinctly show other particular contradictions. But here we are run up to our first principle and have no other to explain the nothingness, or not being of nothing, by. Indeed we can mean nothing else by 'nothing' but a state of absolute contradiction. And if any man thinks that he can think well enough how there should be nothing, I'll engage that what he means by nothing is as much something as anything that ever he thought of in his life. And I believe that, if he knew what nothing was, it would be intuitively evident to him that it could not be. So that we see it is necessary some being should eternally be. And 'tis a more palpable contradiction still to say that there must be being somewhere and not other where; for the words 'absolute nothing' and 'where' contradict each other. And besides, it gives as great a shock to the mind to think of pure nothing being in any one place as it does to think of it in all. And it is self-evident that there can be nothing in one place as well as in another; and so, if there can be in one there can be in all. So that we see this necessary, eternal being must be infinite and omnipresent.

This infinite and omnipresent being cannot be solid. Let us see how contradictory it is to say that infinite being is solid. For solidity surely is nothing but resistance to other solidities. Space is this necessary, eternal, infinite, and omnipresent being.[2] We find that we can with ease conceive how all other beings should not be. We can remove them out of our minds and place some other in the room of them, but space is the very thing that we can never remove and conceive of its not being. If a man would imagine space anywhere to be divided so as there should be nothing between the divided parts, there remains space between, notwithstanding. And so the man contradicts himself. And it is self-

[1] For a discussion of this manuscript see Introduction, pp. xii-xv.

[2] *The Mind*, no. 9 (p. 29, below) seems to refer to this demonstration by the phrase "as has been already observed."

evident, I believe, to every man that space is necessary, eternal, infinite, and omnipresent. But I had as good speak plain. I have already said as much as that space is God.[3] And it is indeed clear to me that all the space there is, not proper to body, all the space there is without the bounds of the creation, all the space there was before the creation, is God Himself. And nobody would in the least stick at it if it were not because of the gross conceptions we have of space*.[4]

---

*Of the Prejudices of Imagination. Lemma to the Whole

Of all prejudices no one so fights with natural philosophy and prevails more against it than that of imagination. 'Tis that which make the vulgar so roar out upon the mention of some very rational philosophical truths. And indeed I have known of some very learned men that have pretended to a more than ordinary freedom from such prejudices so overcome by them, that merely because of them they have believed things most absurd. And truly I hardly know of any other prejudices that are more powerful against truth of any kind than this. And I believe it will not give the lead to any, in any case, except those arising from our ruling self-interest or the impetuosity of human passions. And there is very good reason for it. For opinions arising from imagination take us as soon as we are born, are beat into us by every act of sensation, and so grow up with us from our very births, and by that means grow into us so fast that it is almost impossible to root them out, being, as it were, so incorporated with our very minds that whatsoever is objected to them, contrary thereunto, is as if it were different to the very constitution of them. Hence men come to make what they can actually perceive by their senses or by immediate reflection into their own souls the standard of possibility and impossibility: so that there

---

[3] Compare Berkeley, *A Treatise concerning the Principles of Human Knowledge,* sec. cxvii. Edwards is in agreement with Henry More, Newton, Samuel Clarke, and Locke rather than with Berkeley on this matter. See Locke, *Essay,* II, 15, 3, and John Tull Baker, *English Space and Time Theories from Henry More to Bishop Berkeley,* 1930, *passim.*

[4] After this paragraph was written a note was inserted, cramped between it and the preceding paragraph: "Place this as a lemma where it suits best and let it be more fully demonstr." In the last sentence of the paragraph the original word "imaginations" has been crossed out and "conceptions" substituted. A reference mark at the end of the sentence seems to refer to the little essay entitled, "Of the Prejudices of Imagination." Dwight placed this essay at the beginning of his *Notes on Natural Science,* but it seems to me that such an arrangement is incorrect. I am convinced that, after Edwards had written the original word, "imaginations," he paused to write "Of the Prejudices of Imagination." I am therefore treating the latter as a footnote within *Of Being,* the theme of which is resumed on p. 6, below.

must be no body forsooth bigger than they can conceive of or less than they can see with their eyes, nor motion either much swifter or slower than they can imagine. As for the greatness of bodies or distances, the learned world have pretty well conquered their imagination with respect to that; neither will anybody flatly deny that it is possible for bodies to be of any degree of bigness that can be mentioned. Yet imaginations of this kind among the learned themselves, even of this learned age, hath a very powerful secret influence to cause them either to reject things really true as enormously false or to embrace things that are truly so. Thus some men will yet say they cannot conceive how the fixed stars can be so distant as that the earth's annual revolution should cause no parallax among them, and so are almost ready to fall back into antiquated Ptolemy, his system, merely to ease their imagination. Thus also, on the other [hand], a very learned man and sagacious astronomer, upon consideration of the vast magnitude of the visible part of the world, has in the ecstasy of his imagination been hurried on to pronounce the world infinite. Which, I may say out of veneration, was beneath such a man as he. As if it were any more an argument, because what he could see of the universe wasn't so big as he was assured it was—and suppose he had discovered the visible world, so vast as it is, to be as a globule of water to another, the case is the same—I say, as if it would have been any more of an argument that it was infinite, than if the visible part thereof were no bigger than a particle of the water of this! I think one is no nearer to infinite than the other. To remedy this prejudice I will, as the best method I can think of, demonstrate two or three physical theorem[s] which, I believe, if they are clearly understood, will put every man clean out of conceit with his imagination. In order thereunto these two are prerequisite, as:

First, Proposition 1. There is no degree of swiftness of motion whatsoever but what is possible. That you may not doubt of this, suppose any long piece of matter to move round any point or center, to which one end shall be fixed, with any given degree of velocity. Now that part of this piece of matter that is farthest from the center to which one end is fixed must move swiftest. And then suppose this piece of matter to be lengthened out, and that part of it that moved swiftest before to move on still with the same degree of velocity, 'tis evident that the farther end moves swifter than the farther end did before by so much as the piece of matter is longer. And suppose it to be made longer still, the farther end moves still just so much swifter. So that, as the parcel of matter can be protracted to any degree of length whatsoever, so the farther end of it can be moved with any degree of swiftness whatsoever. So that there is no degree of swiftness whatsoever but what is possible.

Secondly, Proposition 2. There may be bodies of any indefinite degree of smallness. Let two perfect spheres, *A* and *B*, touch each other in some point of their surfaces, at *I*. 'Tis evident that there can be a globule of matter just so big as to reach from the surface of one sphere to the surface of the other sphere at any given distance from the point of contact, *I*, suppose at *e*, let the spheres be greater or smaller. Since therefore that[5] the distance *og* between the surface of one sphere to the surface of the other is less according as the spheres are greater, and since the touching spheres can be of any degree of magnitude, and since consequently the distance *og* can be of any degree of smallness, and since the body that fills up that distance is small accordingly, it follows that there can be a body of any degree of smallness. N.B. This I take to be all that is meant by the divisibility of matter *in infinitum*.[6]

Proposition 3.[7] That it is possible for a body as small as a ray of light to strike the surface of a body as big as the earth, or any indefinite magnitude—supposing it be hard enough to hold the stroke—so as to impel it along with any indefinite degree of swiftness. Let the laws of gravity and motion be mentioned and let it be a postulatum[8] inserted that these laws hold universally in all bodies great or small at how great distance soever and however disproportionate.

Postulatum 2. That there may be bodies of any indefinite degree of smallness, that is, in any of these infinite divisions of matter it is possible that matter or body may extend so far as the extremes of that part and no farther, and that this part will be a distinct body. For instance, let the body *AB* be by you supposed to be as small as 'tis possible for a body to be. No doubt but there is a middle between the two extremes of that body, how small soever it is, at *C*. Now we mean that 'tis possible that matter may not extend any further than to the extremes of the half of that body, in fact only from *B* to *C*. So that 'tis possible there may be a body smaller than *AB*, however small that is.

[5] The word "that" has been retained though it mars the style. It probably represents an unconscious change in grammatical structure as the author wrote the sentence.

[6] My italics. I follow the usual practice of italicising such words and phrases.

[7] The third proposition seems to have been added at a later time, although in the phrase "two or three physical theorems," above, he had already provided for it.

[8] Although unnumbered this appears to be Postulatum 1.

Postulatum 3. That there is no degree of swiftness of motion whatever but what is possible. For instance, suppose the body *AB* to be fixed at the point *B* and to move round the point *B* in an hour. If the body *AB* be made as long again, yet 'tis possible it may be moved round in an hour. So, let it be made never so long, then it is manifest that the longer it is the swifter doth the further extreme move.[9]

Postulatum 4. That the separating of bodies, or the parts of bodies that touch each other, is always by divulsion, or pulling asunder. That is, if of the body *AD* the parts *AC, CD* [are separated], it must be by force pulling one from the other. It cannot be by protrusion because nothing can be between them at that very place where they touch before they are separated. Thus if we suppose them to be separated by the driving in a wedge at C, yet the parts must be separated before the wedge could get between them. Not but that protrusion or impulsion in another place might cause the divulsion in that. Or if we suppose the parts of the body *AD* to be broken thus—

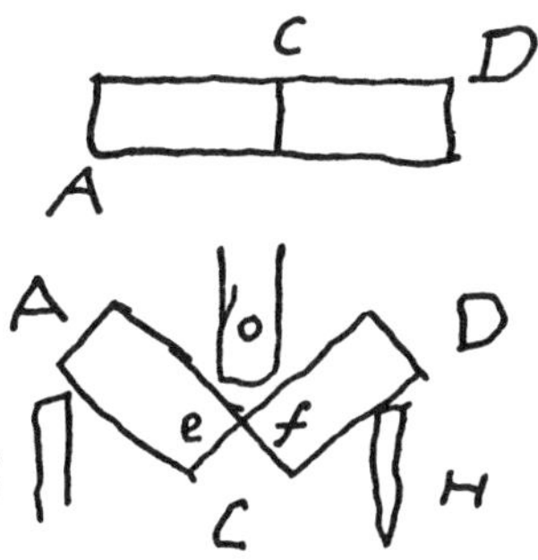

let the two ends *A* and *D* baited, laid upon two other bodies *G, H,* and broken by the striking of the body *O* in the middle, at *C*—even then 'tis manifest that the parts *AC* and *CD* were pulled asunder. The extreme *e* of *AC* was pulled from the extreme *f* of *CD*. This is all I mean by divulsion.

Postulatum 5. A body, everywhere in every other respect equal in there being a possibility of separating the parts, may be most easily separated where 'tis least. For instance, the body *IK* may be more easily pulled in two at *L* than at *M*. And it is least where 'tis most easily separated.

Postulatum 6. A body whose parts may be separated by such a degree of force, that same body still retaining the same degree of inseparableness, or another body with an equal degree of inseparableness, will evermore be separated when that degree of force is applied.

Postulatum 7. Every body and every part of body has length and breadth and thickness. Suppose the body *AB* to be an absolute plenum and the parts *AC* and *CB* to be frustrums of a cone. I say the parts of this body could never be separated. To prove which, let us suppose it separable. Let us suppose it fixed at *B* and every part pulled with equal

[9] The words are slightly confused but the meaning is plain.

force towards *A*. 'Tis manifest by the 5 postulate that it will break first at *C*. Let there be another absolute plenum *DB* being a cone equal that of which *CB* was the frustrum. Let it be fixed at *B* and every part of it be pulled with equal force towards *D*, and with a force equal to that which broke the body *AB* at *C*. 'Tis manifest by the 6 postulate that the body *DB* would be broken at *C* where 'tis equal to *C* of the body *AB*. But if so it would also be broken by the same force in every point betwix *D* and *C* by the fifth postulate because in every point it is less than at *C*. But this is impossible; for if it break at every point the broken parts have no length, breadth, and thickness, contrary to 7 postulate. Such a breaking would be annihilation. All these are certain consequences from the supposition that the parts *AC* and *CB* of the body *AB* can be pulled asunder; but we see that these are impossible, therefore that . . . [10]

Again, let the cylinder *EF* be an absolute plenum and fixed at *F* and let all the parts be pulled towards *E* with equal force. I say that with how great force soever it is pulled it will nowhere break. If it break it will break either in some part only or in every point. Not in some parts only and not in others, for, if so, it will be because some parts were more easily broken than others—for it is supposed that the force is equal everywhere—but some parts would not be more easily broken than others by the 5 postulate; not in every point, for then 'tis manifest the broken parts would be without length, breadth, and thickness.

Neither can be any such thing without consciousness. How is it possible there should something be from all eternity and there be no consciousness of it? It will appear very plain to everyone that intensely considers of it that consciousness and being are the same thing exactly. And how doth it grate upon the mind to think that something should be from all eternity, and nothing all the while be conscious of it? Let us suppose, to illustrate it, that the world had a being from all eternity, and had many great changes and wonderful revolutions, and all the while nothing knew; there was no knowledge in the universe of any such thing. How is it possible to bring the mind to imagine—yea, it

[10] The sentence is not completed. Dwight omits all of Postulatum 7 except the first sentence, perhaps because of an internal confusion in the second sentence due to a slip of the pen by which the symbol *D* is used instead of *B*, which the diagram calls for. I have changed the *D* of the manuscript to a *B* to bring it into conformity with the diagram. The meaning is not in doubt.

is really impossible it should be—that anything should be and nothing know it. Then you'll say, if it be so it is because nothing has any existence anywhere else but in consciousness. No, certainly nowhere else but either in created or uncreated consciousness.

Supposing there were another universe, only of bodies created at a great distance from this, created in excellent order and harmonious motions and a beautiful variety, and there was no created intelligence in it, nothing but senseless bodies, nothing but God knew anything of it: I demand in what respect this world has a being but only in the divine consciousness. Certainly in no respect. There would be figures and magnitudes, and motions and proportions—but where? Where else but in the Almighty's knowledge? How is it possible there should? Then you'll say, for the same reason a room close shut up, that nobody sees, can have nothing in it; there is nothing any other way than in God's knowledge. I answer, created beings are conscious of the effects of what is in the room, for perhaps there is not one leaf of a tree nor spire of grass but what has effects all over the universe, and will have to the end of eternity. But any otherwise there is nothing in a room shut up but only in God's consciousness. How can anything be there any other way? This will appear to be truly so to anyone that thinks of it with the whole united strength of his mind. Let us suppose, for illustration, this impossibility, that all the spirits in the universe be for a time deprived of their consciousness, and God's consciousness at the same time be intermitted. I say the universe for that time would cease to be, of itself; and not only, as we speak, the Almighty could not attend to uphold the world, but because God knew nothing of it. 'Tis our foolish imagination that will not suffer us to see. We fancy there may be figures and magnitudes, relations and properties, without anyone's knowing of it. But it is our imagination hurts us. We don't know what figures and properties are.

Our imagination makes us fancy we see shapes and colors and magnitudes though nobody is there to behold it. But to help our imagination let us thus state the case: let us suppose this world deprived of every ray of light so that there should not be the least glimmering of light in the universe. Now all will own that in such case the universe would be immediately really deprived of all its colors; one part of the universe is no more red, or blue, or green, or yellow, or black, or white, or light, or dark, or transparent, or opaque. There would be no visible distinction between this world and the rest of the incomprehensible void. Yea, there would be no difference in these respects between the world and the infinite void. That is, any part of that void would really be as light and as dark, as white and as black, as red and green, as blue and as brown, as transparent and as oqaque as any part of the universe.

Or, as there would be in such case no difference between the world and nothing in these respects, so there would be no difference between one part of the world and another. All, in these respects, is alike confounded with and undistinguishable from infinite emptiness.

At the same time also, let us suppose the universe to be altogether deprived of motion and all parts of it to be at perfect rest (the former supposition is indeed included in this but we distinguish them for better clearness); then the universe would not differ from the void in this respect. There will be no more motion in one than the other. Then also solidity would cease. All that we mean, or can be meant, by solidity is resistance, resistance to touch, the resistance of some parts of space. This is all the knowledge we get of solidity by our senses and, I am sure, all that we can get any other way. But solidity shall be shown to be nothing else, more fully hereafter.[11] But there can be no resistance if there is no motion. One body can't resist another when there is perfect rest amongst them. But you'll say, though there is not actual resistance yet there is potential existence [resistance?], that is, such and such part of space would resist upon occasion. But this is all I would have, that there is no solidity now, not but that God would cause there to be on occasion. And if there is no solidity there is no extension, for extension is the extendedness of the solidity. Then all figure, and magnitude, and proportion immediately ceases.

Put both these suppositions together, that is, deprive the world of light and motion, and the case would stand thus with the world. There would [be] neither white nor black, neither blue nor brown, bright nor shaded, pellucid nor opaque, no noise or sound, neither heat nor cold, neither fluid, nor wet nor dry, hard nor soft, nor solidity, nor extension, nor figure, nor magnitude, nor proportion, nor body, nor spirit. What then is become of the universe? Certainly it exists nowhere but in the divine mind. This will be abundantly clearer to one after having read what I have further to say of solidity,[12] etc., so that we see that a world without motion can exist nowhere else but in the mind, either infinite or finite.

Corollary. It follows from hence that those beings which have knowledge and consciousness are the only proper and real and substantial beings, inasmuch as the being of other things is only by these. From hence we may see the gross mistake of those who think material things the most substantial beings and spirits more like a shadow, whereas spirits only are properly substance.[13]

---

[11] The reference may be to *The Mind,* no. 61, p. 60, below.

[12] See n. 11.

[13] See *Miscellanies,* f, p. 193, below.

A state of absolute nothing is a state of absolute contradiction. Absolute nothing is the aggregate of all the absurd contradictions in the world, a state wherein there is neither body, nor spirit, nor space, neither empty space nor full space, neither little nor great, narrow nor broad, neither infinitely great space nor finite space, nor a mathematical point, neither up nor down, neither north nor south. I don't mean as it is with respect to the body of the earth or some other great body, but no contrary points nor positions or directions, no such thing as either here or there, this way or that way, or only one way. When we go about to form an idea of perfect nothing we must shut out all these things. We must shut out of our minds both space that has something in it and space that has nothing in it. We must not allow ourselves to think of the least part of space, never so small. Nor must we suffer our thoughts to take sanctuary in a mathematical point. When we go to expel body out of our thoughts we must be sure not to leave empty space in the room of it; and when we go to expel emptiness from our thoughts we must not think to squeeze it over by anything close, hard, and solid, but we must think of the same that the sleeping rocks dream of. And not till then shall we get a complete idea of nothing.

A state of nothing is a state wherein every proposition in Euclid is not true, nor any of those self-evident maxims by which they are demonstrated; and all of the eternal truths are neither true nor false.

When we go to enquire whether or no there can be absolutely nothing, we speak nonsense in enquiring. The stating of the question is nonsense because we make a disjunction where there is none. Either being or absolute nothing is no disjunction, no more than whether a triangle is a triangle or not a triangle. There is no other way but only for there to be existence. There is no such thing as absolute nothing. There is such a thing as nothing with respect to this ink and paper. There is such a thing as nothing with respect to you and me. There is such a thing as nothing with respect to this globe of earth and with respect to this created universe. There is another way besides these things having existence but there is no such thing as nothing with respect to entity, 'being' absolutely considered. We don't know what we say if we say we think it possible in itself that there should not be entity.

Proposition 1.[14] All bodies whatsoever except atoms themselves must, of absolute necessity, be composed of atoms, or of bodies that are

[14] What follows in this section of the text was called "Of Atoms and Perfectly Solid Bodies" by Dwight. The manuscript has no title. A new folding of foolscap, together with slight changes of ink, pen, and handwriting, indicates that this portion of the manuscript was not immediately continuous with the preceding. Some time may have elapsed between the essay *Of Being* and the discussion of atoms.

indiscerpible,[15] that cannot be made less, or whose parts cannot, by any finite power whatsoever, be separated from one another. And this will be fully seen as soon as it is seen what bodies those are that are indiscerpible or what is requisite in order to cause a body to be so. And here we shall lay down this proposition that that body that is absolutely plenum, or that has every part of space included within its surfaces impenetrable, is indivisible, and that the parts thereof cannot, by no means, [be] separated from each other by any force how great soever. As for instance, suppose the body *B* to be what we call an absolute plenum, and suppose the two bodies *A* and *C* to come as impetuously and with as great a force as you please and strike on each side of the body *B*—I say the two bodies *A* and *C* could cause no fraction in the body *B*.

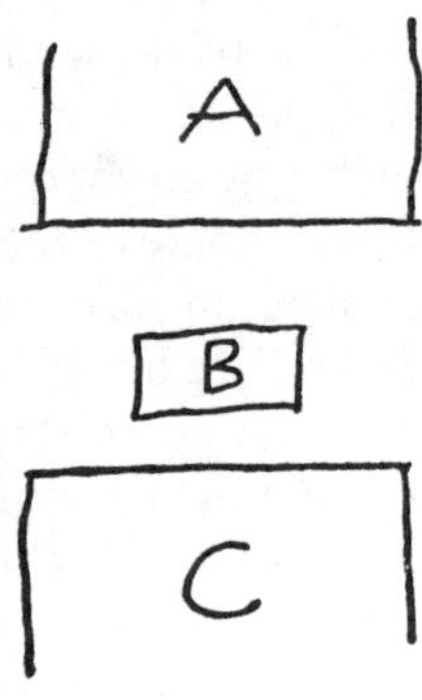

And again[16] suppose the body *D* to be a perfectly solid body and to be as pressingly jammed up as you please between the two bodies *E* and *F*, which are supposed not in the least to give way to the body *D*, and the surfaces of them which touch the body *D* are supposed everywhere perfectly even and plain and to continue parallel to each other and to be every way infinitely extended—I say the body *D* could not broken by the pressure of the bodies *E* and *F*. For suppose the body *D* to begin to be broken and crumbled into parts by the pressure of the bodies *E* and *F*—if the whole body *D* can be broken by that pressure, then the parts of the body *D* can still be broken again by the pressure of the same bodies with equal reason, supposing the bodies still to continue pressing towards each other. And then too, their parts can still be broken into other parts and so on, and that as fast as the motion of the bodies *E* and *F* towards each other shall require. And truly, I think, if it be so that the parts can be broken still finer and finer, they can be broken so fast as not to retard the motion of the *E* and *F* at all. And if so, surely the bodies *E* and *F* will presently

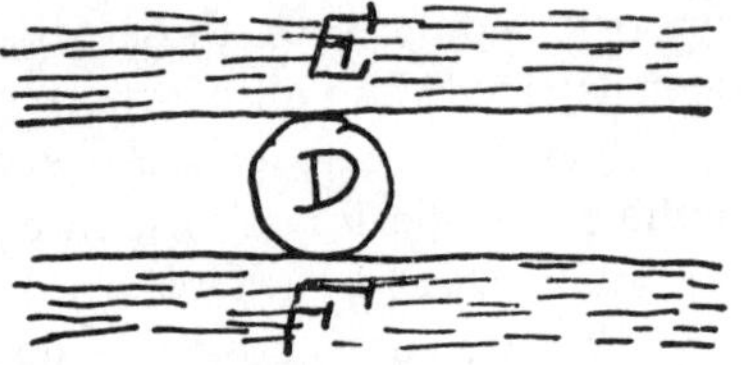

[15] This rather unusual word was used by Henry More in discussing immortality. *The Immortality of the Soul,* 1659, Preface, vol. 1, p. 3; also pp. 4, 6. This book was in the collection of books at Yale when Edwards entered college. Edwards does not seem to use the word with reference to the soul but only with reference to atoms.

[16] This paragraph in the manuscript is a footnote inserted by means of an asterisk. It therefore interrupts the example begun in the previous paragraph.

meet so as to touch intimately everywhere, inasmuch as it was said the surfaces of the bodies were perfectly even and continued parallel. And then, I ask, what is become of the body *D*? I think there can be no other answer but that it is annihilated, since it was said that the two bodies were infinitely extended. So that we see, if the body *D* can be broken by the bodies *E* and *F*, then it can be annihilated by them, which I believe nobody will own, and the case is all one, let the body *D* be of whatsoever figure. Q.E.D.

For if the two bodies *A* and *C* should cause any fractions in the body *B*, those fractions must be in some certain places or parts of the body and not in others. For there cannot be fractions in every part. For I suppose everybody will own that, after the body is supposed to be broken, there remain parts of the broken body which are unbroken. And so it will be; let the body be broken into as fine parts as you please, those fine parts are still unbroken. The fraction is not through the midst of those parts, as it is between them. So the fraction must be, if at all, in some places and not in others. And indeed breaking of a body all over or in every part is the same as to annihilate it. We say then that the body *B* cannot be broken in some parts and not in others by the bodies *A* and *C*, for if it is broken in this part and not in that it must be because it is easier broken in this than in that. But a body perfectly solid, and that is absolutely full, is everywhere equally full, equally solid, and equally strong, and indeed everywhere absolutely alike, so that there is nothing that should cause a fraction in one place sooner than in another. But here I foresee that it will be immediately objected to render what has been said invalid: But what in [if?] the body *B* should begin first to be broken off at the corners where pieces would be more easily cracked off than in other places, and what if it were less in some places than others, or what if the bodies *A* and *C* were applied with much greater force in some places than others? These objections seem at first quite to render all good for nothing. But I must say that, notwithstanding these objections, what has been said does prove that, suppose the perfectly solid body were everywhere equally bulky, and the bodies *A* and *C* were all along applied with equal force, the perfectly solid body could never be broken. And to them that say that it would first break at the corners, I ask how near the corner the first fraction would be? If they tell me so near, I ask why was it not nearer still since that the nearer the corner the easier and sooner broken? If, after that, the place for the first fraction be assigned nearer yet, I ask still, why not nearer still? So that at last they must be forced to say that the first fraction would be infinitely near the corner or that the first piece that would be broken off would be infinitely little. And they had as good say that none at all would be broken off first, for, as I take it, an actually infinitely little body and no body at all are the same thing or rather the same nothing. And as to the other two parts of the objection, it is enough for them if we can discover it to be the nature of perfectly solid bodies not to be broken but to resist any, however great, force, as it will appear rather more plain by another instance. As suppose the body *e* to be a perfect solid in that shape wider at the upper end and by degrees to come quite to a point at the lower, to be thrust with indefinitely great force towards the corner *g* against the sides *fg* and *gh,* which are supposed not at all to give way. It has been proved already that if it would break anywhere it would be the lower point first. And what we have said concerning the corners of the body *B* proves that it would not break there. Now since nothing but the perfect solidity can hinder the body *e* from breaking, we have certainly found out that a perfectly solid body cannot be broken. For the body *e* may be as great or as small, as long and as slender as you please, the case is the same. And let the force that *e* is to withstand be as great as you please—if the weight of the universe falling against it from never so great a distance and as much more as you please—we can prove, and what is said above does prove, that it would neither bend nor break but stiffly bear the shock of it all.

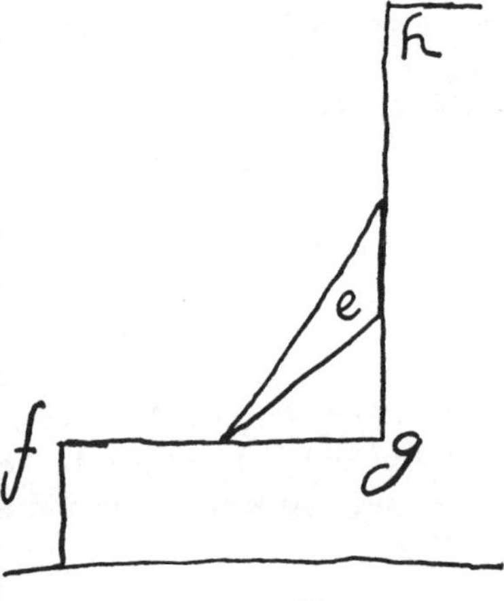

Corollary 1. From what was said concerning the first and second figure it plainly appears that breaking of a perfectly solid [body] and the annihilation of it are the same thing so far that the breaking of it would be the annihilating of it.

Corollary 2. Hence [it] appears that solidity and impenetrability and indivisibility are the same thing if run up to their first principles. For, as in the first figure, the solidity of the body *B* is that whereby it so far resists the bodies *A* and *C* that they shall not be able, till the body *B* is out of the way, closely everywhere to touch each other. That is to say, the force of the two, *A* and *C,* endeavoring to meet could not be the annihilating of the body *B,* for the meeting of them would be the annihilating of it. By the second case, so also the indivisibility of the body *B*, in the first figure, and in the body *D*, in the second figure, has been proved to be that also whereby the bodies *B* and *D* resist that the bodies pressing upon them should touch each other,[17] inasmuch as the breaking of them would certainly admit of it and would be their annihilation.

Corollary 3. It appears from the two demonstrations and the two first corollaries that solidity, indivisibility, and resisting to be annihilated are the same thing, and that bodies resist division and penetration only as they obstinately persevere to be.

Corollary 4. Since that by the preceding corollary solidity is the resisting to be annihilated, or the persevering to be of a body, or, to speak plain, the being of it (for being and persevering to be are the same thing looked upon two, a little different, ways), it follows that the very essence and being of bodies is solidity or rather that body and solidity are the same. If here it shall be said by way of objection that body has other qualities beside solidity, I believe it will appear to a nice eye that it hath no more real ones. What say (say they) to extension, figure, and mobility? As to extension I say I am satisfied it has none more than space without body except what results from solidity; as for figure, it is nothing but a modification of solidity or of the extension of the solidity; and as to mobility, it is but the communicability of this solidity from one part of space to another.

Or thus, since that by corollary 1 annihilation and breaking are the same, their contraries, being and indivisibility, must also be the same; and since by corollary 2 indivisibility and solidity are the same, it follows that the solidity of bodies and the being of bodies is the same, or that body and solidity are the same.

Corollary 5. From what has been said it appears that the nature of an atom or a *minimum physicum* (that is, if we mean by these terms a body that can't be made less, which is the only sensible meaning of the words) does not at all consist in littleness, as generally used to be thought, for by our philosophy an atom may be as big as the universe, because any body of whatsoever bigness were an atom if it were a perfect solid.

N.B. It will be needful here a little to explain what it is that we mean by perfectly solid, absolute plenum, etc., for we have laid down that that is an absolutely full, a solid, body that has every part of space included within its surface solid or impenetrable. Our meaning is very liable to be mistaken unless a little explained. We intend not but that a perfect solid may be very full of pores, though perhaps improperly so called, interspersed up and down in it as in the perfect solid *L*. It is only requisite that every part of the body *L* should intimately be con-

[17] That is, resists the tendency of bodies *A* and *C*, or *E* and *F*, to come together.

joined with some other parts of it so as not only barely to touch in some points or lines thereof (I mean mathematical points or lines) as two perfect globes do, or as a cylindar when it lies on one side does a plane, and as all atoms do each other except the surfaces where they happen to be infinitey exactly fitted to join each other. So that the body *L,* although it may have some little holes in it, yet it has an absolute plenum continued all along between these holes so that it is as impregnable as a body that has no holes at all.[18] And this will be understood more fully after we have proved that two atoms touching each other by surfaces can never be separated.

Now 'tis time to apply what we have said concerning atoms to prove that all bodies are compounded of such. For if we suppose that all those bodies which are anyway familiar to our senses have interstices so interspersed throughout the whole body that some parts of [it] do only touch others and are not conjoined with them, by which they are rendered imperfectly solid, yet we must allow that those parcels of matter that are between the pores (that is, betwixt this and the next adjacent pore) have no pores at all in them and consequently are plenums or absolute solids or atoms. And surely all bodies that have pores are made up of parcels of matter which are between the pores, which we have proved to be atoms.[19]

Proposition 2.[20] Two or more atoms, or perfect solids, touching

---

[18] Another definition appears as no. 29 in the first series of topics on which Edwards proposed to write. It reads, "In definition of an atom: such a body whose parts are no ways separated by pores but has all its parts conjoined by an absolute continuity of matter." See Introduction, above, pp. xii-xiii and notes 22 and 23.

[19] No. 30, first series (see note 18), reads: "Relating to the note of the 5 corollary of the 1st proposition. Hence we may learn that an absolutely solid body may have as much vacuity within its surfaces as any body whatsoever that is not absolutely solid."

[20] In the third part of the manuscript which Dwight called *Notes on Natural Science* (p. 25) there is a possible reference to this proposition. It reads, "Gravity. Let it be a corollary to one of the former propositions. Hence it follows that two atoms or particles, however small, may by the force of their gravity cleave together with any finite degree of strength that can be mentioned, and yet not cleave with infinite strength. For, seeing that when their surfaces touch each other they tend to each other with infinite strength, and the nearer two atoms approach to such touching with so much the greater strength they tend to each other, and amongst the infinite numbers of degrees of nearness there is none but what is possible—all which are short of infinite but which [are] touching: therefore it follows that there is no degree of finite tendency to each other but what the least particles are capable of. And it is no strange thing if two very small particles should cleave together with such strength as to exceed the force of the motion of a comet in its perihelion. So that, if all the force of that motion could be applied to these atoms, it shall not

each other by surfaces—I mean so that every point in any surface of the one shall touch every point in some surface of the other, that is, not only barely in some particular points or lines of their surfaces how many soever (for whatsoever does touch in more than points or lines toucheth in every point of some surface)—by that become one and the same atom or perfect solid, which will be abundantly clear by the figure. As, suppose the perfect solid *AB* and the perfect solid *CD* to be precisely like to the halves of the perfect solid *AD,* to wit *Af* and *cD;* and then suppose the atom *AB* to move up to the body *CD,* so that the surface *gB* shall touch in every point of the surface *Ch.* Now since that these two bodies when separate were precisely every way like the two halves of the body *AD,* it follows that, after they are joined together after the same manner as the two halves of the body *AD* are, they must make up a body every way precisely like the body *AD,* as if it were the same and, consequently, must be a perfect solid as the body *AD* is.

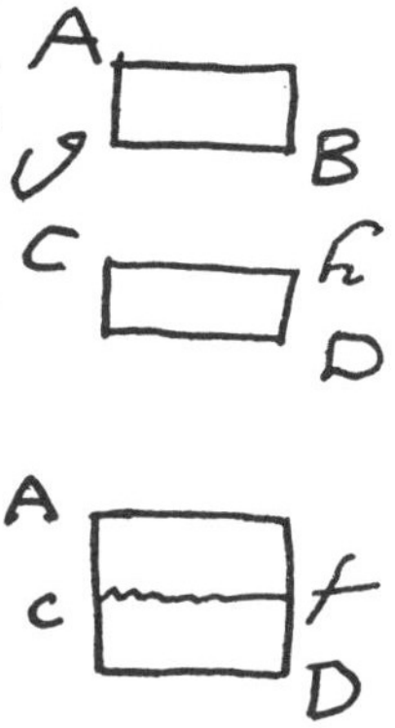

A B g C h D A c f D

But perhaps it will be answered, the halves of the body *AD* are joined and continued but the two bodies *AB* and *CD* only touch each other. But I affirm that the latter are as much joined and continued as the former, for all the way as the former are joined and continued is only as solidity is all along continued from one to t'other without the least intermission. So, as there is not the least vacuity betwixt them, just so also it is in the latter after they touch. For they are supposed to touch in every point of their surfaces and then, I am sure, solidity is continued from one to the other without intermission or vacuity. Neither does the *AB* and *CD* being once separate make any alteration.

Corollary 1. Hence it follows that all atoms that ever happen to touch each other in any surfaces or more than barely in some certain points or lines (millions of millions of which don't make so much as the least surface) can never again be separated by any finite power, since it has been proved that the parts of atoms cannot be torn asunder and since it has been proved that atoms so touching become the same atom.

Corollary 2. From proposition 1 and the preceding corollary we learn that it must needs be an infinite power that keeps the parts of atoms together, or, which with us is the same, that keeps two bodies

be able to rend them asunder—and yet a greater force shall be sufficient for it." Dwight has given this item a number, modified its language, and placed it as corollary 18 of proposition 2 (vol. 1, p. 715).

touching by surfaces in being. For it must be infinite power, or bigger than any finite, that resists all finite how big soever, as we have proved these bodies to do.

Corollary 3. We have already as much as [said] that it is God Himself or the immediate exercise of His power that keeps the parts of atoms or two bodies touching, as aforesaid, together; for it is self-evident that barely two atoms being together, and that alone, is no power at all much less an infinite power, and if any say the nature of atoms is an infinite power [they] say the same that I do. For all the nature of them that is not absolutely themselves must be God exerting His power upon them.

Corollary 4. Since by the foregoing corollary the exercising of the infinite power of God is necessary to keep the parts of atoms together and since by the first corollary, if the dissolution of them would be annihilation, it follows that the constant exercise of the infinite power of God is necessary to preserve bodies in being.

Corollary 5. Hence an incontestible argument for the being of God.

Corollary 6. Since by corollary 4, foregoing, there is need of the exercise of infinite power in order to keep bodies in being, it clearly follows that there was need of an infinite power to bring them into being. So that it was a divine and no created being that created and preserves the world.

Corollary 7. Hence also an incontestable argument for the being, infinite power, and omnipresence of God. Of the two latter, inasmuch as we see that the infinite power [is] actually exerted in an infinite number of places at once, even in every part of every atom of the universe. And since where His power is exercised there His essence must be, His essence can be by nothing excluded.

Corollary 8. Since by corollary 3 of the first proposition solidity [and] indivisibility are the same and since by corollary 3, foregoing, indivisibility is from the immediate exercise of God's power, it follows that solidity results from the immediate exercise of God's power causing there to be indefinite resistance in that place where it is.

Corollary 9. Since by the fourth corollary of the first proposition body and solidity are the same and by the preceding corollary solidity is from the immediate exercise of divine power, it follows that all body is nothing but what immediately results from the exercise of divine power in such a particular manner.

Corollary 10. It follows by the same corollaries that creation is the first exercise of that power in that manner. *Vid.* No. 47.[21]

---

[21] No. 47, first series, reads: "Since, as has been shown, body is nothing but an infinite resistance in some part of space caused by the immediate exercise of

Corollary 11. Since by corollary fourth of the first proposition body and solidity are the same and, by the eighth foregoing, resistance or solidity are by the immediate exercise of divine power, it follows that the certain unknown substance which philosophers used to think subsisted by itself and stood underneath and kept up solidity and all other properties (which they used to say it was impossible for a man to have an idea of) is nothing at all distinct from solidity itself. Or, if they must needs apply that word to something else that does really and properly subsist by itself and support all properties, they must apply it to the divine being or power itself. And here, I believe, all those philosophers would apply it if they knew what they meant themselves. So that this substance of bodies at last becomes either 'nothing' or nothing but the Deity acting in that particular manner in those parts of space where He thinks fit. So that speaking most strictly there is no proper substance but God Himself. We speak at present with respect to bodies only. How truly then is He said to be *ens entium*![22]

Corollary 12. Since, by the eighth and ninth foregoing, solidity or body is immediately from the exercise of divine power causing there to be resistance in such a part of space, it follows that motion also,

---

divine power, it follows that as great and as wonderful power is every moment exerted to the upholding of the world as at first was to the creating of it—the first creation being only the first exertion of this power to cause such resistance; preservation, only the continuation or the repetition of this power every moment to cause this resistance. So that the universe is created out of nothing every moment and, if it were not for our imaginations, which hinder us, we might see that wonderful work performed continually which was seen by the morning stars when they sang together."

[22] No. 26, first series, reads: "To bring in an observation somewhere, in a proper place, that, instead of Hobbes's notion that God is matter and that all substance is matter, that nothing that is matter can possibly be God and that no matter is, in the most proper sense, matter. Relating to the 11th corollary of proposition 2."

No. 44 reads: "To observe that as bodies have no substance of their own, so neither is solidity, strictly speaking, a property belonging to body: and to show how. And if solidity is not so, neither are the other properties of body which depend upon it and are only modifications of it. So that there is neither real substance nor property belonging to bodies; but all that is real is immediately in the first being.

"Corollary 1. Hence see still, how God is said still more properly to be *ens entium* or, if there was nothing else in the world but bodies, the only real being. So that it may be said in a stricter sense than hitherto—Thou art and there is none else besides Thee.

"Corollary 2. Hence, that instead of matter's being the only proper substance and more substantial than anything else because it is hard and solid, that it is truly even nothing at all strictly, and in itself, considered.

"Corollary 3. The nearer in nature beings are to God, so much the more properly are they beings, and more substantial. And that spirits are much more properly beings and more substantial than bodies."

which is the communication of body, solidity, or this resistance from one part of space to another successively (that is, from one part of space to the next immediately adjacent and so on to the next), is from the immediate exercise of divine power communicating that resistance, according to certain conditions which we call the laws of motion. How truly then is it in Him that we live, move, and have our being![28]

Corollary 13. From all which we find that what divines used to say concerning divine concourse had a great deal of truth lay at the bottom of it.

Corollary 14. We by this also clearly see that the creation of the corporeal universe is nothing but the first causing [of] resistance in such parts of space as God thought fit, with a power of being communicated successively from one part of space to another according to such stated conditions as His infinite wisdom directed (and then, the first beginning of this communication) so that ever after it might be continued without deviating from those stated conditions.

Corollary 15. Hence we see what's that we call the laws of nature

---

[28] No. 14, first series, reads: "To show how the motion, rest, and direction of the least atom has an influence on the motion, rest, and direction of every body in the universe. And to show how, by that means, how that everything that happens with respect to motes or straw, and such little things, may be for some great uses in the whole course of things through eternity. And to show how the least wrong step in a mote may in eternity subvert the order of the universe. And to take notice of the great wisdom that is necessary in order thus to dispose every atom at first that they should go for the best throughout all eternity, and in the adjusting, by an exact computation and a nice allowance, to be made for the miracles which should be needful. [In no. 53 of the same series Edwards has meticulously made a memorandum to add the following words to the preceding sentence, "and other ways whereby the course of bodies should be diverted."] And then to show how God who does this must necessarily be omniscient and know every least thing that must happen through eternity. *Vid.* 49; *Vid. The Mind,* p. 12, 13, 14."

No. 49 reads: "*Vid.* 14. In order to this 'tis not only necessary that God should tell the number of the stars, and know the exact bigness, weight, density, number, and distance of those greater bodies of the universe; not only weigh the mountains in exact scales and the hills in perfectly even balances, and measure the seas as in the hollow of His hand: but He must comprehend the dust of the earth; in a measure He must measure the dust of the earth in all these respects. He must know the exact number of particles of dust, the exact dimensions and weight of every atom, the exact distance of every, yea, of every part of every one from every other, yea, from every part of all others in the universe. Thus infinite wisdom is as much concerned, not only in the excellent creation of the world but merely the creation of it, as infinite power. Yea, one single atom cannot have a being without it, one single atom could not move without it, inasmuch as we have shown that motion cannot be without infinite wisdom, and again that no body could have a being without motion any otherwise than as the world had a being from all eternity."

The reference to *The Mind* is omitted by Dwight. The numbers (12, 13, 14) do not correspond to any numbers in Dwight's printed edition. The references are important, however, for they indicate that the manuscript on *The Mind* is earlier than this list of topics.

in bodies, to wit, the stated methods of God's acting with respect to bodies and the stated conditions of the alteration of the manner of His acting.

Corollary 16. Hence we learn that there is no such thing as mechanism if that word is taken to be that whereby bodies act each upon other purely and properly by themselves.

Corollary 17. Since by corollary 1 atoms that happen to touch each other in surfaces or more than barely in points and lines can never by finite force be separated, it follows that all those compound bodies in the universe which can be divided and broken have their parts only touching each other in some points or, at most, lines. Not but that those points and lines in which they touch may be of any number whatsoever—as many, if you please, as a man can note down with his pen in his lifetime—yet these points and lines fall infinitely short of the least surface; and two bodies touching each other in all those points don't touch each other so much, by an infinite deal, as two bodies touching in the least surface. And although perhaps, *ceteris paribus,* the more points bodies touch each other in, the more difficulty separated, yet it must be allowed that those that touch in most points can be separated infinitely easier than bodies touching in surfaces.[24]

Objection. But, you will say, if so we should surely experience something of it. A thousand to one but that some of the atoms of those compound bodies with which we converse, in all their infinite jumbles and colligations and collisions, would happen to touch each other by their surfaces so as not by any finite force to be separated. Why then do we never find any body but what we can divide and divide again as often as we please? Why do the surfaces of two bodies never happen to touch each other so as never to [be] hauled asunder again, for who can imagine but that some atom in the surface of one body in so many innumerable applications should happen to touch some atom in the surface of another body by surfaces?

I answer: 1. I do not think it to be at all rash or absurd to suppose that the Almighty might take care, in the first creation, sufficient to prevent any such fatal or inconvenient consequences, by creating the atoms of which the universe was to be composed of such figures as that no surface of any one should be so suited to the surface of any other as to be able to touch it by surfaces—which would prevent all that is objected.

2. If we suppose that the Almighty took no care at all of that matter, yet it is a thousand to one if, of all the atoms in the universe, there happened to be ever a two whose surfaces were so exactly and nicely suited and adapted to each other as that they should precisely

coalesce. For is it not infinity to one that one surface should be so as to be precisely fitted to another surface when there are infinite other different ways that it could have been as well? And it is all one, let the surfaces be greater or less; and the odds is the same betwixt infinity and one atom and infinity and all the atoms in the universe.[25]

3. Suppose there should be some atoms in the universe which had their surfaces exactly adapted, it is a thousand to one if ever they come together or, if they did, that they should touch on that side where were the correspondent surfaces.

4. If those that had surfaces exactly adapted to each other should come together, a thousand to one if they are not some prominences or some such thing that shall hinder their being exactly applied.

5. If there should happen to get together some of those atoms, yea many millions of them, in a heap so as never again to be got asunder and such heaps should be frequent—that need not hinder but that bodies may be divided more than ever we yet experienced and in finer parts than we can perceive with our senses either naked or assisted by the best instruments. For what hinders but that a compages of millions of millions of atoms should be so little as to be out of the reach of the microscope?

6. Neither would there be any such fatal adhesion if one atom in the surface of one body should happen to touch an atom in the surface of another in this manner, for 'tis but the taking of an atom from the surface of one of these bodies and the separation is made. And I conceive, if it were three or four millions of atoms, it could be done with infinite ease.

---

[24] No. 34, first series, reads: "To show how that by our laws a compound body of any degree of rarity may have any degree of hardness or inseparability and, *vice versa,* a very dense body and of little vacuity may be, in comparison of it, very soft and separable." On Dwight's corollary 18, see note 20 above.

[25] See *Miscellanies,* no. 880, p. 87, below.

The Mind[1]

1. Excellency. There has nothing been more without a definition than excellency, although it be what we are more concerned with than any thing else whatsoever: yea, we are concerned with nothing else. But what is this excellency? Wherein is one thing excellent and another evil; one beautiful and another deformed? Some have said that all excellency is harmony, symmetry, or proportion; but they have not yet explained it. We would know, why proportion is more excellent than disproportion; that is, why proportion is pleasant to the mind and disproportion unpleasant. Proportion is a thing that may be explained yet further. It is an equality or likeness of ratios; so that it is the equality that makes the proportion. Excellency therefore seems to consist in equality. Thus if there be two perfect equal circles or globes together, there is something more of beauty than if they were of unequal, disproportionate magnitudes. And if two parallel lines be drawn, the beauty is greater than if they were obliquely inclined without proportion, because there is equality of distance. And if betwixt two parallel lines, two equal circles be placed, each at the same distance

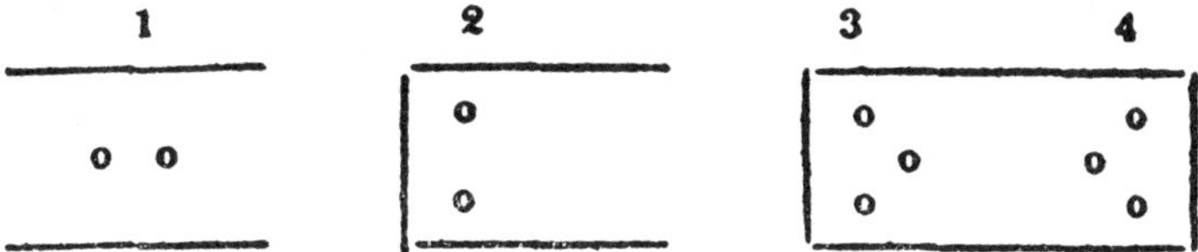

from each parallel line, as in Fig. 1, the beauty is greater than if they stood at irregular distances from the parallel lines. If they stand, each in a perpendicular line going from the parallel lines (Fig. 2), it is requisite that they should each stand at an equal distance from the per-

[1] See Introduction. I find no reason to abandon the commonly accepted theory that this is a work of the young Edwards, although it is probable that it was mainly written after he had expressed his distinctive idealism in the essay *Of Being*. The time relation between *The Mind* and the so-called *Notes on Natural Science* seems to be substantially as E. C. Smyth supposed it to be in his paper (*Proceedings of the American Antiquarian Society,* n.s., vol. 10, 1895, pp. 213-236), that is, that the latter, or at least the parts of it included in this volume, were the earlier, but this does not exclude the possibility that the two documents were written during a rather extended period of time and therefore may be in parts contemporary. Dwight records the fact that the numbers from 61 to the end of *The Mind* were "inserted in the manuscript distinctly from the rest, and were written probably at a somewhat later period of life." (Vol. 1, p. 674n.) The loss of the manuscript leaves us without data for interpretation of *The Mind* such as

pendicular line next to them; otherwise there is no beauty. If there be three of these circles between two parallel lines, and near to a perpendicular line run between them[2] (Fig. 3), the most beautiful form, perhaps, that they could be placed in is in an equilateral triangle with the cross line, because there are most equalities. The distance of the two next to the cross line is equal from that, and also equal from the parallel lines. The distance of the third from each parallel is equal, and its distance from each of the other two circles is equal, and is also equal to their distance from one another, and likewise equal to their distance from each end of the cross line. There are two equilateral triangles: one made by the three circles, and the other made by the cross line and two of the sides of the first[3] protracted till they meet that line. And if there be another like it, on the opposite side, to correspond with it and it be taken altogether, the beauty is still greater, where the distances from the lines, in the one, are equal to the distances in the other; also the two next to the cross lines are at equal distances from the other two. Or, if you go crosswise from corner to corner, the two cross lines are also parallel, so that all parts are at an equal distance.[4] And innumerable other equalities might be found.

This simple equality without proportion is the lowest kind of regularity, and may be called simple beauty. All other beauties and excellencies may be resolved into it. Proportion is complex beauty. Thus, if we suppose that there are two points, *AB,* placed at two inches distance, and the next, *C,* one inch farther (Fig. 1), it is requisite, in order to regularity and beauty, if there be another, *D,* that it should be at half an inch distance. Otherwise there is no regularity, and the last, *D,* would stand out of its proper place, because now the relation that the space *CD* bears to *BC* is equal to the relations that *BC* bears

Fig. 1.

A B C D

Fig. 2.

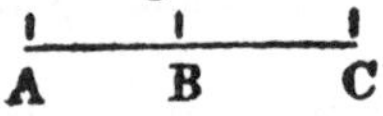

A B C

I found in the manuscript of the *Notes on Natural Science.* The statement of Faust and Johnson (*Jonathan Edwards,* 1935, p. 418) that a transcript of *The Mind* is deposited in the Newton-Andover Theological Library seems to be without foundation, as a search of the library failed to discover it. The original manuscript was apparently not known to Smyth in 1895 (*op. cit.,* p. 212). Writing in 1903 (*Exercises Commemorating the Two-Hundredth Anniversary of the Birth of Jonathan Edwards,* Andover, 1904, Appendix I, p. 3), Smyth says: "The autographs of the papers on the 'External world' are in my possession; those on the 'Mental world' have strangely disappeared."

[2] That is, between the parallel lines.

[3] That is, the "first" equilateral triangle.

[4] Dwight has designated a part of Fig. 3 with the numeral "4" (vol. 1, p. 694). His text, however, does not justify this and the illustration would be clearer if "4" were omitted.

to *AB;* so that *BCD* is exactly similar to *ABC*. It is evident this is a more-complicated excellency than that which consisted in equality because the terms of the relation are here complex, and before were simple. When there are three points set in a right line, it is requisite in order to regularity that they should be set at an equal distance, as *ABC* (Fig. 2), where *AB* is similar to *BC,* or the relation of *C* to *B* is the same as of *B* to *A*. But in the other are three terms necessary in each of the parts between which is the relation, *BCD* is as *ABC*. So that here more-simple beauties are omitted, and yet there is a general complex beauty: that is, *BC* is not as *AB,* nor is *CD* as *BC,* but yet *BCD* is as *ABC*. It is requisite that the consent or regularity of *CD* to *BC* be omitted for the sake of the harmony of the whole. For although, if *CD* was perfectly equal to *BC,* there would be regularity and beauty with respect to them two, yet if *AB* be taken into the idea, there is nothing but confusion. And it might be requisite, if these stood with others, even to omit this proposition[5] for the sake of one more complex still. Thus if they stood with other points where *B* stood at four inches distance from *A, C* at two from *B,* and *D* at six from *C,* the place where *D* must stand in (if *A, B, C, D* were alone, viz. one inch from *C*) must be so as to be made proportionate with the other points

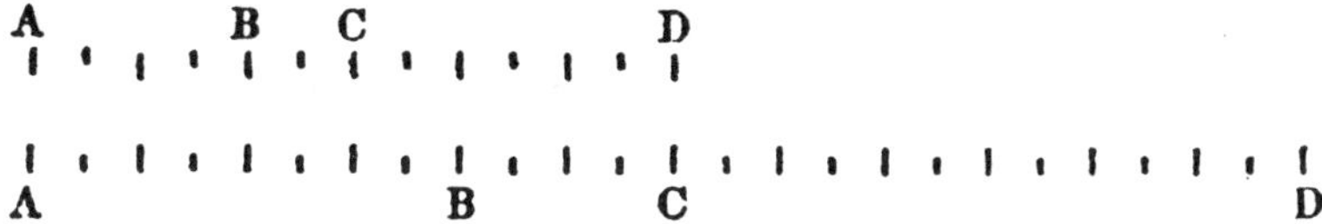

beneath. So that, although *A, B, C, D* are not proportioned but are confusion among themselves, yet taken with the whole they are proportioned and beautiful.

All beauty consists in similarness or identity of relation. In identity of relation consists all likeness, and all identity between two consists in identity of relation. Thus, when the distance between two is exactly equal, their distance is their relation one to another. The distance is the same, the bodies are two; wherefore this is their correspondency and beauty. So, bodies exactly of the same figure: the bodies are two, the relation between the parts of the extremities is the same, and this is their agreement with them. But if there are two bodies of different shapes having no similarness of relation between the parts of the extremities, this, considered by itself, is a deformity because being disagrees with being, which must undoubtedly be disagreeable to perceiving being, because what disagrees with being must necessarily be disagreeable to being in general, to everything that partakes of entity, and of course

[5] The word should probably be "proportion."

to perceiving being; and what agrees with being must be agreeable to being in general, and therefore to perceiving being. But agreeableness of perceiving being is pleasure, and disagreeableness is pain. Disagreement or contrariety to being is evidently an approach to nothing, or a degree of nothing (which is nothing else but disagreement or contrariety of being) and the greatest and only evil; and entity is the greatest and only good. And by how much more perfect entity is, that is, without mixture of 'nothing,' by so much the more, excellency. Two beings can agree one with another in nothing else but relation, because otherwise the notion of their twoness (duality) is destroyed, and they become one.

And so in every case what is called correspondency, symmetry, regularity, and the like may be resolved into equalities, though the equalities in a beauty in any degree complicated are so numerous that it would be a most-tedious piece of work to enumerate them. There are millions of these equalities. Of these consist the beautiful shape of flowers, the beauty of the body of man, and of the bodies of other animals. That sort of beauty which is called natural, as of vines, plants, trees, etc., consists of a very complicated harmony. And all the natural motions and tendencies and figures of bodies in the universe are done according to proportion, and therein is their beauty. Particular disproportions sometimes greatly add to the general beauty, and must necessarily be, in order to a more universal proportion—so much equality, so much beauty. Though it may be noted that the quantity of equality is not to be measured only by the number, but the intenseness, according to the quantity of being. As bodies are shadows of being, so their proportions are shadows of proportion.

The pleasures of the senses, where harmony is not the object of judgment, are the result of equality. Thus in music, not only in the proportion which the several notes of a tune bear, one among another, but in merely two notes there is harmony—whereas it is impossible there should be proportion between only two terms—but the proportion is in the particular vibrations of the air which strike on the ear. And so, in the pleasantness of light, colors, tastes, smells, and touch—all arise from proportion of motion. The organs are so contrived that upon the touch of such and such particles there shall be a regular and harmonious motion of the animal spirits.[6]

[6] In the third part of the manuscript of *Notes on Natural Science,* at the top of the page numbered 22, Edwards wrote, "The pleasure the mind has by the sense arises immediately from an harmonious motion of the animal spirits; their appulse to the brain being in an harmonious order consisting in a regular proportion of time, distance, and celerity. We know it is thus in one of the senses, to wit, hearing, which may lead us to think 'tis so in all the rest; especially considering that we

Spiritual harmonies are of vastly larger extent, i. e., the proportions are vastly oftener redoubled and respect more[7] beings and require a vastly larger view to comprehend them; as some simple notes do more effect one who has not a comprehensive understanding of music.[8]

The reason why equality thus pleases the mind, and inequality is unpleasing, is because disproportion or inconsistency is contrary to being. For being, if we examine narrowly, is nothing else but proportion. When one being is inconsistent with another being, then being is contradicted. But contradiction to being is intolerable to perceiving being; and the consent to being, most pleasing.

Excellency consists in the similarness of one being to another, not merely equality and proportion, but any kind of similarness—thus similarness of direction. Supposing many globes moving in right lines, it is more beautiful that they should move all the same way, and according to the same direction, than if they moved disorderly—one, one way and another, another. This is an universal definition of excellency: The consent of being to being, or being's consent to entity. The more the consent is, and the more extensive, the greater is the excellency.

How exceedingly apt are we, when we are sitting still and accidentally casting our eye upon some marks or spots in the floor or wall, to be ranging of them into regular parcels and figures and, if we see a mark out of its place, to be placing of it right by our imagination; and this, even while we are meditating on something else. So we may catch our-

---

find nothing that the mind loves in things but proportion. Pain is caused either by a motion of the animal spirits that is contrary thereto or by a laceration and dislocation of the parts of the body, which are partly its destruction, which the mind abhors by reason of the law of union between soul and body.

"'Tis certain that, when God first created matter or the various chaoses of atoms, besides creating the atoms and giving of the whole chaos its motion, He designed the figures and shapes of every atom and likewise their places; which doubtless was done with infinite wisdom and with an eye to what should follow from the particular bulk, figure, and place of every atom. And this He so ordered that, without doing any more, the chaoses of themselves, according to the established laws of matter, were brought into these various and excellent forms, adapted to every of God's ends (omitting the more excellent works of plants and animals which it was proper and fit God should have a more immediate hand in). So the atoms of our chaos were created in such places, of such magnitudes and figures, that the laws of nature brought them into this form fit in every regard for them who were to be the inhabitants."

For some unknown reason Dwight divided this item into two parts. He numbered the first paragraph "30" of the first series (vol. 1, p. 721) and the second paragraph "88" of the second series (vol. 1, p. 760). He further supplied a title, "Atoms," for the second paragraph.

[7] Dwight's text reads "mere" but this must be a misprint.

[8] The transition of thought is not explicit; but Edwards seems to mean that stupid or uninformed persons will have difficulty in perceiving complex spiritual beauty, as they have in perceiving the beauty of complex music.

selves at observing the rules of harmony and regularity in the careless motions of our heads or feet, and when playing with our hands, or walking about the room.

Pleasedness in perceiving being always arises either from a perception of consent to being in general or of consent to that being that perceives. As we have shown that agreeableness to entity must be agreeable to perceiving entity, it is as evident that it is necessary that agreeableness to that being must be pleasing to it, if it perceives it. So that pleasedness does not always arise from a perception of excellency in general.[9] But the greater a being is, and the more it has of entity, the more will consent to being in general please it. But God is proper entity itself, and these two, therefore, in Him become the same. For, so far as a thing consents to being in general, so far it consents to Him. And the more perfect created spirits are, the nearer do they come to their Creator in this regard.

That which is often called self-love is exceedingly improperly called love. For they do not only say that one loves himself when he sees something amiable in himself (the view of which begets delight), but merely an inclination to pleasure and averseness to pain they call self-love. So that the devils and other damned spirits love themselves, not because they see anything in themselves which they imagine to be lovely, but merely because they do not incline to pain but to pleasure, or merely because they are capable of pain or pleasure. For pain and pleasure include an inclination to agreeableness and an aversion to disagreeableness. Now how improper is it to say that one loves himself because what is agreeable to him is agreeable to him and what is disagreeable to him is disagreeable to him—which mere entity supposes! So that this that they call self-love is no affection, but only the entity of the thing, or his being what he is.

One alone without any reference to any more cannot be excellent; for, in such case, there can be no manner of relation no way, and therefor no such thing as consent. Indeed, what we call 'one' may be excellent because of a consent of parts, or some consent of those in that being that are distinguished into a plurality some way or other. But in a being that is absolutely without any plurality there cannot be excellency, for there can be no such thing as consent or agreement.

One of the highest excellencies is love, as nothing else has a proper being but spirits. And, as bodies are but the shadow of being, therefore the consent of bodies one to another and the harmony that is among them is but the shadow of excellency. The highest excellency there-

[9] Dwight's punctuation is especially unfortunate here since it obscures Edwards' familiar concept of "excellency in general."

fore must be the consent of spirits one to another; but the consent of spirits consists half in their mutual love one to another. And the sweet harmony between the various parts of the universe is only an image of mutual love. But yet a lower kind of love may be odious because it hinders, or is contrary to, a higher and more general. Even a lower proportion is often a deformity because it is contrary to a more general proportion.

Corollary 1. If so much of the beauty and excellency of spirits consists in love, then the deformity of evil spirits consists as much in hatred and malice.

Corollary 2. The more any doctrine or institution brings to light of the spiritual world, the more will it urge to love and charity.

Happiness strictly consists in the perception of these three things: of the consent of being to its own being; of its own consent to being; and of being's consent to being.

2. Place of minds. Our common way of conceiving of what is spiritual is very gross and shadowy and corporeal—with dimensions and figure, etc.—though it be supposed to be very clear, so that we can see through it. If we would get a right notion of what is spiritual we must think of thought, or inclination, or delight. How large is that thing in the mind which they call thought? Is love square or round? Is the surface of hatred rough or smooth? Is joy an inch or a foot in diameter? These are spiritual things. And why should we then form such a ridiculous idea of spirits as to think them so long, so thick, or so wide; or to think there is a necessity of their being square or round or some other certain figure?

Therefore spirits cannot be in place in such a sense that all within the given limits shall be where the spirit is, and all without such a circumscription, where he is not; but in this sense only, that all created spirits have clearer and more strongly impressed ideas of things in one place than in another, or can produce effects here and not there. And as this place alters, so spirits move. In spirits united to bodies the spirit more strongly perceives things where the body is and can there, immediately, produce effects. And in this sense the soul can be said to be in the same place where the body is. And this law is that we call the union between soul and body. So, the soul may be said to be in the brain because ideas that come by the body immediately ensue only on alterations that are made there; and the soul most immediately produces effects nowhere else.

No doubt that all finite spirits, united to bodies or not, are thus 'in place'—that is, that they perceive, or passively receive, ideas only of created things that are in some particular place at a given time. At least a finite spirit cannot thus be in all places at a time, equally. And doubtless the change of the place where they perceive most strongly and produce effects immediately is regular and successive—which is the motion of spirits.

3. Perception of separate minds. Our perceptions or ideas that we passively receive by our bodies are communicated to us immediately by God while our minds are united with our bodies. But only, we in some measure know the rule: we know that upon such alterations in our minds[10] there follow such ideas in the mind. It need, therefore, be no difficulty with us how we shall perceive things when we are separate. They will be communicated then also, and according to some rule no doubt, only we know not what.

4. Union of mind with body. The mind is so united with the body that an alteration is caused in the body, it is probable, by every action of the mind. By those acts that are very vigorous a great alteration is very sensible. At some times, when the vigor of the body is impaired by disease, especially in the head, almost every action causes a sensible alteration of the body.

5. Certainty. Determined: that there are many degrees of certainty—though not indeed of absolute certainty, which is infinitely strong. We are certain of many things upon demonstration which yet we may be made more certain of by more demonstration; because although, according to the strength of the mind, we see the connection of the ideas, yet a stronger mind would see the connection more perfectly and strongly because it would have the ideas more perfect. We have not such strength of mind that we can perfectly conceive of but very few things. And some little of the strength of an idea is lost in a moment of time as we, in the mind, look successively on the train of ideas in a demonstration.

6. Truth is the perception of the relations there are between ideas. Falsehood is the supposition of relations between ideas that are inconsistent with those ideas themselves, not their disagreement with things without. All truth is in the mind, and only there. It is ideas, or what is in the mind alone, that can be the object of the mind. And what we call truth is a consistent supposition of relations between what is the object of the mind. Falsehood is an inconsistent supposition of relations. The truth that is in a mind must be in that mind as to its

---

[10] Probably "bodies" instead of "minds."

object and everything pertaining to it. The only foundation of error is inadequateness and imperfection of ideas; for if the idea were perfect it would be impossible but that all its relations should be perfectly perceived.[11]

7. Genus. The various distributing and ranking of things and tying of them together under one common abstract idea is, although arbitrary, yet exceedingly useful and indeed absolutely necessary. For how miserable should we be if we could think of things only individually, as the beasts do; how slow, narrow, painful, and endless would be the exercise of thought!

What is this putting and tying things together which is done in abstraction? It is not merely a tying of them under the same name (for I do believe that deaf and dumb persons abstract and distribute things into kinds), but it is so putting of them together that the mind resolves hereafter to think of them together under a common notion as if they were a collective substance; the mind being as sure, in this proceeding, of reasoning well as if it were of a particular substance. For it has abstracted that which belongs alike to all, and has a perfect idea whose relations and properties it can behold as well as those of the idea of one individual. Although this ranking of things be arbitrary, yet there is much more foundation for some distributions than others. Some are much more useful and much better serve the purposes of abstraction.

8. Rules of reasoning. It is no matter how abstracted our notions are, the further we penetrate and come to the prime reality of the thing the better, provided we can go to such a degree of abstraction and carry it out clear. We may go so far in abstraction that, although we may thereby, in part, see truth and reality, and farther than ever was seen before, yet we may not be able more than just to touch it and have a few obscure glances. We may not have strength of mind to conceive clearly of the manner of it. We see farther indeed, but it is very obscurely and indistinctly. We had better stop a degree or two short of this and abstract no farther than we can conceive of the thing distinctly and explain it clearly: otherwise we shall be apt to run into error and confound our minds.

9. Space. Space, as has been already observed,[12] is a necessary being, if it may be called a being; and yet we have also shown that all existence

---

[11] It is apparent that this paragraph was written under the direct influence of Locke. Later, as in nos. 10 and 15, Edwards alters Locke's view radically.

[12] See the second paragraph of the essay *Of Being*, pp. 1-2, above.

is mental—that the existence of all exterior things is ideal.[13] Therefore it is a necessary being only as it is a necessary idea—so far as it is a simple idea that is necessarily connected with other simple exterior ideas and is, as it were, their common substance or subject. It is in the same manner a necessary being as anything external is a being.

Corollary. It is hence easy to see in what sense that is true that has been held by some, that when there is nothing between any two bodies they unavoidably must touch.

10. Truth, in the general, may be defined after the most strict and metaphysical manner: the consistency and agreement of our ideas with the ideas of God. I confess this, in ordinary conversation, would not half so much tend to enlighten one in the meaning of the word as to say: the agreement of our ideas with the things as they are. But it should be enquired, What is it for our ideas to agree with things as they are—seeing that corporeal things exist no otherwise than mentally, and, as for most other things, they are only abstract ideas? Truth as to external things is the consistency of our ideas with those ideas or that train and series of ideas that are raised in our minds according to God's stated order and law. Truth as to abstract ideas is the consistency of our ideas with themselves—as when our idea of a circle, or a triangle, or any of their parts, is agreeable to the idea we have stated and agreed to call by the name of a circle, or a triangle. And it may still be said that truth[14] is the consistency of our ideas with themselves. Those ideas are false that are not consistent with the series of ideas that are raised in our minds by, [i. e.,] according to, the order of nature.

Corollary 1. Hence we see in how strict a sense it may be said that God is truth itself.

Corollary 2. Hence it appears that truth consists in having perfect and adequate ideas of things. For instance, if I judge truly how far distant the moon is from the earth, we need not say that this truth consists in the perception of the relation between the two ideas of the moon and the earth, but in the adequateness.[15]

Corollary 3. Hence, certainty is the clear perception of this perfection. Therefore, if we had perfect ideas of all things at once, that is, could have all in one view, we should know all truth at the same moment, and there would be no such thing as ratiocination, or finding

---

[13] See the corollary of the essay *Of Being*, p. 9, above.

[14] The meaning seems to require the phrase, "as to external things," at this point in the sentence.

[15] The sentence would be clearer if we substitute "their adequateness" for "the adequateness." It means that, if our ideas of the earth and the moon are adequate, then we have the truth about the distance between them.

out truth. And reasoning is only of use to us in the consequence of the paucity of our ideas and because we can have but very few in view at once. Hence it is evident that all things are self-evident to God.

11. Personal Identity. Well might Mr. Locke say that identity of person consisted in identity of consciousness, for he might have said that identity of spirit, too, consisted in the same consciousness. For a mind or spirit is nothing else but consciousness and what is included in it. The same consciousness is, to all intents and purposes, individually the very same spirit or substance as much as the same particle of matter can be the same with itself at different times.[16]

12. Being. It seems strange sometimes to me that there should be being from all eternity; and I am ready to say, What need was there that anything should be? I should then ask myself, Whether it seems strange that there should be either something or nothing? If so, it is not strange that there should be, for that necessity of there being something or nothing implies it.

13. The real and necessary existence of space and its infinity, even beyond the universe, depend upon a like reasoning as the extension[17] of spirits, and to the supposition of the reality of the existence of a successive duration before the universe—even the impossibility of removing the idea out of the mind. If it be asked, if there be limits of the creation, whether or no it be not possible that an intelligent being shall be removed beyond the limits; and then whether or no there would not be distance between that intelligent being and the limits of the universe in the same manner and as properly as there is between intelligent beings and the parts of the universe within its limits—I answer, I cannot tell what the law of nature or the constitution of God would be in this case.

Corollary. There is, therefore, no difficulty in answering such questions as these, What cause was there why the universe was placed in such a part of space? and, Why was the universe created at such a time? For if there be no space beyond the universe it was impossible that it should be created in another place; and if there was no time before, it was impossible it should be created at another time.

The idea we have of space and what we call by that name is only colored space and is entirely taken out of the mind if color be taken away. And so, all that we call extension, motion, and figure is gone if

---

16 This Lockean view was later modified. See no. 72, p. 68, below; see also *Original Sin*, pt. iv, ch. iii, in Dwight, vol. 2, pp. 549ff.

17 Probably "existence" is meant.

color is gone. As to any idea of space, extension, distance, or motion that a man born blind might form, it would be nothing like what we call by those names. All that he could have would be only certain sensations or feelings that in themselves would be no more like what we intend by space, motion, etc., than the pain we have by the scratch of a pin, or than the ideas of taste and smell. And as to the idea of motion that such an one could have, it could be only a diversification of those successions in a certain way—by succession as to time. And then there would be an agreement of these successions of sensations with some ideas we have by sight as to number and proportions. But yet the ideas, after all, [would be] nothing akin to that idea we now give this name to. And as it is very plain color is only in the mind and nothing like it can be out of all mind, hence it is manifest there can be nothing like those things we call by the name of bodies, out of the mind, unless it be in some other mind or minds.

And indeed the secret lies here: that which truly is the substance of all bodies is the infinitely exact and precise and perfectly stable idea in God's mind together with His stable will that the same shall gradually be communicated to us and to other minds according to certain fixed and exact established methods and laws; or, in somewhat different language, the infinitely exact and precise divine idea together with an answerable, perfectly exact, precise, and stable will with respect to correspondent communications to created minds and effects on their minds.

14. Excellence, to put it in other words, is that which is beautiful and lovely. That which is beautiful considered by itself separately and deformed considered as a part of something else more extended, or beautiful only with respect to itself and a few other things and not as a part of that which contains all things—the universe—is false beauty and a confined beauty. That which is beautiful with respect to the university of things has a generally extended excellence and a true beauty; and the more extended or limited its system is, the more confined or extended is its beauty.[18]

15. Truth. After all that has been said and done, the only adequate definition of truth is the agreement of our ideas with existence. To explain what this existence is, is another thing. In abstract ideas it is nothing but the ideas themselves; so their truth is their consistency with themselves. In things that are supposed to be without us, it is the determination and fixed mode of God's exciting ideas in us. So that

[18] Here, as frequently, Edwards employs a chiasmus.

truth in these things is an agreement of our ideas with that series in God. It is existence and that is all that we can say. It is impossible that we should explain a perfectly abstract and mere idea of existence; only we always find this, by running of it up, that God and real existence are the same.

Corollary. Hence we learn how properly it may be said that God is and that there is none else. And how proper are these names of the deity, Jehovah, and I am that I am!

16. Consciousness is the mind's perceiving what is in itself—ideas, actions, passions, and everything that is there perceptible. It is a sort of feeling within itself. The mind feels when it thinks, so it feels when it discerns, feels when it loves, and feels when it hates.

17. Logic. One reason why, at first, before I knew other logic, I used to be mightily pleased with the study of the old logic was because it was very pleasant to see my thoughts, that before lay in my mind jumbled without any distinction, ranged into order and distributed into classes and subdivisions, so that I could tell where they all belonged and run them up to their general heads. For this logic consisted much in distributions and definitions; and their maxims gave occasion to observe new and strange dependencies of ideas, and a seeming agreement of multitudes of them in the same thing, that I never observed before.

18. Words. We are used to apply the same words a hundred different ways and, ideas being so much tied and associated with the words, they lead us into a thousand real mistakes. For where we find that the words may be connected, the ideas being by custom tied with them, we think the ideas may be connected likewise and applied everywhere and in every way as the words.[19]

19. Things that we know by immediate sensation we know intuitively and they are properly self-evident truths: as, grass is green; the sun shines; honey is sweet. When we say that grass is green, all that we can be supposed to mean by it is that, in a constant course, when we see grass the idea of green is excited by it; and this we know self-evidently.

20. Inspiration. The evidence of immediate inspiration that the prophets had when they were immediately inspired by the Spirit of God with any truth is an absolute sort of certainty and the knowledge

[19] See no. 35, p. 40, below; also *Miscellanies,* no. 4, p. 208, below.

is, in a sense, intuitive—much in the same manner as faith and spiritual knowledge of the truth of religion. Such bright ideas are raised and such a clear view of a perfect agreement with the excellencies of the divine nature that it is known to be a communication from Him. All the deity appears in the thing and in everything pertaining to it. The prophet has so divine a sense, such a divine disposition, such a divine pleasure, and sees so divine an excellency and so divine a power in what is revealed, that he sees as immediately that God is there as we perceive one another's presence when we are talking together face to face. And our features, our voice, and our shapes are not so clear manifestations of us as those spiritual resemblances of God that are in the inspiration are manifestations of Him. But yet there are doubtless various degrees in inspiration.

21. Matter. Thought.[20] It has been a question with some, whether or no it was not possible with God to the other properties or powers of matter to add that of thought; whether He could not, if He had pleased, have added thinking and the power of perception to those other properties of solidity, mobility, and gravitation. The question is not here, whether the matter that now is, without the addition of any new primary property, could not be so contrived and modelled, so attenuated, wrought, and moved as to produce thought; but whether any lump of matter, a solid atom for instance, is not capable of receiving by the almighty power of God, in addition to the rest of its powers, a new power of thought.

Here, if the question be whether or no God cannot cause the faculty of thinking to be so added to any parcel of matter so as to be in the same place (if thought can be in place)—and that inseparably—where that matter is, so that, by a fixed law, that thought should be where that matter is and only there, being always bound to solid extension, mobility, and gravity—I do not deny it. But that seems to me quite a different thing from the question, whether matter can think, or whether God can make matter think, and is not worth the disputing. For if thought be in the same place where matter is, yet if there be no manner of communication or dependence between that and anything that is material (that is, any of that collection of properties that we call matter), if none of those properties of solidity, extension, etc., wherein materiality consists (which are matter, or at least whereby matter is matter) have any manner of influence towards the exerting of thought, and if that thought be no way dependent on solidity or mobility, and they no way help the matter, but thought could be as well without

[20] See *Miscellanies,* no. 361, p. 252, below.

those properties—then thought is not properly in matter though it be in the same place. All the properties that are properly said to be in matter depend on the other properties of matter, so that they cannot be without them. Thus figure is in matter: it depends on solidity and extension; and so doth motion; so doth gravity. And extension itself depends on solidity, in that it is the extension of the solidity; and solidity on extension, for nothing can be solid except it be extended. These ideas have a dependence on one another. But there is no manner of connection between the ideas of perception and solidity, or motion, or gravity. They are simple ideas of which we can have a perfect view and we know there is no dependence; nor can there be any dependence, for the ideas in their own nature are independent and alien one to another. All the others either include the rest or are included in them. And except the property of thought be included in the properties of matter, I think it cannot properly be said that matter has thought; or, if it can, I see not a possibility of matter in any other sense having thought. If thought's being so fixed to matter, as to be in the same place where matter is, be for thought to be in matter, thought not only can be in matter, but actually is, as much as thought can be in place. It is so connected with the bodies of men, or at least with some parts of their bodies, and will be forever after the resurrection.

22. Prejudice. Those ideas which do not pertain to the prime essence of things—such as all colors that are everywhere objected to our eyes; and sounds that are continually in our ears; those that affect the touch, as cold and heats; and all our sensations—exceedingly clog the mind in searching into the innermost nature of things, and cast such a mist over things that there is need of a sharp sight to see clearly through. For these will be continually in the mind and associated with other ideas, let us be thinking of what we will. And it is a continual care and pains to keep clear of their entanglements in our scrutinies into things. This is one way whereby the body and the senses observe[21] the views of the mind. The world seems so differently to our eyes, to our ears and other senses, from the idea we have of it by reason that we can hardly realize the latter.

23. The reason why the names of spiritual things are all, or most of them, derived from the names of sensible or corporeal ones—as imagination, conception, apprehend, etc.—is because there was no other way of making others readily understand men's meaning, when they first signified these things by sounds, than by giving of them the names

[21] Probably the word in the manuscript was "obscure" rather than "observe."

of things sensible, to which they had an analogy. They could thus point it out with the finger and so explain themselves, as in sensible things.

24. There is really a difference that the mind makes in the consideration of an universal (absolutely considered) and a species. There is a difference in the two ideas when we say man, including simply the abstract idea, and when we say [man], the human sort of living creature. There is reference had to an idea more abstract. And there is this act of the mind in distributing an universal into species—it ties this abstract idea to two or more less-abstract ideas and supposes it limited by them.

It is not every property that belongs to all the particulars included in and proper to a genus, and that men generally see to be so, that is a part of that complex abstract idea that represents all the particulars or that is a part of that nominal essence. But so much is essential which, if men should see anything less, they would not call it by the name by which they call the genus. This indeed is uncertain because men never agree upon fixing exact bounds.

25. The distribution of the objects of our thoughts into substances and modes may be proper, if by substance we understand a complexion of such ideas which we conceive of as subsisting together and by themselves; and by modes, those simple ideas which cannot be by themselves or subsist in our mind alone.

A part is one of those many ideas which we are wont to think of together. A whole is an idea containing many of these.[22]

26. Cause is that, after or upon the existence of which (or the existence of it after such a manner), the existence of another thing follows.

27. Existence. If we had only the sense of seeing, we should not be as ready to conclude the visible world to have been an existence independent of perception as we do; because, the ideas we have by the feeling are as much mere ideas as those we have by the sense of seeing, but we know that the things that are objects of this sense (all that the mind views by seeing) are merely mental existences because all these things, with all their modes, do exist in a looking glass, where all will acknowledge they exist only mentally.

It is now agreed upon by every knowing philosopher that colors are not really in the things—no more than pain is in a needle—but strictly nowhere else but in the mind. But yet I think that color may

---

[22] This paragraph appears in Dwight's text as no. 25. But, since he has two 25s and they are related in subject matter, I have placed them under the single number.

have an existence out of the mind with equal reason as anything in body has any existence out of the mind, beside the very substance of the body itself, which is nothing but the divine power, or rather the constant exertion of it. For what idea is that which we call by the name of body? I find color has the chief share in it. 'Tis nothing but color, and figure which is the termination of this color, together with some powers, such as the power of resisting and motion, etc., that wholly makes up what we call body. And if that which we principally mean by the thing itself cannot be said to be in the thing itself, I think nothing can be. If color exists not out of the mind, then nothing belonging to body exists out of the mind but resistance, which is solidity; and the termination of this resistance with its relations, which is figure; and the communication of the resistance from space to space, which is motion—though the latter are nothing but modes of the former. Therefore, there is nothing out of the mind but resistance. And not that neither, when nothing is actually resisted. Then, there is nothing but the power of resistance. And as resistance is nothing else but the actual exertion of God's power, so the power can be nothing else but the constant law or method of that actual exertion. And how is there any resistance except it be in some mind, in idea? What is it that is resisted? It is not color. And what else is it? It is ridiculous to say that resistance is resisted. That does not tell us at all what is to be resisted. There must be something resisted before there can be resistance, but to say resistance is resisted is ridiculously to suppose resistance before there is anything to be resisted. Let us suppose two globes only, existing; and no mind. There is nothing there, *ex confessio,* but resistance. That is, there is such a law that the space within the limits of a globular figure shall resist. Therefore, there is nothing there but a power, or an establishment. And if there be any resistance really out of the mind, one power and establishment must resist another establishment and law of resistance, which is exceedingly ridiculous. But yet it cannot be otherwise, if any way out of the mind. But now it is easy to conceive of resistance as a mode of an idea. It is easy to conceive of such a power or constant manner of stopping or resisting a color. The idea may be resisted, it may move, and stop and rebound; but how a mere power, which is nothing real, can move and stop is inconceivable, and it is impossible to say a word about it without contradiction. The world is therefore an ideal one; and the law of creating, and the succession of these ideas, is constant and regular.

28. Corollary 1. How impossible is it that the world should exist from eternity without a mind!

29. Power. We have explained a cause to be that after, or upon the existence of which, or its existence in such a manner, the existence of another thing follows. The connection between these two existences or between the cause and effect is what we call power. Thus the sun above the horizon enlightens the atmosphere. So we say the sun has power to enlighten the atmosphere. That is, there is such a connection between the sun being above the horizon after such a manner and the atmosphere being enlightened that one always follows the other. So the sun has power to melt wax: that is, the sun and wax so existing, the melting of the wax follows. There is a connection between one and the other. So man has power to do this or that—that is, if he exists after such a manner, there follows the existence of another thing; if he wills this or that, it will be so. God has power to do all things because there is nothing but what follows upon His willing of it. When intelligent beings are said to have power to do this or that, by it is meant: the connection between [them is that] this or that [follows] upon this manner of their existing—their willing; in which sense they have power to do many things that they never shall will.[23]

Corollary. Hence it follows that men in a very proper sense may be said to have power to abstain from sin and to repent, to do good works and to live holily, because it depends on their will.

30. Corollary 2. Since it is so and that absolute nothing is such a dreadful contradiction, hence we learn the necessity of the eternal existence of an all-comprehending mind and that it is the complication of all contradictions to deny such a mind.[24]

31. From what is said above,[25] we learn that the seat of the soul is not in the brain any otherwise than as to its immediate operations and the immediate operation of things on it. The soul may also be said to be in the heart, or the affections, for its immediate operations are there also. Hence we learn the propriety of the Scripture's calling the soul the heart, when considered with respect to the will and the affections.

We seem to think in our heads because most of the ideas of which our thoughts are constituted, or about which they are conversant, come by the sensories that are in the head, especially the sight and hearing, or those ideas of reflection that arise from hence; and partly because we feel the effects of thought and study in our head.

---

[23] The suggested addition of words at least makes the sentence express a meaning. And the meaning is plainly in harmony with Edwards' doctrine.

[24] In Dwight's edition, no. 30 follows immediately after no. 28, which is in turn a corollary to no. 27. In serial order it appears to be a corollary to no. 29, but the content does not allow this.

[25] See no. 2, p. 27, above.

32. Seeing human souls and finite spirits are said to be in this place or that only because they are so as to mutual communications, it follows that the Scripture, when it speaks of God being in Heaven, of His dwelling in Israel, of His dwelling in the hearts of His people, does not speak so improperly as has been thought.

33. [Dwight's text has no No. 33.]

34. When we say that the world, i.e., the material universe, exists nowhere but in the mind we have got to such a degree of strictness and abstraction that we must be exceedingly careful that we do not confound and lose ourselves by misapprehension. That [i.e., It] is impossible that it should be meant that all the world is contained in the narrow compass of a few inches of space, in little ideas in the place of the brain, for that would be a contradiction. For we are to remember that the human body and the brain itself exist only mentally, in the same sense that other things do. And so, that which we call place is an idea too. Therefore, things are truly in those places; for what we mean, when we say so, is only that this mode of our idea of place appertains to such an idea. We would not therefore be understood to deny that things are where they seem to be. For the principles we lay down, if they are narrowly looked into, do not infer that. Nor will it be found that they at all make void natural philosophy, or the science of the causes or reasons of corporeal changes. For to find out the reasons of things in natural philosophy is only to find out the proportion of God's acting. And the case is the same, as to such proportions, whether we suppose the world only mental, in our sense, or no.

Though we suppose that the existence of the whole material universe is absolutely dependent on idea, yet we may speak in the old way, and as properly and truly as ever. God in the beginning created such a certain number of atoms, of such a determinate bulk and figure, which they yet maintain and always will, and gave them such a motion, of such a direction, and of such a degree of velocity; from whence arise all the natural changes in the universe forever in a continued series. Yet perhaps all this does not exist anywhere perfectly but in the divine mind. But then, if it be enquired, What exists in the divine mind, and how these things exist there? I answer, there is His determination, His care, and His design that ideas shall be united forever, just so and in such a manner as is agreeable to such a series. For instance, all the ideas that ever were or ever shall be to all eternity in any created mind are answerable to the existence of such a peculiar atom in the beginning of the creation of such a determinate figure and size, and hav[ing] such a motion given it. That is, they are all such as infinite wisdom sees would follow according to the series of nature from such an atom so moved. That is, all ideal changes of creatures are just so as if just such a particular atom had actually all along existed even in some finite mind, and never had been out of that mind, and had, in that mind, caused these effects which are exactly according to nature, that is, according to the nature of other matter that is actually perceived by the mind. God supposes its existence. That is, He causes all changes to arise as if all these things had actually existed in such a series in some created mind, and as if created minds had comprehended all things perfectly. And although created minds do not, yet the divine mind doth, and He orders all things according to His mind and His ideas. And these hidden things do not only exist in the divine idea, but in a sense in created idea; for that exists in created idea which necessarily supposes it. If a ball of lead were supposed to be let fall from the clouds and no eye saw it, till it got within ten rods of the ground, and then its motion and celerity was perfectly discerned in its exact proportion—if it were not for the imperfection and slowness of our minds, the perfect idea of the rest of the motion would immediately and of itself arise in the mind, as well as that which is there. So, were our thoughts comprehensive and perfect enough, our view of the present state of the world would excite in us a perfect idea of all past changes.

And we need not perplex our minds with a thousand questions and doubts that will seem to arise: as, To what purpose is this way of exciting ideas? and, What advantage is there in observing such a series? I answer, it is just all one, as to any benefit or advantage, any end that we can suppose was proposed by the Creator, as if the material universe were existent in the same manner as is vulgarly thought. For the corporeal world is to no advantage but to the spiritual; and it is exactly the same advantage this way as the other, for it is all one as to anything excited in the mind.

35. Seeing the brain exists only mentally, I therefore acknowledge that I speak improperly when I say the soul is in the brain—only as to its operations. For, to speak yet more strictly and abstractly, 'tis nothing but the connection of the operations of the soul with these and those modes of its own ideas, or those mental acts of the deity—seeing the brain exists only in idea. But we have got so far beyond those things for which language was chiefly contrived that, unless we use extreme caution, we cannot speak (except we speak exceedingly unintelligibly) without literally contradicting ourselves.

Corollary. No wonder, therefore, that the high and abstract mysteries of the deity, the prime and most abstract of all beings, imply so many seeming contradictions.

36. Things as to God exist from all eternity alike, that is, the idea is always the same and after the same mode. The existence of things, therefore, that are not actually in created minds consists only in power, or in the determination of God that such and such ideas shall be raised in created minds upon such conditions.

37. Genus and species, indeed, is a mental thing. Yet, in a sense, nature has distributed many things into species without [i. e., outside of] our minds. That is, God evidently designed such particulars to be together in the mind and in other things. But 'tis not so, indeed, with respect to all genera. Some therefore may be called 'arbitrary' genera, other 'natural.' Nature has designedly made a distribution of some things, other distributions are of a mental original.

38. Body infinite? If we dispute whether body is capable of being infinite, let us in the first place put the question whether motion can be infinite; that is, whether there can be a motion infinitely swift. I suppose that everyone will see that if a body moved with infinite swiftness it would be in every part of the distance passed through exactly at once and, therefore, it could not be said to move from one part of it to another. Infinite motion is therefore a contradiction. Supposing, therefore, a body were infinitely great, it could doubtless be moved by infinite power and turned round some point or axis. But if that were possible, it is evident that some part of that infinite body would move with infinite swiftness, which we have seen is a contradiction. Body therefore cannot be infinite.

39. Conscience. Beside the two sorts of assent of the mind, called will and judgment, there is a third arising from a sense of the general beauty and harmony of things, which is conscience. There are some things which move a kind of horror in the mind, which yet the mind wills and chooses; and some which are agreeable in this way to its make and constitution, which yet it chooses not. These assents of will and conscience have indeed a common object which is excellency. Still they differ. The one[26] is always general excellency, this is, harmony taking [i. e., taken] in its relation to the whole system of beings; the other, that excellency which most strongly affects, whether the excellency be more general or particular. But the degree wherein we are affected by

[26] Probably "The one" is conscience.

any excellency is in proportion compounded of the extensiveness and the intensiveness of our view of that excellency.

40. Since all material existence is only idea, this question may be asked, In what sense may those things be said to exist, which are supposed and yet are in no actual idea of any created minds? I answer, they exist only in uncreated idea. But how do they exist otherwise than they did from all eternity, for they always were in uncreated idea and divine appointment? I answer, they did exist from all eternity in uncreated idea, as did everything else, and as they do at present, but not in created idea. But it may be asked, How do those things exist which have an actual existence but of which no created mind is conscious—for instance, the furniture of this room when we are absent, and the room is shut up, and no created mind perceives it—how do these things exist? I answer, there has been in times past such a course and succession of existences that these things must be supposed to make the series complete according to divine appointment of the order of things. And there will be innumerable things consequential which will be out of joint, out of their constituted series, without the supposition of these. For upon supposition of these things are infinite numbers of things otherwise than they would be if these were not by God thus supposed. Yea, the whole universe would be otherwise; such an influence have these things by their attraction—and otherwise. Yea, there must be an universal attraction in the whole system of things from the beginning of the world to the end and, to speak more strictly and metaphysically, we must say in the whole system and series of ideas in all created minds. So that these things must necessarily be put in to make complete the system of the ideal world. That is, they must be supposed if the train of ideas be in the order and course settled by the supreme mind. So that we may answer, in short, that the existence of these things is in God's supposing of them in order to the rendering complete the series of things (to speak more strictly, the series of ideas) according to His own settled order and that harmony of things which He has appointed. The supposition of God, which we speak of, is nothing else but God's acting in the course and series of His exciting ideas as if they (the things supposed) were in actual idea.

But you may object: but there are many things so infinitely small that their influence is altogether insensible, so that whether they are supposed or not there will no alteration be made in the series of ideas. Answer: But, though the influence is so small that *we* do not perceive, yet who knows how penetrating other spirits may be to perceive the minutest alterations? And whether the alterations be sensible or not at present, yet the effect of the least influence will be sensible in time. For instance, let there be supposed to be a leaden globe of a mile in diameter to be moving in a right line with the swiftness of a cannon ball in the infinite void and let it pass by a very small atom supposed to be at rest. This atom will somewhat retard this leaden globe in its motion, though at first, and perhaps for many ages, the difference is altogether insensible. But let it be never so little, in time it will become very sensible. For if the motion is made so much slower that in a million of years it shall have moved one inch less than it would have done otherwise, in a million million it will have moved a million inches less. So now the least atom by its existence or motion causes an alteration, more or less, in every other atom in the universe; so the alteration in time will become very sensible; so the whole universe in time will become all over different from what it would otherwise have been. For if every other atom is supposed to be either retarded or accelerated or diverted, every atom will cause great alterations (however small for the present)[27] as we have shown already of retardation. The case is the same as to acceleration; and so as to diversion, or varying the direction of the motion. For let the course of the body be never so little changed, this course in time may carry it to a place immensely distant from what the other would have carried it to, as is evident enough. And the case is the same still if the motion, that before was never so slow, is wholly stopped; the difference in time will be immense, for this slow motion would have carried it to an immense distance if it were continued.

But the objector will say, I acknowledge it would be thus if the bodies in which these insensible alterations are made were free and alone in an infinite void, but I do not know but the case may be far otherwise when an insensible alteration is made in a body that is among innumerable others and subject to infinite jumbles among them. Answer: The case is the same whether the bodies be alone in a void or in a system of other bodies, for the influence of this insensible alteration continues as steadily forever through all its various interchanges and collisions with other bodies as it would if it were alone in an infinite void, so that in time a particle of matter that shall be on this side of the universe might have been on the other. The existence and motion of every atom has influence, more or less, on the motion of all other bodies in the universe, great or small, as is most demonstrable from the laws of gravity and motion. An alteration, more or less, as to motion is made on every fixed star and on all its planets, primary and secondary. Let the alteration made in the fixed stars be never so

[27] I have changed the order of Dwight's text for the sake of avoiding an ambiguity. He makes the phrase "however small for the present" follow the word "atom" rather than the word "alterations."

small, yet in time it will make an infinite alteration from what otherwise would have been. Let the fixed stars be supposed, for instance, before to have been in perfect rest; let them now be all set in motion, and this motion be never so small yet continued forever, where will it carry those most immense bodies with their systems! Let a little alteration be made in the motion of the planets, either retardation or acceleration; this in time will make a difference of many millions of revolutions. And how great a difference will that make in the floating bodies of the universe!

Corollary. By this we may answer a more difficult question, viz., If material existence be only mental then our bodies and organs are ideas only, and then in what sense is it true that the mind receives ideas by the organs of sense—seeing that the organs of sense themselves exist nowhere but in the mind? Answer: Seeing our organs themselves are ideas, the connection that our ideas have with such and such a mode of our organs is no other than God's constitution that some of our ideas shall be connected with others, according to such a settled law and order, so that some ideas shall follow from others as their cause. But how can this be, seeing that ideas most commonly arise from organs when we have no idea of the mode of our organs or the manner of external objects being applied to them? I answer, our organs and the motions in them and to them exist in the manner explained above.

"Plato, in his 'subterranean cave,' so famously known, and so elegantly described by him, supposes men tied with their backs toward the light placed at a great distance from them, so that they could not turn about their heads to it neither, and therefore could see nothing but the shadows of certain substances behind them projected from it; which shadows they concluded to be the only substance and realities. And when they heard the sounds made by those bodies that were betwixt the light and them, or their reverberated echoes, they imputed them to those shadows which they saw. All this is a description of the state of those men, who take body to be the only real and substantial thing in the world, and to do all that is done in it; and therefore often impute sense, reason and understanding, to nothing but blood and brains in us."[28]

CUDWORTH'S INTELLECTUAL SYSTEM.

41. As there is great foundation in nature for those abstract ideas which we call universals, so there is great foundation in the common circumstances and necessities of mankind, and the constant method of things proceeding, for such a tying of simple modes together to the constituting such mixed modes. This appears from the agreement of

[28] This passage may be found in Cudworth's *True Intellectual System of the Universe,* 1st American ed. 1837, vol. 1, p. 72. Dwight's text does not exactly reproduce the words of Cudworth.

languages; for language is very much made up of the names of mixed modes. And we find that almost all those names in one language have names that answer to them in other languages. The same mixed mode has a name given to it by most nations. Whence it appears that most of the inhabitants of the earth have agreed upon putting together the same simple modes into mixed ones and in the same manner. The learned and polished have indeed many more than others, and herein chiefly it is that languages do not answer one to another.

42. The agreement or similitude of complex ideas mostly consists in their precise identity with respect to some third idea of some of the simples they are compounded of. But if there be any similitude or agreement between simple ideas themselves, it cannot consist in the identity of a third idea that belongs to both, because the ideas are simple; and if you take anything that belongs to them, you take all. Therefore no agreement between simple ideas can be resolved into identity, unless it be the identity of relations. But there seems to be another infallible agreement between simple ideas. Thus some colors are more like one to another than others, between which there is yet a very manifest difference; so between sounds, smells, tastes, and other sensations. And what is that common agreement of all these ideas we call colors whereby we know immediately that that name belongs to them? Certainly all colors have an agreement one to another that is quite different from any agreement that sounds can have to them. So is there some common agreement to all sounds, that tastes cannot have to any sound. It cannot be said that the agreement lies only in this, that these simple ideas come all by the ear so that their agreement consists only in the relation they have to that organ. For if it should have been so that we had lived in the world, and had never found out the way we got these ideas we call sounds, and never once thought or considered anything about it, and should hear some new simple sound, I believe nobody would question but that we should immediately perceive an agreement with other ideas that used to come by that sense (though we knew not which way one of them came) and should immediately call it a sound, and say we had a heard a strange noise. And if we had never had any such sensation as the headache, and should have it, I do not think we should call that a new sound; for there would be so manifest a disagreement between those simple ideas, of another kind from what simple ideas have one with another.

I have thought whether or no the agreement of colors did not consist in a relation they had to the idea of space, and whether color in general might not be defined: that idea that filled space. But I am convinced that there is another sort of agreement beside that; and the more, because there can no such common relation be thought of with respect to different sounds. It is probable that this agreement may be resolved into identity, if we follow these ideas to their original in their organs. Like sensations may be caused from like motions in the animal spirits. Herein the likeness is perceived after the same manner as the harmony in a simple color, but if we consider the ideas absolutely it cannot be.

Corollary. All universals, therefore, cannot be made up of ideas abstracted from particulars, for color and sound are universals as much as man or horse. But the idea of color or sound in general cannot be made up of ideas abstracted from particular colors or sounds; for from simple ideas nothing can be abstracted. But these universals are thus formed: the mind perceives that some of its ideas agree, in a manner very different from all its other ideas. The mind therefore is determined to rank those ideas together in its thoughts; and all new ideas it receives with the like agreement it naturally and habitually and at once places to the same rank and order and calls them by the same name; and by the nature, determination, and habit of the mind the idea of one excites the idea of others.

43. Many of our universal ideas are not arbitrary. The tying of ideas together in genera and species is not merely the calling of them by the same name, but such an union of them that the consideration of one shall naturally excite the idea of others. But the union of ideas is not always arbitrary but unavoidably arising[29] from the nature of the soul, which is such that the thinking of one thing of itself, yea against our wills, excites the thought of other things that are like it. Thus if a person, a stranger to the earth, should see and converse with a man and a long time after should meet with another man and converse with him, the agreement would immediately excite the idea of that other man, and those two ideas would be together in his mind for the time to come, yea, in spite of him. So if he should see a third, and afterwards should find multitudes, there would be a genus or universal idea formed in his mind naturally, without his counsel or design. So I cannot doubt but, if a person had been born blind and should have his eyes opened and should immediately have blue placed before his eyes, and then red, then green, then yellow, I doubt not they would immediately get into one general idea—they would be united in his mind without his deliberation.

Corollary. So that God has not only distributed things into species

[29] The sentence calls for "arises" rather than "arising."

by evidently manifesting (by His making such an agreement in things) that He designed such and such particulars to be together in the mind; but by making the soul of such a nature that those particulars which He thus made to agree are unavoidably together in the mind—one naturally exciting and including the others.

44. [Dwight's text has no No. 44.]

45. Excellence. 1. When we spake of excellence in bodies we were obliged to borrow the word 'consent' from spiritual things. But excellence in and among spirits is, in its prime and proper sense, being's consent to being.[30] There is no other proper consent but that of minds, even of their will; which, when it is of minds towards minds, it is love, and when of minds towards other things, it is choice. Wherefore all the primary and original beauty or excellence that is among minds is love; and into this may all be resolved that is found among them.

2. When we spake of external excellency, we said that being's consent to being must needs be agreeable to perceiving being. But now we are speaking of spiritual things, we may change the phrase and say that mind's love to mind must needs be lovely to beholding mind; and being's love to being in general must needs be agreeable to being that perceives it, because itself is a participation of being in general.

3. As to the proportion of this love—to greater spirits, more and to less, less—it is beautiful as it is a manifestation of love to spirit or being in general. And the want of this proportion is a deformity because it is a manifestation of a defect of such a love. It shows that it is not being in general but something else that is loved, when love is not in proportion to the extensiveness and excellence of being.

4. Seeing God has so plainly revealed Himself to us, and other minds are made in His image and are emanations from Him, we may judge what is the excellence of other minds by what is His, which we have shown is love. His infinite beauty is His infinite mutual love of Himself. Now God is the prime and original being, the first and last, and the pattern of all and has the sum of all perfection. We may therefore, doubtless, conclude that all that is the perfection of spirits may be resolved into that which is God's perfection, which is love.

5. There are several degrees of deformity or disagreeableness of dissent from being. One is, when there is only merely a dissent from being. This is disagreeable to being, for perceiving being only is properly being. Still more disagreeable is a dissent to very excellent being (or, as we have explained, to a being that consents in a high degree to

---

[30] See no. 1, p. 25, above.

being, because such a being by such a consent becomes bigger), and a dissenting from such a being includes also a dissenting from what he consents with, which is other beings or being in general. Another deformity that is more odious than mere dissent from being is for a being to dissent from, or not to consent with, a being who consents with his being. It is a manifestation of a greater dissent from being than ordinary, for the being perceiving knows that it is natural to being to consent with what consents with it, as we have shown. It therefore manifests an extraordinary dissent that consent to itself will not draw its consent. The deformity, for the same reason, is greater still if there be dissent from consenting being. There are such contrarieties and jars in being as must necessarily produce jarring and horror in perceiving being.

6. Dissent from such beings, if that be their fixed nature, is a manifestation of consent to being in general, for consent to being is dissent from that which dissents from being.

7. Wherefore all virtue, which is the excellency of minds, is resolved into love to being. And nothing is virtuous or beautiful in spirits any otherwise than as it is an exercise or fruit or manifestation of this love. And nothing is sinful or deformed in spirits but as it is the defect of, or contrary to, these.

8. When we speak of being in general we may be understood [to speak] of the divine being, for He is an infinite being. Therefore all others must necessarily be considered as nothing. As to bodies, we have shown in another place that they have no proper being of their own. And as to spirits, they are the communications of the great original Spirit, and doubtless, in metaphysical strictness and propriety, He is and there is none else. He is likewise infinitely excellent and all excellence and beauty is derived from Him in the same manner as all being. And all other excellence is, in strictness, only a shadow of His. We proceed, therefore, to show how all spiritual excellence is resolved into love.

9. As to God's excellence, it is evident it consists in the love of Himself, for He was as excellent before He created the universe as He is now. But if the excellence of spirits consists in their disposition and action, God could be excellent no other way at that time, for all the exertions of Himself were towards Himself. But He exerts Himself towards Himself no other way than in infinitely loving and delighting in Himself, in the mutual love of the Father and the Son. This makes the third—the personal Holy Spirit, or the holiness of God—which is His infinite beauty. And this is God's infinite consent to being in general. And His love to the creature is His excellence or the communication of Himself. His complacency in them [is] according as they partake more or less of excellence and beauty; that is, of holiness

which consists in love; that is, according as He communicates more or less of His Holy Spirit.

10. As to that excellence that created spirits partake of, that it is all to be resolved into love, none will doubt that knows what is the sum of the Ten Commandments; or believes what the apostle says, that love is the fulfilling of the law; or what Christ says, that on these two, loving God and our neighbor, hang all the law and the prophets. This doctrine is often repeated in the New Testament. We are told that the end of the commandment is love; that to love is to fulfill the royal law; and that all the law is fulfilled in this one word, love.

11. I know of no difficulties worth insisting on except pertaining to the spiritual excellence of justice, but enough has been said already to resolve them. Though injustice is the greatest of all deformities, yet justice is no otherwise excellent than as it is the exercise, fruit, and manifestation of the mind's love or consent to being; nor injustice deformed any otherwise than as it is the highest degree of the contrary. Injustice is not to exert ourselves towards any being as it deserves, or to do it contrary to what it deserves, in doing good or evil or in acts of consent or dissent. There are two ways of deserving our consent, and the acts of it (by deserving anything, we are to understand that the nature of being requires it): by extensiveness and excellence, and by consent to that particular being. The reason of the deformity of not proportioning our consent and the exercise of it may be seen in paragraphs 3 and 5. As to the beauty of vindictive justice, see paragraph 6.

12. 'Tis peculiar to God that He has beauty within Himself (consisting in being's consenting with His own being, or the love of Himself in His own Holy Spirit), whereas the excellence of others is in loving others, in loving God, and in the communications of His Spirit.

13. We shall be in danger, when we meditate on this love of God to Himself as being the thing wherein His infinite excellence and loveliness consists, of some alloy to the sweetness of our view, by its appearing with something of the aspect and cast of what we call self-love. But we are to consider that this love includes in it, or rather is the same as, a love to everything, as they are all communications of Himself. So that we are to conceive of divine excellence as the infinite general love, that which reaches all proportionally, with perfect purity and sweetness; yea, it includes the true love of all creatures, for that is His Spirit or, which is the same thing, His love. And if we take notice when we are in the best frames, meditating on divine excellence, our idea of that tranquility and peace which seems to be overspread and cast abroad upon the whole earth and universe naturally dissolves itself into the idea of a general love and delight everywhere diffused.

14. Conscience is that sense the mind has of this consent—which sense consists in the consent of the perceiving being to such a general consent (that is, of such perceiving beings as are capable of so general a perception as to have any notion of being in general) and the dissent of his mind to a dissent from being in general. We have said already that it is naturally agreeable to perceiving being that being should consent to being, and the contrary, disagreeable. If by any means, therefore, a particular and restrained love overcomes this general consent, the foundation of that consent yet remaining in the nature exerts itself again, so that there is the contradiction of one consent to another. And as it is naturally agreeable to every being to have being consent to him, the mind, after it has thus exerted an act of dissent to being in general, has a sense that being in general dissents from it, which is most disagreeable to it. And as he is conscious of a dissent from universal being and of that being's dissent from him, wherever he is he sees what excites horror. And by inclining or doing that which is against his natural inclination as a perceiving being, he must necessarily cause uneasiness, inasmuch as that natural inclination is contradicted. And this is the disquiet of conscience. And, though the disposition be changed, the remembrance of his having so done in time past and the idea being still tied to that of himself, he is uneasy. The notion of such a dissent anywhere, as we have shown, is odious, but the notion of its being in himself renders it uneasy and disquieting. But when there is no sense of any such dissent from being in general, there is no contradiction to the natural inclination of perceiving being and, when he reflects, he has a sense that being in general doth not dissent from him—and then there is peace of conscience. Though he has a remembrance of past dissentions with nature, yet, if by any means it be possible when he has the idea of it to conceive of it as not belonging to him, he has the same peace. And if he has a sense not only of his not dissenting but of his consenting to being in general or nature, and (acting accordingly) he has a sense that nature in general consents to him, he has not only peace but joy of mind wherever he is. These things are obviously invigorated by the knowledge of God and His constitution about us and by the light of the Gospel.

46. [Dwight's text has no No. 46.]

47. The foundation of the most-considerable species, or sorts in which things are ranked, is the order of the world—the designed distribution of God and nature. When we, in distributing things, differ from that design we don't know the true essences of things. If the world had been created without any order, or design, or beauty, indeed all species would be merely arbitrary. There are certain multitudes of things that God has made to agree very remarkably in something, either as to their outward appearance, manner of acting, the effects they produce or that other things produce on them, the manner of their production, or God's disposal concerning them, or some peculiar perpetual circumstances that they are in. Thus diamonds agree in shape; pieces of gold, in that they will be divided in *aqua regia;* loadstones, in innumerable strange effects that they produce; many plants, in the peculiar effects they produce on animal bodies; men, in that they are to remain after this life. That inward conformation that is the foundation of an agreement in these things is the real essence of the thing. For instance, that disposition of parts, or whatever it be, in the matter of the loadstone from whence arises the verticity to the poles and its influence on other loadstones and iron is the real essence of the loadstone. That is unknown to us.

48. Definition. That is not always a true definition that tends most to give us to understand the meaning of a word, but that which would give anyone the clearest notion of the meaning of the word if he had never been in any way acquainted with the thing signified by that word. For instance, if I was to explain the meaning of the word, 'motion,' to one that had seen things move but was not acquainted with the word, perhaps I should say, motion is a thing's going from one place to another. But, if I was to explain it to one who had never seen any thing move (if that could be), I should say, motion is a body's existing successively in all the immediate contiguous parts of any distance, without continuing any time in any.

49. It is reasonable to suppose that the mere perception of being is agreeable to perceiving being, as well as being's consent to being. If absolute being were not agreeable to perceiving being, the contradiction of being to being would not be unpleasant. Hence there is in the mind an inclination to perceive the things that are, or the desire of truth. The exercise of this disposition of the soul to a high degree is the passion of admiration. When the mind beholds a very uncommon object, there is the pleasure of a new perception with the excitation of the appetite of knowing more of it—as the causes and the manner of production and the like—and the uneasiness arising from its being so hidden. These compose that emotion called admiration.

50. [Dwight's text has no No. 50.]

51. It is hardly proper to say that the dependence of ideas of sensation upon the organs of the body is only the dependence of some of our ideas upon others. For the organs of our bodies are not our ideas, in a proper sense, though their existence be only mental. Yet there is no necessity of their existing actually in our minds, but they exist mentally, in the same manner as has been explained. *See Appendix, p. 669, No. 34.*[31] The dependence of our ideas upon the organs is the dependence of our ideas on our bodies, after the manner there explained, mentally existing. And if it be enquired, to what purpose is this way of exciting ideas? I answer, to exactly the same purpose as can be supposed if our organs are actually existing in the manner vulgarly conceived, as to any manner of benefit or end that can be mentioned.

It is not proper at all, nor doth it express the thing we would, to say that bodies do not exist without [i.e., outside of] the mind. For the scheme will not allow the mind to be supposed determined to any place in such a manner as to make that proper; for place itself is mental, and within and without are mere mental conceptions. Therefore, that way of expressing will lead us into a thousand difficulties and perplexities. But when I say, the material universe exists only in the mind, I mean that it is absolutely dependent on the conception of the mind for its existence, and does not exist as spirits do, whose existence does not consist in, nor in dependence on the conception of other minds. We must be exceedingly careful lest we confound ourselves in these by mere imagination. It is from hence I expect the greatest opposition.[32] It will appear a ridiculous thing, I suppose, that the material world exists nowhere but in the soul of man, confined within his skull; but we must again remember what sort of existence the head and brain have. The soul, in a sense, has its seat in the brain and so in a sense the visible world is existent out of the mind, for it certainly, in the most proper sense, exists out of the brain.

52. [Dwight's text has no No. 52.]

53. Sensation. Our senses when sound and in ordinary circumstances are not properly fallible in anything—that is, [if] we mean our experience by our senses. If we mean anything else, neither fallibility nor certainty in any way belongs to the senses. Nor are our senses certain

[31] Dwight's text goes beyond the manuscript in adding a page reference to his own text; but the reference to no. 34 could have been in the manuscript.

[32] This item furnishes ample evidence that Edwards thought of his idealistic doctrines as novel and that he was considering an announcement to the world.

in anything at all any other way than by constant experience by our senses—that is, when our senses make such or such representations we constantly experience that things are in themselves thus or thus. So, when a thing appears after such a manner, I judge it to be at least two rods off, at least two feet broad, but I only know by constant experience that a thing that makes such a representation is so far off and so big. And so my senses are as certain in everything, when I have equal opportunity and occasion to experience. And our senses are said to deceive us in some things because our situation does not allow us to make trial, or our circumstances do not lead us to it, and so we are apt to judge by our experience in other and different cases. Thus, our senses make us think that the moon is among the clouds because we cannot try it so quick, easily, and frequently as we do the distance of things that are nearer. But the senses of an astronomer who observes the parallax of the moon do not deceive him but lead him to the truth. (Though the idea of the moon's distance will never be exercised so quick and naturally upon every occasion, because of the tediousness and infrequency of the trial; and there are not so many ways of trial, so many differences in the moon's appearance from what a lesser thing amongst the clouds would have, as there are in things nearer.) I can remember when I was so young that, seeing two things in the same building, one of which was twice so far off as the other, yet, seeing one over the other, I thought they had been of the same distance, one right over the other. My senses then were deceitful in that thing though they made the same representations as now, and yet now they are not deceitful. The only difference is in experience. Indeed, in some things our senses make no difference in the representation where there is a difference in the things, but in those things our experience by our senses will not lead us to judge at all, and so they will deceive. We are in danger of being deceived by our senses in judging of appearances by our experience in different things, or by judging where we have had no experience, or the like.

54. Reasoning. We know our own existence, and the existence of everything that we are conscious of in our own minds, intuitively. But all our reasoning with respect to real existence depends upon that natural, unavoidable, and invariable disposition of the mind, when it sees a thing begin to be, to conclude certainly that there is a cause of it; or if it sees a thing to be in a very orderly, regular, and exact manner, to conclude that some design regulated and disposed it. That a thing that begins to be should make itself, we know, implies a contradiction; for we see intuitively that the ideas that such an expression excites

are inconsistent. And that anything should start up into being, without any cause at all—itself, or anything else—is what the mind, do what we will, will forever refuse to receive but will perpetually reject. When we therefore see anything begin to be, we intuitively know there is a cause of it, and not by ratiocination or any kind of argument. This is an innate principle, in that sense that the soul is born with it—a necessary, fatal propensity so to conclude, on every occasion.

And this is not only true of every new existence of those we call substances, but of every alteration that is to be seen. Any new existence of any new mode we necessarily suppose to be from a cause. For instance, if there had been nothing but one globe of solid matter which in time past had been at perfect rest, if it starts away into motion, we conclude there is some cause of that alteration—or if that globe, in time past, had been moving in a straight line and turns short about at right angles with its former direction; or if it had been moving with such a degree of celerity, and all at once moves with but half that swiftness. And it is all one, whether these alterations be in bodies or in spirits, their beginning must have a cause: the first alteration that there is in a spirit after it is created, let it be an alteration in what it will; and so the rest. So if a spirit always in times past had had such an inclination—for instance, always loved and chosen sin—and then has a quite contrary inclination, and loves and chooses holiness, the beginning of this alteration, or the first new existence in that spirit towards it, whether it were some action, or whatsoever, had some cause.

And, indeed, it is no matter whether we suppose a being has a beginning or no, if we see it exists in a particular manner (for which way of existing we know that there is no more reason, as to anything in the thing itself, than any other different manner), the mind necessarily concludes that there is some cause of its *so* existing, more than any other way. For instance, if there is but one piece of matter existing from all eternity and that be a square, we unavoidably conclude there is some cause why it is square, seeing there is nothing in the thing itself that more inclines it to that figure than to an infinite number of other figures. The same may be said as to rest, or motion, or the manner of motion. And for all other bodies existing, the mind seeks a cause why.

When the mind sees a being existing very regularly and in most exact order, especially if the order consists in the exact regulation of a very great multitude of particulars, if it be the best order as to use and beauty that the mind can conceive of that it could have been—the mind unavoidably concludes that its cause was a being that had design: for instance, when the mind perceives the beauty and contrivance of the world. For the world might have been one [of an] infinite number of confusions, and not have been disposed beautifully and usefully; yea, infinite times an infinite number, and so, if we multiply infinite by infinite, *in infinitum*. So that, if we suppose the world to have existed from all eternity and to be continually all the while without the guidance of design, passing under different changes, it would have been, according to such a multiplication, infinite to one whether it would ever have hit upon this form or no. Note: this way of concluding is a sort of ratiocination.

55. Appetite of the mind. As all ideas are wholly in the mind, so is all appetite. To have appetite towards a thing is as remote from the nature of matter as to have thought. There are some of the appetites that are called natural appetites that are not indeed natural to the soul—as the appetite to meat and drink. I believe, when the soul has that sort of pain which is in hunger and thirst, if the soul never had experienced that food and drink remove that pain, it would create no appetite to any [such] thing. A man would be just as incapable of such an appetite as he is to food he never smelt nor tasted. So the appetite of scratching when it itches.

56. Number is a train of differences of ideas, put together in the mind's consideration, in orderly succession and considered with respect to their relations one to another, as in that orderly mental succession. This mental succession is the succession of time. One may make which they will the first, if it be but the first in consideration. The mind begins where it will and runs through them successively one after another. It is a collection of differences; for it is its being another in some respect that is the very thing that makes it capable of pertaining to multiplicity. They must not merely be put together in orderly succession; but it's only their being considered with reference to that relation they have one to another as differences, and in orderly mental succession, that denominates it number. To be of such a particular number is for an idea to have such a particular relation (and so considered by the mind) to other differences put together with it, in orderly succession. So that there is nothing inexplicable in the nature of number but what identity and diversity is, and what succession, or duration, or priority and posteriority is.

57. Duration. Pastness, if I may make such a word, is nothing but a mode of ideas. This mode, perhaps, is nothing else but a certain veterascence attending our ideas. When it is, as we say, past, the idea after a particular manner fades and grows old. When an idea appears

with this mode, we say it is past; and according to the degree of this particular inexpressible mode, so we say the thing is longer or more lately past. As in distance, it is not only by a natural trigonometry of the eyes, or a sort of parallax, that we determine it, because we can judge of distances as well with one eye as with two; nor is it by observing the parallelism or aperture of rays, for the mind judges by nothing but the difference it observes in the idea itself, which alone the mind has any notice of; but it judges of distance by a particular mode of indistinctness, as has been said before. So it is with respect to distance of time, by a certain peculiar inexpressible mode of fading and indistinctness which I call 'veterascence.'

I think we find by experience that, when we have been in a sound sleep for many hours together, if we look back to the time when we were last awake the ideas seem farther off to us than when we have only ceased thinking a few minutes—which cannot be because we see a longer train of intermediate ideas in one case than in the other, for I suppose we see none in neither. But there is a sort of veterascence of ideas that have been a longer time in the mind. When we look upon them they do not look just as those that are much nearer. This veterascence consists, I think, in blotting out the little distinctions, the minute parts and fine strokes of it. This is one way of judging of the distance of visible objects. In this respect, a house, a tree, do not look at a little distance as they do very near. They not only do not appear so big, but a multitude of the little distinctions vanish that are plain when we are near.[33]

58. Reasoning does not absolutely differ from perception any further than there is the act of the will about it. It appears to be so in demonstrative reasoning because the knowledge of a self-evident truth, it is evident, does not differ from perception. But all demonstrative knowledge consists in, and may be resolved into, the knowledge of self-evident truths. And it is also evident that the act of the mind in other reasoning is not of a different nature from demonstrative reasoning.

59. Judgment. The mind passes a judgment in multitudes of cases, where it has learned to judge by perpetual experience, not only exceedingly quick, as soon as one thought can follow another, but absolutely without any reflection at all, and at the same moment without any time intervening. Though the thing is not properly self-evident, yet it judges without any ratiocination, merely by force of habit. Thus

[33] This paragraph is numbered 65 in Dwight's text; but, since he has two no. 65s and since the subject matter of this paragraph is a recognizable continuation of no. 57, it may well be placed here.

when I hear such and such sounds or see such letters, I judge that such things are signified without reasoning. When I have such ideas coming in by my sense of seeing, appearing after *such* a manner, I judge without any reasoning that the things are further off than others that appear after *such* a manner. When I see a globe I judge it to be a globe though the image impressed on my sensory is only that of a flat circle appearing variously in various parts. And in ten thousand other cases the ideas are habitually associated together and they come into the mind together. So likewise in innumerable cases men act, without any proper act of the will at that time commanding, through habit. As when a man is walking there is not a new act of the will every time a man takes up his foot and sets it down.

Corollary. Hence there is no necessity of allowing reason to beasts in many of those actions that many are ready to argue are rational actions—as cattle in a team are wont to act as the driver would have them upon his making such and such sounds, either to stop or go along or turn hither or thither, because they have been forced to do it by the whip upon the using of such words. It is become habitual so that they never do it rationally, but either from force or from habit. So of all the actions that beasts are taught to perform—dogs, and horses, and parrots, etc. And those that they learn of themselves to do are merely by virtue of appetite and habitual association of ideas. Thus a horse learns to perform such actions for his food because he has accidentally had the perceptions of such actions associated with the pleasant perceptions of taste. And so his appetite makes him perform the action without any reason or judgment.

The main difference between men and beasts is that men are capable of reflecting upon what passes in their own minds. Beasts have nothing but direct consciousness. Men are capable of viewing what is in themselves, contemplatively. Man was made for spiritual exercises and enjoyments and therefore is made capable, by reflection, to behold and contemplate spiritual things. Hence it arises that man is capable of religion.

A very great difference between men and beasts is that beasts have no voluntary actions about their own thoughts, for it is in this only that reasoning differs from mere perception and memory. It is the act of the will in bringing its ideas into contemplation and ranging and comparing of them in reflection and abstraction. The minds of beasts, if I may call them minds, are purely passive with respect to all their ideas. The minds of men are not only passive but abundantly active. Herein probably is the most distinguishing difference between men and beasts. Herein is the difference between intellectual or rational will and mere animal appetite: that the latter is a simple inclination to, or aversion from, such and such sensations, which are the only ideas that they are capable of that are not active about their ideas; the former is a will that is active about its own ideas in disposing of them among themselves, or appetite towards those ideas that are acquired by such action.

The association of ideas in beasts seems to be much quicker and stronger than in men—at least in many of them. It would not suppose any exalted faculty in beasts to suppose that like ideas in them, if they have any, excite one another. Nor can I think why it should be so any the less for the weakness and narrowness of their faculties in such things, where to perceive the argument[34] of ideas requires neither attention nor comprehension. And experience teaches us that what we call thought in them is thus led from one thing to another.

60. The Will.[35] It is not that which appears the greatest good, or the greatest apparent good, that determines the will. It is not the greatest good apprehended, or that which is apprehended to be the greatest good; but the greatest apprehension of good. It is not merely by judging that anything is a great good that good is apprehended or appears. There are other ways of apprehending good. The having a clear and sensible idea of any good is one way of good's appearing, as well as judging that there is good. Therefore, all those things are to be considered: the degree of judgment by which a thing is judged to be good, and the contrary, evil; the degree of goodness under which it appears, and the evil of the contrary; and the clearness of the idea and strength of the conception of the goodness and of the evil. And that good of which there is the greatest apprehension or sense (all those things being taken together) is chosen by the will. And if there be a greater apprehension of good to be obtained or evil escaped by doing a thing than in letting it alone, the will determines to the doing of it. The mind will be for the present most uneasy in neglecting it. And the mind always avoids that in which it would be for the present most uneasy. The degree of apprehension of good, which I suppose to determine the will, is composed of the degree of good apprehended and the degree of apprehension. The degree of apprehension, again, is composed of the strength of the conception and the judgment.

Will, its determination. The greatest mental existence of good—the greatest degree of the mind's sense of good—the greatest degree

---

[34] The word should be "agreement."

[35] The first paragraph of this item is no. 21 in Dwight's text; but, since he has two no. 21s and since the subject matter is continuous with no. 60, it has been placed here.

of apprehension, or perception, or idea of [one's] own good always determines the will: where three things are to be considered that make up the proportion of [the] mental existence of [one's] own good. For it is the proportion compounded of these three proportions that always determines the will: 1. The degree of good apprehended or the degree of good represented by idea. This used to be reckoned by many the only thing that determined the will. 2. The proportion or degree of apprehension or perception—the degree of the view the mind has of it, or the degree of the ideal perceptive presence of the good in the mind. This consists in two things: (1) In the degree of the judgment. This is different from the first thing we mentioned, which was the judgment of the degree of good; but we speak now of the degree of that judgment, according to the degree of assurance or certainty. (2) The deepness of the sense of the goodness; or the clearness, liveliness, and sensibleness of the goodness or sweetness; or the strength of the impression on the mind. As one that has just tasted honey has more of an idea of its goodness than one that never tasted, though he also fully believes that it is very sweet, yea, as sweet as it is. And he that has seen a great beauty has a far more clear and strong idea of it than he that never saw it. Good, as it is thus most clearly and strongly present to the mind, will proportionally more influence the mind to incline and will. 3. There is to be considered the proportion or degree of the mind's apprehension of the propriety of the good, or of its own concernment in it. Thus the soul has a clearer and stronger apprehension of a pleasure that it may enjoy the next hour than of the same pleasure that it is sure it may enjoy ten years hence, though the latter doth really as much concern it as the former. There are usually other things concur, to make men choose present before future good. They are generally more certain of the good and have a stronger sense of it. But if they were equally certain, and it were the very same good and they were sure it would be the same, yet the soul would be most inclined to the nearest, because they have not so lively an apprehension of themselves, and of the good, and of the whole matter. And then there is the pain and uneasiness of enduring such an appetite so long a time that generally comes in. But yet this matter wants to be made something more clear—Why the soul is more strongly inclined to near than distant good?

It is utterly impossible but that it should be so that the inclination and choice of the mind should always be determined by good as mentally or ideally existing. It would be a contradiction to suppose otherwise, for we mean nothing else by good but that which agrees with the inclination and disposition of the mind. And surely that which agrees with it must agree with it. And it also implies a contradiction to suppose that that good whose mental or ideal being is greatest does not always determine the will; for we mean nothing else by greatest good but that which agrees most with the inclination and disposition of the soul. It is ridiculous to say that the soul does not incline to that most which is most agreeable to the inclination of the soul. I think I was not mistaken when I said that nothing else is meant by good, here, but that that agrees with the inclination and disposition of the mind. If they do not mean that that strikes the mind, that that is agreeable to it, that that pleases it and falls in with the disposition of its nature, then I would know, What is meant?

The will is no otherwise different from the inclination, than that we commonly call that the will that is the mind's inclination with respect to its own immediate actions.

61. Substance. It is intuitively certain that if solidity be removed from body nothing is left but empty space. Now, in all things whatsoever, that which cannot be removed without removing the whole thing, that thing which is removed is the thing itself, except it be mere circumstance and manner of existence, such as time and place—which are in the general necessary because it implies a contradiction to existence itself to suppose that it exists at no time and in no place. And therefore, in order to remove time and place in the general, we must remove the thing itself; so [also] if we remove figure and bulk and texture in the general (which may be reduced to that necessary circumstance of place).

If, therefore, it implies a contradiction to suppose that body or anything appertaining to body, beside space, exists when solidity is removed, it must be either because body is nothing but solidity and space, or else that solidity is such a mere circumstance and relation of existence which the thing cannot be without, because whatever exists must exist in some circumstances or other, as at some time or some place. But we know, and everyone perceives, it to be a contradiction to suppose that body or matter exists without solidity; for all the notion we have of empty space is space without solidity, and all the notion we have of full space is space resisting.

The reason is plain; for, if it implies a contradiction to suppose solidity absent and the thing existing, it must be because solidity is that thing (and so it is a contradiction to say the thing is absent from itself), or because it is such a mode, or circumstance, or relation of the existence as it is a contradiction to suppose existence at all without it—such as time and place, to which both figure and texture are reduced. For nothing can be conceived of so necessarily in an existence that it is a contradiction to suppose it without it but the existence itself, and those general circumstances or relations of existence which the very supposition of existence itself implies.

Again, solidity or impenetrability is as much action, or the immediate result of action, as gravity. Gravity by all will be confessed to be immediately from some active influence. Being a continual tendency in bodies to move, and being that which will set them in motion, though before at perfect rest, it must be the effect of something acting on that body. And it is as clear and evident that action is as requisite to stop a body that is already in motion, as in order to set bodies amoving that are at perfect rest. Now we see continually that there is a stopping of all motion at the limits of such and such parts of space, only this stoppage is modified and diversified according to certain laws; for we get the idea and apprehension of solidity, only and entirely, from the observation we make of that ceasing of motion, at the limits of some parts of space, that already is, and that beginning of motion that till now was not, according to a certain constant manner.

And why is it not every whit as reasonable that we should attribute this action or effect to the influence of some agent, as that other action or effect which we call gravity—which is likewise derived from our observation of the beginning and ceasing of motion according to a certain method? In either case there is nothing observed but the beginning, increasing, directing, diminishing, and ceasing of motion. And why is it not as reasonable to seek a reason, beside that general one that it is something—which is no reason at all? I say, Why is it not as reasonable to seek a reason or cause of these actions, as well in one as in the other case? We do not think it sufficient to say, it is the nature of the unknown substance in the one case. And why should we think it a sufficient explication of the same actions or effects in the other? By substance, I suppose it is confessed, we mean only something; because of abstract substance we have no idea that is more particular than only existence in general. Now why is it not as reasonable, when we see something suspended in the air set to move with violence towards the earth, to rest in attributing of it to the nature of the something that is there, as when we see that motion, when it comes to such limits, all on a sudden cease, for this is all that we observe in falling bodies? Their falling is the action we call gravity; their stopping upon the surface of the earth, the action whence we gain the idea of solidity. It was before agreed on all hands that there is something there that supports that resistance. It must be granted now that that something is a being that acts there as much as that being that causes bodies to descend towards the center. Here is something in these parts of space that of itself produces effects without previously being acted upon;

for that being that lays an arrest on bodies in motion and immediately stops them when they come to such limits and bounds certainly does as much as that being that sets a body in motion that before was at rest. Now this being, acting altogether of itself producing new effects that are perfectly arbitrary and that are no way necessary of themselves, must be intelligent and voluntary. There is no reason in the nature of the thing itself why a body when set in motion should stop at such limits more than at any other. It must therefore be some arbitrary, active, and voluntary being that determines it. If there were but one body in the universe, that always in time past had been at rest and should now without any alteration be set in motion, we might certainly conclude that some voluntary being set it in motion, because it can certainly be demonstrated that it can be for no other reason. So with just the same reason in the same manner we may conclude, if the body had hitherto been in motion and is at a certain point of space now stopped. And would it not be every whit as reasonable to conclude, it must be from such an agent, as if in certain portions of space we observed bodies to be attracted a certain way and so at once to be set into motion or accelerated in motion? And it is not at all the less remarkable because we receive the ideas of light and colors from those spaces; for we know that light and colors are not there, and are made entirely by such a resistance, together with attraction, that is antecedent to these qualities and would be a necessary effect of a mere resistance of space without other substance.

The whole of what we any way observe whereby we get the idea of solidity, or solid body, are certain parts of space from whence we receive the ideas of light and colors, and certain sensations by the sense of feeling. And we observe that the places whence we receive these sensations are not constantly the same, but are successively different, and this light and colors are communicated from one part of space to another. And we observe that these parts of space from whence we receive these sensations resist and stop other bodies, which we observe communicated successively through the parts of space adjacent, and that those that there were before at rest, or existing constantly in one and the same part of space, after this exist successively in different parts of space, and these observations are according to certain stated rules. I appeal to anyone, that takes notice and asks himself, whether this be not all that ever he experienced in the world whereby he got these ideas? And this is all that we have or can have any idea of in relation to bodies. All that we observe of solidity is that certain parts of space from whence we receive the ideas of light and colors, and a few other sensations, do likewise resist anything coming within them. It therefore follows that, if we suppose there be anything else than what we thus observe, it is but only by way of inference.

I know that it is nothing but the imagination will oppose me in this. I will therefore endeavor to help the imagination thus: Suppose that we received none of the sensible qualities of light, colors, etc., from the resisting parts of space (we will suppose it possible for resistance to be without them) and they were to appearance clear and pure; and all that we could possibly observe was only and merely resistance; we simply observed that motion was resisted and stopped, here and there, in particular parts of infinite space. Should we not then think it less unreasonable to suppose that such effects should be produced by some agent present in those parts of space, though invisible? If we, when walking upon the face of the earth, were stopped at certain limits and could not possibly enter into such a part of space nor make any body enter in it, and we could observe no other difference, no way, nor at any time between that and other parts of clear space, should we not be ready to say, What is it stops us? What is it hinders all entrance into that place?

The reason why it is so exceedingly natural to men to suppose that there is some latent substance, or something that is altogether hid, that upholds the properties of bodies is because all see, at first sight, that the properties of bodies are such as need some cause that shall every moment have influence to their continuance, as well as a cause of their first existence. All therefore agree that there is something that is there and upholds these properties. And it is most true, there undoubtedly is. But men are wont to content themselves in saying merely that it is something. But that something is He "by whom all things consist."

62. As bodies, the objects of our external senses, are but the shadows of beings, that harmony wherein consists sensible excellency and beauty is but the shadow of excellency. That is, it is pleasant to the mind because it is a shadow of love. When one thing sweetly harmonizes with another, as the notes in music, the notes are so conformed and have such proportion one to another that they seem to have respect one to another as if they loved one another. So the beauty of figures and motions is, when one part has such consonant proportion with the rest as represents a general agreeing and consenting together—which is very much the image of love in all the parts of a society united by a sweet consent and charity of heart. Therein consists the beauty of figures—as of flowers drawn with a pen—and the beauty of the body and of the features of the face.

There is no other way that sensible things can consent one to another but by equality or by likeness or by proportion. Therefore the lowest or most simple kind of beauty is equality or likeness, because by equality or likeness one part consents with but one part. But by proportion one part may sweetly consent to ten thousand different parts. All the parts may consent with all the rest and, not only so, but the parts taken singly may consent with the whole taken together. Thus, in the figures or flourishes drawn by an acute penman, every stroke may have such a proportion, both by the place and distance, direction, degree of curvity, etc., that there may be a consent in the parts of each stroke, one with another, and a harmonious agreement with all the strokes and with the various parts composed of many strokes and an agreeableness to the whole figure taken together.

There is a beauty in equality, as appears very evident by the very great respect men show to it in everything they make or do. How unbeautiful would be the body if the parts on one side were unequal to those on the other; how unbeautiful would writing be if the letters were not of an equal height, or the lines of an equal length, or at an equal distance, or if the pages were not of an equal width or height; and how unbeautiful would a building be if no equality were observed in the correspondent parts!

Existence or entity is that into which all excellency is to be resolved. Being or existence is what is necessarily agreeable to being; and when being perceives it, it will be an agreeable perception. And any contradiction to being or existence is what being, when it perceives, abhors. If being, in itself considered, were not pleasing, being's consent to being would not be pleasing nor would being's disagreeing with being be displeasing. Therefore, not only may greatness be considered as a capacity of excellency, but a being, by reason of his greatness considered alone, is the more excellent because he partakes more of being. Though if he be great, if he dissents from more general and extensive being or from universal being, he is the more odious for his greatness because the dissent or contradiction to being in general is so much the greater. It is more grating to see much being dissent from being than to see little; and his greatness, or the quantity of being he partakes of, does nothing towards bettering his dissent from being in general; because there is no proportion between finite being, however great, and universal being.

Corollary 1. Hence it is impossible that God should be any otherwise than excellent, for He is the infinite, universal, and all-comprehending existence.

2. Hence God infinitely loves Himself because His being is infinite. He is in Himself, if I may so say, an infinite quantity of existence.

3. Hence we learn one reason why persons who view death merely as annihilation have a great abhorrence of it though they live a very afflicted life.

63. Sensible things, by virtue of the harmony and proportion that is seen in them, carry the appearance of perceiving and willing being. They evidently show at first blush the action and governing of understanding and volition. The notes of a tune or the strokes of an acute penman, for instance, are placed in such exact order, having such mutual respect one to another, that they carry with them into the mind of him that sees or hears the conception of an understanding and will exerting itself in these appearances. And were it not that we by reflection and reasoning are led to an extrinsic intelligence and will that was the cause, it would seem to be in the notes and strokes themselves. They would appear like a society of so many perceiving beings sweetly agreeing together. I can conceive of no other reason why equality and proportion should be pleasing to him that perceives but only that it has an appearance of consent.

64. Excellency may be distributed into greatness and beauty: the former is the degree of being; the latter is being's consent to being.

65. Motion. If motion be only mental, it seems to follow that there is no difference between real and apparent motion, or that motion is nothing else but the change of position between bodies. And then of two bodies that have their position changed, motion may with equal reason be ascribed to either of them and the sun may as properly be said to move as the earth. And then returns this difficulty: If it be so, how comes it to pass that the laws of centrifugal force are observed to take place with respect to the earth considered as moving round the sun, but not with respect to the sun considered as moving round the earth? I answer, it would be impossible it should be so, and the laws of gravitation be observed. The earth cannot be kept at a distance from a body so strongly attracting it as the sun any other way than by such a motion as is supposed. That body therefore must be reputed to move that can be supposed so to do according to the laws of nature universally observed in other things. It is upon them that God impresses that centrifugal force.

N.B. This answers the objection that might be raised from what Newton says of absolute and relative motion and that distinguishing property of absolute circular motion (that there was a centrifugal force in the body moved). For God causes a centrifugal force in that body that can be supposed to move circularly (consistently with the laws of motion in that and in all other things on which it has a near or a remote dependence) and which must be supposed to move in order to the observance of those laws in the universe. For instance, when a bushel with water in it is violently whirled round, before the water takes the impression there is a continual change of position between the water and the parts of the bushel. But yet that [i.e., water][36] must not be supposed to move as fast as that position is altered because, if we follow it, it will not hold out consistent with the laws of motion in the universe; for if the water moves, then the bushel does not move; and if the bushel does not move, then the earth moves round the bushel every time that seems to turn round; but there can be no such alteration in the motion of the earth created naturally or in observance of the laws of nature.

66. Ideas. All sorts of ideas of things are but the repetitions of those very things over again—as well the ideas of colors, figures, solidity, tastes, and smells, as the ideas of thought and mental acts.

67. Love is not properly said to be an idea any more than understanding is said to be an idea. Understanding and loving are different acts of the mind entirely. And so pleasure and pain are not properly ideas, though pleasure and pain may imply perception in their nature; yet it does not follow that they are properly ideas. There is an act of the mind in it. An idea is only a perception wherein the mind is passive or, rather, subjective. The acts of the mind are not merely ideas. All acts of the mind about its ideas are not themselves mere ideas. Pleasure and pain have their seat in the will and not in the understanding. The will, choice, etc., is nothing else but the mind's being pleased with an idea, or having a superior pleasedness in something thought of, or a desire of a future thing, or a pleasedness in the thought of our union with the thing, or a pleasedness in such a state of ourselves and a degree of pain while we are not in that state, or a disagreeable conception of the contrary state at that time when we desire it.

68. Reason. A person may have a strong reason and yet not a good reason. He may have a strength of mind to drive an argument and yet not have even balances. It is not so much from a defect of the reasoning powers as from a fault of the disposition. When men of strong reason do not form an even and just judgment, 'tis for one of these two reasons: either a liableness to prejudice through natural temper or education or circumstances; or for want of a great love to

---

36 See Newton, *Principia,* Definition VIII and the Scholium. See also A. E. Taylor, *A Commentary on Plato's Timaeus,* 1928, Appendix 4 and the notes.

truth and of [a] fear of error that shall cause a watchful circumspection that nothing relative to the case in question, of any weight, shall escape the observation and just estimation to distinguish with great exactness between what is real and solid and what is only color and shadow and words.

Persons of mean capacities may see the reason of that which requires a nice and exact attention and a long discourse to explain—as, the reason why thunder should be so much feared and many other things that might be mentioned.

69. Memory is the identity, in some degree, of ideas that we formerly had in our minds with a consciousness that we formerly had them, and a supposition that their former being in the mind is the cause of their being in us at present. There is not only the presence of the same ideas that were in our minds formerly, but also an act of the judgment that they were there formerly; and that judgment not properly from proof, but from natural necessity arising from a law of nature which God hath fixed.

In memory, in mental principles, habits, and inclinations, there is something really abiding in the mind when there are no acts or exercises of them, much in the same manner as there is a chair in this room when no mortal perceives it. For when we say, there are chairs in this room when none perceives it, we mean that minds would perceive chairs here according to the law of nature in such circumstances. So when we say, a person has these and those things laid up in his memory, we mean they would actually be repeated in his mind upon some certain occasions, according to the law of nature—though we cannot describe, particularly, the law of nature about these mental acts so well as we can about other things.

70. That it is not uneasiness in our present circumstances that always determines the will, as Mr. Locke supposes, is evident by this: that there may be an act of the will in choosing and determining to forbear to act or move when some action is proposed to a man, as well as in choosing to act. Thus, if a man be put upon rising from his seat and going to a certain place, his voluntary refusal is an act of the will which does not arise from any uneasiness in his present circumstances, certainly. An act of voluntary refusal is as truly an act of the will as an act of choice; and indeed there is an act of choice in an act of refusal. The will chooses to neglect—it prefers the opposite of that which is refused.

71. Knowledge is not the perception of the agreement or disagreement of ideas, but rather the perception of the union or disunion of

ideas—or the perceiving whether two or more ideas belong to one another.

Corollary. Hence it is not impossible to believe or know the truth of mysteries or propositions that we cannot comprehend, or see the manner how the several ideas that belong to the proposition are united. Perhaps it cannot properly be said that we see the agreement of the ideas unless we see how they agree, but we may perceive that they are united and know that they belong one to another, though we do not know the manner how they are tied together.

72. Identity of person is what seems never yet to have been explained. It is a mistake that it consists in sameness or identity of consciousness—if by sameness of consciousness be meant having the same ideas hereafter that I have now, with a notion or apprehension that I had had them before, just in the same manner as I now have the same ideas that I had in time past by memory. It is possible, without doubt, in the nature of things for God to annihilate me and after my annihilation to create another being that shall have the same ideas in his mind that I have, and with the like apprehension that he had had them before, in like manner as a person has by memory, and yet I be in no way concerned in it, having no reason to fear what that being shall suffer or to hope for what he shall enjoy. Can anyone deny that it is possible after my annihilation to create two beings in the universe, both of them having my ideas communicated to them, with such a notion of their having had them before (after the manner of memory) and yet be ignorant one of another? And in such a case will anyone say that both these are one and the same person, as they must be if they are both the same person with me? It is possible there may be two such beings, each having all the ideas that are now in my mind in the same manner that I should have by memory if my own being were continued, and yet these two beings not only be ignorant one of another but also be in a very different state: one in a state of enjoyment and pleasure, and the other in a state of great suffering and torment. Yea, there seems to be nothing of impossibility in the nature of things but that the Most High could, if He saw fit, cause there to be another being who should begin to exist in some distant part of the universe, with the same ideas I now have after the manner of memory, and should henceforward co-exist with me (we both retaining a consciousness of what was before the moment of his first existence in like manner) but thenceforward should have a different train of ideas. Will anyone say that he, in such a case, is the same person with me when I know nothing of his suffering and am never the better for his joys?

TITLE.[37] THE NATURAL HISTORY OF THE MENTAL WORLD, OR OF THE INTERNAL WORLD: BEING A PARTICULAR ENQUIRY INTO THE NATURE OF THE HUMAN MIND WITH RESPECT TO BOTH ITS FACULTIES—THE UNDERSTANDING AND THE WILL—AND ITS VARIOUS INSTINCTS, AND ACTIVE AND PASSIVE POWERS.

Introduction. Concerning the two worlds—the external and the internal: the external, the subject of natural philosophy; the internal, our own minds; how the knowledge of the latter is in many respects the most important; of what great use the true knowledge of this is, and of what dangerous consequence errors here are, more than in the other.

Subjects to be handled in the Treatise on the mind.[38]

1. Concerning the difference between pleasure and pain, and ideas, or the vast difference between the understanding and the will.

2. Concerning prejudices: the influence of prejudice to cloud the mind; the various sorts of prejudices in particular and how they come to cloud the mind; particularly prejudices of interest—the true reason why they cloud the judgment; prejudices of education and custom, their universal influence on wise and learned and rational, as well as other men, demonstrated from fact and experience; of their insensible influence, how it is insensible on great men; how difficultly a people are got out of their old customs—in husbandry, how difficult to persuade that a new way is better; another prejudice is the general cry and fashion and vogue of an age—its exceeding strong influence like a strong stream that carries all that way, this influence on great men, prejudices of people in favor of individual great men, to the contempt of others; again, the voice of men in power, riches, or honorable place; how some churches would laugh at their ceremonies if they were without them; how a man's being rich or in high place gives great weight to his words; how much more weighty a man's sayings are after he becomes a bishop, than before; another prejudice is from ridicule or an high, strong, overbearing, contemptuous style.

3. Either after or before this, to have a dissertation concerning the exceeding vanity, blindness, and weakness of the mind of man; what poor fallible creatures men are; how every man is insensible of his own, thinks himself best; concerning the pride of men, how ready to think they shall be great men and to promise themselves great things.

4. How some men have strong reason but not good judgment.

5. Concerning certainty and assurance: how many things that are demonstrations in themselves are not demonstrations to men and yet are strong arguments—no more demonstrations than a boy may have that a cube of two inches may

---

[37] This series of topics comes ahead of *The Mind* in Dwight's edition, although he records the fact that it came "at the close of the work" (vol. 1, p. 668n). It probably represents an effort by Edwards, after he had written *The Mind,* to rearrange and systematize his thoughts on the subject, and is therefore probably homologous to a similar series appended to *Notes on Natural Science.* See Introduction, n. 22.

[38] It is not certain from Dwight's edition whether this was found in Edwards or was supplied by Dwight (vol. 1, p. 664).

be cut into eight cubes of one inch, for want of proper clearness and full comprehension of the ideas;[39] how assurance is capable of infinite degrees—how none have such a degree but that it might be heightened—even of that that two and two make four; it may be increased by a stronger sight or a greater clearness of ideas; minds of clearer and stronger sight may be more assured of it than those of more obscure vision; there may be beings of a thousand times stronger sight than we are; how God's sight only is infinitely clear and strong; that which is demonstration at one time may be only probable reasoning at another by reason of different degrees of clearness and comprehension; it is almost impossible that a long demonstration should beget so great assurance as a short one, because many ideas cannot be so clearly comprehended at one time as a few; a very long demonstration may beget assurance by a particular examination of each link of the chain, and so by recollection that we were very careful and assured in the time of it—but this is less immediate and less clear.

6. Why it is proper for orators and preachers to move the passions—needful to show earnestness, etc.; how this tends to convince the judgment, and many other ways is good and absolutely necessary.

7. Of the nature of the affections or passions—how only strong and lively exercises of the will—together with the effect on the animal nature.

8. In treating of human nature, treat first of being in general and show what is in human nature necessarily existing from the nature of entity; and then, concerning perceiving or intelligent beings in particular and show what arises from the nature of such; and then, animal nature and what from that.[40]

9. Concerning enthusiasm, inspiration, grace, etc.

10. Concerning a two-fold ground of assurance of the judgment—a reducing things to an identity or contradiction as in mathematical demonstrations; and by a natural, invincible inclination to a connection, as when we see any effect, to conclude a cause—an opposition to believe a thing can begin to be without a cause —this is not the same with the other and cannot be reduced to a contradiction.

11. Difference between natural appetities and rational desires.

12. Whether any difference between the will and inclination; imperate acts of the will, nothing but the prevailing inclination concerning what should be done that moment; so hath God ordained that the motions of the body should follow that.

---

[39] This illustration is elaborated in *Miscellanies,* no. 652. Edwards had reached this number in the *Miscellanies* after 1733, as indicated by the fact that no. 625 refers to a sermon preached "June, 1733." Dexter records the fact that a manuscript of a sermon preached in November 1734 refers to no. 668 (*Massachusetts Historical Society Proceedings,* 2nd series, vol. 15, p. 10n). If the two bits of evidence are taken together, it is fairly certain that no. 652 was written in 1733 or 1734. This suggests, even if it does not prove, that the outline of topics at the end of *The Mind* was drawn up later than has often been supposed, perhaps as late as 1735. No. 652 is printed in Dwight's edition (vol. 7, p. 219) substantially as found in the manuscript, except for the omission of two sentences at the end and the "improvement" of style.

[40] This paragraph may be referred to in *Miscellanies,* no. 361, where "8" has been written and crossed out (see below, p. 252). In any case Gardiner's suggestion that the paragraph refers to *Of Being* deserves credence. See H. N. Gardiner, "The Early Idealism of Jonathan Edwards," *Philosophical Review,* vol. 9, 1900, p. 578.

13. Concerning the influence which nearness or remoteness of time has in determining the will, and the reason of it.

14. Concerning speculative understanding and sense of heart; whether any difference between the sense of the heart and the will or inclination; how the Scriptures are ignorant of the philosophic distinction of the understanding and the will; and how the sense of the heart is there called knowledge or understanding.

15. Of what nature are ideas of what is internal or spiritual; how they are the same thing over again.

16. Concerning liberty, wherein it consists.

17. Concerning the prime and proper foundation of blame.

18. How far men may be to blame for their judgments or for believing or not believing this or that.

19. Concerning great prejudices from the ambiguous and equivocal use of words—such as liberty, force, power, etc.; how from this many things seem to be, and are called, natural notions, that are not so.

20. Concerning beauty and deformity, love and hatred, the nature of excellency or virtue, etc.

21. Whether or no self-love be the ground of all love.

22. Concerning the corruption of man's nature; how it comes to be corrupt; what is the positive cause of corruption.

23. How greatly things lose their influence on the mind through persons being used to them—as miracles, and the evidence of the being of God which we daily behold; the greatest demonstrations, most plain and direct proofs; use makes things fail of their influence on the understanding, so on the will and affections; things most satisfying and convincing; things otherwise most moving.

24. Consider of what nature is that inward sensation that a man has when he almost thinks of a thing—a name or the like—when we say it is at our tongue's end.

25. Concerning moral sense; what moral sense is natural.

26. How natural men have a taste of and delight in that external beauty that is a resemblance to love.

27. Sensitive appetites: how far they consist in some present pain attended with the idea of ease habitually connected or associated with the idea of such an object; whether the sight of food excites the appetite of one who is hungry, any other way; by what means persons come to long after a particular thing, either from an idea of pleasure, or the removal of pain, associated—not immediately after the thing itself, but only the pleasure or the removal of pain.

28. Judgment. Wherein an act of the judgment consists, or an assent to a thing as true or a dissent from its as false; show it to be different from mere perception, such as is in the mere presence of an idea in the mind—and so, not the perception of the agreement and disagreement of ideas.

29. Sensation. How far all acts of the mind are from sensation; all ideas begin from thence and there never can be any idea, thought, or act of the mind unless the mind first received some ideas from sensation, or some other way equivalent, wherein the mind is wholly passive in receiving them.

30. Separate state. How far the soul in a separate state must depend on sensation or some way of passively receiving ideas equivalent to sensation in order to conversing with other minds—to the knowing of any occurrence—to beholding any of the works of God—and to its farther improvement in knowledge.

31. Sensation. Whether all ideas wherein the mind is merely passive and which

are received immediately without any dependence on reflection are not ideas of sensation or external ideas; whether there be any difference between these; whether it be possible for the soul of man in this manner to be originally, and without dependence on reflection, capable of receiving any other ideas than those of sensation or something equivalent, and so some external idea; and whether the first ideas of the angels must not be of some such kind.

32. Angels. Separate spirits. How far the angels and separate spirits--being in some respects *in place* in the third Heaven where the body of Christ is, their moving from place to place, their coming down from Heaven then ascending to Heaven, their being with Christ at the day of judgment, their seeing bodies, their beholding the creation of the material universe, their having in their ministry to do with the bodies of men [and] with the body of Christ and other material things, and their seeing God's works of providence relating to the material universe—how far these things necessarily imply that they have some kind of sensations like ours, and whether these things do not show that, by some laws or other, they are united to some kind of matter?

33. Concerning the great weakness and fallibility of the human mind in its present state.

34. Concerning beauty.

35. How the affections will suggest words and expressions and thoughts, and make eloquent.

36. The manifest analogy between the nature of the human soul and the nature of other things; how laws of nature take place alike; how it is laws that constitute all permanent being in created things, both corporeal and spiritual.

37. Wherein there is an agreement between men and beasts—how many things in men are like instincts in brutes.

38. Whether the mind perceives more than one object at a time.

39. How far the mind may perceive without adverting to what it perceived—as in the winking of the eyelids and many other like things.

40. How far there may be acts of the will without our adverting to it—as in walking, the act of the will for each individual step and the like.

41. The agreement between objects of sight and objects of feeling—or visible magnitude and figure and tangible magnitude and figure—as to number and proportion.

42. How far imagination is unavoidable in all thinking and why.

43. Connection of ideas. Concerning the laws by which ideas follow each other or call up one another, in which one thing comes into the mind after another in the course of our thinking; how far this is owing to the association of ideas and how far to any relation of cause and effect or any other relation; and whether the whole may not be reduced to these following—association of ideas, resemblance of some kind, and that natural disposition in us, when we see anything begin to be, to suppose it owing to a cause; observe how these laws by which one idea suggests and brings in another are a kind of mutual attraction of ideas; concerning the importance and necessity of this mutual attraction and adhesion of ideas—how rarely our minds would serve us if it were not for this; how the mind would be without ideas except as suggested by the senses; how far reasoning, contemplation, etc., depend on this.

44. How far the love of happiness is the same with the faculty of the will; it is not distinct from the mere capacity of enjoying and suffering, and the faculty of the will is no other.

45. Whether it be possible for a man to love anything better than himself and in what sense it is so.

46. Example. To enquire what are the true reasons of so strong an inclination in mankind to follow example; how great its influence over men in their opinions, their judgment, their taste, and the whole man; how by this means, at certain times, a particular thing will come to be in great vogue and men's passions will all, as it were, be moved at once as the trees in the wood by the same wind or as things floating with the tide, the same way—men follow one another like a flock of sheep; how sometimes the vogue lasts an age, at other times but a short time, and the reason of this difference.

47. In what respects men may be and often are ignorant of their own hearts, and how this comes to pass.

48. Concerning the soul's union with the body, its laws and consequences.

49. One section particularly to show wherein men differ from beasts.

50. In how many respects the very being of created things depends on laws, or stated methods fixed by God, of events following one another.

51. Whether all the immediate objects of the mind are properly called ideas, and what inconvenience and confusion arises from giving every subjective thought that name—what prejudices and mistakes it leads to.

52. In what respects ideas or thoughts and judgments may be said to be innate and in what respects not.

53. Whether there could have ever been any such thing as thought without external ideas—immediately impressed by God either according to some law or otherwise; whether any spirit or angel could have any thought if it had not been for this; here particularly explain what I mean by external ideas.

54. How words came to have such a mighty influence on thought and judgment—by virtue of the association of ideas or from ideas being habitually tied to words.

55. How far through habit men move their bodies without thought or consciousness.

56. Whether beauty, natural and moral, and the pleasure that arises from it in ourselves or others be not the only object of the will, or whether truth be not also the object of the will.

Miscellanies[1]

Being of God

pp. God. We know there was being from eternity and this being must be intelligent, for how doth our mind refuse to believe that there should be being from all eternity without its being conscious to itself that it was. That there should be from all eternity and yet nothing know, all that while, that anything is—this is really a contradiction. We may see it to be so though we know not how to express it. For in what respect has anything a being when there is nothing conscious of its being? And in what respect has anything a being that angels nor men nor no created intelligence know nothing [of], but only as God knows it to be? Not at all; [any more] than there are sounds where none hears or colors where none sees. Thus, for instance, supposing a room in which none is, none sees in that room, no created intelligence; the things in the room have no being any other way than only as God is conscious [of them], for there is no color, nor any sound, nor any shape, etc.[2]

27a. God is a necessary being because it's a contradiction to suppose Him not to be. A being is a necessary being whose nonentity is a contradiction. We have shown that absolute nothing is the essence of all contradiction.[3] But being in order is all that we call God, who is, and there is none else besides Him.

91. Being of God. 'Tis acknowledged by all to be self-evident that nothing can begin to be without cause. Neither can we prove it any other way than by explaining it. When understood, 'tis a truth that irresistably will have place in the assent. Thus, if we suppose a time wherein there was nothing, a body will not of its own accord begin to be; 'tis what the understanding abhors, that it should be when there was no manner of reason why it was. So 'tis equally self-evident that a being cannot begin to be, as to the manner of its being, without a cause, [as] that when a body has been perfectly at rest that it should begin to move without any reason, either within itself or without. So that, 'because it so happened' will not satisfy the mind at all. The mind asks what was the reason. So it is equally self-evident, if equally under-

---

1 For a discussion of the manuscript see Introduction, pp. xvi-xviii, above.

2 See no. 94, p. 254, below.

3 See *Of Being,* p. 1, above.

stood, that there must be a reason why a body should be after this manner and not after another. Thus, if a body is a moving body there must be some reason or cause why it is a moving body, and not a resting body. It must be because of something, otherwise there is something without a cause, as much as when a body starts into being of itself. Supposing there are two globes, the one is a moving globe, the other is resting; the mind asks why the one moves and the other rests. It is natural to the mind to say something is the reason why this body moves and not the other; and if it should be said, no, there is not, nor ever was, any reason or cause why this being should move more than why the other should, the mind immediately returns: If there be no reason why one should move more than the other, why then does one move and the other rest? It abhors the supposition that there is none. So if two bodies are of different figures, there is some reason why this is of this shape and that of the other; so when one body moves with one degree of velocity and another of another; when one body is of one bigness and another of another; when one body moves with one direction and another of another; one rests on this place, another, another. 'Tis exceeding evident that there must be some cause or other for these things. Wherefore now I ask the question of the different bodies in the world: Why is this body in this place and not in any or some other; why is this body of such dimensions and not of others; why is this body of this figure and that of that; why doth this move and that rest; why doth this body move with just such a degree of velocity; why doth the planets move west to east and not from east to west? Something must be the reason of it. If it be said it is so because it was so from all eternity, or because there was such a succession of alterations from eternity as to cause it to be so now, how came it to be so from all eternity? If there can be absolutely no reason or cause why it should be so any more than why it should be infinite other ways, then I say it wasn't so from eternity. And why was there not another succession of alterations from eternity so as to cause another sort of alteration now?

124. Existence of God. There is just the same sort of knowledge of the existence of an universal mind in the world, from the action of the world and what is done that is objected to our senses and that is effected by this mind, as there is of the existence of a particular mind in an human body from the observation of the actions of that in gesture, look, and voice. And there wants nothing but a comprehensive view to take in the various actions in the world and look on them at one glance, and to see them in their mutual respects and relations. And these would as naturally, as quick, and with as little ratiocination, and more as-

suredly indicate to us an universal mind than human actions do a particular.

125. God's existence. 'Tis certain with me that the world exists anew every moment, that the existence of things every moment ceases and is every moment renewed. For instance, in the existence of bodies there has to be resistance or tendency to some place. 'Tis not numerically the same resistance that exists the next moment. 'Tis evident because these existences may be in different places, but yet its existence is continued so far that there is respect had to it in all the future existences. 'Tis evident in all things continually, how past existence can't be continued so that respect should be had to it otherwise than mentally. If the world this moment should be annihilated so that nothing should really and actually exist any more, the existence of the world could not be continued so that, if another world after a time should be created, that world should exist after this or that manner from respect to the manner of the existence of this, or should be so only because this had been thus or thus. Indeed, we every moment see the same proof of a God as we should have seen if we had seen [Him] create the world at first. 'Tis only this way that respect can be had to existence, distant as to place as well as time. But as much respect is had to distant existence in one sense as in another.

149. Being of God. 'Tis evident that none of the creatures, none of the beings that we behold, are the first principle of their own action, but all alterations follow in a chain from other alterations. Now, therefore, there must necessarily be something in itself active so as that it is the very first beginning of its own actions, or some necessary being that has been the cause of all the rest, which cannot be matter as it don't have the nature of matter.

199. God's existence. The existence of our own souls, which we know more immediately than anything, is an argument of exceeding glaring evidence for the existence of a God. Our souls were not always, but they are wonderful beings, certainly exceeding in contrivance everything that is seen or can be seen with eyes. They are pieces of workmanship so curious and of such amazing contrivance that their operation infinitely exceeds those of any machines that are seen. Let us consider what has been done and what is daily done by human souls. What strange contrivance is this, to take in the sun, moon, and stars, and the whole universe, and bring all distant things together, and to make past and future things present, to move the body after such a

manner, to produce such strange effects on other souls and in the corporeal world! If our souls are material machines, certainly they are so curious that none will deny that they are the effect of contrivance. Let them be created immediately, or let them be by propagation, the contrivance is wonderful. What contrivance is necessary to make such machines that will produce and propagate other such machines in an infinite succession! And if they be not material, whence are they if not from a superior immaterial being? And if we say our souls existed from eternity, who is it orders it so that upon every generation a soul shall be brought and united to such a parcel of matter? Or if we say our souls existed in the bodies from eternity, existing one within another *in infinitum,* who contrived this matter so?

200. God's existence. If the atheist will not acknowledge any great order and regularity in the corporeal world, he must acknowledge that there is in spirits, in minds, which will be as much an argument for a contriver as if the contrivance was in bodies. He must acknowledge that reason, wisdom, and contrivance are regular actions. But they are the actions of spirits. Many of the works of men are wonderfully regular, but certainly no more regular than the contrivance that was the author of them. And who made those beings that they should act as regularly as the nicest machines of men? Did such nice beings come into existence by chance or were they not the effect of a superior contrivance?

Corollary. Hence we see that all man's works and human inventions and artifices are arguments of the existence of God, as well as those that are more immediately the works of God, for they are only the regular actings of God's works. When we walk in stately cities or admire curious machines and inventions, let us argue the wisdom of God as well as of the immediate contrivers; for those spirits who were the contrivers are the most wonderful contrivances.

254. Faith over the being of God can be made most rationally and demonstratively evident by divine revelation and by gracious spiritual illumination after the same manner as we have shown the Christian religion.[4] The superstructure built upon that foundation is evident. Suppose all the world had otherwise been ignorant of the being of God before, yet now they might know it because God has revealed Himself; He has shown Himself; He has said a great deal to us and conversed much with us. And this is every whit as rational a way of being convinced of the being of God as it is of being convinced of the

[4] See no. 42, p. 238, below.

being of a man who comes from an unknown region and shows himself to us and converses with us for a long time. We have no other reason to be convinced of his being than only that we see a long series of external concordant signs of an understanding, will, and design, and various affections. The same way God makes known Himself to us in his Word. And if we have a full and comprehensive knowledge of the revelation made, of the things revealed, and of the various relations and respects, of the various parts, their harmonious congruities and mutual concordances, these appear most indubitable signs and expressions of a very high and transcendent understanding, together with a great and mighty design, an exceeding wisdom, a most-magnificent power and authority, a marvelous purity, holiness, and goodness. So that, if we never knew there was any such being before, yet we might be certain that there must be such an one.

267. God's existence. The mere exertion of a new thought is a certain proof of a God. For certainly there is something that immediately produces and upholds that thought. Here is a new thing, and there is a necessity of a cause. It is not in antecedent thoughts, for they are vanished and gone; they are past, and what is past is not. But if we say 'tis the substance of the soul, if we mean that there is some substance besides that thought that brings that thought forth, if it be God, I acknowledge it; but if there be meant something else that has no properties, it seems to me absurd. If the removal of all properties, such as extension, solidity, thought, etc., leaves nothing, it seems to me that no substance is anything besides them; for if there be anything besides, there might remain something when these are removed.

268. God's existence. Innate ideas. That sweet intimation and sort of inward testimony that men have, upon occasion, of the being of a God, and [which] is in the mind of all men however they may endeavor to root it out, is this: In the first place, the arguing for the being of a God according to the natural powers from everything we are conversant with is short and easy, and what we naturally fall into; and in the next place, it appears decorous and orderly that it should be so, and that natural inclination that persons have to excellence and order does, as it were, prejudice in favor of it. 2. When we suffer great injustice, we look to some superior being to set things to rights, because there is a great resistance of the soul against that sort of indecorum and we don't know how to believe if injustice should be done without ever being mended. 'Tis so abhorrent to nature. So when we have done good or evil, we naturally expect from some superior being reward or punishment. 3. There is a habit of the mind in reasoning. We are wont every day,

from our very infancy, to argue causes from effects after the same manner, in general. And we have such a habit that we believe this or that without standing to argue about it. Thus we do in many other cases, and as long [as] we are thus forced to judge in other things continually, it will return upon us inevitably when we think anything about the being of a God.

269. God's existence. If we allow generation to be merely mechanically performed, yet that the bodies of men and of all animals and plants should be so contrived that there should spring endless successions of the same kind of like curious frames from them is an exceeding bright argument of a deity.

274. God's existence. The being of God may be argued from the desirableness and need of it. This we see in all nature everywhere, that great necessities are supplied. We should be miserably off without our light in the night, and we have the moon and stars. In Egypt and India they are very much without rain, and they have the floods of Ganges and Nile and great deserts. In Greenland the sun's rays are exceeding oblique, and he is above the horizon so much the longer to make it up. Moles have poor eyes, and they have little occasion for them. Beasts are without reason, and they are guided by instinct that supplies its place as well. Men are without natural weapon to fight, and they have reason and hands to make weapons. The young of insects are not able to provide for themselves nor do their dams take care of them, but they, by instinct, are laid where they have their food round about them. Camels are forced, being in dry countries, to go long without water, and they have a large vessel within them which, being filled, supplies them a long time. And so it is in everything. Therefore we can't think there should be so great and essential and universal and eternal defect that there should be no wise, just, and good being to govern the world; that the miseries amongst reasonable creatures, both through the defect of nature and through wickedness and injustice (which are infinitely more than [in] all the rest of the creation), can never be relieved.

312. Being of God. If we should suppose that the world is eternal, yet the beauty, contrivance, and useful disposition of the world would not less strongly conclude for the being of an intelligent author. It will appear in this question: Whether or no, if we should see such a poem as Vergil's *Aeneid*, it would be any more satisfying to us if we were told that it was from eternity, transcribed from copy to copy (though we

supposed that a succession of men had actually existed from eternity), I say, would it be at all more satisfying than if we were told that it was made by the casual falling of ink on paper?

333. Scriptures. Being of God. Christian religion. The being of God is evident by the Scriptures, and the Scriptures themselves are an evidence of their own divine authority, after the same manner as the existence of a human thinking being is evident by the motions, behavior, and speech of a body of a human form and contexture, and that the body is animated by a rational mind. For we know this no otherwise than by the consistency, harmony, and concurrence of the train of actions and sounds, and that according to all that we can suppose to be in a rational mind. These are a clear evidence of an understanding and design that is the original of those actions. So there is that wondrous universal harmony and consent and concurrence in the Scriptures; such an universal appearance of a wonderful glorious design; such stamps everywhere of exalted and divine wisdom, majesty, and holiness in matter, manner, contexture, and aim—that the evidence is the same that the Scriptures are the word and work of a divine mind to one that is thoroughly acquainted with them, as 'tis that the words and actions of an understanding man are from a rational mind to one that has, of a long time, been his familiar acquaintance. An infant, when it first comes into the world and sees persons and hears their voices, before it is so much acquainted with their action and voice, before it has so much comprehension of them as to see something of their consistence, harmony, and concurrence, makes no distinction between their bodies and other things, their motion and sounds, and the motions and sounds of inanimate things. But as its comprehension increases, the understanding and design begin to appear. So 'tis with men that are so little acquainted with the Scriptures, as in infants with the actions of human bodies: they can't see any evidence of a divine mind as the original of it because they have not comprehension enough to apprehend the convincing evidence, etc.

365. Being of God. The only reason why we are ready to object against the absolute, indivisible, unconditional necessity of God's being is that we are ready to conceive as if there were some second. We are ready to say, why could not there have been nothing, as if this were a second. But 'tis because of the miserableness of our conceptions that we are ready to imagine any such supposition. 'Tis but talk whether there be any such supposition or no, except we knew what nothing was; but we can't have any such knowledge because there is no such thing.

383. Being of God. That the first supreme and universal principle of things from whence results of the being, the nature, the powers and motions, and sweet order of the world is properly an intelligent willing agent such as our souls, only without our imperfections, and not some inconceivable, unintelligent, necessary agent, seems most rational; because, of all the beings that we see or know anything of, man's soul only seems to be the image of that supreme universal principle. These reasons may be given why we should suppose man's soul to be the image of that first principle. In the first place, it is evidently the most perfect and excellent of all the beings in the lower world. 'Tis very plain that the other creatures are put in subjection to him and made to be subservient to him. 'Tis rational to conclude that the most perfect of things that proceed from this principle should bear most of the image of itself. 2. 'Tis only the soul of man that does as that supreme principle does. This is a principle of action, has a power of motion in itself as that first principle has, and which no unperceiving being in this lower world has. Man's soul determines things in themselves indifferent, as motion and rest, the direction of motion, etc., as the supreme cause does. Man's soul has an end in what it does, pursues some good that is the issue of its actions, as the first universal principle doth. Man's soul makes, forms, preserves, disposes, and governs things within its sphere as the first principle does the world. Man's soul influences the body, continues its nature and powers and constant regular motions and productions, and actuates it as the supreme principle does the universe.

So that, if there be anything amongst all the beings that flow from this first principle of all things, that have any sort of resemblance to it or have anything of a shadow of likeness to it, spirits or minds bid abundantly the fairest for it.

587. Being of God. Necessary existence. God is a necessary being, as it is impossible but that God should exist because there is no other way. There is no second to make a disjunction; there is nothing else supposable. To illustrate this by one of God's attributes, take eternity. It is absolutely necessary that eternity should be, and it is because there is no other way. To say eternity or not eternity is no disjunction, because there is no such thing to make a proposition about as no eternity. Nor can we, in our minds, make any such supposition as not any eternity. We may seem to make such a supposition in words, but it is no supposition because the words have no sense in thought to answer them. They are words as much without any sense in thought that they should signify as these: a crooked straight line, or a square circle, or a six-angled triangle. If we go to suppose that there is no eternity, it is the same as if we should say or suppose that there never was any such thing as

duration, which is a contradiction, for the word 'never' implies eternity, and 'tis the same as to say there never was any such a duration from all eternity. So that in the very doubting the thing we affirm it.

650. Being of God. Necessary existence. 'Tis from the exceeding imperfect notion that we have of the nature or essence of God, and because we can't think of it but we must think of it far otherwise than it is, that arises the difficulty in our mind of conceiving of God's existing without a cause. 'Tis repugnant to the nature of our souls and what our faculties utterly refuse to admit that anything that is capable of being one part of a proper disjunction should exist and be as it is, rather than not exist or exist otherwise, without causes. Our notions we have of the divine nature are so imperfect that our imperfect idea admits of a disjunction, for whatsoever is not absolutely perfect doth so. [In] everything that is imperfect there is dependence or contingent existence implied in the nature of it, and we can conceive of its being a part of a disjunction. There is a 'thus' and an 'otherwise' in the case. As soon as ever we have descended one step below absolute perfection, possibility ceases to be simple: it divides and becomes manifold. Thus, for instance, we can't conceive of God without attributing succession to Him, but that notion brings along with it contingent existence and introduces with it a manifold possibility. There is nothing that exists in a successive duration but it will necessarily follow from thence that 'tis entirely possible that it might exist infinite other ways than it doth, and that it might not exist at all.

It is a contradiction to suppose that being itself should not be. If anyone says, no, there may be nothing, he supposes at the same time nothing has a being. And indeed nothing, when we speak properly, or when the word has any meaning, i.e., when we speak of nothing in contradiction [to] some particular being, has truly a being.

749. Being of God. The first cause an intelligent voluntary agent. Nothing can be more plain than [that] the make and constitution of the world, in all parts of it, is with respect to final causes or with an aim at these and these ends to be obtained. And therefore it seems to be plain that the world must have a cause, and that this cause is an intelligent and voluntary or designing agent. 1. It shows that the world must have an efficient cause; for how can anything but an efficient cause have respect to an end in an effect? If the world be disposed and ordered for an end, then there must have been some being that has disposed and ordered it for that end. Its being ordered for a future end must be from something that has some regard to futurity, or to what as yet is not. For the end is what is not as yet obtained when the disposal first is, but is a

consequence of the disposal. It can't be without any cause or from nothing, for in nothing there can in no respect be any regard or relation to a future thing. It can't be from the thing itself that is disposed, for the relation to futurity is, by the supposition, the thing that governs the disposal. And therefore the relation or regard to futurity can't be consequent on the disposed or be from the thing itself disposed. As for instance, the clock's disposal to tell the hour of the day can't be from the clock disposed, because a respect to the notification of the hours of the day is supposed to govern the disposal of the clock. The world, therefore, being so disposed that respect is had to final causes or to future good must be from something prior to the world, for any other supposition carries in it a contradiction. To suppose it is from the world itself carries a contradiction. And to suppose that it is from nothing is a contradiction, for it supposes that nothing carries in it some regard or respect or relation to future good to be obtained, so as to govern in the disposal of things in order to that good.

2. It shows that the efficient cause of the world must be an intelligent voluntary agent; for, in the first place, by things being disposed to an end, something that is future and that as yet has no actual being has influence and governs in the effect that is produced. For the good that is the final cause as yet is future. But this future thing that has no actual existence yet has a present existence some way or other; otherwise it could have no present influence in any effect at all. For that which in no respect whatsoever *is* can in no respect whatsoever have influence in an effect. For it is a contradiction to suppose that that which absolutely and in all respects is not, or is nothing, should have influence or causality, or that mere nothing can do something. But there is no other way that that which has no actual existence can have existence but only by having existence in the understanding or in some idea. For instance, there is no way that things that are first to begin to be the next year can be now, before they begin to be, but by their being foreseen. Therefore, if any cause be now seen acting with evident respect to something that is first to begin to be the next year, so as that its effects shall be disposed in order to it, and the production of that future thing governs in the ordering and disposal of the effect, it argues that that cause is intelligent and that he foresees that future thing, or that it exists already in his idea just as much as if he foretold it. To foretell an event to come is to hold forth those things that are signs conformed to the future event, and by their conformity manifestly show that that future event is present with the efficient of those signs; and that there is an aim or respect of the efficient to the event in directing and ordering and designing those things wherein the sign consists, in conformity to the event signified,

and for an end, viz., to signify or give notice of that future event. There is nothing in foretelling events, however particularly or exactly, that manifests intelligence and design any other ways than these two: viz., 1. conforming things present, viz., sounds or marks, to things future; and 2. doing that with a certain design, viz., giving notice. But there is the very same evidence of an intelligent and voluntary agent in ordering and disposing *things* in conformity to future events, as *words;* as much in conforming other things, as sounds or marks. Things are so disposed to future ends, so perfectly ordered to bring about such and such necessary and good ends, that there [is], as it were, as exact and perfect [a] conformity, or rather correspondence, between the means and the end as there is between a stamp and the picture that is designed to be stamped with it, or as there is in the types in the press and the impression intended by it, or as there is between the letters and their combinations on paper and the words that are intended should be spoken by him that shall read them.

We may as well and as reasonably suppose that words, yea, a great multitude of them, may be in exact and precise conformity, in innumerable particulars, to something future without understanding, as that a great multitude of things shall be in as exact and particular conformity to future events without understanding. There are two things in foretelling future events that argue intelligence, viz., conformity to something future and design or aim at an end. And there is the same in directing or ordering things for future good or for final causes.

If a cause may conform and direct effects to final causes without understanding, as if it had exceeding great understanding, then there is nothing that we expect of intelligent beings but what we may expect from such an unintelligent cause. For there is nothing whatsoever that we look upon as a sign or mark of intelligence in any being but it is in thus directing and ordering things for final causes. For we can see no signs of intelligence in any but these three, viz., 1. that he acts and produces effects. And 2. that, in acting or producing effects, he shows that things not present in their actual existence are yet some way present with him, as in idea, by a conformity of his acts to things distant or future; as it is in one that conceives of things distant and future. And 3. that he acts with design, as aiming at that which is future. But he that evidently acts for final causes does all these things. If a cause without understanding can do all these things, then we may expect that he will do all the acts that intelligent beings do in as great perfection as they, viz., determine between good and bad, reward, punish, instruct, counsel, comfort, give answers, and converse. For all that, in any or all of these things, argues intelligence is a conformity of actions to things absent or future as if present in idea, and acting with design or ends. And though the designs or ends in such a way of acting is exceeding various or manifold, yet the multiplicity and variety of ends argues intelligence no otherwise than as it the more plainly manifests that there is indeed a presence of things absent, as in idea; and that there is indeed an ordering of effects for final causes, as in design. But this is not the thing now in question. But the question is, Whether or no, if it be granted that future things are manifestly so present as if in idea, and they are indeed so ordered for final causes, it argues intelligence? Not but that there is [as] great an evidence of real intelligence and design in God's works of creation and providence by multiplicity and variety of good ends evidently aimed at, as there can be in conversing as intelligent beings do.

In an efficient cause disposing things for a final cause, it appears that things not actually in being are present with it, but present with it so as to determine it in acting, just as intelligent beings are determined by choice, and by a wise choice rejecting the bad and choosing the good (and choosing the good with admirable distinction, choosing the best in millions of cases) out of an infinite variety that are equally possible and equally before this cause. It argues perception in the cause that thus selects the best out of infinite numbers in all cases; because 'tis good that governs the determination of this cause, but things are neither good nor bad but only with relation to perception. There is no other way that a being can exist before its actual proper existence but only [by] existing in some representation. For if the thing itself is not, nor anything that represents it, then surely it is not at all or in any wise. But there is no representation present with an efficient to make that aim at the thing represented, as that for which he effects, but an idea—no other representation but a perceived representation. The representation of the future thing aimed at by the first cause is no otherwise present with that first cause, before actual existence, than all other possible beings not actually existing. But only that is selected by the first cause, out of all other possible things, for its goodness, which argues that the first cause perceives the goodness. For goodness has no existence but with relation to perception.

Why should there be a backwardness in us to conceive of this first cause of things as a properly intelligent and voluntary agent, or why should we look upon it as a strange thing that it should be so? Is it because 'tis a strange thing that there should be any intelligent and voluntary beings at all? If it be so, it argues against the first cause being such a being no otherwise than it argues against there being any such being at all. And if it ben't forceable against the existence of any such being, then it is not against the first cause being such a being. But we know that there are intelligent and voluntary beings, and that more certainly than we know the existence of any other kind of being, because we know it by our own immediate consciousness. And we, that are intelligent and voluntary beings, are the effects of this first cause; 'tis it that has made [us] and made us intelligent beings. And why is it more strange that the cause should be intelligent than the effect? Why should it appear strange that the intelligent creatures that it has made are more in His image than any other effects that it hath made? We see they are so in its image in all other things far more than any unperceiving beings. They are so in the manner of their acting. The first cause acts from Him[self]; so these act more from themselves than any other beings. The first cause acts for final causes; so do these His creatures and these only. The first cause is chief of all beings; these intelligent beings that He has made are chief among creatures and so in His image in that respect. And [they] are next to the first cause; and 'tis more likely that those effects of the first cause that are nearest to it should be most like it. These intelligent creatures are evidently set over the rest. The rest are put more in subjection to them than to any other and more in their power. In this respect they bear the image of the first [cause] who has all things under it and in its power.

We have all reason to think that this first cause of all things, that is the cause of all perception and intelligence in the world, is not only not an unintelligent, unknowing, and insensible being, but that He is infinitely the most intelligent and sensible being of all; that He is more perceiving than any; that His perception is so much more sensible and lively and perfect that created minds are, in comparison of Him, like dead, senseless, unperceiving substances; and that He infinitely more exceeds them in the sensibility and life and height (if I may so speak) of His perception than the sun exceeds the planets in the intensive degree of his brightness, as well as the bulk or extent of his shining disk. And as He is more sensible, so He is, as I may express it, more voluntary than created minds. He acts more of Himself, infinitely more purely active, and in no respect passive as all created minds are in a great measure passive in their acts of will. And the acts of will are more voluntary. Though there be no proper passions, as in created minds, yet voluntariness is exercised to an infinitely greater height. The divine love, which is the sum of all the exercises of the divine will, is infinitely stronger, more lively, and intense, as not only the light of the sun but his heat is immensely greater than that of the planets whose light and heat is derived from him.

880. Being of a God. Concerning the external existence.[5] Concerning that objection against the form of the argument from the order and final causes of things, to prove the being of a God, viz., that this order might happen in an infinite number of changes of the fortuitous positions of the parts of the matter that the universe is composed of, in their endless wanderings in infinite space:

To this it may be answered, 1. that matter could not be from eternity of itself without any cause, having no necessary existence or there being no reason, without supposing an efficient cause, why matter should have existence. 'Tis absurd to suppose that anything is and there is absolutely no reason why it is. When there are two parts of a disjunction, one of them will not be and not the other, unless there be some reason why one should be rather than the other. There must be something to preponderate with respect to that part of the disjunction that has prevailed. If one scale of a balance descends and the other ascends, it is a sure evidence that there is a preponderation. There is a reason to be given why God should have a being. The reason is because there is no other way. There is nothing else supposable to be put with the being of God as the other part of the disjunction. If there be, it is absolute and universal nothing. A supposition of something is a supposition of the being of God. It don't only presuppose it but it implies it. It implies it not only consequently but immediately. God is the sum of all being and there is no being without His being. All things are in Him, and He in all. But there is no such thing supposable as an absolute universal nothing. We talk nonsense when we suppose any such thing. We deceive ourselves when we think we do in our minds suppose it, or when we imagine we suppose it to be possible. What we do when we go to think of absolute nihility (if I may so speak) is only to remove one thing to make way for and suppose another. In this case there is no such thing as two parts of a disjunction. When we are come to being in general we are come to one single point without a disjunction. Therefore, God is, because there is no other way. God is, because there is nothing else to make a supposition of.

But we know that it is not so with respect to the matter of which the universe is composed. If nothing else can be supposed but the existence of such matter as we find in some places, then why is it not everywhere alike? If this matter can be supposed not to be in such a part of space, then surely it is in the nature of things supposable that it should not be in other parts of space. It is not in itself necessary that there should be matter in other places more than in this place which is empty.

---

[5] This item is reminiscent of the earlier discussion of the nature of atoms in *Of Being*. Compare it also with *Freedom of Will*, part 4, sec. 8.

If it be in itself necessary that matter should be, why is there no more of it? There is room for a great deal more. Or why is there so much: why is there not less? Surely here is a supposable disjunction: so much or not so much, or so much and more. You have room for infinite different sorts of a disjunction or distribution, all equally supposable, viz., infinite different quantities of matter of which there is no more reason in the thing itself that any one should be rather than any other. Therefore, to suppose that one certain particular of all this infinite number should be and all the rest not be, without any disposing cause, is infinitely absurd. Again, why should the matter that there is be so disposed of as to occupy just such particular parts of space in such a situation and not be disposed in any of the other infinite manners equally supposable? Here again is one particular of an infinite number of particulars, equally supposable, which can't be without a reason.

By these things it appears that matter is not a thing of necessary existence. Therefore, if matter exists, it exists accidentally without any reason at all, which is absurd. 'Tis absurd to suppose one atom of matter to exist accidentally, to have being and there be no cause for it. Therefore, the absurdity seems to appear still greater that there should be so many millions, such an infinite number of such causeless existences. What we see often come to pass we are more ready to think there is some cause for, than what happens but once.

Again, 2. The objection supposes not only that the matter of which the universe consists could have being from eternity without any cause, but also that it could be in motion from eternity without a cause, which is more palpably absurd. The objection supposes that the numberless parts of matter were in motion from eternity and so have been subject to endless changes in their situation with respect one to another. But it may justly be inquired, What set 'em in motion, or what caused 'em to move rather than to stand still? When we see an arrow or a stone flying through the air we conclude, yea we know, that there must be some cause of its motion, and some cause why it flies in such a direction and so swiftly and at such a time. 'Tis plain that the being of matter is not necessary but that the contrary, viz., its not being, is a thing supposable. But 'tis more plain and manifest to everyone, with less reflection, that 'tis not necessary that matter should be in motion, that it may be supposed to be still. And it is more palpably manifest still that it is not necessary that matter should move in such a direction and with such a degree of velocity. 'Tis self-evident that matter in itself is indifferent to an infinite number of directions; and therefore, when we see matter actually determined to one particular direction and proceeding on one path [out of] all the rest of that infinity of paths, it is certain that 'tis not absolute perfect indifference that thus determines it to one rather than all the rest, but some determining cause. And so it is as plain that matter, if it moves, is in itself no more disposed to move in the degree of velocity that it has than in infinite numbers of other degrees. And therefore there is some cause why it moves in such a degree of velocity.

The unreasonableness of supposing matter and motion (which are not necessary existences) to be from eternity without any cause has been illustrated by the similitude of a chain hung up or hanging down from an infinite height, and we observed the last link was suspended in the air without falling down. We argue that this must be the effect of some cause. The supporting of that link is not of the link itself; for, supposing gravity be the nature of the link, then we know that supporting the link is something added besides what is in the link itself, and therefore it must be from some other cause. Now it don't satisfy to say that the preceeding link is the cause of this effect on that, and the next the cause of the support of that, and so on, *in infinitum*. For still a cause is justly demanded of this effect in [the] whole infinite chain which has not this effect in itself, because the whole is supposed to have gravity in itself, which is a tendency to descend. The case is exactly parallel, because 'tis not a thing in dispute whether things that now are or are existing in any part of the infinite extension of things exist of themselves or need a cause as much as the suspension of any one of the links of the chain, for by supposition they both need a cause. For instance, the existence of the present generation of men needs a cause just as much as the suspension of the last link of the chain. For 'tis not a thing now in dispute whether a generation of men come into being of themselves. And therefore the ascribing the suspension of the last link to the suspension of the foregoing, and this on the next, and so on *in infinitum,* is just so sufficient to account for the suspension of the whole as to ascribe the existence of the present generation to the preceding, and of that to the preceding, and so on, is to account for the existence of the whole infinite succession. Or it is just the same thing as if (supposing all things by gravitation tended in the same direction) it should be asked what holds up the earth, and it should be answered that it lay on something else, and that on something, and so *in infinitum*; and yet all those things that lie one upon another by gravitation tend to sink one from under another. And it's still the same thing if we should suppose the body of the earth to be heaved up contrary to its supposed tendency by gravitation, and it should be solved in the same manner, viz., that it was lifted by something under it, and that by something under that, and so *in infinitum.* For the holding it up, contrary to its natural tendency, is an effect that needs a cause as much as moving it contrary to its natural tendency. The latter is only the like effect (viz., opposing the natural tendency of the earth) to a further degree. Yea, the atheists do actually solve the existence of the motion of bodies that is observed in the world this very way. For they suppose it is to be accounted for thus: that one body moved another by percussion, and that, another, and so *in infinitum.* And that so the present motion that is observed in the bodies of the universe is to be accounted [for], though there be no reason in the nature of things as they are in themselves why they should move and not be at rest or, if they do move, why they should move in these and those directions and with such degrees of velocity and not in any other of the infinite number of directions or degrees of velocity equally possible.

Now therefore let us a little more particularly consider how unreasonable this is. If there was a row of perfectly elastic bodies of infinite length, and at last at a certain moment that next to us, though till then it had always been at rest, move and of a sudden start forward out of its place, we should conclude that this could not be without a cause. And would it at all satisfy anyone to say that the next to it moved and struck against that, and the preceding struck against that, and so *in infinitum*? The case is the same if we should suppose a chain infinitely long that had, till this moment, always remained at rest, but now we observe the link next to us starts out of its place, and the reason ascribed should be that the last link was drawn and put in motion by the next, and that by the next, and so *in infinitum.* And still the case is the same if we should suppose a solid cylinder infinitely long, with one end near to us but protracted to an infinite length from us, and we observe that the end next to us on a sudden moves forward, and it should be asked, what was the cause, and answer should be made that the parts next adjoining to it moved and moved that, and the parts next to that moved that, and so *in infinitum.* But would it not be reasonable in such a case to ask why the whole moved? And so we should have this reason to conclude that the cylinder had some cause of its motion without itself—that it moved only just at such a moment when there was no more reason in itself that it should move than at any other moment when it was at rest. So it is with respect to an infinite row of bodies: there is no more reason that the motion of the row should be so ordered as to set that next to us in motion just at this moment rather than any other moment. If we should see such a cylinder infinitely long, as we supposed, thus of a sudden put in motion, would not such a motion as plainly show a cause without itself as if we saw a cylinder of a finite length or a short one of two feet long, after it had been at rest, suddenly to start out of its place? By which it appears that 'tis just so unreasonable to suppose an infinite succession of beings, not existing of themselves, to be without an efficient cause without themselves, as a finite succession.

What we observed just now of the unreasonableness of supposing an infinite row of bodies striking one against another and setting one another in motion without any external cause is applicable, with an exact parity of reason, to a circular row of bodies in motion by percussion—if one of these bodies be observed to move, and it should be inquired why it did so, and it should be said it was moved by the next, and that by the next, and so moved round *in infinitum*. And the case is still the same if we should suppose one single body in motion from eternity with a particular direction and degree of velocity, and it should be asked why that body was thus moved, and it should be answered that its motion this moment was caused by the motion it had the last moment, and that by the motion it had the preceding moment, and so *in infinitum*.

The absurdity of an infinite procession of beings having existence without any external cause, by having it one from another when yet no one of them could have it of themselves, or have [it] by any necessity or reason in the nature of things in themselves considered, will further appear by this: Supposing there had existed an eternal succession of generations of blind men, and the present generation were able to tell the number, magnitude, and position of the stars, and it should be inquired how they came by this knowledge which no one could have of themselves because they were all blind and so all insufficient for such knowledge of themselves, and it should be answered that the present generation were instructed in it by the foregoing, and they had it from the preceding, and so on *in infinitum*. This is very absurd and foolish and the only reason why it is so is this: because here it is supposed that those successive generations of men are possessed of something that is transmitted from one to another which no one of all the infinite succession are sufficient to obtain of themselves, and yet that they have it without communication from any cause that is sufficient to have it of himself. The case is just the same with respect to existence of this eternal succession of generations of men as it is with respect to this knowledge. For by the supposition no one generation has in itself more sufficiency to obtain existence than a blind man has to obtain that knowledge of himself. Nor is there anything more in the nature of things to direct, or determine, or make necessary such an effect as the existence of such a generation of men than there is to direct and determine such an effect as blind men's having such ideas. And therefore there is [as] much necessity that their existence, which is not at all necessary, should have some cause without the whole succession as that such knowledge should have a cause without the whole succession of generations of blind men.

An infinite succession of dependent beings don't only require an external efficiency as much as a finite succession of beings, or a number of beings existing without succession, but it requires a much greater efficacy; for the whole effect, whether it be eternal or a temporary beginning, is dependent on an external efficiency, and the greater the effect is the greater efficiency does it require to produce it. Thus to hold up an infinite chain is required infinitely greater efficiency than to hold up a finite one; so to move a cylinder of infinite length; so in the supposition of an infinite succession of beings that give existence one to another. The farther we go back, the greater efficiency is required in the cause to give being such an existence and power as that they shall have power to produce others, with power to produce others like them, and so on.

3. If we suppose that both matter and motion might possibly have been from eternity of themselves, yet that won't help the objection that is made against the force of the argument from the order and final causes of things to prove the being of a God. The objection supposes that this order and regularity that is found in the creation may well enough be supposed to happen without any designing, contriving cause once in a whole eternity, in an infinite number of changes of the fortuitious positions of the parts of the matter that the universe is composed of in their endless wanderings in infinite space; and that, [as] it is supposable that the various parts of matter, having so much room or opportunity as there is in an infinite duration to change their situations and come into an infinite number of various forms and contextures, that 'tis not unreasonable to suppose that they might of themselves jostle into that beautiful, convenient order and wonderful contexture in which they now are, so as to produce such a general frame of the universe—the heavenly bodies to such forms, in such a system, with such proportion, such motions, and with such properties, and so particularly with those wonderful phenomena of such a mutual regular attraction by some strange, unsearchable mechanism, and such a wonderful thing as the light, with all that is observed of its properties, powers, and effects, and all that belongs to the particular planets, and this earth in particular with its various elements of earth, air, and water, with all their convenient dispositions and phenomena; and also

all that belongs to the smaller systems that are the particular parts of the greater and more general systems, such as the bodies of man and the other innumerable kinds of animals, great and small, visible to the naked eye and discernible by the microscope; with the infinite number of vegetables, with such a mechanism or wonderful disposition as that all of them have a power to propagate their species to endless ages. The objection supposes that it is not unreasonable to suppose that the various parts of matter fortuitously existing and fortuitously moving might, in infinite duration, of themselves, without any designing or contriving cause, jumble into such a contexture as this. Not but that it would be very unreasonable to suppose that this should come to pass of itself in a short space of time; but the whole weight of the objection is laid on the infinity of the room or opportunity there is for parts of matter to wander in and come into an infinite variety of positions and contextures.

But if we thoroughly consider the matter, it will appear that, whether we suppose an infinite duration or never so short an opportunity, it is very much the same thing as to the present argument. The supposed infinite duration will make but infinitely little difference as to the probability of such an event as the various parts of matter coming of themselves into such an infinitely regular, beautiful, and convenient frame. The difference is so small that it is as nothing, and really worthy of no consideration.

And to avoid absurdity and repeated circumlocutions I would explain in what sense I use the word 'particle' in what follows. Hereby I intend the least parcel of matter that is of such a quantity as that its particular position or situation is of any consequence in the frame and system of things, so that its being placed so or otherwise should make some difference worthy to be regarded with respect to the regularity, conveniency, or excellency of the frame, either the general frame or the particular parts in which regularity is in fact observed, as in the bodies of animals, vegetables, etc. Or, in other words, by particle I mean the particular parcels or quantities of matter whose particular and exact positions are actually that wherein that regularity, beauty, and convenience of the frame and composition of the universe that are observed does partly consist, or on which the good ends, that we see are obtained by its disposition and contexture, do partly depend.

Having explained the sense in which I would in this place use the word 'particle,' I proceed to observe:

1. If we suppose but two particles in all, and there were some certain positions or distances one from another that was more convenient than any other, supposing that convenient distance to be the

length of ten of both their diameters, and suppose, moreover, these two particles from all eternity to be confined to one certain right line of an infinite length, supposing these particles could exist without a cause, and supposing also that they could have motion without a cause, it would be an infinite number to one whether these two particles would lie in that most convenient situation at this time—because there is but one convenient distance and an infinite number of other possible distances in that infinite line, and it is at least a thing as likely never to have been as to have been that these two particles should ever have come to this convenient situation at all at any time throughout all the past eternity. For it is manifest that the whole line that is infinitely extended both ways, and without any beginning or any end, is a length in extension that is equivalent to eternity, that is, an infinite length of duration that is infinitely extended both ways and without beginning or end. And one part of that line taken from any particular point and extended infinitely but one way is a length that proceeds to eternity *in parte ante,* or past eternity. An eternal duration is an infinite length of single points of duration, joined together and following one another, extended to an infinite length in a manner equivalent to the single points following one another in a right line of infinite length. Now if we should suppose that the two particles that exist in that right line that is infinite both ways might probably, at some moment in the whole infinite duration from eternity to eternity, come into that proposed convenient situation (because in such a duration the two particles might come into all possible situations in that right line, there being as many moments in that infinite duration as there are different parts, and so of situations and distances in that infinite line), if we allow it to be thus more likely than not that, in all eternity without beginning or end, those two particles might come once into that convenient situation, yet if we take but half this duration, viz., only eternity *a parte ante,* we must suppose the probability not to be more than half so great, and consequently that, at most, the probability of their ever coming into this situation is more than ever equal to that of their not coming into it. Or, in other words, the probability of the affirmative is to that of the negative no more than one to one. (N.B. It alters not the case as to what has been asserted whether we suppose these particles of matter in their motions to observe the laws of motion that now appear to be observed in the universe, and so to move in the same direction perpetually, or no; for if this be supposed, it is at best as probable that these two particles that move in this right line should from eternity move from one another as towards one another, and so still the probability of their never coming into a convenient propinquity is at best as great as the affirmative—as was said before, as one to one. Yet it must be more than so, for the chance is one to one whether the particles will move at all or no, for matter in itself is indifferent to motion or rest, and, if so, the probability of their not coming into the convenient situation is as two to one; but to avoid all occasion for disputes we will suppose it to be as one to one.)

2. Supposing those two particles not to be confined to any certain infinite line but to a certain infinite plane, the probability then is infinitely less than ever those two particles would come into that convenient situation, because an infinite plane contains an infinite number of such lines, as many such lines as that infinite line did points, so that, as before the probability was to the improbability as one to one, so now it is an infinite number to one; or, in other words, though we allow an infinite duration for those two particles to move and wander and change distance, yet confining them to one certain plane it would be infinitely unlikely that ever they should come at all, throughout a whole eternity, into that most convenient distance one from another, or infinitely more likely that they should not, than that they should.

3. Let us suppose these two particles not to be confined either to any certain line or plane, but to have the whole infinite solid to wander in. Then it is infinitely more improbable still that ever they would come throughout eternity once into that convenient situation, because there are an infinite number of infinite planes in an infinite solid, as there are an infinite number of infinite lines in an infinite plane, and an infinite number of points in an infinite line. So that now the degree of improbability of the convenient situation ever happening throughout eternity, beyond the chance there is that ever it would happen, is expressed by an infinite number multiplied by an infinite number to one.

And now if instead of two particles we add a third, and the thing required be that these three come at once into a convenient situation one with another, as that the former two should at some time or other come into that convenient distance before spoken of, and also that this third do, at the same time, be so posited with them as to form such a certain convenient figure as, suppose, an equicrural triangle having one right angle, all these having an infinite solid extension to wander in—this will most prodigiously increase the account and magnify the improbability. For let us suppose the two first particles fixed at their due distances as though each were fastened at the two ends of a rod of a proper length and so to remain fixed throughout eternity waiting for the third to come into its proper point or proper situation with respect to them. Then the remaining thing required is equivalent to the third particle's coming into a certain individual point in infinite space. And that chance is just the same whether we suppose the point be fixed or moving, because just so much advantage as is gained by its being movable in one way is lost another. The advantage gained is that the points, being movable, may move towards the particle and meet it. But on the contrary, if in its motion it should happen to fly from it, there would be as great a disadvantage. But its motion is just so likely to be from, [so] as to increase the distance, as towards it so as to approach nearer to it. So that it appears that the coming of the third particle into a due position with the other two that remained fixed at the same distance one from another is equivalent to this third particle's coming into a certain and fixed point in infinite space. But the improbability that lies against that is to the probability there is for it (as appears by what has already been said) as an infinite number mutiplied by an infinite, twice over. For if it were confined to a certain plane that had that fixed point in it, it would be as one infinite number to one; but if wandering at liberty in an infinite solid, it is as an infinite number multiplied by an infinite number to one that expresses the improbability of the third particle coming into its due position with them, supposing the others to be fixed at a due position one with another throughout eternity. But if the other two come into their due position but at one point of time in an eternity (supposing that it be certain that it would be once), it is still infinitely more unlikely that the third should come into its due position with them at that individual point of time than if they were so tied together through all eternity, because a whole eternity includes an infinite number of points of time. So that now, upon this supposition, the improbability is expressed as an infinite number multiplied by an infinite number and the product again multiplied by an infinite number to one. Thus the matter would stand on the supposition that it was certain that the two first particles would, some time in eternity, come into their due position one with respect to another. But it has been shown that that is so far from being certain that the degree of improbability of it is expressed by an infinite number of infinite numbers to one, which improbability, if added to the foregoing, it makes still so many more times improbable. So that now the degree of the whole improbability of the three particles ever coming into such a position as to form such an equicrural triangle as has been mentioned is increased by an infinite number of infinite numbers multiplied again by an infinite number, and that again by an infinite number, and this last product still by another infinite—so unlikely is it that but only three particles would ever come into so simple a regularity as this fortuitously, though there should be an whole eternity of opportunity for it.

It appears, from what has been observed, that the eternity of opportunity makes so little part as to the probability of but three particles coming into so simple a regularity as that of a certain kind of equicrural triangle, that the addition of one single particle to the frame does infinitely more than overbalance it. The improbability of the regular position of the two particles with an eternity of opportunity, as was before observed, is expressed by an infinite once multiplied by an infinite to one. But if we suppose there had been no eternity of opportunity and but one single moment, the opportunity would have been infinitely less still, so that then the improbability would be so added to, that infinites must be multiplied by infinites twice instead of once. But the addition of another particle makes an infinitely greater odds than this; for, by this means, instead of multiplying infinite by infinite thrice the multiplication must be made four times.

And in this manner does the system's becoming more complex increase the improbability. The addition of every single particle that goes to the making up of the regularity or convenience of the system increases the improbability so much that the increase of it is not expressed by multiplying the improbability by an infinite number three times, but by multiplying the improbability by an infinite number, and that product by another infinite, and that product by another infinite. To illustrate this by adding a fourth particle to the three forementioned: I have already showed, if there were but three particles, how great the improbability would be that ever they should come into such a situation one with respect to another as to form a right-angled equicrural triangle. We will now suppose there to be four particles in all, and the thing required be that they should come into such a situation, one with respect to another, as to form an exact square of such a bigness that each of the sides should be equal to the two equal sides of the forementioned equicrural triangle, or (which is the same thing) the thing required is that the three first particles should come at the same moment into the forementioned situation of an equicrural triangle, and also that the fourth should come into that individual point that makes the fourth angle of the square with these three, and also at that individual moment wherein the other three come into their requisite situation. And in order to judge how great the improbability of all this is, we must in the first place consider how great the improbability is that the three first particles should ever come into their requisite situation of such an equicrural triangle, which is necessary in order to there being any such point as the fourth angle of a square with them. But the degree of that improbability we have considered already and shown it to be expressed by the proportion of the product of an infinite number multiplied into itself three times to an unit. This is the degree of improbability of there ever being any such point given as the fourth angle required. But now if we suppose there to be such a point given at some moment in eternity, the additional improbability is of the fourth particle's coming into that point at that individual moment. If the point was fixed and unmoved, waiting through eternity, it appears by what has already been demonstrated it would be an infinite number multiplied by an infinite number to one whether ever it would come into any fixed individual point at any time through eternity. But as the point is supposed to be given but one moment in eternity, this makes it yet infinitely more improbable. So that the improbability of the fourth particle's coming into that point at the right time is expressed by an *infinite* number (which multiplies the preceding), and this multiplied by an *infinite* number, and that product by an *infinite* number. And this is the addition of the improbability of the whole system. The preceding improbability is expressed by an infinite × infinite × infinite × infinite × infinite, and the additional improbability is first an *infinite,* which we must conceive of as multiplying the preceding product and then this multiplied by infinite, and this still by infinite so that the whole degree [of] improbability of the four particles ever happening to be so situated as to make the requisite square at any one time through eternity is expressed by an infinite number × infinite × infinite × infinite infinite × infinite × infinite × infinite × infinite to one.

And in like manner the improbability would be increased if we should go on and to the four particles should suppose a fifth to be added at some certain point requisite to make out the regularity, suppose in the center of the square. It will easily appear that the improbability will be increased by multiplying of it by infinites a like number of times. So that the improbability of five particles coming into this or any other determinant regular system, though there be an eternity of opportunity, or the probability of the contrary, is expressed by an infinite number × infinite × infinite × infinite × infinite × infinite × infinite × infinite × infinite × infinite × infinite.

If there be so great an improbability of a regular system so simple, consisting of but five parts, ever coming into existence through the fortuitous wandering of the parts in infinite space, though there be an eternity of opportunity given for it, then how great would be the improbability of so many millions of different parts of matter as must be supposed in so complex a frame as that of an animalcule coming of themselves, or by mere accident, into a situation of such marvelous exactness of contrivance and regularity and such wonderful mechanism, as not only to perform all those functions of life that are performed, but also (which the atheists must suppose) [so] as to have a power through the mechanism to make other forms like itself, still with a power to make others like them, and so on through thousands of generations? And how great then is the improbability of the whole frame of the universe—its coming into such a regularity as it exists in, containing so many myriads of millions of millions of millions of such animal bodies and also as many if not more bodies of plants, with all that mechanism whence arises all those phenomena that are seen in them, and particularly the like power of producing the species through thousands of generations as in animals, and also many millions of such frames of matter (as the atheists suppose) so curious as to have a power of understanding, remembering, refining, and contriving and performing all the intelligent operations of mankind, with a power of producing the like frames from generation to generation for so many thousand years? Besides, the frame of the world about them every way so wonderfully fitted for their habitation and use, with such a variety of substances, earth, water, air, fire, light, and innumerable others, some of which are of such wonderful form, power, and use, as the water, air, and many others (and especially the use) and all disposed in such a manner, in such parts, situations, and with such motions so excellently insuring all ends—I say how unreasonable will it appear, from what has been observed, to suppose that all this came to pass fortuitously, by mere chance, without any contriving, disposing cause?

It appears from what has been said that the parts of matter wandering in infinite space being supposed to have an eternity of opportunity to get into this regularity makes no odds of any moment or worthy of any consideration as to the improbability of such an event's ever coming to pass, or the unreasonableness of supposing [it] any more than if we suppose the opportunity only of a single moment. For it has been demonstrated from things that have been observed that the addition of the minutest particle that goes to the making up the complex frame adds infinitely more to the improbability than an eternity of opportunity diminishes it. So that, if we only suppose the whole frame to be less complex by one single particle than [it] is, then the infinite opportunity that is in eternity is balanced, and infinitely more than balanced; and it is infinitely less likely that the whole frame, taking in that single particle, should ever exist with an eternity of opportunity than that the frame without that one single particle, as being less complex by one particle, should come into existence with but a single moment's opportunity. Surely, therefore, the difference that is made in the improbability of the existence of the frame of the universe through a casual concourse of particles by supposing an eternity of opportunity is absolutely of no moment, and worthy of no consideration in the argument between us and atheists.

We have supposed, hitherto, that all the particles that have any existence throughout the whole of infinite space do go to make up the frame of the universe. But if we suppose a surplusage of particles, it will not help the cause of the atheist; for [if] the supposition of a surplusage of particles seems to give a better chance for such a regular frame to come accidentally into existence through a fortuitous jumbling of particles, and so to less[en] the improbability one way, yet it seems as much to increase it another. For let us suppose that, besides the particles that belong to the frame of this universe, the whole of infinite space is possessed by particles as thick, take one part of space with another, as they are in this universe, or that it has as many particles at all parts of space equal to the extent of this universe, take one part with another, as there are particles in the universe, then these two things must come to pass by mere accident: 1. that all those particles of which the universe is constituted should come into such a regular and exact situation as to constitute such a wonderful, infinitely complex, and exact frame as this, and 2. that all the other particles that fill space in general as full as this universe is, all particles that are unserviceable and are not needed to make up the frame, should agree to absent themselves and keep at a distance, to leave so vast a vacuity for the regular frame, and none of them interpose so as to hinder the regularity and beauty and disturb the order of the parts, so that so vast a room should be left and avoided by all irregular particles as much as if they were fenced out—and that although other parts of space, take one with another, are as full of particles as that universe is which has such an immense and, as it were, infinite multitude. And if we suppose there to be a surplusage of particles, but not so many as to fill up space in general so full as this universe is, but elsewhere to be very thin and so therein to be less likely to interpose to disturb the order of this regular frame, it is to be considered that, as on that supposition the probability of disturbing the frame is diminished, so the probability [of] their helping it by their numbers is as much diminished. So that, whether we suppose the particles to be thick or rare, it comes to the same thing. The thicker they are the less likely it is that they would leave such vast room to be occupied only by regular particles and the more likely to thrust themselves among those that are regularly situated one with respect to another; and the thinner or more rare they are the less do they, through their multitude, help the chance for the existence of a regular situation of some particles or others. Thick particles, jumbling together without any direction, in some respects tend more to confusion than if they were very rare, as they tend more to intrude and so to disturb and break any regularity that might happen. A multitude of particles, all without rule or direction, tend more to interfere with any regularity of frame, that they are conjoined with or encompass, than a small number.

It is to be considered that the universe is one vast general frame consisting of an innumerable multitude of lesser regular frames. There is a multitude of particular regular frames that constitute the body of an animal—as the frame of the eye, the ear, the lungs, the heart, etc.; and so it also is with the body of a plant—the root, the stem, the leaf, flower, fruit, and seed. And then the innumerable multitude of bodies and plants and animals that live upon earth go to constitute another more general frame, viz., the animate world, and this goes to the constitution of another larger frame together with the habitation provided for it and the many various provisions made in it for their proper abode, life, preservation, nourishment in growth, propagation, increase, motion, mutual subserviency, and all the good they receive and use they are of through the provision of a proper variety of substances and their proper situation, composition, regular motions, and alterations—such as the earth, water, air, wind, sea, springs, rivers, light, heat, cold, vapors, dew, rain, day, night, summer, winter, etc. And the whole frame of this terraqueous globe, with its atmosphere, is a part of another regular frame, viz., the planetary system, and this of another made up of innumerable enlightened systems, each from one fountain of light like the sun, all posited at such a distance one from another as to enlighten and advance one another, and yet not to disturb one another sensibly for 6,000 years.

Now the supposition of infinite space being filled, in general thick with particles wandering at random, though it may seem to lessen the improbability of such a frame coming by chance one way, yet it exceedingly increases it another, for this whole universe is no other than an immense multitude of particular regular systems all with a convenient mutual vicinity and a proper relation and exact situation and commensuration. But now the supposition of infinite space being filled thick with particles all moving without rule or direction does, in a way, vastly increase the improbability of such a multitude of regular frames happening in such a mutual neighborhood and relation; for if certain particles fall into a due situation for one particular regular frame, 'tis the more likely for the multitude of irregular particles about it that others will interpose among those regularly situated particles to disturb and destroy the harmony. And if there should, notwithstanding the multitude of irregular busy wandering particles, happen to be two systems of particles in a due regular situation, it is still the more likely that other particles will interpose to disturb the order and mutual subserviency, either by intruding among these regular particles or interposing between the two frames; and if we suppose three systems, still the probability is greatly increased.

But how great is the improbability that, in such an universe, numbers of millions of millions of particles in very complex and wonderfully regular frames, which the universe consists of, should all happen at once fortuitously, in a proper and exact proportion and convenient situation and relation, and none of the surplusage of particles with which infinite space is filled should interfere or interpose to disturb the harmony and subserviency, or obscure the beauty—and that although the room be so vast and the opportunity so great?

So that the objection made from the eternity of opportunity against the force of the argument from the wonderful contrivance of the world to prove the being of a God is but a mere amusement. Such order and contrivance plainly shows a contriving and disposing cause and is a demonstration of intelligence and wisdom, whether we suppose an eternity of existence of wandering atoms or no. An infinite length of time has no tendency to alter the case. If we should suppose people traveling in the snow, one after another, thousands in a day for thousands of years together, and all should tread exactly without the least variation in one another's steps so as, in all this time, to make no beaten path but only steps with the snow not broken between, this is a demonstration of intention, design, and care. Of if we suppose that, in the showers of rain that fall out of the clouds on all the face of the earth for a whole year, the drops should universally fall in order on the ground so as to describe such figures that would be Roman letters in such exact order as to be Vergil's *Aeneid* written on every acre of ground all over the world, or so as exactly to write the history of the world and all nations and families in it through all ages without departing from truth in one fact or minutest circumstance—that would distinctly demonstrate a designing cause. Length of time has no tendency at all to produce such an effect of itself. If we multiply years never so much to give large opportunity, it helps not the case without a designing cause. 'Tis no more likely to bring about such a year's rain as that than if we suppose the opportunity of one year only.

And as that objection against the force of the argument for the being of a God from the order and contrivance of the frame of the universe, viz., that there has been an eternity of opportunity for this to come to pass in, of itself is vain and insignificant—so would it be as vain to say that the world has existed in this regular, beautiful, and convenient frame from eternity. For still continuance shows wisdom and intelligence, and to say that the world exists in such a regular frame because it did so always no more solves the difficulty of its being so without wisdom and intelligence than if there were a blind man that had lived from eternity, and always blind, that was able exactly to describe visible things as if he saw, without ever having been informed—as particularly the number and diverse magnitude, position and motion of the stars—and any should ask how he came to know this and it should be answered that there never was a time when he came to know it, for he knew it from eternity and never needed the information of his senses or of his fellow creatures. This is a mere put off and in no wise removes the difficulty, for seeing it is as necessary, in order to his knowing it from eternity, as to his receiving the knowledge of it in time. So the orderly, convenient, and excellent disposing of things in order to obtain good ends is a thing that depends as much on knowledge and understanding as the knowledge of visible things depends on sight, and therefore the former can no more be from eternity without understanding than the latter without sight.

976. Unity of God. Being of God. Unity of the world. The uniformity, concord, and perfect harmony which appears in the constitution and conservation of things, their conspiring to one end, their continuing in the same order and course do plainly declare the unity of God: as the lasting peace of a commonwealth composed of persons different in affection and humor argues one law that regulates and contains them; as the orderly march of an army shows it managed by one conduct; as the uniformity of an house declares it contrived by one architect. (Barrow's *Works,* vol. 2, p. 96.)[6] This is most apparent concerning the solar, or our planetary, system. 'Tis plain 'tis one system. We will therefore consider the union there is in the whole visible universe or between the fixed stars. And first, I will show wherein there is a manifest agreement between these distant parts of the universe, whereby it is evident that there is oneness in the cause of all. And secondly, I would take notice wherein these distant systems are united one with another, whereby they all become one great system.

I. I would observe wherein there is a manifest and marvelous agreement in those distant parts of the universe whereby it is evident that they agree in their cause. And they do so agree in these following respects:

1. They agree in this, that they all of them are, in comparison of the expanse of the heavens, but little spots or specks separated one from another. Why should it so happen concerning so many millions; and

[6] The first sentence of this item is a close paraphrase of a paragraph from Barrow. See *The Theological Works of Isaac Barrow, D.D.,* 1859, vol. 7, p. 52.

that there should appear no other matter in the universe but what is thus collected? Why should it not have happened as well that one side of the heavens should be all one lurid body, the rest vacant; or one part of the heavens a continued body, another full of spots; or here and there a continuity of matter, and here and there a vacancy; here and there spots of many different kinds, etc.—were it not for some common cause ordering it so that all the bodies that should appear through the immense expanse of the universe should be in such small, compact collections of matter?

2. They not only all agree in this that they are all distinct, compact, and comparatively very small bodies or little particles, but they are also all of them exactly of the same figure, all round. Now whether we suppose that this is owing to the mutual gravitation of their parts or not, it clearly, in either supposition, argues the oneness of the efficient cause. Their being all of a round figure is indeed most probably owing to the mutual gravitation of their parts, for that is evidently the cause of the round figure of all the heavenly bodies near us, as of the earth and all the rest of the planets primary and secondary, and in the sun that is by far the most like the fixed stars of any body near us. 'Tis demonstrable that a mutual gravitation of the parts of matter according to the quantity of matter and the square of distance obtains on all these, and the round figure in all of them appears evidently, in all of them, to be the consequence of this. Therefore, seeing we behold the same effect, the same round figure, in the many millions of heavenly bodies that are far distant, there is all reason to conclude it to be from the same cause. Now in this supposition that such a wondrous power or law should take place everywhere through the whole universe and all the matter that is contained in it in all the innumerable distant systems that are in it, which power is demonstrably not from matter itself but from the established law and continued power of the Creator, I say this shows the whole corporeal universe to be but one, and that all is created and upheld and governed by the same first cause, and every moment under the influence of the same divine power. But upon the other supposition that no such law obtains in other parts of the universe but only in this solar system, then the universal agreement of the many millions of fixed stars in the same round figure is a clear argument of one common first cause. For if there be no such internal cause or power belonging to the nature of these bodies themselves that should, as it were, naturally incline 'em to such a figure rather than any other, then it would be a strange thing if any two of them should happen to be of the same figure; for in themselves they must be supposed indifferent to all kinds of possible figures, which are infinite, and therefore are as likely to be in one of all those infinite figures

as another. But much more strange would it be that every one of such a vast multitude, not only that are seen with the naked eye but the more and more that are discovered by telescopes, should, without the exception of one, be exactly of the same figure without a common cause.

3. Another remarkable instance of their agreement is their all being perfectly at rest without the least sensible motion or change of their situation from one thousand years to another. Upon whatever supposition we go as the next or immediate reason of this, yet such an agreement in so many millions of such bodies will argue a common cause. If we suppose that the law of gravitation holds throughout the universe, then this is a wonderful thing that they don't run together by virtue of that mutual gravitation, and must be owing to the law of some one common disposer, whether it be by limiting that power and causing that it shall not take place beyond such bounds, lest these distant bodies should disturb one another, or otherwise. For if their gravitation don't reach one another, it must be by an arbitrary limitation contrary to the laws of gravitation in the respective systems. For the grand law is that every part of matter should tend to every other part according to square of distance, however vast the distance is, in proportion to the bigness of those parts. Thus 'tis demonstrable that the countless parts of the matter of this solar system tend to all other parts, however distant and however small. Thus if we divide the two globes of the earth [and sun] into never so small parts, parts never so many million times small[er] than rays of light, yet 'tis evident that each of these small parts in the globe of the earth tends to each of these small parts in the globe of the sun according to the square of distance, because 'tis evident by experience that these two whole globes tend to each other according to the quantity of matter and square of distance. But the whole matter of both globes is made up of these small parts. But these small parts are as far distant one from another, in proportion to their diameters, as the fixed stars are; and the case is exactly the same between two fixed stars as to their situation, proportion, and respect they have one to another, as between two similar parts of this solar system whose distance is in the same proportion to their diameters. But we see that with respect to the one the law of gravitation holds, and if it don't with regard to the other it must be by an arbitrary limiting and cutting off this power at certain limits, contrary to the law that obtains elsewhere, on design. And if there be this arbitrary designed limitation of such a power everywhere at certain limits between so many millions of heavenly bodies to prevent mutual disturbance, this shows a common disposer, and that the whole is regu-

lated by a common wisdom and a common will and a common power that governs everywhere.

Gravitation is a power of that nature that, unless it be arbitrarily limited in some places contrary to its own laws that universally and immutably obtain in other places, must extend itself infinitely, because we see that it in fact does, in some places, extend itself infinitely in the solar system. For the matter of the mutually attracting globes is infinitely divisible, and therefore [we] may say that there are some parts of matter that are infinitely small in proportion to the distance to which their attraction is extended; but [i.e., for] that attraction may be looked upon as infinitely extended that is extended to a distance that is infinite in proportion to the bigness of the attracting body.

And furthermore, the rest of the fixed stars, upon this supposition of their not being attracted one by another, is a great evidence of the ordering of one common cause. For all allow that matter in itself is indifferent to motion or rest; yea, 'tis indifferent to rest or any of the infinitely various degrees of motion. Hence, if there appeared but one body suspended in free space in the midst of the expanse of the heavens, it would be a strange thing if that should happen to be in a state of perfect rest. It would be an infinite number to one whether it would or no, because it would be as likely that it would be in either of the infinite number of degrees of motion as at rest. So that a state of rest is to be reckoned but as one state amongst an infinite number of other states to all which the body, in itself, is indifferent and as likely to be in one of them as another. Hence we see nothing in this world or system like every body's being suspended in free space yet remaining at rest, excepting the sun that is one of the fixed stars. But how can we conceive of so many millions of bodies suspended in the open expanse of the universe, and all of them so fixed in their places that there shall be no sensible motion from one thousand years to another, without the ordering of a voluntary, wise disposer—and that every one should agree in it—without one common cause?

But upon the supposition that gravitation extends and obtains through the whole universe, acting everywhere by the same laws that are universally and invariably maintained (which is most likely), still the rest of the fixed stars will be an evidence of one common cause that disposes all. Or if we suppose that the fixed stars are placed at so vast a distance one from another that their mutual attraction should disturb them so [little] that their motion, occasioned hereby, should be so small as not to be discerned by us at this distance in many thousand years, such a disposal everywhere through the whole innumerable multitude of those bodies shows a common care extending through the whole as the cause. Or if we suppose, besides their great distance one from another, such an artful disposal among them that their attractions should balance one another so wonderfully as to keep all in rest and quietness (which is the most probable supposition of all), this still more evidently and remarkably shows the care, influence, and government of a common cause. Or if, lastly, we suppose these stars to be all fixed in a solid sphere, that shows the universe all to be one building and that 'tis one architect that has thus built such a bespangled arch or roof to encompass this our system on every side.

4. Another thing wherein they all agree is that they all shine by their own light with an exceeding great and sparkling brightness and luster. Matter does not seem in itself to have any great tendency to this. Here in our world we see very few things that shine by their own light; and those that do don't shine with one ten-thousandth or millionth part of this brightness—none of them. We see here very few bodies that will of themselves enkindle and burn; and those that do continue so to do but a little while before they go out. But we behold in the heavens, either with naked eyes or glasses, many thousands and millions of bodies all alike in this, all shining with their own light, and shining from age to age, and all shining with a brightness like the light of the sun. This seems to show a common cause.

5. Though there is so vast a number of them and they are so vastly distant one from another, yet all seem remarkably to agree in their internal nature, being replete with a like kind of particles and all agreeing in the laws of the intestine motion and mutual action of their minute parts. This appears because the effects of that intestine motion and mutual action of their minute parts is exactly the same. From that intestine action, they all continually send forth, as it were, an infinite quantity of their minute parts, parts of the same kind, in like manner affecting the organ of our sight and all causing the like sensation in us, and in like manner reflected and refracted by glass, water, and other bodies. They are all emitted in the same manner: all with, as it were, an infinite celerity and in like manner disposed to pierce both transparent bodies and to be absorbed by opaque and dark bodies, and in every respect subject to the same laws with the particles of matter emitted by the sun. Whatever the powers be by which the internal minute parts of the sun act on one another, by which many of these minute parts leap forth to such a distance, if it be a mutual attraction and repulsion, these are most evidently the same powers or the same laws of intestine motion by which the inward parts of the fixed stars act on one another, because the effects are so exactly the same. And the minute parts of these bodies, that by means of that action are emitted, even to such a distance as we are, are still here governed in their motions by just the same laws as the rays of the sun, being reflected and refracted by

different degrees of refrangibility, causing the same different colors or sensations in us. This exact agreement of the inward nature which creating power has given all these bodies, and the laws of the motion of their minute parts producing such wonderful effects, is a most remarkable evidence that one common cause has made and does uphold and influence and actuate and govern all. Such an unity of invention and device shows the unity of the causes. Light is a strange work of God. There [is] nothing in the whole external creation wherein appears a more admirable contrivance than this. [It] appears to be the same in this solar system and in all those infinitely distant systems.

II. I would observe wherein these distant systems do not only agree together but are united one to another so as to become one great system, which is a further evidence that they all have one cause.

1. The parts of these different systems are communicated to or diffused through each other by the rays of light that are transmitted. Thus I suppose there are beams of light from several millions of fixed stars diffused every moment through every part of this solar system so that there is not a hair's breadth distance of [i. e., between] some of their beams [for] one second of time, unless where the beams are intercepted by some opaque body, which is but a very small part of the system; and consequently we may suppose that each star thus diffuses her parts through millions of the systems of other stars.

Now upon a supposition of several gods as the creators of the several systems, then we must suppose that the same gods that made these different stars have clothed 'em with their light, and have created and do maintain their beams because of their power. Hence, we must either suppose that many millions of gods that are the authors of the diverse systems are present in each system at once and throughout that system, each one, by his powers and energy, accompanying the rays of his own system, maintaining their motion and action in every part of it, every moment—and so, that the god of each distinct system is present every moment by his mighty power and energy throughout every minute part of the systems of millions of other gods, at the same time that these millions of other gods are, all of 'em, also in like manner present, by a like power and energy, all of them, through every part of each system; or else we must suppose that all these many millions of gods, though entirely distinct and independent, have by mutual, perfect, and immutable consent, agreed to observe the parts of the systems of the other gods and, at the boundaries of the systems and from these limits to take care of them, and by their power and energy to uphold them and actuate them—both which appears very absurd.

2. The parts of these different systems are not only communicated to and diffused through one another, but act upon one another; and

there is a mutual action and reaction between their different blended parts by the same laws of matter and motion. Thus, for instance, the rays of the fixed stars don't only enter this system and are diffused through it, but they act upon the parts of it, and the parts of this react upon them by the laws of this system. So the rays of the fixed stars act on our organs of sight; and so there is action and reaction between them and our air, as appears by the brilliancy of the fixed stars and the refraction of their rays by the atmosphere, and between them and water and glass and other transparent bodies, and also between them and all opaque bodies that do reflect them, as appears by their being enlightened by them in a starlight night. Now how unreasonable it is to suppose any other than that this action and reaction are both by the laws and influence of the same God!

3. These parts of different systems that are continually transmitted into and diffused through each other are liable to be converted into parts of these other systems (as Sir Isaac Newton has shown how rays of light after frequent reflection and refraction do at length cease their motion and do stick to the solid parts of other bodies).[7] And what can be supposed in this case but absurdity [in] supposing the matter of different systems [to] be created and upheld by different gods?

4. Ancient observation shows that fixed stars have a great influence upon, and a sort of government over, sublunery things—the weather, and the frame and temperament of the bodies of plants and animals.

These things show that all these different systems take hold of one another and influence and act upon one another as the different wheels of a machine. It is reasonable, therefore, to suppose that all have one maker. Since we see the machine to be one, 'tis unreasonable to suppose any other than [that] one and the same artificer made it, and that one and the same owner possesses and takes care of its motions, and not that one made and takes care of one wheel, and another another.

Common Illumination

116. Preparatory work. This with me is established, that grace and the exercise of grace is given entirely by the Spirit of God by His free and most arbitrary motions; but that His ordinary method, notwithstanding, is to give grace to those that are much concerned about it, and earnestly and for a considerable time seek it or continue to do things in order to it. That is, 'tis the Spirit's ordinary method first to

[7] Sir David Brewster in his *Life of Sir Isaac Newton,* 1831, p. 108, quotes Newton as holding that "gross bodies and light were convertible into one another." Edwards could have gotten his information about the corpuscular theory of light from papers and controversies before the Royal Society from 1671 to 1675.

make them concerned about it so as to convince them that 'tis best to seek it, so far as to make them seek it much, and then to bestow it. Wherefore 'tis established that, in those that are brought up under the Gospel, God's ordinary way is thus first to convince them; so that there is doubtless ordinarily a preparatory work of conviction. This conviction that causes men to think it worth the while to seek salvation is hardly ever a conviction of the worth of the reward but of the dreadfulness of the punishment. So that there is doubtless in God's ordinary way a preparatory conviction of sin, that is, the danger of it, before conversion. In the more unthinking people, such as husbandmen and the common sort of people who are less used to much reasoning, God commonly works this conviction by begetting in their minds a dreadful idea and notion of the punishment. In the more-knowing and thinking men, the Holy Spirit makes more use of rational deductions to convince them that 'tis worth their while to seek earnestly for salvation. For God makes use of those things, viz., good nature, a good understanding, a rational brain, moral prudence, etc., as far as they hold.

353. Law of nature. The Apostle says (Rom. 2:14, 15) that the gentiles which have not the law do by nature the things contained in the law. Those having not the law are a law unto themselves, which shows the work of the law written in their hearts, their conscience also bearing witness. In order to men's having the law of God made known to them by the light of nature, two things are necessary: the light of nature must not only discover to them that these and these things are their duty, i. e., that they are right, that there is a justice and equality in them, and the contrary unjust; but it must discover to 'em also that 'tis the will of God that they should be done, and that they shall incur His displeasure by the contrary. For a law is a signification of the will of a lawgiver, with the danger of the effects of his displeasure in case of the breach of that law. The gentiles had both these. Their natural consciences testified to the latter after this manner. Natural conscience suggests to every man the relation and agreement there is between that which is wrong or unjust and punishment. This naturally disposes man to expect it. To think of wrong and injustice, especially such as often is seen without any punishment to balance it, is shocking to men's minds. Men, therefore, are naturally averse to thinking that there will be no punishments, especially when they themselves are great sufferers by injustice and have it not in their power to avenge themselves. And the same sense made guilty persons zealous lest they should meet with their deserved punishment. And this kept up in the world among all nations the doctrine of superior powers that

would revenge iniquity. This sense of men's consciences kept alive that tradition and made it easily and naturally received. The light of nature discovered the being of a deity otherwise, but this sense of conscience upheld this notion of Him—that He was the avenger of evil. And it also made them the more easily believe the being of a deity itself. God also gave many evidences, in His providence amongst the heathen, that He was the revenger of iniquity. When the light of nature discovered to 'em that there was a God that governed the world, they the more easily believed Him to be a just being, and so that He hated injustice because it appeared horrid to think of a supreme judge of the universe that was unjust. Gen. 18:25, "Shall not the judge of all the earth do right?"

626. Spirit's operation. Nature. Grace. Common grace. Special regeneration. (*Vid.* No. 471.)[8] Natural men may have convictions from the Spirit of God, but 'tis from the Spirit of God only as assisting natural principles and not infusing any new and supernatural principle. That conviction of guilt which a natural man may have from the Spirit of God is only by the Spirit's assisting natural conscience the better and more fully to do its office. Therein common grace differs from special. Common grace is only the assistance of natural principles; special is the infusing and exciting supernatural principles; or, if these words are too abstruse, common grace only assists the faculties of the soul to do that more fully which they do by nature. Man's natural conscience will, by mere nature, render him in a degree sensible of guilt; it will accuse a man and condemn him when he has done amiss. The Spirit of God, in those convictions which natural men sometimes have, assists conscience to do this in a further degree and helps the natural principles against those things that tend to stupify it and to hinder its free exercise. But special grace causes the faculties to do that that they do not by nature; causes those things to be in the soul that are above nature and of which there is nothing of the like kind in the soul by nature; and causes them to be in the soul habitually and according to such a stated constitution or law that lays such a foundation for a continued course of exercises as is called a principle of nature—such as a principle of life in a plant or animal, or a principle of sensation or natural appetites, etc.

732. Common illumination. The nature of the work of the Spirit may be learnt from the nature of His work in legal conviction. 'Tis the same common enlightening assistance of both, but only one is of

[8] No. 471 is not included in this text because it is repetitious.

evil and the other of good. Those legal convictions that natural men have are from the common illumination of the Spirit of God concerning evil. Those pleasant religious affections and apprehensions that natural men sometimes have are from the common illuminations of the Spirit of God concerning good. The assistance given is of a like sort in both, but only the object is different. One respects good and the other evil, both [of] which natural men are equally capable of apprehending without any supernatural principle. The mind of man without a supernatural principle is capable of two things with respect to conviction of evil:

1. The judgment is capable of being convinced of evil; man's natural reason is capable of discerning force in those arguments that prove it, though sin greatly clouds the judgment concerning these things. A natural man's reason, by common assistance of it against the clouding, prejudicing, and stupifying nature of sin, is capable of seeing the force of many arguments that prove God's anger and future punishment, and the greatness of these things. And so a natural man is capable of being convinced how much there is in him contrary to God's law, and to how great a degree it is contrary, and what connection there is between these faults and God's anger and future punishment.

2. Besides a conviction of truth respecting evil in the judgment, a natural man, as such, is capable of a sense of heart of this evil, i. e., he is capable of a deeply impressed and lively and affecting idea and sense of these things which is something more than a mere conviction in the judgment concerning their truth. The mind of a natural man is capable of a sense of the heart of natural [things], or of those things that are terrible to nature.[9] And, therefore, what the Spirit of God does in legal conviction or, which is the same thing, common illuminations of evil is to assist those principles, viz., the natural reason or judgment, against the prejudicing, blinding tendency of sin, and to assist the sense of the heart against the stupefying nature of sin.

And it is the same kind of influence or assistance that is given in common convictions and illuminations of good, whereby the souls of natural men are affected with thoughts of God's love and pity and kindness to them or others, of benefits offered or bestowed on them, of being beloved of God, of being delivered from calamity, of having honor put upon them of God, and the like. For the mind of man, without any supernatural principles, is in like manner capable of two things, viz., 1. of a conviction of the judgment by reasons that evince

[9] Although this sentence is confused, Edwards seems to mean that even the "natural" man can detect the evil in acts "that are terrible to nature."

the truth of the things of religion that respect natural good, and 2. of a sense of heart of natural good. And so God assists these principles in common illumination. And 'tis to be noted that a conviction of evil abundantly makes way for such a conviction of good. A conviction of sin and guilt makes way for a conviction of the greatness of mercy held for them; and a conviction of danger of misery prepares for a more sensible, affecting idea of God's pity appearing either in comfortable words of Scriptures, or in the great works of God in redemption, or in His particular providence towards the person affected.

Such a conviction and illumination of the mind or such an assistance of the soul to a sense of the good or evil things of religion is the proper work of the Spirit of God. For the Spirit of God is indeed the author of our capacity of discerning or having a sense of heart of natural good or evil. For this really differs not from the faculty of man's will. And it was especially the work of the Spirit of God in creation, wherein the three persons of the Trinity were conjunct, to infuse this principle—this part of the natural image of God. For herein man is made in the image of God who has understanding and will, which will is the same with the Holy Ghost. And therefore the assisting this principle in its acting and in giving a sense of good and evil is proper to the Holy Ghost.

782. Ideas. Sense of the heart. Spiritual knowledge or conviction. Faith. Great part of our thoughts and the discourse of our minds concerning [things] is without the actual ideas of those things of which we discourse and reason; but the mind makes use of signs instead of the ideas themselves. A little attentive reflection may be enough to convince anyone of this. Let any man, for his own satisfaction, take any book and read down one page of it as fast as he ordinarily is wont to read with understanding. He finishes perhaps the whole page in about a minute of time, wherein, it may be, were many such terms as God, man, angel, people, misery, happiness, salvation, distinction, consideration, perplexity, sanctification, and many more such like. And then let him consider whether he has had the actual ideas of all those things, and things signified by many other words in the whole page, in this short space of time. And particularly let him consider whether or no, when in the course of his reading he came upon the word 'God' in such a line, which his mind dwelt not a moment upon, whether or no he had an actual idea of God, i. e., whether he had an actual idea, that moment, of those things that are principally essential in an idea of God; as, whether he had an actual idea of supremacy, of supreme power, of supreme government, of supreme knowledge, of will, etc. I apprehend

that diligent attention will convince him that he has no actual idea of one of these things when he understandingly reads, or hears, or speaks the word 'God.' I will instance but in one thing that seems most found a notion of all [i. e., most commonly found] in the idea of God, viz., understanding or knowledge. He will find that in such cases he had no actual idea at all of this. For if he had an actual idea of understanding or knowledge, then he had an actual idea of ideas—of ideas of perception or consciousness; of judging or perceiving connections and relations between different ideas; and so had an actual idea of various ideas and relations between them. So when he read the word 'people,' let him inquire whether he had any actual idea of that which was signified by this word. In order to this he must have an actual idea of man. I don't mean only a confused idea of an outer appearance like that of man; for, if that was all, that was not an idea of man properly but only a sign made use of instead of an idea. But he must have an actual idea of those things wherein manhood most essentially consists, as an idea of reason, which contains many other actual ideas—as an actual idea of consciousness, an actual idea of a disposal of ideas in the mind, an actual idea of a consequent perception of relations and connections between them, etc. And so he must have an actual idea of will, which contains an actual idea of pleasure and pain, agreeableness and disagreeableness, and a consequent command or imperate act of the soul, etc. So when he read the word 'perplexity,' let him consider whether he had an actual idea of that actual thing signified by that word which contained many actual ideas—as an actual idea of thought and an actual idea of intenseness of thought, and also earnestness of desire, an actual idea of disappointment or crossness to desire (which contains many other actual ideas), and an actual idea of manifoldness of troubles and crosses, etc. So when he read the word 'sanctification,' the actual idea of which contains a great many actual ideas, viz., an actual idea of what is implied in the faculties of an intelligent voluntary being, and then an actual idea of holiness, which contains a great number of other actual ideas.

But I need not insist on more instances. I should think that these might be enough to convince anyone that there is very often no actual idea of those things when we are said to think of them, and that the thought is not employed about things themselves immediately, or immediately exercised in the idea itself, but only some sign that the mind habitually substitutes in the room of the idea. Our thoughts are oftentimes ten times swifter than our reading or speech. Men oftentimes think that in a few minutes which it would take 'em a long time to speak. And if there be no room to suppose that all the ideas signified by the words of a discourse can be actually excited in the mind in reading or speaking, much less can it be in such swift discourse of thought.

We thus, in the discourse of our minds, generally make use of signs instead of ideas, especially with respect to two kinds of subjects of our thoughts, viz., 1. with respect to general things, or kinds and sorts; such are kinds of substances and such also are what Mr. Locke calls 'mixed modes.' When we, in the course of our thoughts, in reading or hearing or speaking or meditation, think of any sort of substance or distinct beings, as particularly of men, instead of going about with attention of mind actually to excite the ideas of those things that belong to the nature of man, that are essential to it, and that distinguish it from other creatures, and so having actually such an abstract idea as Mr. Locke speaks of, we have only an idea of something in our mind, either a name or some external sensible idea that we use as a sign to represent that idea; so when, in the discourse of our minds, there passes a thought of that sort of creatures called lions, or that sort of natural bodies called metal, or that called trees; so in mixed modes such as compassion, decency, harmony, and the like.

2. 'Tis commonly so in our discourses of those things that we can know only by reflection, which are of a spiritual nature, or things that consist in the ideas, acts, and exercises of minds. It has been shown elsewhere[10] that there is no actual idea of those things but what consists in the actual existence of the same things, or like things, in our own minds. For instance, to excite the idea of an idea we must have that very idea in our minds; we must have the same idea. To have an actual idea of a thought is to have that thought, that we have an idea of, then in our minds. To have an actual idea of any pleasure or delight, there must be excited a degree of that delight; so to have an actual idea of any trouble or kind of pain, there must be excited a degree of that pain or trouble; and to have an idea of any affection of the mind, there must be then present a degree of that affection. This alone is sufficient to show that, in great part of our discourses and reasonings on things, [we] are without the actual ideas of those things of which we discourse and reason. For most of our discourses and reasonings are about things that belong to minds or things that we know by reflection; or at least do involve some relation to them in some respect or other. But how far are we, when we speak or read or hear or think of those beings that have minds (or intelligent beings), or of their faculties and powers, or their dispositions, principles, and acts, and those mixed modes that involve relations to these things, from actually having present in our minds those mental things, those thoughts, and those mental acts that

[10] See no. 123, p. 245; no. 201, p. 247; and especially no. 238, p. 247, below.

those spiritual things do consists in or are related to! Very commonly we discourse about them in our minds and argue and reason concerning them, without any idea at all of the things themselves in any degree, but only make use of the signs instead of the ideas. As for instance, how often do we think and speak of the pleasure and delight or pain and trouble that such have, or have had, in such and such things, or things that do in some respect involve pleasure or pain in their idea, without the presence of any degree of that pleasure or that trouble, or any real idea of those troublesome or pleasing sensations!

Those signs that we are wont to make use of in our thoughts for representations of things, and to substitute in the room of the actual ideas themselves, are either the ideas of the names by which we are wont to call them or the idea of some external sensible thing that some way belongs to the things—some sensible image or resemblance, or some sensible part, or some sensible effect, or sensible concomitant, or a few sensible circumstances. We have the ideas of some of those excited, which we substitute in the room of those things that are most essential, and use 'em as signs as we do words, and have respect to 'em no further in our discourse. Hence we don't stand at all on the clearness and distinctness of that external idea that we thus make use of, but commonly 'tis very dim and transient and exceeding confused and indistinct—as when in a course of meditations we think of man, angels, nations, conversion, conviction. If we have anything further in our thoughts to represent those things than only the words, we commonly have only some very confused, passing notion of something external, some[thing] we don't at all insist on the clearness and distinctness of. Nor do we find any need of it, because we make use of that external idea no otherwise than as a sign of the idea or something to stand in its stead. And the notion need not be distinct in order to that, because we may habitually understand the use of it as a sign without it; whereas it would be of great consequence that it should be clear and distinct if we regarded it as an actual idea and proper representation of the thing itself. The signs that those that have the use of speech do principally make use of in their thoughts are words or names, which are indeed very frequently accompanied with some slight confused glance of some sensible idea that belongs to the thing named; but the name is the principal sign the mind makes use of. Others that are deaf and dumb do probably make use of the ideas of those signs which they have been accustomed to signify the thing by, or (if we may judge by what we find in things that we have no names for, and there are many such) they make use of some sensible effect, part, concomitant, or circumstance as the sign.

'Tis something external or sensible that we are wont to make use [of] for signs of the ideas of the things themselves; for they are much more ready at hand and more easily excited than ideas of spiritual or mental things, which for the most part can't be without attentive reflection. And very often the force of the mind is not sufficient to excite them at all, because we are not able to excite in our minds those acts, exercises, or passions of the mind that we think of.

We are under a necessity of thus putting signs in our minds instead of the actual ideas of the things signified, on several accounts: partly by reason of the difficulty of exciting the actual ideas of things, especially in things that are not external and sensible, which are a kind of things that we are mainly concerned with; and also because, if we must have the actual ideas of everything that comes in our way in the course of our thought, this would render our thoughts so slow as to render our powers of thinking in a great measure useless, as may be seen in the instance mentioned of a man reading down a page. Now [if] we use signs instead of the actual ideas themselves, we can sufficiently understand what is contained in that page in a minute of time, and can express the same thoughts to another in as little time by our voices, and can think ten times as swiftly as we can read or speak. But if, in order to an understanding of what was contained in that page, we must have an actual idea of everything signified by every word in that page, it would take us up many hours to go through with it. For taking in all the ideas that are either directly signified, or involved in relations that are signified by them, it would take us up a considerable time before we could be said to understand one word. But if our understandings were so slow, it would frustrate all use of reading or writing and all use of speech—yea, and all improvement of a faculty of thinking, too. And if all our thoughts must have proceeded after this slow manner from our infancy, we must have remained infants all the days of our lives, and seventy years would have been sufficient to have proceeded but a few steps in knowledge.

This way of thinking by signs, unless as it is abused to an indulgence of a slothful inattentive disposition, may well serve us to many of the common purposes of thinking; for in many respects we, without the actual presence of the idea, know how to use the sign as if it were the idea itself. Having learned by frequent experience, our minds in the presence of the sign being habitually led to the relations and connections with other things, the presence of the sign in the mind does by custom as naturally and spontaneously suggest many relations of the thing signified to others, as the hearing of such a certain sound or seeing such letters does by custom and habit spontaneously excite such a thought. But if we are at a loss concerning a connection or consequence, or have a new inference to draw, or would see the force of some new argument, then commonly we are put to the trouble of exciting the actual idea and making it as lively and clear as we can. And in this consists very much of that which we call attention of the mind in thinking. And the force or strength of a mind consists very much in an ability to excite actual ideas so as to have them lively and clear; and its comprehension, whereby it is able to excite several at once to that degree as to see their connections and relations.

Here, by the way, we may observe the exceeding imperfection of the human understanding and one thing wherein it appears immensely below God's understanding, in that He understands Himself and all other things by the actual and immediate presence of an idea of the things understood. All His understanding is not only by actual ideas of things without ever being put to it to make use of signs instead of ideas (either through an inability or difficulty of exciting those ideas, or to avoid a slow progress of thoughts that would arise by so manifold and exact an attention), but He has the actual ideas of things perfectly in His mind without the least defect of any part and with perfect clearness, and without the imperfection of that fleetingness or transitoriness that attends our ideas, and without any troublesome exertion of the mind to hold the idea there, and without the trouble we are at to have in view a number at once that we may see the relations. But He has the ideas of all things at once in His mind, and all in the highest possible perfection of clearness, and all permanently and invariably there without any transitoriness or fading in any part. Our understandings are not only subject to the imperfections that consist in those things which necessitates us to make use of such signs as we have been speaking [of], but this is a source of innumerable errors that we are subject to. Though, as was said before, such a use of signs serves us well to many purposes, yet the want of the actual ideas, and making use only of the signs instead of them, causes mankind to run into a multitude of errors, the falsity of which would be manifest to them if the ideas themselves were present.

From what has been said, we see that there are two ways of thinking and understanding, especially of spiritual or mental things that we receive a notion of by reflection or consciousness: viz., 1. that wherein we don't directly view the things themselves by the actual presence of their ideas or (which is the same thing in mental matters) sensation of their resemblances, but apprehend them only indirectly in their signs, which is a kind of a mental reading wherein we don't look on the things themselves but only on those signs of them that are before our eyes. This is a *mere cogitation* without any proper apprehension of the things thought of. 2. There is that which is more properly called *apprehension,* wherein the mind has a direct *ideal view* or *contemplation* of the thing thought of.

This ideal apprehension or view of mental things is either: 1. of things that pertain merely to the faculty of understanding, or what is figuratively called the head, including all the modes of mere discerning, judging, or speculation; or 2. of things that appertain to the other faculty of the will, or what is figuratively called the heart, whereby things are pleasing or displeasing, including all agreeableness and disagreeableness, all beauty and deformity, all pleasure and pain, and all those sensations, exercises, and passions of the mind that arise from either of those. An ideal apprehension or view of things of this latter sort is what is vulgarly called a having a sense. 'Tis commonly said, when a person has an ideal view of anything of this nature, that he has a sense of it in his mind, and 'tis very properly so expressed. For, by what has been said already, persons can't have actual ideas of mental things without having those very things in the mind. And seeing all of this latter sort of mental things that belong to the faculty of will or the heart do, in great part at least, consist in a sensation of agreeableness or disagreeableness, and a sense or feeling of the heart of pleasedness or displeasedness, therefore it will follow that everyone that has an ideal view of those things has therein some measure of that inward feeling or sense.

Hence arises another great distinction of the kinds of understanding of mental things, or those things that appertain or relate to spiritual beings, which is somewhat diverse from the former, viz., of speculative and sensible: or 1. that understanding which consists in mere speculation or the understanding of the head; and 2. that which consists in the sense of the heart. The former includes all that understanding that is without any proper ideal apprehension or view and all that understanding of mental things of either faculty that is only by signs. And also all ideal views of things that are merely intellectual or appertain only to the faculty of understanding, i. e., all that understanding of things that don't consist in or imply some motion of the will or, in other words (to speak figuratively) some feeling of the heart, is mere speculative knowledge, whether it be an ideal apprehension of them or no. But all that understanding of things that does consist in or involve such a sense or feeling is not merely speculative but sensible knowledge. So is all ideal apprehension of beauty and deformity, or loveliness and hatefulness; and all ideas of delight or comfort, or pleasure of body or mind, pain, trouble, or misery; and all ideal apprehensions of desires and longings, esteem, acquiescence, hope, fear, contempt, choosing, refusing, assenting, rejecting, loving, hating, anger, and the idea of all the affections of the mind, and all their motions and exercises; and all ideal views of dignity or excellency of any kind; and also all ideas of terrible greatness, or awful majesty, meanness, or contemptibleness, value and importance. All knowledge of this sort, as it is of things that concern the heart or the will and affections, so it all relates to the good or evil that the sensible knowledge of things of this nature involves. And nothing is called a sensible knowledge upon any other account but on the account of the sense or kind of inward tasting or feeling of sweetness or pleasure, bitterness or pains, that is implied in it or arises from it. Yet 'tis not only the mere ideal apprehension of that good or evil that [is] included in what is called 'being sensible of,' but also that ideal apprehension of other things that appertain to the thing known, on which the goodness or evil that attends them depends. As for instance, some men are said to have a sense of the dreadfulness of God's displeasure. This apprehension of God's displeasure is called having a sense, and is to be looked upon as a part of sensible knowledge because of that evil or pain in the object of God's displeasure, or that is connected with that displeasure—an idea of what God is supposed to feel in His own heart in having that displeasure. But yet, in a sense of the terribleness of God's displeasure there is implied an ideal apprehension of more things than merely of that pain or misery, or sense of God's heart. There is implied an ideal apprehension of the being of God and of some intellectual existence, and an ideal apprehension of His greatness and of the greatness of His power. An ideal apprehension or view of those things is, in vulgar speech, called an having a sense of them. And in proportion to the intensive degree of this ideal apprehension or the clearness and liveliness of the idea of them, so persons are said to have a greater or lesser sense of 'em. And according to the easiness or difficulty of persons receiving such a sense of things, especially things that it much concerns them to be sensible of, are they called either sensible or stupid.

This distribution of the human knowledge into speculative and sensible, though it seems to pertain [to] only one particular kind of the objects of our knowledge—viz., those things that appertain or relate to the will and affections—yet indeed may be extended to all the knowledge we have of all objects whatsoever. For there is no kind of thing that we know but what may be considered as in some respect or other concerning the wills or hearts of spiritual beings. And indeed we are concerned to know nothing on any other account. So that perhaps this distinction of the kinds of our knowledge into speculative and sensible, if duly weighed, will be found the most important of all. The distribution is with respect to those properties of our knowledge that immediately relate to [the] end of all our knowledge, and [to] that in the objects of our knowledge on the account of which alone they are worthy to be known, viz., their relation to our wills and affections and interest —as good or evil, important or otherwise—and the respect they have to our happiness or misery.

The will, in all its determinations whatsoever, is governed by its thoughts and apprehensions of things with regard to those properties of the objects of its thoughts wherein the degree of the sense of the heart has a main influence.

There is a twofold division or distribution [that] may be made of the kinds of sensible knowledge of things that men have.

The first is with respect to the ways we come by it. 1. There's that which is purely natural; either such as men's minds come to be impressed with by the objects that are about them, by the laws of nature; or when they behold anything that is beautiful or deformed, by a beauty and deformity that men by nature are sensible of, then they have sensible knowledge of that beauty or deformity—as when the ear hears a variety of sounds harmoniously proportioned, the soul has a sensible knowledge of the excellency of the sound; when it tastes any good or ill savor or odor, it has a sensible knowledge of the excellency or hatefulness of that savor or odor. So it may have a sensible knowledge of many things by memory and reflection. So a man may have a sensible apprehension of pleasure or sorrow that others are the subjects of, indirectly by reflection, either by exciting from the memory something that he has felt heretofore which he supposes is like it, or by placing himself in other's circumstances, or by placing things about himself in his imagination and, from ideas so put together in his mind, exciting something of a like pleasure or pain transiently in himself. And if those ideas come so together into the mind by the senses, or by the relation of others, such a sensation will spontaneously arise in the mind. In like manner men may have a sense of their own happiness or misery conceived as future. So men may, by mere nature, come to have a sense of the importance or terribleness or desirableness of many things. 2. That sense of things which we don't receive without some immediate influence of the Spirit of [God], impressing a sense of things that do concern our greatest interest on our minds. 'Tis found very often a very difficult thing to excite a sense of temporal things in the mind, requiring great attention and close application of thought. And many times it is not in our power. And in many instances wherein we have a sense of temporal things that is purely natural, it depends not merely on the force of our thoughts but the circumstances we are in, or some special accidental situation and concurrence of things in the course of our thoughts and meditations, or some particular incident in providence that excites a sense of things or gives an ideal view of them in a way inexplicable. But the exciting a sense of things pertaining to our eternal interest is a thing that we are so far from and so unable to obtain of ourselves (by reason of the direction of the inclinations and natural dispositions of the soul [away] from those things as they are, and the sinking of our intellectual powers, and the great subjection of the soul in its fallen state to the external senses), that a due sense of those things is never attained without immediate divine assistance.

'Tis in this that the ordinary work of the Spirit of God in the hearts of men consists, viz., in giving a sense of spiritual and eternal things, or things that appertain to the business of religion and our eternal interest. The extraordinary influence of the Spirit of God in inspiration imparts speculative knowledge to the soul, but the ordinary influence of God's Spirit communicates only a sensible knowledge of those things that the mind had a speculative knowledge of before. And an imagination that some have of speculative knowledge received from the Spirit of God in those that have no real inspiration is that wherein enthusiasm consists.

Secondly, the other distribution that may be made of the kinds of sensible knowledge is according to the different nature of the objects of it: into a sense of things with respect to the natural good or evil that is in them or that relates to them; or, a sense of them with respect to spiritual good or evil. By spiritual good I mean all true moral good, all real moral beauty and excellency, and all those acts of the will or that sense of the heart that relates to it and the idea of which involves it, and all sense of it, all relish and desire of it and delight in it, happiness consisting in it, etc. By natural good and evil I mean all that good or evil which is agreeable or disagreeable to human nature as such, without regard to the moral disposition—as all natural beauty and deformity such as a visible, sensible proportion or disproportion in figures, sounds, and colors; any good or evil that is the object of the external senses; and all that good or evil which arises from gratifying or crossing any of the natural appetites; all that good and evil which consists in gratifying or crossing a principle of self-love and consisting in others' esteem of us and love to us, or their hatred and contempt; and that desirableness or undesirableness of moral dispositions and actions so far as arising from hence; and all that importance, worth, or terribleness arising from a relation to this natural good or evil.

Persons are capable of sensible knowledge of things of religion of the former sort—viz., with respect to the natural good or evil that attends them—of themselves, with the same improvement of their natural powers that they have of that sensible knowledge of temporal [things], because this good and evil consists in an agreeableness or disagreeableness to human nature as such; and therefore no principles are required in men beyond those that are contained in human nature to discern them. But yet by reason of the natural stupidity of the soul with respect to things so diverse from all the objects of sense and so opposite to the natural disposition of the heart, 'tis found by experience that men never will obtain any very considerable sense of them without the influence of the Spirit of God assisting the faculties of human nature and impressing a lively sense of them. But as to the other, viz., a sense of divine things with respect to spiritual good and evil, because these don't consist in any agreeableness or disagreeableness to human nature as such, or the mere human faculties and principles, therefore man, merely with the exercise of those faculties and his own natural strength, can do nothing towards getting such a sense of divine things. But it must be wholly and entirely a work of the Spirit of God, not merely as assisting and co-working with natural principles, but infusing something above nature.

By the things that have been said, we may see the difference between the influences of the Spirit of God on the minds of natural men in awakenings, common convictions, and illuminations, and His spiritual influences on the hearts of the saints at and after their conversion. 1. Natural men, while they are senseless and unawakened, have very little sensible knowledge of the things of religion, even with respect to the natural good and evil that is in them and attends them. And indeed, [they] have very little of any ideal apprehension of any sort of divine and eternal things, by reason of their being left to the stupifying influence of sin and the objects of sense. But when they are awakened and convinced, the Spirit of God, by assisting their natural powers, gives 'em an ideal apprehension of the things of religion with respect to what is natural in them, i.e., of that which is speculative in them, and that which pertains to a sensibleness of their natural good and evil, or all but only that which involves a sense of their spiritual excellency. The Spirit of God assists to an ideal view of God's natural perfections wherein consists His greateness, and gives a view of this as manifested in His works that He has done and in the words that He has spoken, and so gives a sensible apprehension of the heinousness of sin and His wrath against it, and the guilt of it, and the terribleness of the sufferings denounced against it. And so they have a sense of the importance of things of religion in general. And herein consists what we commonly call conviction and a sense of the natural good that attends the things of religion, viz., the favor of so great a being, His mercy, as it relates to our natural good or deliverance from natural evil, the glory of Heaven with respect to the natural good that is to be enjoyed there, and like[wise] those affecting, joyful common illuminations that natural men sometimes have. In thus assisting men's faculties to an ideal apprehension of the natural things of religion, together with what assistance God may give men's natural reason and judgment to see the force of natural arguments, consists the whole of the common work of the Spirit of God in man. It consists only in assisting natural principles without infusing anything supernatural. 2. The spiritual work of the Spirit of God, or that which is peculiar to the saints, consists in giving the sensible knowledge of the things of religion with respect to their spiritual good or evil, which indeed does all originally consist in a sense of the spiritual excellency, beauty, or sweetness of divine things. This is not by assisting natural principles but by infusing something supernatural.

The ideal apprehension and sensible knowledge of the things of religion will give that conviction of their truth or reality which can no otherwise be obtained, and is the principal source of that conviction of the truth of the things of religion that is given by the immediate influence of the Spirit of God on men's hearts.

1. An ideal apprehension and sensible knowledge of the things of religion with respect to what is natural in them, such as natural men have that are under awakenings, will give some degree of conviction of the truth of divine things further than a mere notion of them in their signs, or only a speculative apprehension of them, because by this means men are enabled to see in many instances the agreement of the declarations and threatenings of the word of God with the nature of things, that, without an ideal and sensible knowledge of them, they could not have—as for instance, they that, from the tokens of God's greatness, His power, and awful majesty in His works and in His words, have an idea or sense of that greatness and power and awful majesty, and so see the agreement between such works and such words and such power and majesty, and therefore have a conviction of that truth that otherwise they could not have, viz., that it is a very great being that made those things and spoke those things. And so from a sense they may hence have of the dreadfulness of the wrath of such a being, they have a conviction of the truth of what the Scripture teaches about the dreadfulness of God's wrath and of the punishment of Hell. And from the sense they hereby have of the heinousness or dreadfulness of sin against such a God, and the natural agreement between affronts of such a majesty and the suffering of extreme misery, it appears much more credible to them that there is indeed an extreme misery to be suffered for sin. And so a sense of the natural good that there is in the things of religion,

such as is given in common illuminations, makes what the Scriptures declare of the blessedness of Heaven, etc. more credible.

2. An ideal and sensible apprehension of the spiritual excellency of divine things is [the] proper source of all spiritual conviction of the truth of divine things, or that belief of their truth that there is in saving faith. There can be no saving conviction without it, and it is the great thing that mainly distinguishes saving belief from all other. And the thing wherein its distinguishing essence does properly lie [is] that it has a sense of the divine or spiritual excellency of the things of religion as that which it arises from. All saving conviction of divine truth does most effectively arise from the spiritual sense of the excellency of divine things. Yet this sense of spiritual excellency is not the only kind of ideal apprehension or sense of divine things that is concerned in such a conviction; but it also partly depends on a sensible knowledge of what is natural in religion—as this may be needful to prepare the mind for a sense of its spiritual excellency and, as such, a sense of its spiritual excellency may depend upon it. For as the spiritual excellency of the things of religion itself does depend on and presuppose those things that are natural in religion, they being, as it were, the substratum of this spiritual excellency, so a sense or ideal apprehension of the one depends in some measure on the ideal apprehension of the other. Thus a sense of the excellency of God's mercy in forgiving sin depends on a sense of the great guilt of sin, the great punishment it deserves; a sense of the beauty and wonderfulness of divine grace does in great measure depend on a sense of the greatness and majesty of that being whose grace it is, and so indeed a sense of the glory of God's holiness and all His moral perfections; a sense of the excellency of Christ's salvation depends on a sense of the misery and great guilt of those that are the subjects of this salvation. And so that saving conviction of the truths of things of religion does most directly and immediately depend on a sense of their spiritual excellency; yet it also, in some measure, more indirectly and remotely depends on an ideal apprehension of what is natural in religion, and is a common conviction.

Common conviction, or an ideal and sensible apprehension of what is natural in the things of religion, contributes to a saving conviction of the truth of the Gospel, especially this way: men, by being made sensible of the great guilt of sin or the connection or natural agreeableness there is between that and a dreadful punishment, and how that the greatness and majesty of God seems to require and demand such a punishment, they are brought to see the great need of a satisfaction or something to intervene to make it honorable to that majesty to show 'em favor; and being for a while blind to the suitableness of Christ's satisfaction in order to this, and then afterwards having a sense given them of Christ's divine excellency and so of the glorious dignity of His person and what He did and suffered for sinners, hereby their eyes are, as it were, opened to see the perfect fitness there is in this to satisfy for sin or to render their being received into favor consistent with the honor of God's offended majesty. The sight of this excellent congruity does very powerfully convince of the truth of the Gospel. This way of satisfying for the sins, which now they see to be so congruous, is certainly a real way—not a mere figment but a divine contrivance—and [convinces] that there is indeed acceptance to be had with God in this. And so the soul savingly believes in Christ. The sight of this congruity convinces the more strongly when at last it is seen because, though the person was often told of it before, yet [he] could see nothing of it, which convinces that it was beyond the invention of men to discover it. For by experience they found themselves all their lifetime wholly blind to it, but now they see the perfect suitableness there is, which convinces 'em of the divine wisdom (that is beyond the wisdom of men) that contrived it.

The truth that the soul is most immediately convinced of in this case by a sense of the divine excellency of Christ, with a preparatory sense of the need of satisfaction for sin, is not that the Gospel is the word of [God]. But this is the truth the mind firstly and more directly falls under a conviction of, viz., that the way of salvation that the Gospel reveals is a proper, suitable, and sufficient way, perfectly agreeable to reason and the nature of things, and that which tends to answer the ends proposed. And the mind being convinced of this truth, which is the great subject of the Gospel, it then naturally and immediately infers from this fitness and sufficiency of this salvation, which the mind has experienced to be so much [beyond] the power of human reason of itself to discover, that it is certainly a contrivance of a superhuman excellent wisdom, holiness, and justice, and therefore God's contrivance.

End of the Creation

tt. Devotion. It has been said that there may be not much of devotion, and this reason has been given for it: that man was made to be useful to the rest of the universe, was made for the common good of the whole frame, and that there may be a degree of devotion that may hinder one from their being so useful to the rest of the creatures as they might otherwise. Neither are agreeable to reason. As for the first, that the highest end of a particular creature was to be useful to the common good of creatures in general (which, I think, is the same thing as to say that the world was made that the parts of it might be mutually useful to each other; that is, that the world was made to have all the parts of it nicely hanging together and sweetly harmonious and corresponding; that is, that the world was nicely contrived that the parts might nicely hang together; that is, that the world was nicely contrived that when it was done it might be a nicely contrived world; that is, that the world was nicely contrived for nothing at all—so that it must be, according to that opinion, the highest end of every particular being to be useful to the whole) is the same as to say that the whole, with all its parts useful to each other, is good for nothing at all. Who can't see this? For most certainly, if the highest end of the world be to have its parts useful to each other, the world in general is good for nothing at all. To illustrate it by example: if the highest end of every part of a clock is only mutually to assist the other parts in their motions, that clock is good for nothing at all. The clock in general is altogether useless, however every part is useful to turn round the other parts. So, however useful all the parts of the world are to each other, if that be their highest end, the world in general is altogether useless. I am sure there is the same reason for one as for the other. Yea, it is a contradiction and nonsense to say the highest end of a particular part of the world is to be useful to the rest; for if that is the highest end, they are not useful. So it is not sense to say of a machine that the highest end is to have one part move the rest; for the whole is useless, and so every part, however they correspond together. But, as in a clock, one wheel moves another and that another till at last we come to the hands, and there we end. The use of that immediately respects the eye of man.

So it is in the world. Some inanimate beings are useful to the more perfect and they to beasts; one beast to another, and they to man. And what is man made for? Where shall we go next? Surely men are not made for beasts. We must not go back again. Or is man good for nothing at all? The next immediate step is to the Creator. He was undoubtedly made to glorify the Creator, so that devotion must be his highest end. The hand of the clock was not made to move the wheels. We must not go back after we are come from wheel to wheel at last to the hand. The next immediate step is to the eye. In the creation there is an immediate communication between one degree of being and the next degree of being. Every wheel immediately communions with the next wheel, man being the top. So that the next immediate step from him is to God. Without doubt there is an immediate communication between the Creator and this highest of creatures according to the order of being. As the intelligent being is exercised immediately about the Creator, so, without doubt, the Creator immediately influences the intelligent being, immediately influences the soul—for 'tis but an immediate step from the soul to God. Those that call this enthusiasm talk very unphilosophically.

As for the other thing that is said, that there may be a degree of devotion that may hinder one from being useful to the rest of the universe, I suppose they will not dislike devotion if it only hinders one for but half a minute and makes one much more useful ever after. I mean, if it only makes us useless during our life upon earth and much more useful to eternity afterwards. Not that I believe that a man would be the less useful, even in this world, if his devotion was to that degree as to keep him all his lifetime in an ecstasy.

87. Happiness. 'Tis evident that the end of man's creation must needs be happiness, from the motive of God's creating the world, which could be nothing else but His goodness. If it be said that the end of man's creation might be that He might manifest His power, wisdom, holiness, or justice, so I say too. But the question is, Why God would make known His power, wisdom, etc.? What could move Him to will that there should be some beings that might know His power and wisdom? It could be nothing else but His goodness. This is the question: What moved God to exercise and make known those attributes? We are not speaking of subordinate ends but of the ultimate end of it, or motive into which all others may be resolved. 'Tis a very proper question to ask what attribute moved God to exert His power; but 'tis not proper to ask what moved God to exert His goodness, for this is the notion of goodness—an inclination to show goodness. Therefore, such a question would be no more proper than this, viz., what inclined God to exert His inclination to exercise goodness? What nonsense, for it is an asking and answering a question in the same words. God's power is shown no otherwise than by His powerfully bringing about some end. The very notion of wisdom is nicely contriving for an end, and if there be no end proposed, whatever is done is not wisdom. Wherefore, if God created the world primarily from goodness, every whit of this goodness must, necessarily, ultimately terminate in the consciousness of the creature, for the world is no other way capable of receiving goodness in any measure. But intelligent beings are the consciousness of the world. The end, therefore, of the creation must necessarily be that they may receive the goodness of God and that they may be happy. It appears also from the nature of happiness, which is the perception of excellency. For intelligent beings are created to be the consciousness of the universe, that they may perceive what God is and

does. This can be nothing else but to perceive the excellency of what He is and does. Yet He is nothing but excellency and all that He does nothing but excellent.

92. How then can it be said that God has made all things for Himself, if it is certain that the highest end of the creation was the communication of happiness? I answer, that which is done for the gratifying of a natural inclination of God may very properly be said to be done for God. God takes complacence in communicating felicity and He made all things for this complacence. His complacence in this making happy was the end of the creation. Revelations 4:11, "For thy pleasure they are and were created."

208. Glory of [God]. God loves His creatures so, that He really loves the being honored by them, as all try to be well thought of by those they love. Therefore, we are to seek the glory of God as that which is a thing really pleasing to Him.

243. Glory of God. The first part of the 14th chapter of John, and the 28th verse of the 12th chapter and Isai. 48:11, and Isai. 42:8, and many other such passages of Scripture make me think that God's glory is a good independent of the happiness of the creature; that it is a good absolutely, and in itself, and not as subordinate to the creature's happiness, but [a] good—not only because 'tis the creature's highest good—a good that God seeks (if I may so speak) not only as He seeks the creature's happiness, but for itself, seeks absolutely as an independent ultimate good. And though [there are] many passages in the Old Testament that seem to speak as if the end of His doing this or that was His honor's sake or His name's sake, it still appears to me exceeding plain that to communicate goodness is likewise an absolute good and what God seeks for itself, and that the very being of God's goodness necessarily supposes it. For to make happy is not goodness if it be done purely for another, superior end.

247. Glory of God. For God to glorify Himself is to discover Himself in His works or to communicate Himself in His works, which is all one. For we are to remember that the world exists only mentally, so that the very being of the world implies its being perceived or discovered. For God to glorify Himself is in His acts *ad extra* to act worthy of Himself, or to act excellently. Therefore, God don't seek His own glory because it makes Him the happier to be honored and highly thought of, but because He loves to see Himself, His own excellencies and glories, appearing in His works—loves to see Himself communi-

cated. And it was His intention to communicate Himself that was a prime motive of His creating the world. His own glory was the ultimate, Himself was His end—that is, Himself communicated. The very phrase 'the glory' seems naturally to signify [this]. Glory is a shining forth, an effulgence. So the glory of God is the shining forth or effulgence of His perfections or the communication of His perfections, as effulgence is the communication of light. For this reason, that brightness whereby God was wont to manifest Himself in the wilderness, and in the tabernacle and temple, was called God's glory. So the brightness of the sun, moon, and stars is called their glory . . . [11] So that the glory of God is the shining forth of His perfections. The world was created that they might shine forth—that is, that they might be communicated.

332. The great and universal end of God's creating the world was to communicate Himself. God is a communicating being.[12] This communication is really only to intelligent beings. The communication of Himself to their understandings is His glory, and the communication of Himself with respect to their wills (the enjoying faculty) is their happiness. God created this world for the shining forth of His excellency and for the flowing forth of His happiness. It don't make God the happier to be praised, but it is a becoming and condecent, worthy thing for infinite and supreme excellency to shine forth. 'Tis not His happiness but His excellency so to do.

346. Creation. Providence. It's most agreeable to the Scripture to suppose creation to be performed every moment. The Scripture speaks of it not only as past but as a present, remaining, continual act . . . [13]

445. There is a necessity of supposing that the exercise of God's goodness or the communication of His happiness is not merely a subordinate end, but stands in the place of an ultimate end, though there is no necessity of supposing it the only ultimate end. But if God's making His glory to appear be an ultimate end, this must stand not in subordination to it, but fellow to it and in the same rank with it. For to suppose that God's communication of goodness is wholly subor-

---

[11] A series of Biblical references is omitted.

[12] An exceedingly interesting discussion of communication may be found in a chapter entitled, "Of the Medium of Moral Government—Particularly Conversation" in Dwight's edition, vol. 7, pp. 277-298. The text of this chapter in Dwight is approximately what is found in *Miscellanies,* no. 1338. Because of its length and the substantial correctness of the Dwight text, I have not included no. 1338 in this text.

[13] A series of Biblical references is omitted.

dinate to some other end is to suppose that it is not from God's goodness. That which is done by any being entirely in subordination to some other end, and that is not done at all for the sake of itself, is wholly and only for some other thing that is more ultimately in view. The attribute or disposition that excites to that action is wholly that which seeks that more ultimate end. Thus, if God makes the creature happy only for a further end, viz., that He may manifest His own perfections by it, then His making the creature happy is not indeed from His goodness or His disposition to communicate good, but wholly from that attribute or disposition of the divine nature whereby He is disposed to show forth His own excellency. It is not consistent with the nature of goodness to be wholly moved and excited by something else that is not goodness.

If it be said that God communicates good to the creature only to manifest that part of His essential glory, viz., His goodness, this implies a great absurdity; for it supposes that God is good only to manifest His own goodness, which goodness is only an inclination to manifest His glory this way. So that now it comes to this, that God is good in order to manifest His inclination that He has to manifest His inclination to communicate good. He communicates good for this end that He may glorify His goodness, which goodness itself is nothing else but an inclination to communicate good for this end, viz., to glorify His inclination to communicate good to this end. And so we may run on to endless nonsense. If God is good only to manifest the glory of His goodness, then this would be that glory which was manifested, even His inclination to manifest His own glory. God has an inclination to manifest His own glory and the glory which He manifests is this, viz., His disposition to manifest His own glory; for His goodness is nothing else, if the sole ultimate end of communicating good be to glorify Himself or to show forth the glory of His goodness. Surely God's glory that is to be manifested must be considered as something prior to His disposition or design to manifest it. God's inclining, or designing, or exerting Himself to show His glory surely is not that very glory which He shows. The glory must be something else besides the manifestation of it.

You will say, why mayn't the same be said of God's justice; why can't the exercise of that be argued to be an ultimate end of the creation? I answer that, when the world is already created, merely the glorifying His justice cannot be the only motive to His acting justly—though the glorifying that attribute might be the motive for His giving Himself occasion for the exercise of that attribute by making the creatures. Indeed the glory of God cannot be considered as the proper end of God's acts of justice; for if it be, 'tis the glory of His justice is the end, which will imply those absurdities mentioned concerning God's goodness being altogether for the glory of His goodness. A view to the glorifying of God's justice is not the sole motive to God's acting justly when there is occasion; for He acts justly because 'tis agreeable to His nature and He delights so to do, though God's glorifying Himself might be His end in giving Himself occasion for the exercise of His justice. So that, although God's glorifying and communicating Himself were the sole ends for which He created the world, yet they cannot be properly considered as the sole ends of all that God does in the world. Thus God, when He speaks the truth to His creatures, the sole motive to His speaking the truth, when He does speak, is not to glorify His truth; for 'tis impossible that He should speak anything else. He speaks the truth because He delights in truth for its own sake.

But the attribute of justice, or a just disposition of the divine nature, can't be directly the motive to God's creating the world, as His goodness may. For a just disposition has for its object only being, existing either in act or design. 'Tis absurd to suppose that an inclination to do justice upon all occasions should properly be the motive to give creatures being, that there may be occasion. For that is not any part of the notion we have of justice—a disposition to make occasions for the exercise of justice. It must be some other disposition that does that; and in God it is His disposition to cause His attributes to shine forth, or to glorify Himself. But now goodness, or an inclination to communicate good, has merely possible being as much its proper object as actual or designed being. A disposition to communicate good will move a being to make the occasion for the communication; and indeed giving being is one part of the communication. If God be in Himself disposed to communicate Himself, He is therein disposed to make the creatures to communicate Himself to, because He can't do what He is in Himself disposed to without it. God's goodness is not an inclination to communicate Himself as occasion shall offer, or a disposition conditionally to communicate Himself, but absolutely.

But God's just and righteous disposition is only His disposition to act justly upon every occasion. If God be in Himself just, that supposes no more than that He will certainly act justly whenever there is occasion for His being concerned with the rights or deserts of any. It don't imply in its nature a disposition to make occasions for it. If God be disposed to make occasions for the exercise of that attribute, that must be only because He is disposed to cause His excellencies to shine forth, or to glorify himself. *Vid.* 461[14] *Vid.* note on the cxxxvi Psalm.

---

[14] See p. 134, below.

448. God is glorified within Himself these two ways: 1. By appearing or being manifested to Himself in His own perfect idea, or in His Son who is the brightness of His glory. 2. By enjoying and delighting in Himself, by flowing forth in infinite love and delight towards Himself, or in his Holy Spirit.

So God glorifies Himself towards the creatures also two ways: 1. By appearing to them, being manifested to their understanding. 2. In communicating Himself to their hearts, and in their rejoicing and delighting in, and enjoying, the manifestations which He makes of Himself. They both of them may be called His glory in the more extensive sense of the word, viz., His shining forth or the going forth of His excellency, beauty, and essential glory, *ad extra.* By one way it goes forth towards their understandings, by the other it goes forth towards their wills or hearts. God is glorified not only by His glory's being seen, but by its being rejoiced in. When those that see it delight in it, God is more glorified than if they only see it. His glory is then received by the whole soul, both by the understanding and by the heart. God made the world that He might communicate, and the creature receive, His glory; and that it might [be] received both by the mind and heart. He that testifies his idea of God's glory don't glorify God so much as he that testifies also his approbation of it and his delight in it. Both these ways of God's glorifying Himself come from the same cause, viz., the overflowing of God's internal glory, or an inclination in God to cause His internal glory to flow out *ad extra.* What God has in view in either of them, either in His manifesting His glory to the understanding or His communication of it to the heart, is not that He may receive but that He go forth. The main end of His shining forth is not that He may have His rays reflected back to Himself, but that the rays may go forth. And this is very consistent with what we are taught of God's being the alpha and omega, the first and the last. God made all things; and the end for which all things are made, and for which they are disposed, and for which they work continually, is that God's glory may shine forth and be received. From Him all creatures come, and in Him their well being consists. God is all their beginning, and God, received, is all their end. From Him and to Him are all things. They are all from Him, and they are all to be brought to Him. But 'tis not that they may add to Him, but that God might be received by them. The damned, indeed, are not immediately to God, but they are ultimately. They are to the glorified saints and angels, and they to God, that God's glory may be manifested in them unto the vessels of mercy.

It is said that God hath made all things for Himself; and in the revelation it is said they are created for God's pleasure. That is, they are made that God may in them have occasion to fulfill His good pleasure in manifesting and communicating Himself. In this God takes delight, and for the sake of this delight God creates the world, but this delight is not properly from the creature's communication to God, but in His to the creature. It is a delight in His own act. Let us explain the matter how we will, there is no way that the world can be for God more than so. For it can't be that He can receive anything from the creature.

461. *Vid.* 445.[15] If God delights in the creatures' participation of His happiness for its own sake, then it is evident that the communication of good is not merely a subordinate end, but must be allowed the place of an ultimate end. For if it be for its own sake, then it is not wholly for the sake of something else as its end. But 'tis evident that God delights in goodness for its own sake by such places: Micah 7:18, "He delighteth in Mercy;" Ezek. 18:23, "Have I any pleasure at all that the wicked should die, saith the Lord, and not that he should return from his ways and live;" and again, Ezek. 33:11, "Say unto them as I live, saith the Lord God, I have no pleasure in the death of the wicked; but that the wicked turn from his way and live: turn ye, turn ye from your evil ways, for why will ye die, O house of Israel;" Lam. 3:33, "For he doth not afflict willingly nor grieve the children of men." Such passages of Scripture show that God delighteth in the creatures' happiness in a sense that He doth not in their misery. 'Tis true that God delights in justice for its own sake as well as in goodness, but it will by no means follow from thence that He delights in the creatures' misery for its own sake as well as happiness; for goodness implies, in its nature, that the good of its object be delighted in for its own sake. But justice don't carry that in its nature—that the misery of those it's exercised about is delighted in for its own sake—as is evident because justice procures happiness as well as misery, according as the qualification of the object is. But it carries the contrary in its nature, viz., that misery be not delighted in for itself, but only for further ends.

547. There is doubtless some design that God is pursuing, and scheme that He is carrying on, in the various changes and revolutions that from age to age happen in the world. There is some certain great design to which providence subordinates all the successive changes that come to pass in the state of affairs of mankind. All revolutions from the beginning of the world to the end are doubtless but various parts of one scheme, all conspiring for the bringing to pass the great event which is ultimately in view. And the scheme will not be finished

---

[15] See p. 130, above.

nor the design fully accomplished, the great event fully brought to pass, till the end of the world, and the last revolution brought about. The world, it is most evident, is not an everlasting thing. It will have an end. And God's end in making and governing the world will not be fully obtained nor His scheme be finished till the end of the world comes. If it were, He would put an end to it sooner; for God won't continue the world, won't continue to uphold it and dispose and govern it and cause changes and revolutions in it, after He has nothing further that He aims at by it. God don't fully obtain His design in any one particular state that the world has been in at one time, but in the various successive states that the world is in, in different ages, connected in a scheme. 'Tis evident that He don't fully obtain His end, His design, in any one particular state that the world has ever been in; for, if so, we should have no change. But God is continually causing revolutions. Providence makes a continual progress, and continually is bringing forth things new in the state of the world, and very different from what ever were before. He removes one that He may establish another. And perfection will not be obtained till the last revolution, when God's design will be fully reached. Nor yet are the past states of the world abolished by the revolutions because they are in vain, or don't do anything towards promoting His design in creating the world. If so, providence would never have ordered them. The world never would have been in such a state. There remains, therefore, no other way but that the various successive states of the world do in conjunction, or as connected in a scheme together, attain God's great design.

Corollary 1. Hence it may be argued that the intelligent beings of the world are everlasting and will remain after the world comes to an end. If the perception and intelligence of the world don't remain after the world comes to an end, then as soon as ever the world comes to an end, the world and all that pertains to it, and its successive states and revolutions, the whole absolutely ceases and comes to nothing. Nothing remains of it all. It is at once as if nothing had been, so that, when the world and all its revolutions are finished, nothing is obtained— as soon as ever the last revolution or the last of the scheme is finished. When, [as] we have but now supposed, God first perfectly reaches His great design and accomplishes what He had in view in making the world, He reaches nothing, He accomplishes nothing, but only is just where He was before He made the world or so much as entered upon His scheme. There is nothing remains that can be supposed to be the thing reached or brought forth as the great thing aimed at in all that God had for so many ages been doing. The great event that is struck out at last in the consummation of all things is the same nothing from which things began. No benefit nor glory nor honor to God Himself, nor to any other, remains. God has no benefit, that He enjoys, remaining; He has gained no knowledge, no new idea by all that has happened. There remains no declarative glory of God, nor any benefit to any other being, but all is just as it was before God set out in His work. So that at the end of the world, at the close of all things, when the great design of the whole scheme is to be fully attained, nothing at all is attained.

Corollary 2. It is an argument of the truth of the Christian revelation; for there is nothing else that informs us what God designs by that series of revolutions and events that are brought to pass in the world, what ends He seeks, and what scheme He has laid out. 'Tis most fit that the intelligent beings of the world should be made acquainted with it. They are the beings that are principally concerned in it. The thing that is God's great design is something concerning them, and the revolutions by which it is to be brought to pass are revolutions amongst them, and in their state. The state of the inanimate, unperceiving part of the world is nothing regarded any otherwise than in a subserviency to the perceiving or intelligent parts. And then, 'tis most rational to suppose that God should reveal the design He was carrying on to His rational creatures, [so] that, as God has made them capable of it, they may actively fall [in] with it and promote it, acting herein as the subjects and friends of God . . .[16]

553. There are many of the divine attributes that, if God had not created the world, never would have had any exercise—the power of God, the wisdom of God, the prudence and contrivance of God, the goodness and mercy and grace of God, and the justice of God. It is fit that the divine attributes should have exercise. Indeed God knew as perfectly that there were those attributes fundamentally in Himself before they were in exercise as since. But God, as He delights in His own excellency and glorious perfections, so He delights in the exercise of those perfections. 'Tis true that there was from eternity that act in God, within Himself and towards Himself, that was the exercise of the same perfections of His nature. But it was not the same kind of exercise. It virtually contained it, but was not explicitly the same exercise of His perfection. God, who delights in the exercise of His own perfection, delights in all the kinds of its exercise. That eternal act or energy of the divine nature within Him, whereby He infinitely loves and delights in Himself, I suppose does imply, fundamentally, goodness and grace towards creatures—if there

[16] A paragraph declaring that the Christian revelation informs man of God's plan is omitted.

be that occasion—which infinite mind sees fit. But God, who delights in His own perfection, delights in seeing those exercises of His perfection explicitly in being that are fundamentally implied.

581. When God is said (Prov. 16:4) to make all things for Himself, no more is necessarily understood by it than that He made all things for His own designs and purposes, and to put them to His own use. 'Tis as much as to say that everything that is, that comes to pass, is altogether of God's ordering, and God has some design in it. 'Tis for something that God aims at and will have obtained, that this or the other thing is or happens, whatever it be—even sin and wickedness itself. It comes to pass because God has a use for it, a design and purpose to accomplish by it. Things don't happen merely to fulfil the desires or designs of some other being, some adversary of God. But all that is or comes to pass, 'tis of God's will and for His pleasure that it happens, and for His ends, and 'tis not primarily of the will of some others and for their purposes. But then we are taught nothing by that addition "for Himself." If it had been said God has made all things, that would have implied as much as that God made them for His own ends; for if God made things designedly it must be for some end. *Vid.* No. 586.

586. *Vid.* 581. Answer: This seems to be added because some things seem to come to pass thwarting God's designs and purposes, as particularly the sin and wickedness there is in the world. This is added to obviate such a thought as though God were frustrated or His aims thwarted by wicked men. And therefore it follows that God made all things for Himself (even the wicked), i. e., that He may be the owner and user of it, which is true of everything, for He never ceases to be the owner of anything that He hath made. And when He gives things to others, 'tis not as when we give. He don't cease still to be the owner and user of it. He continues to dispose of it for His own ends as much as ever. When Solomon says that God made all things for Himself, it seems to be an expression of much the same import as that in Revelation 4:11, "Thou hast created all things, and for Thy pleasure they are and were created," i.e., all things come into being at Thy will and pleasure, and for Thy will and pleasure, and for the accomplishment of what Thou wilt of Thine own designs and purposes . . .[17]

662. Glory of God. It may be inquired, why God would have the exercises of His perfections and expressions of His glory known and published abroad.

[17] A series of Biblical quotations is omitted.

Answer: It was meet that His attributes and perfections should be expressed; it was the will of God that they should be expressed and should shine forth. But if the expressions of His attributes are not known, they are not expressions; the very being of the expression depends on the perception of created understandings. And so much the more as the expression is known, so much the more it is.

679. Goodness of God. Love of God. Happiness of Heaven. God stands in no need of creatures and is not profited by them. Neither can His happiness be said to be added to by the creature, but yet God has a real and proper delight in the excellency and happiness of His creatures. He hath a real delight in the excellency and loveliness of the creature, in His own image in the creature, as that is a manifestation, an expression, and shining forth of His own loveliness. God has a real delight in His own loveliness and He also has a real delight in the shining forth and glorifying of it. As it is a fit and condecent thing that God's glory should shine forth, so God delights in its shining forth. So that God has a real delight in the spiritual loveliness of the saints, which delight is not a delight distinct from what He has in Himself, but is to be resolved into the delight He has in Himself. For He delights in His image in the creature as He delights in His own being glorified, or as he delights in it that His own glory shines forth. And so He hath real, proper delight in the happiness of His creatures, which also is not distinct from the delight that He has in Himself; for 'tis to be resolved into the delight that He has in His own goodness. As He delights in His own goodness, so He delights in the exercise of His goodness, and therefore He delights to make the creature happy and delights to see him made happy as He delights in exercising goodness or communicating happiness. This is no proper addition to the happiness of God, because 'tis that which He eternally and unalterably had. God, when He beholds His own glory shining forth in His image in the creature, and when He beholds the creature made happy from the exercise of His goodness, [is delighted?] . . .[18] This delight in God can't properly be said to be received from the creature, because it consists only in a delight in giving to the creature. Neither will it hence follow that God is dependent on the creature for any of His joy, because 'tis His own act only that this delight is dependent on, and the creature is absolutely dependent on God for that excellency and happiness that God delights in. God can't be said to be the more happy for the creature, because He is infinitely happy in Himself. He is not dependent on the creature for anything, nor has He received any addition from the creature. And yet in one sense

[18] A few words at this point are illegible.

it can be truly said that God has the more delight for the loveliness and happiness of the creature, viz., as God would be less happy if He were less good, or if it were possible for Him to be hindered in exercising His own goodness or to be hindered from glorifying Himself. God has no addition to His happiness when He exercises any act of holiness towards His creatures, and yet God has a real delight in the exercise of His own holiness and would be less happy if He were less holy, or were capable of being hindered from any act of holiness . . .[19]

699. Glory of God. God don't seek His own glory for any happiness He receives by it, as men are gratified in having their excellencies gazed at, admired, and extolled by others; but God seeks the display of His own glory as a thing in itself excellent. The display of the divine glory is that which is most excellent. 'Tis good that glory should be displayed. The excellency of God's nature appears in this, that He loves and seeks whatever is in itself excellent. One way that the excellency of God's nature appears is in loving Himself or loving His own excellency and infinite perfection. And as He loves His own perfection, so He loves the effulgence or shining forth of that perfection, or loves His own excellency in the expression and fruit of it. 'Tis an excellent thing that that which is excellent should be expressed in proper act and fruit. Thus 'tis an excellent thing that infinite justice should shine forth and be expressed in infinitely just and righteous acts, and that infinite goodness should be expressed in infinitely good and gracious deeds.

1066. Language seems to be defective and to want a proper general word to express the supreme end of the creation and of all God's works, including both these two as branches of it, viz., God's glorifying Himself or causing His glory and perfection to shine forth, and His communicating himself or communicating His fullness and happiness. The one supreme end of all things is the infinite good, as it were flowering out, or the infinite fountain of light, as it were shining forth. We need some other words more properly and fully to express what I mean. This one supreme end consists in two things, viz., in God's infinite perfection being exerted and so manifested, that is, in God's glorifying Himself; and second, His infinite happiness being communicated and so making the creature happy. Both are sometimes in Scripture included in one word, namely, God's being glorified. Both these things are plainly signified by God's glory in Isai. 6:3.

[19] Three corollaries which follow this passage are repetitious and have been omitted.

1182. Glory of God. Many argue that it must be that all men should make their own happiness their highest end in all things, because in whatever end men pursue they seek to gratify some inclination. They pursue it because they are inclined to it. They seek it as what pleases them and what they conceive would be well pleasing to 'em if obtained. Thus, when a man from benevolence seeks the prosperity of another, he seeks the other's happiness because it is agreeable to him and would, if obtained, be pleasing to him or, which is the same thing, would contribute to his pleasure or happiness. Therefore, still he seeks his own happiness and seeks nothing any otherwise than as something that would be pleasing and happifying to him. And so they suppose that 'tis evident from the very nature of benevolence that, when a man acts from it, he therein seeks his own happiness and makes it his ultimate end. And yet some of those that are in this scheme strangely insist that God cannot make His own glory His ultimate end, for this reason, because He can't make His own happiness His end. Being already infinitely happy, He does not need any manifestation of His glory to make Him more happy and, therefore, He must act only from benevolence, seeking the happiness of His creatures and making that His ultimate end, and not His own happiness. And so [they] run into great inconsistence, for: 1. They suppose it may be argued from the very nature of benevolence—which is to have pleasure or happiness in the happiness of another—that he that acts from benevolence makes his own happiness his ultimate end. And yet [2.] they insist that God can't make His own happiness His ultimate [end] but must act only from benevolence—speaking these two in opposition one to another; speaking [as] if God's acting from benevolence was opposite to His making His own happiness His ultimate end and excluded and disproved it, which yet in the other case they suppose necessarily infers and implies it. God's making His own glory His end no more implies His seeking His own happiness than His making the creature's good His end. 'Tis true that His seeking His own glory implies that He is well pleased and gratified in glorifying Himself, as herein He does what appears in His eyes beautiful and fit to be accomplished. And doubtless 'tis fit in itself that infinite glory should be manifested. So in making the creature's happiness [His end] He, by the supposition, does as really please and gratify Himself as in the other, inasmuch as by His benevolence He delights in the happiness of the creatures.

1208. Glory of God. Nature of redemption. Satisfaction of Christ. Nature of true virtue and religion. When we are considering with ourselves what it would have been fit or proper for God to have a chief respect to and make His highest end in creating a world (if He did create one), and in establishing a system of intelligent creatures, and what He should have the greatest regard to in His governing the world and regulating things in this created system of intelligence, and what they should make their highest end, and whom they and what they should have chief regard to, and what regard or regard to what being or beings should reign in their hearts and have the chief rule and dominion in their behavior, it may help us to judge of this matter with the greater satisfaction and ease to consider what would be determined by some third being of perfect wisdom (if such an one were possible), different both from the Creator and the created system, not interested in or concerned with either, but only occasionally stepping in to decide this matter. Or if we make the supposition thus, that perfect and infinite wisdom, justice, and rectitude were a distinct person or being not interested either in the Creator or His created system, any otherwise than only that it was his office to decide or order these matters between both most properly and suitably, and to be a kind of umpire between them to determine and settle what is most proper and agreeable to natural reason and rectitude with respect to one another without partiality, without favor or affection to either side—would not such a being or person in such an office, in judging of the forementioned matters that he might determine what is most fit and worthy, equally view the whole that is there before him, i. e., the sum of all being, the universality of existence as together making one whole, consisting of created and creating existence which all together is the whole of what is to be the object of regard? And now, in order to determine what sort and what measure of regard each part of this whole is to be the object of (or how every individual belonging to this universality, or sum total, is to share regard or respect of those intelligences that are concerned with this whole, that each part may have its proper portion and the portion that it is worthy of, that in the nature of things it is most fit and suitable that it should have, and that all things may be most properly disposed in the most proportionable, reasonable, and beautiful manner), everything must be weighed in an even balance. And in adjusting the proper measures and kinds of regard that every part of the sum of existence is to have, care must be taken that greater existence, or more existence, should have a greater share than the less; that a greater part of the whole is worthy to be more loved and respected than a lesser part (and that in proportion, other things being equal); and that the more excellent is more worthy to be regarded than the less excellent.

And in adjusting the degree of regard, these two things are to be considered conjunctly, viz., greatness and goodness, or the degree of existence and the degree of excellence. Such an arbiter, in considering the system of created beings by itself, would determine that the general system, consisting of many millions, was of greater importance and was to have a greater share of regard than only one individual. For however considerable some of the individuals might be, so that they might be much greater and, as it were, have a greater share of the sum total of existence than another, yet one don't exceed another so much as to be in any measure worthy to be put in the balance with all the rest of the system. And in adjusting the degrees of regard proper for the individual, the degree of the importance and excellence of each must be considered, so that the greater and more excellent should have a greater share than the less worthy. And in adjusting the measures of regard due to every part of the sum total of universal existence, including the infinite and eternal Creator and Lord of all, then this supreme being, with all in Him that is great and considerable and excellent and in any respect worthy, is to be, as it were, put into the balance against the creation, against individuals and against the whole system; and, according as He is found to outweigh, in such proportion is He to have a greater share of regard. And as it would be found in such a case that the whole system of created beings, in comparison of Him, is as the light dust of the balance (which is taken no notice of by him that weighs with the balance and is as nothing but vanity), so must the arbiter determine the regard He must have. And as He is infinite and has all possible existence, perfection, and excellence, so He must have all possible regard. As He is every way the first and supreme being, and His excellence is in all respects the original excellence, the fountain of all good, and the supreme beauty and glory, so He must in all respects have the supreme regard. As he is God over all, at the head of all, reigning with most absolute dominion and power, on whom all are dependent and all perfectly subordinate and subject, so it is fit that He should be the object of regard in such a manner that respect to Him reign over all our respect to other things, and that regard to creatures should be universally and perfectly subordinate and subject to our regard to Him.

When I speak of the regard proper in this manner to be showed and directed towards different parts of the sum total of intelligent existence, I mean regard in general or the regard of the whole, not only the regard of individual creatures or of all creatures but the regard of all intelligent existence, created and uncreated. 'Tis fit it should be thus with respect to the regard of the Creator as well as the creature. For 'tis as fit that His regard should be proportionable to the worthiness of objects as that the regard of creatures should. And thus such an arbiter as I supposed must be supposed to decide the matter as He [i.e., the Creator] would decide [what is] most properly beautiful and agreeable to truth. Such a judge would determine, and therefore He [i.e., the Creator] must determine, that all things should proceed accordingly, that all that is done and acted by this universality of existence, all proceedings, managements, and conduct through the whole ought to be according to such a rule, that all intelligent creatures should thus make the supreme being the object of their supreme regard and perfectly subordinate to it their regard to everything, and consequenlty that they should make Him their supreme end in all things; and also that the Creator Himself should supremely regard Himself and act in all things supremely with regard to Himself, making Himself his supreme end in creating and governing the world and all that He does with respect to the created system. Such an arbiter as I have supposed, as he would decide how things should proceed most fitly, according to the nature of things, would determine that the whole created system, the whole universe, including all creatures animate and inanimate, should in all its proceedings or revolutions and changes, great and small, that come to pass in it, as it were, act with and from such an absolutely supreme regard to God as its last end, that every wheel both great and small of the vast machine should in all their motions move with a constant, immutable regard to God as the ultimate end, as much as if the whole system were animated and actuated by one common soul that was possessed of such perfect wisdom and rectitude. And if such an arbiter as was before supposed, being possessed of such perfect wisdom and rectitude, becomes the common soul of the universe and animates and actuates it in all its proceedings, then such a supreme arbiter and director as I have supposed must determine that things should proceed, [and] he would determine that things should proceed most beautifully. See papers on the End of the Creation, p. 22, 23, 24 . . .[20]

Hitherto I have gone on a supposition of there being a third person besides the Creator and the creature, a person of perfect discerning and comprehension, of understanding and rectitude of disposition, not interested or concerned with either the Creator or the created system, only as having it for his office to state the highest propriety, fitness, and beauty with regard to their concerns one with another, and acts one towards another. The thing which has been supposed is impossible; but the case is nevertheless just the same, as to what is most fit and suitable in itself, as if there were such an arbiter to state and determine it. And therefore 'tis as proper for God to act according to this greatest fitness, and accordingly to give rules to His creatures, and make estab-

[20] The reference corresponds to *The Dissertation on the End for which God Created the World,* ch. 1, sec. 1. Two paragraphs which make special application to sin have been omitted.

lishments for them and regulate all things in the system of created intelligences and with relation to the intercourse between Him and them, as much as if He were dictated and directed in everything by such a third person, and as much as if such an arbiter were not only the soul of the world but were a common spirit animating the sum total of existence, consisting of God and the creatures. There is no such third person to be umpire in the affairs, . . .[21] nor can there be any, nor is there need of any, seeing God Himself is possessed of that perfect discerning and rectitude. And on this account it belongs to Him to be supreme arbiter, supreme lawgiver, and 'tis His own infinite wisdom and rectitude [that] should state all rules and all methods of proceeding and mutual intercourse between Him and the creature. There must be some supreme arbiter of right, fitness, and propriety, or else those things will be liable to fail and not take place in some instances. And if there must be such an one, it must be God. It belongs to Him and 'tis proper for Him to state all things according to the highest propriety, rectitude, reason, and beauty of things without partiality to either side; and if He should fail He would, as it were, fail of the business of His proper office. Though He is not animated by the spirit of a third person of infinite wisdom and rectitude, yet He is animated and directed by a spirit of infinite wisdom and rectitude, though it be His own spirit. And seeing it is a spirit of infinite wisdom and rectitude, [it] does not the less infallibly direct Him according to wisdom and rectitude than if it were not His own.

'Tis not the less belonging to God to act in all those things, just as an indifferent, perfectly wise arbiter between God and creatures would do, because He is, as it were, interested and is one party concerned; because a being interested unfits one to be a determiner or judge no otherwise than as interest tends either to blind a person and mislead him to think that is most reasonable and suitable which is not, or to incline him to act contrary to his judgment. But that God should be in danger of either of these is contrary to the supposition; for it is supposed that He is possessed of the most absolutely perfect discerning, and that supposes that He can't be blinded or misled in His judgment. And 'tis also supposed that He is possessed of the most perfect rectitude of heart, and that supposes that He can't be inclined to go contrary to His judgment.

Objection I. Some may be ready to say that, seeing God Himself is the supreme determiner of all things, who is one party in transactions between Him and His creatures, it may be proper for Him not to determine in every respect as it would be proper for an independent being no way interested to do, because that would too much limit His gener-

---

[21] Some repetitious phrases have been omitted.

osity. An indifferent third being might fitly determine that 'tis proper that God should be the supreme object of respect, that all creatures should make Him their supreme end, and that He should be the supreme end of all things, to whom all the course of nature and the whole frame of the universe in all its motions should have respect and tendency as its last end—that this would [be] no other than equal and just in itself; but yet that it might show a noble generosity in God when He Himself orders and regulates all things to deny Himself, forego His own right, and make the good of His creatures His last end. Seeing it is so that God Himself is the supreme determiner in His own cause, it would look like selfishness in Him, in His actions to prefer Himself to all other beings.

Answer. I answer, such an objection must arise from a very inconsiderate ignorant notion of the vice of selfishness and the virtue of generosity. If by selfishness he meant a being's disposition to regard for himself, this is no otherwise vicious or unsuitable than as the public weal exceeds the value or importance of self. As to created beings, one single person must be looked upon as vastly less, and so his interest of less importance than the interest of the whole system. Therefore a contracted, confined spirit, a disposition to prefer self as if that were more than all, is exceeding vicious. And a foregoing one's own interest for the sake of others is no further excellent, no further worthy of the name of generosity, than it is treating things according to reason and a prosecuting what is worthy to be prosecuted, and an expression of a disposition to prefer something to self-interest that is more worthy to be valued. If God be so great and so excellent that all other beings are as nothing to Him, and all other excellency be as nothing and less than nothing and vanity in comparison of His excellency, and God be omniscient and infallible, then He knows that He is infinitely the most valuable being. Therefore, if it is fit that His heart should be agreeable to this infallible, all-comprehensive understanding, this clear and perfect and infinitely bright light, then 'tis suitable that He should value Himself infinitely more than His creatures, and act accordingly in all His proceedings with respect to His creatures, and that He should require an answerable disposition and conduct in His intelligent creatures.

Objection II. Some may object and say: If the case were so that God needed anything, or His happiness could be advanced by the world that He hath made, or the goodness of His intelligent creatures extended to Him, or they could be profitable to Him, it might be fit that God should make Himself or His own interest His highest end in creating and governing the world, and it might be proper for His creatures to make Him their highest end in what they do. But seeing it is not so, but God is above all need and all capacity of being added to or advance[d] as to His welfare or interest, therefore it cannot be suitable that God or His creatures should make this their supreme end. For it would be improper and foolish in either to seek that which can't possibly be obtained and which don't need to be obtained. The highest good that can be brought to pass by anything that can be done by either God or created beings is the happiness of the creature. Therefore that is properly made the highest end by both.

Answer 1. Though it be true God's happiness is infinite, eternal, unchangeable, and independent, and so can't properly be added to, nor can He be dependent on the creature for it, yet something seems to be supposed in the objection that is not true, and that is that God is not happy in anything that He sees in the creature, in what He sees of the creature's qualifications, dispositions, state, and action, or that no part of God's happiness (to speak of God according to our manner of conception) consists in which He sees of these things in the creature. God may have a true, proper, and real delight (and so a part of his happiness) in seeing the state of the creature, in seeing its happy state; or He may delight in the exercise of His own goodness (and so gratifying the inclination of His own heart); and yet all His happiness be eternal and immutable. He eternally has this disposition and eternally sees and enjoys this future gratification of it as though it were present. Indeed all things are present to Him; with Him is no succession, no past and future, and He is independent in this delight. He brings the thing to pass by which He is gratified by His own independent power. And as it is with the Creator's happiness, so it is with His holiness. God really delights in it in the same manner. So it is in God's being glorified. His glories shining forth, being expressed, exhibited, and communicated—that is in itself fit and excellent, and therefore God delights in it. But as He accomplishes it Himself by His independent power, so God is independent in this delight. Although the dispositions and voluntary actions of His creatures are made the means of it, yet these are perfectly in God's hands and disposed of by God's independent power, so that still God is independent on it, and as if He sees it perfectly from eternity. His delight in it is eternal and immutable. And if it should here be said that it seems reasonable to suppose that God's infinite happiness should be in Himself, that He should be His own infinite and self-subsistent, complete, objective good, and that the creature, or any of its beauty or anything it does, should not be any part of it or be requisite to make the objective happiness full and complete, I answer that, although God has truly delight in the creature's happiness and holiness, yet still, His happiness is in Himself; for those are but communications of Himself—they are wholly being from the fountain. God's delight in these things is only a delight in His own brightness, communicated and reflected, and in His own action of communicating, which is still to be resolved into a delight in Himself. (See what I have formerly written on this subject.)

2. Let it be considered whether our not being able to profit God is any good evidence that God ought not to be supremely loved, and our love to God ought not to be as much as may be answerable to His infinite superiority to all other beings in greatness, excellency, and the subordination of all things in Him, and the dependence of all on Him, i.e., whether love and benevolence to Him ought not absolutely to reign in our hearts and all our regard to creatures and all our affections and actions be subordinate to that? If it be so, then our not being able to profit God is no argument that we should not make those things that love and benevolence to God most naturally and directly tends to, and seeks, our supreme end—or what we have a supreme respect to in what we do from this love. Indeed 'tis an inconsistence to suppose otherwise, for doubtless love ought to seek that which love tends to. Love should seek to gratify itself. Love is not fit to be had and cherished any further than it is fit to be gratified. The nature of love is a disposition or tendency, but that tendency is not to be sought and cherished as excellent which, when we have it, must be opposed and not allowed of. Therefore, if we ought to love God, we ought to make what love to God tends to our end, in that ratio or in that manner that therein we have respect to God and gratify our regard—which is the same thing as to make Him our end. Love seeks to please and honor the beloved, it is averse to His displeasure and dishonor and therein seeks God; and that, whatever we think about God being added to by anything we can do, love in seeking to please and honor God seeks God; and if we ought to have supreme love to God, then we ought supremely to seek what love to God tends to; and that is supremely to seek God; and that is to make God our supreme good; and that, in whatever way we do this, if it be chiefly in showing kindness to our neighbors, yet if this be done chiefly from love to God, then herein we make God our highest end. There is no other way. If our regard to God ought to be supreme we must make Him our highest end.

Corollary 1. The things which have been observed show plainly that a supreme regard to the deity is essential to true virtue, and that those schemes of religion or moral philosophy, however much in some respects they may treat of benevolence to mankind and other virtues depending on it, yet if a supreme respect to God and love to Him ben't laid in the foundation, and all other virtues handled in connection with this and [in] subordination to it and dependence on it, are not true schemes of philosophy but are fundamentally wrong. And whatever other benevolence or generosity towards mankind, and other virtues or qualifications which go by that name, any are possessed of that are not attended with a love to God, which is altogether above them, and to which they are subordinate, and on which they [are] dependent, there is nothing of the nature of true virtue and religion therein. And it may be asserted in general, that nothing is of the nature of true virtue or religion in which God is not the first and the last, or which with regard to its exercise in general has not their [i.e., its] first foundation and source in apprehension of God's supreme glory and worthiness and an answerable supreme esteem of and love to Him, and which has not respect to God as the supreme end.

Corollary 2. What has been observed may serve to show the reasonableness of the doctrine of the satisfaction of Christ. It is rational to suppose that, if God did determine to forgive such as had cast contempt on His infinite majesty and on His authority as the infinitely high Lord over all, and to take such into favor, infinite wisdom would some way or other so contrive the matter that the injury done to the appearance or exhibition of the dignity and sacred authority of this great king should be fully repaired, and His majesty entirely vindicated and set forth in all awfulness, inviolable sacredness, and worthiness of regard and reverence.

It can't here be reasonably objected that God is not capable of properly receiving any satisfaction for an injury because He is not capable of receiving any benefit—that a price offered to men satisfies for an injury because it may truly be a price to them or a thing valuable and beneficial, but that God is not capable of receiving a benefit—for God is as capable of receiving satisfaction as an injury. 'Tis true He can't properly be profited, so neither can He be properly hurt; but a rebelling against Him may properly be looked upon as of the nature of an injury or wrong done to God. And as God is capable in some proper sense of being the object of injuriousness, so He is as capable of being the object of that which is the opposite of injuriousness or of the repairing of an injury. If you say, what need is there that God have any care for repairing the honor of His majesty when it can do Him no good and no addition can be made to His happiness by it, you might as well say, what need is there that God care when He is despised, dishonored, and His authority and glory trampled on, since it does Him no hurt? 'Tis a vain thing here to pretend that God cares only because it hurts the creature's own happiness for 'em to cast contempt on God. Is it agreeable to the natural light of all men's minds, the natural sense of their hearts, and the dictates of conscience, which unavoidably and necessarily arise after some very direct, most profane, and daring opposition to and reproach of the Most High, that God is now angry and much provoked only because the audacious person has now greatly hurt himself and hurt his neighbors that happen to see him? No, this is entirely diverse and opposite from the voice of natural sense in such a case, which inevitably suggests that God is provoked as one will regard himself for himself, as having a direct respect to His dignity and majesty. This is agreeable to the strictest reason. 'Tis impossible, if God infinitely loves and honors Himself as one infinitely worthy to be loved and esteemed, but that He should, from the same principle, proportionably abhor and oppose opposition to Himself and condemning of Himself. If it be in its own nature decent and proper for Him thus to love Himself, then it is in its own nature fit and becoming in Him to hate opposition to Himself, and for the same reason and from the same principle. God, when He is condemned and injured and His authority and glory are trampled in the dust, will be disposed to repair the injury done His honor and raise His injured majesty out of the dust again.

As I observed before, 'tis requisite that there should be some supreme arbiter of absolute rectitude and fitness, with regard to the sum total of existence, that should determine and fix what is most proper to take place in all that is acted or comes to pass with relation to God and the creatures. Otherwise, supreme fitness and rectitude might be liable to fail and give place to something else, and to be jostled out of the universality of things and have no place. And 'tis fit that the supreme being, who is first, independent, and self-existent, and infinitely wise, and infinitely and immutably holy and just, should be this supreme arbiter. But it is not necessary that this office should belong to each person of the Trinity. 'Tis most proper that He that is the first person, from whom the other two are, should be the person that should have this office to determine rectitude and propriety for the three persons and for all creatures. Consequently, nothing is in the way but that one of the other persons should act under Him in affairs relating to rectitude between God and the creature, as in repairing the dishonor done to God by the sin and rebellion of the creature, making satisfaction, etc.

1218. It can't be properly said that the end of God's creating of the world is twofold, or that there are two parallel coordinate ends of God's creating the world: one, to exercise His perfections *ad extra,* another to make His creatures happy. But all is included in one, viz., God's exhibiting His perfections or causing His essential glory to be exercised, expressed, and communicated *ad extra.* 'Tis true that we must suppose that, prior to the creature's existence, God seeks occasion to exercise His goodness and opportunity to communicate happiness, and that this is one end why He gives being to creatures. And so we must conceive this prior to the creature's existence. He seeks occasion to exercise other attributes of His nature that can have none but creatures for their objects, as His justice, His faithfulness, His wisdom, etc. But a disposition to seek opportunities and occasion for the exercise of goodness towards those that now have no being, and so a being disposed to give being to creatures that there may be such an opportunity, is not the same attribute that we commonly call goodness, any more than a disposition to seek opportunity or occasion to exercise justice, and so to give being to creatures that there may be such occasion, is not the same attribute that we call justice. God seeks occasion for the exercise of one and the other of those attributes by giving existence to beings that may be capable objects of this exercise, in the same manner and from common reason, viz., because it is in itself fit and suitable that those attributes of God should be exerted and should not be eternally dormant.

'Tis true 'tis from an excellent disposition of the heart of God that God seeks occasion to exercise His goodness and beauty, and also His wisdom, justice, and truth—and this, in one word, is a disposition to glorify Himself according to the Scripture sense of such an expression, or a disposition to exercise and communicate Himself *ad extra.*

I know there is an inconsistence in supposing that God inclines to exercise goodness, i.e., good to others, merely for the sake of the honor of His goodness; for the very notion of goodness is an inclination of heart to do good to others, and therefore the existence of such an inclination must be conceived of as prior to an inclination to honor it. There must first be an inclination of the heart to do good before God desires to honor that inclination. So in like manner it is an inconsistence to suppose that God is inclined to exercise justice and do justly only for the sake of the honor of His justice itself. 'Tis an inclination to do justly which must exist before God is inclined to honor it. Therefore God's glorifying Himself, which is the end of the motion, is a different thing from properly seeking His honor.

They that suppose God's inclination to make occasion for the doing good, or communicating Himself by giving being to capable subjects of it, to be what is properly called God's goodness, seem to have a notion of a bountiful disposition in the heart of God disposed to increase the sum of happiness which is to be found in the universality of existence. But there is no such thing. Man's benevolence and bounty, taking his own good and the good of the person benefited by him together, increases the sum of good; and therefore 'tis necessary to conceive of a benevolent disposition in a creature wishing for the being of new subjects of kindness, because the goodness of his nature causes him to love to see a great deal of happiness. But God has no more by making His creatures that they may be happy. He hath in His Son an adequate object for all the desires of that kind that are in His heart, and in His infinite happiness He sees as much happiness as can be. When new beings are made that are infinitely less, and there is opportunity to do them good, God sees not the sum of happiness increased.

The more-proper notion signified by all such words as goodness, kindness, bounty, favor, grace, etc. includes love, benevolence, or good will. But that is not properly love or good will that has the existence of the object loved first supposed. A disposition to make an object that it may be loved, and that we may have good will towards, must be prior to another, and properly different from love and good will itself. It may be an excellent quality, but it must be quality of some other denomination. If it be called goodness and grace, it must be in a less proper sense. To desire new beings to communicate happiness to 'em, especially without increasing the sum of happiness, don't agree with the notion mankind have of goodness, benevolence, grace, etc. Men may call this disposition in the heart of God by the name of goodness if they please; but 'tis properly referred to another perfection of which it is one sort of exercise, viz., the disposition that is in the infinite fountain of good and of glory and excellence to shine forth and to flow out— which shining forth and flowing out of God's infinite fullness is called God's glory in Scripture.

Indeed God in making the creature happy seems, as it were, to express or exhibit Himself *ad extra* two ways. Not only does one of His perfections exercise itself in it, viz., His goodness, but there is something of good actually communicated, some of that good that is in God that the creature hereby has communion in, viz., God's happiness. The creature partakes of the happiness of God, at least an image of it. And we must therefore conceive that there is a disposition in God, not only to exercise His attributes and perfections in this, but also to communicate of His divine good. But then, it is to be considered that God don't only communicate of [His] happiness, but also His holiness and His understanding and power, or an image of those. And we must conceive that there is truly a disposition in God to communicate of these as well as happiness, which general disposition, though in itself excellent, seems to be a disposition besides the goodness of God, or at least is called so in a less proper sense, and in a more extensive sense than that which is more frequently called God's goodness. But although there are several kinds of good in God that are communicated, and though, according to our manner of conceiving things, these are two ways of God's exhibiting Himself *ad extra* (1. His perfections that we conceive to be an active nature are exercised *ad extra,* as His power, wisdom, justice, goodness, happiness; 2. the good that is in Him is communicated *ad extra*), and though this good be of various kinds according to our manner of conceiving, yet, as all this good that is in God of whatever kind belongs to His essential glory and brightness, and there is the same fitness that each part of His brightness or glory should shine forth in every possible way and be both exercised and communicated, and that all that good should flow out, and that God is disposed that each part should do so, [it] may well be referred to one general disposition and the effect may well be called by one name, viz., God's glory.[22]

Both these dispositions of exerting Himself and communicating Himself may be reduced to one, viz., a disposition effectually to exert Himself, and to exert Himself in order to an effect. That effect is the communication of Himself *ad extra,* which is what is called His glory. This communication is of two sorts: the communication that consists in understanding an idea, which is summed up in the knowledge of God; and the other is in the will consisting in love and joy, which may be summed up in the love and enjoyment of God. Thus, that which proceeds from God *ad extra* is agreeable to the twofold subsistences which proceed from Him *ad intra,* which is the Son and the Holy Spirit—the Son being the idea of God, or the knowledge of God, and the Holy Ghost which is the love of God and joy in God.

Although the things which God inclines to and aims at are in some respects two . . . ,[23] yet these may be reduced to one, i.e., God's exerting Himself in order to the effect. The exertion and the effect ought not to be separated as though they were two ends. One is so related to the other and they are so united that they are most properly taken together as one end, and the object of one inclination in God. For 'tis not an ineffectual exertion that God aims at or inclines to. And God aiming at these makes Himself his end. 'Tis Himself exerted and Himself communicated. And both together are what is called God's glory. The end, or the thing which God attains, is Himself in two respects. He Himself flows forth, and He Himself is pleased and glorified. For God's pleasure all things are and were created.

God has made intelligent creatures capable of being concerned in these effects, as being the willing, active subjects or means, and so they are capable of actively promoting God's glory. And that is what they ought to make their ultimate end in all things.

1225. Glory of God. It is a thing in itself infinitely valuable and worthy of regard that God's glory should be known by elect creatures to all eternity. The increasing knowledge of God in all elect creatures

---

[22] Edwards has added a Greek and Hebrew word, which I have omitted.

[23] Some repetitious phrases have been omitted.

to all eternity is an existence, a reality infinitely worthy to be in itself, worthy to be regarded by Him to whom it belongs to order that to be which, of all possible things, is fittest and best and most valuable. See back, 1218. If existence is more worthy than defect and nonentity, and if any created existence is in itself worthy to be, then this knowledge of God and His glory is worthy to be. The existence of the created universe consists as much in it as in anything, yea, it is one of the highest, most real and substantial parts of all created existence, most remote from nonentity and defect.

Free Will

16. Foreknowledge. This is most certain, that if there are any things that are so contingent that there is an equal possibility both of their being or not being, so that they may be or they may not be, God foreknew from all eternity that they may be thus, and also that they may not. All will grant that we need no revelation to teach us this. And furthermore, if God knows all things that are to come to pass, He also foreknows whether those contingent things will come to pass or no, at the same time that they are contingent and that they may or may not come to pass. But what a contradiction is this to say that God knows a thing will come to pass, and yet at the same time knows that it is contingent whether it will come to pass or no. That is, He certainly knows it will come to pass, and yet certainly knows it may not come to pass. What a contradiction is it to say that God certainly foreknew that Judas would betray his master, and yet certainly knew that it might be otherwise, certainly knew that He might be deceived. I suppose it will be acknowledged by all that for God certainly to know that a thing will be, and yet certainly to know that it may not be, is the same as certainly to know that He may be deceived. I suppose it will also be acknowledged that certainly to know a thing, and also at the same time to know that we may be deceived in it, is the same thing as certainly to know it and certainly to know that we are uncertain of it, or that we do not certainly know it; and that that is the same thing as certainly to know it, and not certainly to know it at the same time, which we leave to be considered whether it ben't a contradiction.

29. Decrees. The meaning of the word 'absolute' when used about the decrees wants to be stated. 'Tis commonly said that God decrees nothing upon a sight of anything in the creature, as this, they say, argues imperfection in God; and so it does, taken in the sense that they commonly intend it. But nobody, I believe, will deny but that God

decrees nothing that He would not have decreed if He had not foreknown and foredetermined such and such other things. What we mean we completely express thus: that God decrees all things harmoniously and in excellent order, one decree harmonizes with another, and there is such a relation between all the decrees as makes the most excellent order. Thus, God decrees rain in drought because He decrees the earnest prayers of His people, or thus, He decrees the prayers of His people because He decrees rain. I acknowledge [that] to say, God decrees a thing because, is an improper way of speaking, but not more improper than all our other ways of speaking about God. God decrees the latter event because of the former no more than He decrees the former because of the latter. But this is what we mean: when God decrees to give the blessing of rain, He decrees the prayers of His people; and when He decrees the prayers of His people, He may very comparably decree rain; and thereby there is an harmony between these two decrees of rain and the prayers of God's people. Thus also, when He decrees diligence and industry, He decrees riches and prosperity; when He decrees prudence, He often decrees success; when He decrees striving, then often He decrees the obtaining of the Kingdom of Heaven; when He decrees the preaching of the Gospel, then He decrees the bringing home of souls to Christ; when He decrees good natural faculties, diligence, and good advantage of them, He decrees learning; when He decrees summer, then He decrees the growing of plants; when He decrees conformity to His Son, He decrees calling; and when He decrees will, He decrees justification; and when He decrees justification, He decrees everlasting glory. Thus all the decrees of God are harmonious. And it is all that can be said for or against absolute or conditional decrees. But this I say, it's as improper to make one decree a condition of another as to make this, either, a condition of that; but there is a harmony between both.

31. Free will. Freedom of will, to speak very improperly, don't infer an absolute contingency, nor is it inconsistent with an absolute necessity of the event that is to be brought about by this free will. For most certainly God's will is free, and is no more bound than the will of His creatures; yet there is the greatest and most absolute necessity imaginable that God should always will good and never evil. But if this instance will not be allowed, 'tis certain that the will of the man Christ Jesus was free, who was a man as well as we, and of the same faculties as we; yet, as free as His will was, it was impossible that He should will sin.

71. Free will. 'Tis very true that God requires nothing of us as condition of eternal life but what is in our own power, and yet 'tis very true at the same time that it's an utter impossible thing that ever man should do what is necessary in order to salvation, nor do the least towards it, without the almighty operation of the Holy Spirit of God—yea, except everything be entirely wrought by the Spirit of God. True and saving faith in Christ is not a thing out of the power of man, but infinitely easy. 'Tis entirely in a man's power to submit to Jesus Christ as a savior if he will. But the thing is, is [it] man's will that he should will it, except God works it in him? To will it, as to do it, depends on a man's will and not on his power; and however easy the thing be and however much in a man's power, 'tis an impossibility that he should ever do it except he wills it, because submission to Christ is a willing. There are many things that are entirely in our power, of which things yet it may be said that 'tis an impossibility they should be, because of our dispositions. Perhaps some may say that 'tis a contradiction to say that that is in our power which yet 'tis an impossibility they [i.e., it] should be. 'Tis according to what they mean by being in our power. I mean this: that that is in our power which we can do when we please, and I think those mean very improperly who mean otherwise. Now it is no contradiction to say that we can do such a thing when we please, and yet that 'tis an impossibility that it should be what we please. And, although it may be the easiest thing in the world, yet it is not contradictory to say that it is impossible that we should please to do it, except God works it in us, according as I have explained. It is altogether in a man's power, when he has a cup of poison offered to him, whether he will drink it or no, and yet by reason of the man's internal disposition—the ideas and notions of things that he then has—it may be an impossibility that he should will to drink it. If a man who is a servant, exceeding wicked, debauched, and licentious, who has it offered to him whether he will choose a man of most exemplary holiness and strict piety for his master and submit to his government, it is perfectly (in my sense) in the servant's power whether he will take him for his master and governor or no; and yet it may be an impossible thing that it should be as long as the servant has such and such inclination and desire, judgment, and ideas.

The world has got into an exceeding wrong and confused way of talking about will and power, not knowing what they mean by them. They say man can will such a thing and man can't will it, which is dreadful confusion. When we say a man can't will such a thing, the notion that is raised in our mind by such an expression is that the man might heartily and truly desire to will it but could not; that is, he truly willed to will it but could not; that is, he truly willed it but could not will it. I am sure that when we say a man can or cannot do such a thing we don't mean that he wills or does not will it. We say, and truly often, he can do such a thing when yet he wills it not; and yet 'tis an impossibility that he should do when he wills it not. But you'll say he could will it if he would. 'Tis most certainly true if he does will it he can will it. And you'll say, if he does not will it, he can will it. I say 'tis true things may so happen, circumstances or ideas may so fall, as to cause him to will it, but it is no act of his own power that he wills it, though it be necessary there should be a capacity, because will is the first spring of the voluntary exertions of the active power in man and the cause of it. And therefore, 'tis impossible that active power should cause the will to spring, except the effect causes its own cause, however we are compelled, unavoidably, thus to express—that of ourselves we can do nothing, that we have no power—and however this manner of expression, as well as the contrary, carries often a wrong idea in the mind; so that all that men do in real religion is entirely their own act and yet every tittle is wrought by the Spirit of God. Neither do I contradict myself by saying that all that men do in religion is entirely their own act. I mean that everything they do, they themselves do, which I suppose none will contradict. 'Tis the exertion of their own power.

75. Decree. If it will universally hold that no one have absolutely perfect and complete happiness at the same time that anything is otherwise than as he desires at that time they should be; or thus, if it is true that he has not absolute perfect, infinite, and all possible happiness now, who has not now all that he wished to have now—then God, if anything is now otherwise than He willed to have it now, is not now absolutely, perfectly, and infinitely happy. If God is infinitely happy now, then everything is now as God would have it to be now; if everything, then those things that are contrary to His commands. If so, it is not ridiculous to say that things that are contrary to God's command are yet in a sense agreeable to His will. Again, let it be considered whether it be not certainly true that everyone that can, with infinite ease, have a thing done and yet will not have it done, wills it not; that is, whether or no he that *wills not* to have a thing done, properly wills *not* to have a thing done?[24] For example, let the thing be this—that Judas should be faithless to his Lord—whether it be not true that, if God could with infinite ease have it done if He would, but would not have it done as He could if He would, it be not proper to say that God would not have it be that Judas should be faithful to his Lord?

[24] My italics.

82. Decree. They say, To what purpose are praying and striving and attending on meeting if all was irreversibly determined by God before? But to say that all was determined before those prayers and strivings is a very wrong[25] way of speaking and begets ideas in the mind which correspond with no real thought with respect to God. Decrees of our everlasting state were not before our prayers and strivings, for these are as much present with God from all eternity as they are the moment they are present with us; they are present or not as He decrees, or rather are the same, and they did as really exist in eternity with respect to God as much at one time as another. Therefore, we can no more further argue that these will be in vain because God has foredetermined than we can that they would be in vain if they existed as law or the decree; for so they do, inasmuch as they are a part of it.

85. Decree. That we should say that God has directed every action of men, yea every action that they do that is possible, and every circumstance of those actions—that He determines that they shall be in every respect as they are, or were and are—that He determines that there shall be such actions, and just so sinful as they are—and yet that God don't decree the actions that are sinful as sin, but decrees them as joined, is really consistent. For we do not mean by decreeing an action as sinful the same as decreeing an action so that it shall be sinful. In decreeing an action as sinful, I mean decreeing it for the sake of the sinfulness of the action. God decrees that they shall be sinful for the sake of the good that He causes to arise from the sinfulness of the acts, whereas man decrees them for the sake of the evil that it intends.

342. Axiom. Let this be laid down first as a postulate before treating of those doctrines about free will: that whatever is, there is some cause or reason why it is; and prove it.[26]

436. *Vid.* 291.[27] Adam's fall. Original sin. Free will. *Vid.* 501. Adam's will was free in a respect that ours, since the fall, is not. Now man has, as it were, two wills. He has a will against a will. He has one will arising merely from a rational judgment of what is best for him.

---

[25] Here Edwards wrote "rong" as on previous pages of the manuscript, then crossed it out and wrote "wrong."

[26] See *Freedom of Will,* part 2, sec. 3. Thus early, probably before the age of 30, Edwards had formulated a statement which would one day appear in his *Treatise.*

[27] No. 291 is not included in this text. It asserts that Adam's will was freer than ours because his "reason and judgment never was held down by the inferior inclinations." No. 501, also omitted, is to the same effect.

This may be called the rational will. And he has another will or inclination arising from the liveliness and intenseness of the idea of, or sensibleness of the good of, the object presented to the mind, which we may call appetite, which is against the other rational will and in fallen man in his natural state overcomes it and keeps it in subjection. So that, although man with respect to his whole will compounded of those two (either arising from the addition of them together when they concur, or the excess of one above the other when they are opposite) is always a free agent, yet with respect to his rational will, or that part of his inclination which arises from a mere rational judgment of what is best for himself, he is not a free agent but is enslaved, he is a servant of sin. Thus our first parents were not, but were perfectly free agents with respect to their rational will—the inclinations, which we call appetites, were not above, did not keep in subjection.

And this must be what is meant when we say that God gave our first parent sufficient grace, though He withheld an efficacious grace, or a grace that should certainly uphold him in all temptations he could meet with. I say this must be meant by his having sufficient grace, viz., that he had grace sufficient to render him a free agent, not only with respect to [his] whole will but with respect to his rational, or the will that arose from a rational judgment of what was indeed best for himself.

When I say, his judgment of what is best for himself, I don't mean his judgment of what is best absolutely, and most lovely in itself; for the mind's sense of the absolute loveliness of a thing directly influences only the will of appetite. If the soul wills it merely because it appears lovely in itself, it will be because the loveliness draws the appetition of the soul. It may indirectly influence what I call the rational will, or the judgment may be convinced that what is most lovely in itself will be best for him and most for his happiness. Merely the rationally judging that a thing is lovely in itself, with a sensibleness of the beauty and pleasantness of it, signifies nothing towards influencing the will except it be this indirect way, that he thinks it will therefore be best some way or other for himself—most for his good. Therefore, if a man has only a rational judgment that a thing is beautiful and lovely, without any sensibileness of the beauty, and at the same time don't think it best for himself, he will never choose it. Though, if he be sensible of the beauty of it to a strong degree, he may will it though he thinks 'tis not best for himself. Persons, from a sensibleness of the good and pleasantness of sense enjoyments, will them though they are convinced they are not best for themselves. Hence it follows that a person with respect to his rational will may be perfectly free, and yet may refuse that which he at the same time rationally judges to be in itself most lovely and becoming, and will[s] that which he rationally knows to be hateful.

Therefore man, having that sufficient grace as to render him quite free with respect to his rational will, or his will arising from mere judgment of what was best for himself, could not fall without having that judgment deceived, and being made to think that to be best for himself which was not so, and so having his rational will perverted. Though he might sin without being deceived in his rational judgment of what was most lovely in itself or, which is the same thing, without having his conscience deceived and blinded, [he] might rationally know at the same time that what he was about to do was hateful, unworthy, etc.; or, in other words, he might know that it was what he ought not to do. *Vid.* the next.

437. Perfection of holiness, or how much grace a person must have in order to be sinless. In order to our first parents having grace sufficient to their being free with respect to their rational will, and in order to their being without habitual sin, they must have so much sense of spiritual excellencies and beauties, and so much inclination or appetite to them, as that that should be of itself above any of the inferior kind of appetites, so as to keep the same in subjection without the help of the rational will. If the gracious appetite ben't above other appetites, although those appetites may constantly be kept under and ruled with the help of the rational will, yet 'tis with difficulty, and there is a war and struggle. 'Tis labor for the rational will to maintain its ground, so that that will is not entirely free. The excess of the inferior appetites above the gracious is lust—is a principle of sin. 'Tis an enemy in the soul and makes a great deal of disturbance there. To have a sinful inclination is sin, but the inclination of the man is to be found in compositions of inclinations. The excess of one above another of them is the inclination of the man. If the excess of inclination be to inferior objects in many cases, the prevailing inclination will be [away] from God; and though the man might do his duty in such a case, constantly with the help of the rational will, yet 'twould be grievous to him, which would be a sinful and abominable defect in the manner of doing it.[28]

The case must be thus, therefore, with our first parents: when tempted, their sense of their duty to good and their love to it must be above inferior appetite, but so that that inferior appetite of itself was not sufficient to master the holy principle. Yet the rational will, being

[28] This section suggests an interesting comparison with Kant's ethical theory. See M. M. Curtis, "Kantian Elements in Jonathan Edwards," *Philosophische Abhandlungen*, 1906, pp. 34-62,

perverted and by a deceived judgment fitting in with the inferior appetite, overcame and overthrew the greater inclination. Besides, the holy inclination to obedience (as to its arise at least) must be greatly diminished by their error of judgment concerning God, and their doubting that He was true in what He threatened, and their error as though He were not good in faith and love to man. So Satan's suggestion, "yea, hath God said, etc." Satan suggested that He had forbid them because He was unwilling that they should be so much like Himself in honor and happiness.

573. Free will. I don't scruple to say that God has promised salvation to such things as are properly in men's own powers. Those things in men unto which salvation is promised, or the conditions of [them], are of two sorts: they are either [1.] those acts which consist and are complete in the mere immediate exercise of the will or inclination itself. Such are the internal breathings of love to God and exercise of faith in Christ. These are absolutely necessary to salvation, and salvation is promised to them. These, in the most ordinary way of using the expression, can't be said to be in a man's own power or not in his power; because, when we speak of things being in man's power or not in his power, in our common discourse we have respect only to things that are consequential to his will, that are considered as the effect of his will, and not of the mere simple and first motions of the will itself. If we say a thing is in a man's power, we mean that he can do it if he will. And so a prior act of the will determining is supposed. Neither can those things, in the vulgar and ordinary use of the expression, be said not to be in a man's power; because, when we say a thing is not in anyone's power, we mean that he can't do it if he will. But this is absurd to say of the very simple and mere acts of the will itself, that we can't do them if we will, for the willing is the doing, and the doing of 'em consists in the willing of 'em.

Or 2. the other kind of conditions to which salvation is promised are those actions, or a way and course of those actions, that are the effects of the will and depend upon it, which flow from it, [and] which are properly called voluntary actions. These also are conditions of salvation, and have salvation promised to them. Thus salvation is very often promised to an universal obedience and a steadfast and faithful perseverance in it through the changes, difficulties, and trials of life. Now this sort of condition a man may be said properly to have in his own power, in the vulgar and more ordinary use of such an expression; for if we say a man has it in his own power to do or not, we ordinarily mean no other than that he can do it if he has a mind to do it or chooses to do it or, all things considered, had rather do it than not. If we can't be properly said to have everything in our power that we can do if we choose to do it, then we can't be said properly to have it in our own power to [do] anything but only what we actually do. And so a man may be said properly to have it in his power to do that which he surely will not, as the case may be or the case being as it is. Thus a man may have it in his own power to sell his estate and give the money to his poor neighbor, and yet the case may be so at the same time [that] he may have so little love to his neighbor and so great a love to his possessions and the like that he certainly will not do it. There may be as much of a connection between these things in the qualities and circumstances of the man and his refusing to give his estate to his neighbor as between any two theorems in the mathematics. He has it in his power as much as he has other things, because there wants nothing but his having a mind to do it, or his being willing to do—and that is required in all other things, and in this no more than in everything else. So a man has it in his power, in the voluntary actions of his life, universally and steadfastly and faithfully to obey God's commands and cleave to and follow Christ through all difficulties and trials, though it be certain that without love to God and faith in Jesus Christ no man will do it. And there is some connection between one being without these (as we all are naturally) and a not thus universally and perseveringly obeying God and cleaving to Christ. A man can avoid drunkenness if he will, and he can avoid fornication if he will, and so he can all other ways of wickedness if he chooses to avoid 'em, every one, and he can persevere in it if he holds of that mind, if he continues to choose to avoid them all. And God has promised salvation to 'em if they will thus do. If one should promise another a certain reward if he would appear himself his faithful friend by a persevering adherence to his interest, the case might be so that there might be such remarkable trials, and such a succession of 'em, that the man certainly would not fulfill this condition unless he be a sincere friend, but yet the fulfilling is in his own power and at his own choice.

631. Free will. It don't at all excuse persons for not doing such duties as loving God, accepting of Christ, etc., that they can't do it of themselves, unless they would if they could, i.e., unless they would do it from good principles; for that woulding is as good as no woulding at all that is in no wise from any good principle. But unless men would love God from some real respect to God or sense of duty, that is, of the goodness of that duty, or disposition to their duty as in itself good and lovely, and not merely from an aversion to pain and desire of pleasure, it is in no wise from any good principle.

657. Free will. To place human liberty in a contingency of the will, or the will having nothing to determine it but its being left to happen this way or that, without any determining cause, is contrary to all use and custom of language. It is as far from the meaning of the words 'freedom' or 'liberty' in their original and common acceptation as the east is from the west. The original and proper meaning of a man's being free or at liberty is that he is in such a state that he may act his pleasure and do what he will, and there never was any other meaning thought of till philosophers and metaphysicians took it in hand to fix a new meaning to the words.

And besides, when liberty is understood not for this but for that contingency or sovereignty of the will, as some call it, it not only has not its original true meaning but no meaning at all. The word 'liberty' used in that way is without any sense. It is a word without any notion or distinct consistent meaning to answer it. For the will to be determined without any determining cause is what nobody has any notion of any more than they have of a thing's coming out of nothing without any cause. And to suppose that the will does firstly determine itself, or determine itself in its first volition or choice, is a contradiction; for it supposes that there [is] a volition or act of the will before the first act which is the determining cause of that first act.

830. Free will. According to the present prevailing notion of liberty, it consists in a state of indifference that the soul was in, antecedent to the act of choice. So that if, when the two opposites are proposed set before the will in order to its determination or choice, the soul is not found hitherto in a state of indifference and don't so remain till it has determined itself by its own act of choice, the proposal did not find the soul in a state of liberty, neither is the choice that is made upon it a free choice. And that thing done can be no further blameworthy than it is the fruit of a choice made by the will, in this sense left to itself and to its own sovereignty without any weight lying upon it (antecedent to its own determination and act of choice) to put it out of its balance, to bias and sway it one way, and in any measure by its power to govern its determination—because they suppose that a free will must be determined only by itself, and that nothing but its own sovereign command of itself can have any hand in its determination. But in case of such an antecedent biasing power affecting the will to turn it one way, the will is, in some measure at least, determined by something out of itself. So that according to this notion of liberty, if there be an original corruption, any evil inclination of nature, that so far as it prevails excuses any evil act of choice, because so far the corruption of nature took from

the liberty of the will. And hence it will follow that, if a man be naturally a very ill-natured man, and from that ill nature does often treat his neighbors maliciously and with great indignity, his neighbors ought to excuse and not to be angry with him so far as what he does is from ill nature. And so if he be naturally of a very proud, haughty spirit, 'tis unreasonable in his neighbors to resent his haughty, contemptuous carriage towards them, so far as it arises from a proud natural temper. And so, on the other hand, if any person be naturally of an excellent spirit, a disposition strongly inclining him to virtue and the most amiable actions, so far does it take from the commendableness and praiseworthiness of his actions. And so none of the holy excellent actions or voluntary sufferings of Jesus Christ are worthy of any reward or commendation, because He was naturally perfectly holy. He had a nature so strongly inclining Him to holiness that it certainly and indeclinably determined Him to holy actions. And so of the holy actions of the angels, and above all of the holy and righteous and excellent acts of God Himself; for He by nature is infinitely holy. He is so far from exercising liberty in any of His holiness or virtue, according to this notion of liberty, that He is infinitely far from it, for His will antecedently to the act is infinitely out of the balance. An inclination one way is so strong, and makes it so necessary that he should choose on the holy side, that 'tis infinitely impossible that His will should be determined the other way.

And so 'tis equally against this notion of liberty if there was, previous to the act of choice, a preponderancy in those visible circumstances of the two opposite proposed objects of choice, so that, antecedent to its act of choice, there was more, manifested or apparent to the soul, on one side that naturally tended to bias and sway the choice on that side than on the other. When the will proceeds in its act of choice according to such a bias, it is not a free choice because it was not determined only by itself but partly at least by something without itself, viz., that apparent preponderance of circumstances that put the will out of its balance so that it was not under equal advantages to choose either, in the mere exercise of its own sovereignty. A preponderance in visible circumstances that naturally tend to sway the disposition on one side is equivalent to a preponderance of the natural disposition on one side. And indeed it is the same thing, for 'tis supposed that in such circumstances nature preponderates that way. To say that there is a preponderance of such circumstances as naturally tend to turn the disposition that way is the same thing as to say that the disposition in the view of such circumstances naturally tends that way. As for instance, when the circumstances of a case proposed to the will for its choice are such that most of the visible pleasure and advantage, which we naturally incline to, is on one side, this is equivalent to a preponderating of nature towards one side and can't be distinguished from it, because it is supposed that the natural inclination preponderated towards the greatest apparent advantage. Hence it is scarcely worth the while to offer any arguments to persuade men to choose that which is good and refuse that which is evil. 'Tis not worth the while to set before men the wisdom of ways of virtue and piety and the folly of ways of vice by showing the great advantages and benefits of the former and the mischievous tendency of the latter—no, nor the deformity of the one and the beauty and amiableness of the other; for men naturally incline to what appears beautiful to them and abhor deformity. This notion of liberty seems to frustrate all such endeavors to persuade men to virtue; for though these things may induce 'em to what is materially virtuous, yet at the same time they take away the form of virtue, because they put the soul out of its equilibrium wherein its liberty consists, and occasion something else to determine the will besides its own sovereignty. And the more powerful the arguments are, the more likely are they to be in vain in this respect; for the more is the inclination put out of its balance and the greater hand has something external in determining the will, and so the more effectually is the form of virtue destroyed. And so likewise when men are led into the practice of virtue or vice by powerful example, the form of virtue and vice are wanting because men naturally incline to follow example. But how absurd are these things!

Corollary 1. From the absurdity of this notion of liberty we may infer that it is false, and that the liberty of men don't at all consist in, or depend upon, such an equilibrium but is entirely of another nature, and that, whether the will or inclination be more or less out of its equilibrium before the act of choice, it don't at all concern the liberty of that act of choice.

Corollary 2. And from hence it follows that necessity (if by necessity is meant only certain connections of nature between one thing and another) is not a thing opposite to liberty or at all inconsistent with it, though compulsion or force be inconsistent with it. For, as has been just shown, it is not in any measure inconsistent with liberty that the soul be out of an equilibrium, or that its nature preponderates before the act of choice (let it preponderate more or less). But no one will deny that the preponderance may be, and often is, such as to imply a necessity or certain connection with an act of choice agreeable to it.

Corollary 3. From what has been said, also it appears that 'tis not against human liberty for the will to be determined by something out of itself, as when it is determined by such a preponderating of circumstances.

Corollary 4. Hence it is not at all inconsistent with human liberty for man's will to be determined by the ordering of divine providence, as when providence orders that the prevailing natural inclination or that preponderating visible circumstances should be on one side—yea, though providence should so order it as that a particular determination of the will should in nature be certainly connected with such a disposal of providence. And so neither the commendableness nor blameworthiness of the acts of the will is hereby infringed.

Corollary 5. Hence it is not at all against human liberty for God absolutely to decree that such a determination of the will shall come to pass, or to decree to order circumstances so that such a determination of the will shall certainly follow.

1075b. Freedom of the will. Self-determining power. If the will determines its own acts, that determination is an act of the will. For, by the supposition of those that hold this, self-determining power is that wherein consists the will's exercise of its liberty and sovereignty (as some of them speak). Now undoubtedly the exercise of liberty and sovereignty is some act. The will can't exercise any liberty in that wherein it don't act, or wherein it don't exercise itself. If this determination be no act, then it is no exercise of liberty, and then all that it is introduced for fails. Neither does the supposition of it at all help their cause or make out their scheme of the liberty of the will, consisting in a self-determining power. But the soul exercises as much liberty without it as with it, so that in denying this determination to be an act of the will they will entirely overthrow their own scheme. For if there be no act or exercise of the will in its determining its own acts, then no liberty is exercised in the will's determining its own acts. And if no liberty be exercised in the will's determining its own acts, then it follows that no liberty consists in the will's power to determine its own acts, and consequently that the liberty of the will does not consist in a self-determining power in the will.

1153.[29] Moral inability. Free will. Self-determining power. The following positions may be laid down as most clear and evident, relating to voluntary agents as subject to moral government.

[29] No. 1153 is included, notwithstanding the fact that some of it appears almost word for word in *Freedom of Will* (part 2, sec. 5), because it is the first formulation of Edwards' doctrine and presents interesting variations from the printed text. The manuscript has been mutilated, parts of pages being cut out. While Dwight was preparing his edition of Edwards, he employed an amanuensis to copy

There is no command given by God or men, or that ever is given by one intelligent being to another, that does directly and properly respect anything further than the disposition and acts of the will of that intelligent being that is commanded, i.e., nothing else, by any command given to an intelligent voluntary substance, is directly and properly the thing commanded and required of that substance but such acts of its will. It is the soul (that is, an intelligent substance) only that is properly commanded, that only is a capable subject of commands. For that being only is properly a capable subject of commands that is capable of perceiving commands given. But when commands thus are given to the soul, nothing else is required by those commands but its own acts. For a command is to do something, i.e., to do something itself. A command is not given to one thing, that another thing should do something. Though the actions of one thing may have respect to the actions or motions of another, and have influence upon them, yet the [action], directly and properly, is the action of the thing commanded itself, and not the effects of its actions. Though the effects may be connected with the actions, all that a command given to an intelligent thing properly respects is what that thing should do or act. And therefore the commands that are given to the soul of man do proper[ly] respect or reach nothing further than the acts of the soul, and therefore respect nothing directly and properly beyond such and such acts of the will. For the soul itself has no other acts that are its own whereby to fulfill any command. And although the motions of the body follow the acts of the will by the law of nature which the Creator has established, yet that don't make the motions of the body the acts of the soul. The acts of the will, therefore, only are properly the acts that are required by any command God gives us. For our actions and all our duties and performances that are required or commanded, so far as they are properly ours, are no other than such and such acts of the will.

Things beside the habit and acts of the will are respected by the commands of God only indirectly, viz., as connected with the will. So far, therefore, as any good thing is connected with the will and its acts, so far, and so far only, is it the subject of a command, obligation, or duty. And so far, and so far only, as any good exercise of the faculties of the soul or members of the body is not implied in or connected

---

selected items from the *Miscellanies,* among them no. 1153. Probably he considered publishing all of the items copied, but rejected this one and many others. The mutilation of this item in the manuscript must have occurred after the copy was made, although the copy of what is left of the original is not verbally faithful. I have resorted to Dwight's copy to supply the missing parts. The material taken from the copy is enclosed in brackets: < >. The copy is in the Andover-Newton Theological Library.

with the will and its acts, it is not the proper subject of a command or matter of a duty, but is what we are justly excused and free from. And that, for that reason and that only, because it is not implied in or connected with the good will, and so is not what we can be properly voluntary in.

Hence it follows that no other sort of inability to any action or performance, consisting in the exercise of the faculties of the soul or members of [the] body, renders that performance not properly the matter of a command or duty, but such an one as implies want of a connection between that action or performance and the disposition and act of the will. If there be any sort of inability to that good thing that does in no wise interfere with, hinder, or stand in the way of a close, proper, and immediate connection with or implication in the act of the will, then that sort of inability does in no wise hinder any good thing from being the proper subject matter of a command. And with respect to any command supposed to require any such performance, 'tis in vain for any to plead their inability and to say they can't do it, unless they would if they could. For willing, as has just now been shown, is all the thing directly required of 'em. Let 'em perform this. Let 'em exhibit the compliance of the will and they have done their duty; and that is all that is directly required of the soul in all commands whatsoever. And if there be anything else desirable that don't attend this compliance of the will and inclination, that don't prove to [be] implied in it or connected with it, from that they are excused.

From the things that have been already laid down and proved, it also follows that, as to those things that are not the subject matter of duty and commands directly, as the dispositions and acts of the will themselves, but only indirectly, as other good actions and performances of the human nature (consisting either in any exercise of the faculties of the soul or motions of the body), no other sort of inability to them renders them improperly the subject matter of prescription and command, but only the inability that consists in the want of connection between them and those good acts of the will that are proper to be in such a nature as man's, and are fit exercises of his faculties. It has been already shown that those good acts of his that are proper to be in such a nature as man's, and not beyond the capacity of his faculties, are the proper matter of command. It has also been already shown that all such things as are connected with such acts of the will are also properly the subject matter of command. Therefore, certainly it follows that those things only that are not connected with such acts of the will are not the proper matter of command. And this implies that no other sort of inability to them but such as implies a want of such connection, makes 'em to be not the proper subjects of command. So that, if there be anything that man is supposed to be required to do, any exercise, affection, or exertion of mind that he is required to have, or any outward deed that he is required to perform, that he may in any sense be said to [be] unable to, that don't excuse him or render the thing not properly the matter of his duty and prescription to him, unless the inability be such as implies a want of connection between that thing and the good act of will that is properly required of him, so that he may properly have that good act of will fully exerted and yet can't do the thing required, there being no connection between his will and the performance. If there be the good act of will that is properly required, fully exerted, and the performance ben't connected and don't follow, then the man is excused, but otherwise not.

Again it is further evident that, if there be some act of will about this performance required that the performance don't prove to be connected with, so that in some kind of sense the person may be said to be willing to do it or to desire to do it and can't, yet is he not excused unless his act of will be a properly good act, and that act relating to this thing that is properly required of him. If there be some sort of act of will about it that the performance is not connected with, that don't at all excuse the man for want of the performance as long as the good act properly required is absent which, if it were present, the performance would be found to be connected with it. For if this other act of will don't excuse for the want of the proper act required, no more can it excuse for the want of performance that is connected with the proper act required. For it is the connection of the performance with this proper act, and that only, that causes our duty to be concerned in it, and not its connection with some other act of the will that is diverse from the proper act required. Therefore, 'tis the want of a connection with this proper act of the will, and not its want of connection with some other act diverse from that, [which] causes our duty not to be concerned in it.

Thus, for instance, if an old notorious drunkard that is under the power of a violent and invincible appetite after strong [drink] be supposed to be commanded entirely to forsake his drunkenness, and required so to do under pain of eternal damnation, and has some kind of willingness to forsake this vice, i.e., his reason tells him that the pain of eternal damnation will be so great an evil that it will far more than countervail all the pleasure or good that he shall have from this vice, and therefore wishes he could forsake it, but his actually forsaking it don't prove to be connected with such a sort of act of will, this don't excuse him unless this be the proper act of will that is required of him, relating to this matter; but [if] the act of will required of him be not such an indirect willingness, which is not so properly a willingness to do the thing commanded to be done as a willingness to escape the punishment threatened; [if] the act of will required of him be a proper, direct, and full willingness actually to forsake this vice and all those deeds that belong to it—if this be the volition required, and he has this, and the performance don't prove to be connected with it, then is the man excused, but not otherwise. Or we will suppose the violent lust the man is under the invincible power of is not any sensitive appetite, but some malice and an insatiable devilish malignancy of spirit against some excellent and most worthy person, and very highly deserving of him, and the thing required of him, under pain[30] <of damnation is to leave off injuring that person; and he finds the same sort of willingness to it that, in the forementioned instance, the drunkard has to forsake his cups, but the performance does not prove to be connected with it; it does not at all excuse him, because his willingness is no proper, direct, and full willingness actually to comply with the command.

The case is the same and equally evident, and the evidence more direct and plain, if the thing required be not any external performance that is connected with some act of the will, but only the act of the will itself, or some good compliance of the heart, that is properly required of him. According to the foregoing positions, if this act of the will required be wanting, but yet [there] is some other indirect act of the will, which the person to escape punishment or on some foreign considerations is willing to will, or wishes he was willing, but yet remains without the proper act of will required—his indirect willingness in such a case cannot excuse the want of the proper willingness that is required. As for instance, suppose a man has a most amiable and agreeable and every way deserving woman for his wife, and be required to love her and choose her above all other women, to cleave to her in the choice and acquiescence of his will, as relinquishing all other women; but he, instead of this, is overpowered by a violent lust for some vile and notorious strumpet, whereby he has his heart alienated from his wife and has no delight in her, but an aversion to her; but yet he is sensible that its being with him as it is, in this respect, is like to prove the utter ruin of himself and his family, and he therefore wishes it was otherwise; he wishes that he loved his wife as he does his harlot, and that his heart cleaved to her with so full a choice and entire compliance that he could have as much pleasure and delight in her as in the other; this indirect willingness to cleave to his wife in his love and choice does not > at all excuse him for the want of actual love and choice. Or if a child has an

[30] See note 29.

excellent father that has ever been kind to him, and has every way in the highest degree merited the respect and honor and love of his child, and this child be commanded by God to love and honor his father, but he is of so vile a disposition that he notwithstanding inveterately hates him, but, being sensible that his hatred of his father will prove his ruin by his father's disinheriting him, wishes it was otherwise but remains still under the invincible power of his cursed disposition, and so in a settled hatred of his father—his indirect willingness to love and honor his father don't excuse for the want of the actual compliance of his heart with the duty required of him towards his father. And further we will suppose [the] thing required be that a man make choice of God as his highest portion and chief good, or that his heart should cleave to Christ Jesus and acquiesce in Him as his savior, his guide, his lord, and best friend, and, through fear of damnation as the consequence of the want of such an act of will or choice of heart, he wishes he could find it in himself but yet remains destitute of it; that indirect willingness he has don't at all excuse him for the want of the proper act of will required.

It is further evident that such an indirect willingness, as has been spoken of, can't at all excuse for the want of that good act of will that is required, provided that good act of will be properly and fitly required (which is a thing supposed), for this reason, that this other indirect willingness don't answer the command fitly given or (which is the same thing) it don't answer the man's duty. If the man's duty is not answered by what he does, then what he does don't excuse or acquit him; for 'tis his doing something that answers the obligation only that acquits him with respect to that obligation, and not his doing something else that does not answer it. But now this other indirect willingness don't answer the man's duty, or satisfy the command that requires of him another willingness quite diverse from that.

And as to such good acts of the will, or exercises of the heart as have been mentioned, viz., a man's making choice of God as his portion and highest [good], his heart cleaving to Christ as a most excellent savior, or any other holy exercise of the will, inclination, or affection that are proper to be in the heart of man, it will further appear that such an indirect willingness to those things as has been spoken [of], or their wishing, by strong fear of punishment, they could exercise such a will and disposition but find themselves unable, i.e., they don't find such exercises to be connected with such wishings and wouldings—I say, it will further appear that such a willingness or desire for those things cannot excuse for the want of them or at all acquit the person that remains destitute of them, let his willingness and desires through such fear be never so true and real, and so in that respect sincere, because, if they excuse and acquit the person, it must be on one of these two accounts: either 1. because those desires are in effect the thing required, or 2. that there is that virtue or goodness in them that balances the goodness and virtue of the thing required, and so countervails the want of it.

As to the first of these, that those indirect desires from foreign considerations are not in effect the same thing that is required, has been observed already as contrary to the supposition; and therefore, if such a willingness excuses persons, it must be on the other account, viz., that there is some virtue or goodness in such an indirect willingness to balance the goodness of the exercise required or countervail the want of it. A willingness to do a good thing required of us can't countervail the want of that good thing, unless it be a good willingness. It has nothing to countervail the want of true goodness and virtue. A kind of willingness that is not truly a good willingness can't excuse for the want of a good willingness.

Supposing a son is possessed by a most inveterate enmity against a wealthy and excellent father, that is so great as hinders his behaving towards him as a dutiful child, which provokes his father to shut up his hand towards [one] who otherwise might have his pockets full of money; supposing also the son to be a person of violent and impetuous lust but is not under advantage to gratify his lust, not having money to spend upon his whores by reason of the penury which his undutifulness brings upon him, which causes him to wish that his heart was otherwise towards his father; but yet so rooted and vehement is his devilish malignity of spirit towards his honorable father that he still remains under the power and government of it—I suppose that willingness he has to love and honor his father (though he sincerely, i.e., really and truly, desires it for that end, that he may gratify his violent lust) don't at all excuse the want of that love or countervail his remaining enmity. The plain reason is that there is no virtue or goodness in it to make up for the want of the virtue required or countervail the badness of his enmity. This is the proper reason; and therefore, if he had the same indirect willingness from some other principle not so heinous as this, yet, if it was from no good principle, and so it was a willingness that had no goodness in it, still it would not excuse or countervail for the want of the goodness required, and that because the reason holds good, viz., that there is no goodness at all in the willingness, and consequently nothing at all to countervail the defect of goodness, and so no excuse at all.

Sincerity and reality in this willingness don't make it the better —that which is real and hearty is sincere whether it be in virtue or vice;

some persons are sincerely bad and others are sincerely good; others may be sincere and hearty in things in their own nature indifferent—but being sincere in a thing that is virtuous. A man may be sincere and hearty in subscribing to a covenant offered him by a crew of pirates or gang of robbers, obliging himself to join with them, and yet there can be no virtue in his sincerity. The devils are sincerely and heartily willing and desirous to be freed from the torments of hell, but this don't make their will or desires virtuous.

And as an having a real, sincere, and hearty willing to one's duty don't make his willingness to be virtuous, or such as can excuse him in a defect of compliance with any supposed duty, unless that willingness be from a good principle, so it is with endeavor arising from such a will. The endeavors have no more goodness in them than the will that the endeavors arise from. If a young man hates his father (as was represented before) from the violence of lust and, that he may be under advantage to gratify that, is willing to love his father, his willingness has no goodness in it, nor can excuse for the want of the required love. And if from such a willingness he endeavors to love his father, neither have his endeavors, though as sincere as his willingness, any virtue in them or excuse for the want of the required love, any more than his willingness. The endeavor considered as the act of the willing agent can't be any better than the will it proceeds from, for his endeavor is no further his act than as it is an expression of his will. But certainly there is no more goodness or virtue in the exercises and expressions of a will than there is in the will itself that is exercised and expressed. And therefore the sincerity of endeavors, or a person's truly endeavoring a thing, and doing what they can from a real willingness to obtain the thing they endeavor for, don't render those endeavors at all virtuous unless the will itself that the endeavors proceed from (the reality of which denominates the endeavors sincere) be virtuous, and can't excuse a person in this defect of the thing endeavored for, any more than the will itself. The devils that possessed the Gadarene were doubtless afraid Christ was going to torment 'em, and were sincerely willing to avoid it. If we also suppose they were sincere in their endeavors to avoid it when they cried, "Thou Son of God most high we beseech thee torment us not," those endeavors, however sincere, had not more virtue in them than the will they proceeded from. And if we suppose they did whatever they could in their endeavors, still it alters not the case.

That such indirect desires and wishing from mere fear and self-love, and from no other principles than are as much in the hearts of devils as angels, haven't any virtue or goodness in them that be a balance for the goodness of those holy exercises of heart required, though never so real and sincere, is easily proved. (Here largely show the evidence of this, if ever I should write anything on this subject to be published.) Their being sincere alters not the case unless a being sincerely afraid of Hell be a virtue. The sincerity of the act don't make it virtuous unless the sanctity of the principle makes it virtuous.

Sincerity.[31] From what has been said, it is evident that persons' endeavors, however sincere and real, and however great, and though they do their utmost, unless the will that those endeavors proceed from be truly good and virtuous, can avail to no purposes whatsoever with any moral validity, as anything in the sight of God morally valuable and so of weight through any moral value, to merit, recommend, satisfy, excuse, or make up for any moral defect, or anything that should abate resentment or render it any way unjust or hard to execute punishment for any moral evil or want of any moral good. Because, if such endeavors have any such value, weight, or validity in the sight of God, it must be through something in them that is good and virtuous in His sight. For surely that which in His sight is good for nothing is in His sight wholly and entirely vain and without any positive moral value, weight, or validity, and can have no weight at all in a moral sense positively and properly—though there may be something negative in it, as through those endeavors persons may avoid some positive evils that otherwise would be committed and so may in some respects avoid incurring further guilt. He that saves his neighbor from drowning, not from love to him but merely from covetousness and because his own interest is concerned, though what he does is nothing good in the sight of God, yet hereby he avoids the greater guilt that would arise in the sight of God through such a degree of murder as he would actually be guilty of if he should stand by and see him drown when he could easily help him.

There is an exceeding great and unknown deceit arises from the use of language, from the great ambiguity of the word 'sincere.' Indeed, there is a vast indistinctness, unfixedness, and ambiguity in most (or at least very many) of the terms that are used to express these 'mixed modes' (as Mr. Locke calls them) that appertain to moral and spiritual matters, whence arise innumerable mistakes, strong prejudices, and endless controversy and inextricable confusion.

The word 'sincere' is commonly used to signify something good and virtuous. Men are habituated to such an understanding of it, so that the expression, whenever it is used, excites that notion and naturally suggests something to the mind that is indeed very excellent. (Much the same with the words 'honest' and 'upright'.) Yea, something more

[31] Compare *Freedom of Will*, part 3, sec. 5.

we conceive by it—not only something that is honestly and truly good, and good in the sight of Him that sees not only the outward appearance but the heart, but also good with all the heart and from the bottom of the heart. Therefore men think that, if a person be sincere in his endeavors to do his duty or to obtain any moral qualification that is supposed to be requisite, he is altogether to be justified, and it would be hard and unreasonable to blame him, much more to punish him, for being unsuccessful. For to say he is thus sincere suggests to the mind as much as that his heart and will is good. There is no defect of duty as to his virtuous inclination. He honestly and uprightly desires and endeavors to do as he is required. His will and heart fully comply with his duty, but only the thing supposed to be required don't prove to be connected.

Whereas, it ought to be observed that the word 'sincere' has these different significations: 1. Sincerity, as the word is often used, signifies no more than reality of will and endeavor with respect to anything that is professed or pretended, without any consideration of the nature of the principle or aim whence this real will and true endeavor arises. If the man has some real will or desire to obtain a thing, either direct or indirect, or does really endeavor after a thing, he is said sincerely to desire it and endeavor it, without any consideration of the goodness and virtuousness of the principle he acts from, and the excellency of the end he acts for. What is meant by the man's being sincere in his desire or endeavor is no more than that the appearance and show there is of a desire or endeavor is not a mere pretence and dissimulation, when indeed he don't at all desire or endeavor the thing that he pretends to. Thus, a man that is kind to his neighbor's wife that is sick and languishing is very helpful in her case, and makes a show of desiring and endeavoring her restoration to health and vigor, and not only makes such a show, but there is a reality in his pretence—he does heartily and earnestly desire her restoration and uses his true and utmost endeavors for it—he is said sincerely to desire and endeavor it because he does so truly, through perhaps the principle he acts from is no other than a vile and scandalous lust, he having secretly maintained a criminal intercourse and lived in adultery with her and earnestly wishes for her restored health and vigor that he may return to his criminal pleasure. So a man that don't merely pretend to it may be said sincerely to hate his neighbor.

Or secondly, by sincerity is meant not merely a reality of will and endeavor of some sort or other, from some consideration or other, but a virtuous sincerity. That is, that in a man performing those particular acts that are the matter of virtue or duty, there is not only the reality of the matter or thing to be done, but also the reality of the form and essence of the virtue [that] appertains to it, consisting in the aim that governs the act and the principle that is exercised in it. There is not only the reality of the act that is, as it were, the body of the duty, but also the soul that should properly belong to such a body, or those inward principles wherein consists the real virtue that properly should belong to the act. In this sense a man is said to be sincere when he acts with a pure intention, not from sinister views or for by-ends. He not only, in reality, desires and endeavors after the thing to be done or the qualification to be obtained, but he wills the thing directly and properly, as neither forced nor bribed. His choice is free in the matter. He seeks it as virtue, and chooses it for its own [sake], as delighting in virtue. So that not only the thing itself in the matter of it, upon some account or other, is the object of the willing, but the virtue of the thing is properly the object of the will.

In the former sense, a man is said to be sincere in opposition to a mere pretence and show of the particular thing to be done or exhibited, without any real desire or endeavor at all. In the latter sense, a man is said to be sincere in opposition to that show of virtue there is in merely doing the matter of duty without the reality of the virtue itself in the soul and essence of it that there is a show of. A man may be sincere in the former sense, and yet in the latter be in the sight of God, who searches the heart, a vile hypocrite, and his deeds and endeavors, though in some sort sincere, may before God be good for nothing and of no significancy or avail.

In the latter kind of sincerity only is there any true virtue, and this is the thing that in the Scripture is called sincerity, uprightness, integrity, truth in the inward parts, and being of a perfect heart. If a man be sincere in his will, desires, and endeavors in this respect, this is of some virtue in the sight of God. And if there be such a sincerity and such a degree of it as there ought to be, and it be found that anything that might be supposed to be required is not connected with it, the man indeed is wholly excused and acquitted in the sight of [God]. His will shall surely be accepted for the deed. For such a will is all that is in strictness required of him by any command of [God], as we showed before. The commands of God given to any spiritual voluntary being respect nothing else directly and properly but the habits and acts of the will. But as to the other kind of sincerity of desires and endeavors, as was observed before, it being good for nothing in God's sight, is not accepted with Him as <of any weight or value to recommend, satisfy, excuse, or

counterbalance any good thing that is mentioned. See Bk. I on *Free Will,* p. 54.[32]>

If there be any act or determination of the soul, or any exertion or alteration whatsoever prior to the act of the will, or any voluntary act in the case, as it were, directing and determining what the will shall be, that exertion or determination is not what any command does properly respect, because it is no voluntary act (because by the supposition it is prior to any voluntary act), or act of the will, being that which determines the will in its acts and directs it how to act.

<If the soul is self-determined in its own acts of will, as some suppose, that determination is an act of the soul, for certainly it is an active determination that is supposed; and therefore, if the act of the will be determined by the soul itself, it is determined by some antecedent act or act prior to the particular volition directed and determined. (See No. 1155.[33]) If any say, no, there is no necessity of supposing that the soul's determination of the act of will is anything prior to the act of will itself; but the soul determines the act of will in willing, or directs its own volition in the very act of volition; so that, in willing as it does, it determines its own will—they that say thus can mean no more than that the soul's determination of its act of will is in the very time of the act of will itself and not before it in the order of time. But that does not make it the less before it in the order of nature, so that the particular act of volition should really be consequent upon it, as an effect is on the cause that it depends on. Thus that act of the will which determines the direction of a motion of a body may not be prior to the motion itself in order of time, but it may direct the motion of the body in moving it; but yet the act that determines the motion is not the less before the motion directed and determined in the order of nature, as that by which the determined motion is caused and on which it depends. Nothing else can be meant but this, by such an objection against the priority of the determination of the act of will to the act of will itself—unless any will say that the soul's determining its own act is not anything at all diverse from the soul's exerting an act of will, and that the determination of the act of the will is the very same with

[32] Notice that the reference is found in Dwight's copy. The identification of the reference is difficult and not entirely satisfactory. The book is undoubtedly *An Essay on the Freedom of Will in God and in Creatures,* 1732, by Isaac Watts (1674-1748). The difficulty arises from the fact that the symbol "p." as it appears in the text cannot mean "page." Assuming that it means "part" and further assuming that it is a careless equivalent for "section," the reference bears the interpretation section 5, subsection 4. These assumptions identify the relevant passages in Watts. Edwards was usually very meticulous in citing other authors, but for some reason this citation and the ones found below, pp. 179, 182, are careless.

[33] See p. 182, below.

the act of the will itself that is determined. But this is to talk nonsense. If the particular act of will that appears or comes into existence> be something properly directed or determined at all, then it has some cause of its being in such a particular determined manner and not another, and that determination or deciding what the particular manner of its existence shall be is not the very same with the thing determined, but something prior to it and on which it depends. If the particular determined or precise act of will that exists is not consequent or dependent on something preceding determination and direction, or the determination of the act be nothing at all, either preceding or diverse from the very act of will itself, then that particular act of will is an existence that has no cause, and so is no effect at all, but is absolutely something that has started up into existence without any cause determinate in reason, or foundation of its existence—which is as great an absurdity as to suppose the world, that had from eternity been nonexistent, to start into existence all at once at a particular moment absolutely without any cause. And besides, to insist and contend earnestly [that] the soul determines its own acts of will, and then to say that its determination of its acts of will is the very same with the acts of will themselves, is to dispute and contend about nothing. For thus the dispute is not at all about the reason or ground of the acts of will, or any of the soul's acts; but what is contended for, it seems, comes to no more than this, that the soul wills what it wills, and determines what it determines, or that the mind acts what it acts, and that it has those acts that it has, and is the subject of what it is the subject of, or what is, is.

<But if any shall insist that the act of the soul, that is, in determining its own acts of will, is subject to the command of God—that that determining exertion or directing act that directs the consequent volition is either obedience or disobedience to the command of God—I desire such persons to consider that, if there be any obedience in that determining act, it is, to be sure, obedience wherein the will has no share. Because, by the supposition, it precedes each act of the will, since each act depends on it as its determining cause, and therefore it is wholly an involuntary act; so that, if in these acts the soul either obeys or disobeys, it obeys or disobeys wholly involuntarily; it is no willing obedience or rebellion, no compliance or opposition of the will. And what sort of obedience and rebellion is this?>

But no command does properly, directly, and immediately respect any action or exertion whatsoever but that which is voluntary. For what a command requires is that the will of the being commanded should be conformed to the will of him that gives the command. What a command has respect to and seeks is compliance and submission; but there is no compliance, submission, or yielding in that which is not voluntary. Hence 'tis plain that, if there be any sort of act or exertion of the soul prior to its acts of will or voluntary acts, directing and determining those acts of the will, they cannot be subject to any command. If they are properly subject to commands and prescriptions at all, it must be only remotely as those prior acts and determinations are connected with and dependent on some acts of the will in the soul prior to them. But this is contrary to the supposition, for it is supposed that these acts of the soul are prior to all acts of the will—all acts of the will being directed and determined thereby.

It will prove according to all schemes that the necessity, negative or positive (i.e., the necessity or impossibility), of such acts of the will as are fit and proper to be in such a nature as man's, and not beyond the capacity to his faculties, don't render them improperly the subject matter of prescription and command, if by necessity be meant only a prior certainty, determination, or fixedness. For according to the scheme of those that hold what they call a sovereignty of the will, and hold that the soul determines its own volitions or acts of will, if this be true in any proper sense, then there is some act of the soul prior to those volitions that it determines. For the soul's volition[s], by this supposition, are effects of something that passes in the soul, some act or exertion of the soul prior to the volitions themselves, directing, determining, and fixing the consequent volition. For, according to them, the volition is a determined effect; and, if it be, it is determined by some act, for a cause lying perfectly dormant and inactive does or determines nothing any more than that which has no being. Whatever determines the acts of the will, yet the acts of the will themselves, being determined effects or effects decisively fixed by some prior determining cause, the acts themselves must be necessary. And whatever that be that determines or decides what those acts shall be, whether the soul itself or something else, it alters not the case as to the acts themselves being fixed and necessary events. The determination of the act of will must be prior to the act determined, as has been demonstrated; and by the supposition of the act of the will being determined by it, it is dependent on it and necessarily consequent upon it. If it be wholly determined by it, as it is by the supposition, then it is wholly dependent on it and altogether necessarily consequent upon it. If the acts of the will are determined by any cause whatsoever deciding what they shall be, and ben't events absolutely without any cause, then there is a fixed connection between these effects and their causes—as when, in a body in motion in a particular direction, if that direction of motion ben't absolutely without a cause, something has determined the motion to such a course, and the direction of motion depends [on], and is necessarily connected with, the preceding action of something that gave the moving body that direction. And whether we suppose the moving body to determine the direction of its own motion or to be determined by something else, it alters not the case as to the dependence of the effect itself on its cause, or of the direction of motion on the determination or determining act by which it is decided. If there be any meaning at all in any talk about determining the will as to its acts, the meaning must be determining which way it shall act or what the particular acts shall be, whether thus or thus. This plainly supposes that there is some cause of the particular acts of the will, or some cause, ground, or reason that the will is exerted this way and not the other, something that causally determines and decides which way the act shall be. So that, according to the scheme even of those that hold a sovereignty of the will in this sense, the volition and acts of the will themselves are all determined effects fixed by something preceding, and so, in the sense that has been spoken of, are either necessary or impossible. (See book on the Freedom of the Will, p. 539 :2.[34] See Chubb, p. 389, a little past the middle—"self-determining power becomes a necessary cause, etc.")[35]

And again, if any are in that scheme that the acts of the will themselves don't come to pass by any determining or directing cause at all, and arise purely accidentally, yet still they are necessary to the soul that is the subject. For if the soul be subjected to chance after this manner, that its volitions arise by pure accident without any determining cause whatsoever, then to be sure the soul has no hand in them and neither causes nor prevents them, but is necessarily subjected to what chance brings to pass from time to time, as much as the earth (that is inactive) is subject to what falls upon it, and necessarily without what falls not upon it. That which is by chance without dependence on determining cause is, by the supposition, not caused nor prevented by any determination of the subject of it, nor can be, so far as it is by chance without dependence on a determining cause. (See paper of minutes N. 4, p. 8,9.) So that it is evident to a demonstration on all suppositions that, if the volitions or acts of the will of any creature are ever properly the subject matter of duty, prescription, or command, merely the necessity or impossibility of those volitions, in that sense that their being or not being is determined by a prior certainty and fixation, does not hinder any of

[34] Isaac Watts, *op. cit.* in note 32. The notation means section 5, subsection 3 and paragraph 2 of subsection 9.

[35] Thomas Chubb (1679-1729) was an inveterate tractarian. A collection of his tracts was made in 1730. This is doubtless the work to which Edwards refers. Indeed the very reference (i.e., p. 389) is found in his *Freedom of Will,* Dwight edition, vol. 2, p. 95. Part 2, sec. 10 is an extended examination of Chubb's theories.

those volitions that are proper to be in a thing of such a nature as man's soul from being properly the matter of divine prescription and command.

Hence it follows that no inability to any good act of will—that don't consist in any incapacity of human nature and faculties to be the subject of such an act, but amounts to no more than such a kind of negative necessity, certainty, and fixation as has been spoken of, either through an unsuitable and hateful aversion already fixed and settled, or any other cause that don't bring such a necessity by making the volition impossible, by rendering the thing required such as the faculties of human nature are not capable to be made the subjects of, but only by determining the will against it—I say it follows from what has been said, that no such sort of inability to any good act of the will does in any wise render it improperly the matter of divine prescription and command. For that is what I have just now shown—that an act of the will being either necessary or impossible in that sense, merely that the act of the will or the absence of the act is certain by some determination and fixation, don't make it the less the matter of divine prescription.

<Hence that the absolute decrees of God, foreordaining or foredetermining the volitions of men, are in no wise inconsistent with God's moral government as exercised with respect to those volitions, as commanding or forbidding, rewarding or punishing them. I say, absolute decrees are not inconsistent with those merely because they infer such fixation and certainty of those volitions. If they are inconsistent with such a divine moral government with regard to those volitions, it must not be on account of such a certainty or necessity, but on some other account. For it has been now proved that such a necessity of particular volitions does not render such volitions or acts of the will properly the matter of duty, and so of prescription and command, and consequently of the proper enforcements of commands and sanctions of law.>

1154. Events without a cause cannot be foreseen. If anything could come to pass at a particular time without a cause, I scruple not to affirm that it could not be foreseen. As for instance, we will suppose that till 5750 years ago there was no other being excepting the divine being, and then this world, or some particular body or spirit, all at once started out of nothing, without any concern of God in this matter, but absolutely without cause or any reason at all why it started into being then rather than sooner or later, or why such a thing came into being and not something else, why of such dimensions rather than less or greater, etc., or why anything should come into being at all—I say, if this be supposed, it will follow that such an event could not be foreknown. It could not be foreseen that such a thing would at that time come into being. It could not be foreseen that that thing would come into being rather than another, when there was absolutely no more reason why that should rather than another. It could not be foreseen that it should come into being at such a time rather than another, when there was absolutely nothing to give any superior right or value to that moment, to cause that to preponderate rather than any other with respect to that event. Such a future event as has been supposed could not be known because it would be absolutely in its own nature unknowable by the supposition, as some things can't be done because they are absolutely and in their own nature impossible. I call that absolutely and in its own nature impossible which, with the greatest degree of strength supposable, has no tendency to, and which no increase of strength makes any approach to. So I call that absolutely unknowable, to the knowledge of which the greatest capacity of discerning supposable has no tendency and which no increase of discerning makes any approach to. But if something thus comes into existence, absolutely without any cause or anything prior as the reason why it should come into existence, its futurity is such a thing that no increase of discerning causes any approach or tendency to the knowledge of it. And that appears because a great degree of discerning has a greater tendency to the knowledge of things, or enables better to know things, no otherwise than it enables better to discern the evidence of things. But an increase of discerning has no tendency to a discerning evidence where there is none. But in the case of the supposition before us of a future existence that is absolutely without any reason why it should be, there is, even by the supposition, absolutely no preceding evidence of it. If there be no reason why such an existence should be, rather than another, then all things at present are exactly equal and the same with respect to that and other supposed existences, and therefore there is at present no more evidence that that will be than something else that never will be. If there be at present no reason why that existence should be rather than another, then no reason can be seen why it should be rather than another. If there be at present some more evidence that that will be [rather] than another, that prevailing evidence consists in something. But this is contrary to the supposition, for by the supposition at present all things are equal with respect to each, and there is nothing whatsoever preponderating with respect to either. If there be evidence at present of this futurity (as I said), the evidence consists in something, and therefore either consists in the thing itself or something else. If it be self-evident, then the evidence that now is of the future existence consists in the thing itself, foreseen by the evidence there is in the thing itself. But this is contrary to the supposition, for it is supposed that the thing itself at present is not. There is no such thing at present in any respect for the evidence of it to be seen in it. And there is no evidence of it in anything else, for by the supposition there is at present nothing else—for by the supposition there is nothing at all at present in existence that is in any respect, whatsoever, connected with it or related to it. And therefore there can be no evidence or proof or argument of it, for the very notion of proof or argument implies relation and connection with the truth proved or argued. God, therefore, on this supposition, by His infinite capacity of discerning, can't discern any proof or evidence of this futurity because there is none to be discerned. He can't discern it in Himself, for by the supposition He is not the author of it, nor is any way concerned, nor is there anything in Himself connected with it. He can't discern it in anything else, for there is by the supposition nothing else.

If anyone shall say that God, by His omniscience, can know things without evidence, I desire that he would consider again what he says. For to say that God knows things without evidence is the same thing as to say that things are known to Him without being evident to Him, i.e., they are very clear, evident, and certain when they are not at all evident. If things are evident to God, then He sees evidence of 'em—there is something that is evident in His eyes though it may be not in the eyes of others. But we may be sure that that which is evident in His eyes is good and real evidence in its own nature. See book concerning *Free Will* at the beginning, but especially p. 6, etc.[36] See Stebbing, p. 236,[37] and Dr. Clark's Dem., prop. 10. [38]

1155. Free will. Self-determining power. They that hold a self-determining power in the will would be understood, that the will is active in determining itself or that it determines its own volitions by its own act. For they are strenuous in it, that the soul is not merely passive in conversion and turning of the will to good, etc. They cry out at the Calvinists for making men passive. They insist upon it that men are active in it, so that there is another act preceding the act of the will according to them.

Again, if the will determines the will, then the will in so determining itself does something. For determining the will is to do something. And therefore this determination is a doing or act of the will, so that here we have plainly an act of the will determining an act of the will, and the

[36] Isaac Watts, *op cit.* in n. 32, sec. 6.

[37] Henry Stebbing (1687-1763) published from about 1720 to 1759. There was a collected edition of his works in 1737, London, *fol.*

[38] Samuel Clarke (1675-1729), *A Discourse concerning the Being and Attributes of God,* 1705-1706.

will determining all its own acts by some preceding act of its own—which is a contradiction, because this supposes an act of the will before the first or determining one. If the will determines its own acts by its own acts, then it determines its own acts prior to its volitions. For if the will be determined by an act of the will, 'tis determined by its volition—that is, by an act of the will and not an act of the understanding or any other faculty—'tis purely an act of the will or volition.

God's Nature

89. Justice. It appears plain enough that an omnipotent and omniscient being can have no desire of having us seek for His own ends, because He can as easily bring about all His ends without it. And this appears of every and all objects. And if we consider the case of excellency (which is being's consent to entity, and we have shown that this must necessarily be consistent and agreeable to existing being, and [on] the contrary, contradiction, dissent to entity, must necessarily be disagreeable to it), from hence it follows that all excellency, when perceived, will be agreeable to perceiving being, and all evil, disagreeable. But God being omnipotent must necessarily perfectly perceive all excellency and fully know what is contrary to it, and therefore all excellency is perfectly agreeable to His will, and all evil perfectly disagreeable. Therefore, He cannot will to do anything but what is excellent; but justice is all excellency.

150. Deity. Many have wrong conceptions of the difference between the nature of the deity and created spirits. The difference is no contrariety, but what naturally results from His greatness and nothing else, such as [i.e., which] created spirits come nearer to or more imitate, the greater they are in their powers and faculties. So that, if we should suppose the faculties of a created spirit to be enlarged infinitely, there would be the deity to all intents and purposes, the same simplicity, immutability, etc.

194. God. That is a gross and an unprofitable idea we have of God, as being something large and great as bodies are, and infinitely extended throughout the immense space. For God is neither little nor great with that sort of greatness, even as the soul of man—it is not at all extended, no more than an idea, and is not present anywhere as bodies are present, as we have shown elsewhere.[39] So 'tis with respect to the uncreated spirit. The greatness of a soul consists not in any extension, but its com-

[39] See *The Mind*, no. 2, p. 27, above.

prehensiveness of idea and extendedness of operation. So the infiniteness of God consists in His perfect comprehension of all things and the extendedness of His operation equally to all places. God is present nowhere any otherwise than the soul is in the body or brain; and He is present everywhere, as the soul is in the body. We ought to conceive of God as being omnipotence, perfect knowledge, and perfect love, and not extended any otherwise than as power, knowledge, and love are extended, and not as if it were a sort of unknown thing that we call substance, that is extended.

453. Free grace. The righteousness of a judge consists in his judging according to law, or to the rule of judgment which has been fixed by rightful legislators, especially if the law and rule of judgment fixed be good, whatever good principles influenced the legislators in making such laws, whether justice or goodness and mercy. But God, in the blessings He adjudges to His people, judges according to the fixed rule of judgment which is His covenant. God shows His holiness by fulfilling His promises to His people. God's faithfulness is part of His holiness, and this is what is meant by righteousness.

1077. God's holiness is His having a due, meet, and proper regard to everything, and therefore consists mainly and pre-eminently in his infinite regard or love to Himself—He being infinitely the greatest and most excellent being—and therefore a meet and proper regard to Himself is infinitely greater than to all other beings. Now as He is, as it were, the sum of all being, and all other positive existence is but a communication from Him, hence it will follow that a proper regard to Himself is the sum of His regard.

1196. God's moral government. So much evidence of the most perfect exactness of proportion, harmony, equity, and beauty in the mechanical laws of nature and other methods of providence, which belong to the course of nature, by which God shows His regard to harmony and fitness and beauty in what He does as the governor of the natural world, may strongly argue that He will maintain the most strict and perfect justice in proportion and fitness in what He does as the governor of the moral world.

1263. God's immediate and arbitrary operation, in all instances of it at least in this lower world, whether through all ages on men's minds by His spirit, or at some particular season extraordinarily requiring it in what is called miracles, is that which there is a strong and strange disposition in many to object against and disbelieve. But for what reason, unless it be something in the disposition of the heart, is hard to imagine. (See concerning such prejudices, McLaurin's *Discourses,* p. 314, 315, etc.[40]) If there be a God who is truly an intelligent, voluntary, active being, what is there in reason to incline us to think that He should not act, and that He should not act upon His creatures, which, being his creatures, must have their very being from His actions, and must be perfectly and most absolutely subject to and dependent on His action? And if He acted once, why must He needs be still forever after and act no more? What is there in nature to disincline [us] to suppose He mayn't continue to act towards the world He made? And if under His government, and if He continues to act at all towards His creatures, then there must be some of His creatures he continues to act upon immediately. 'Tis nonsense to say He acts upon all mediately, because in so doing we go back *in infinitum* from one thing acting on another without ever coming to a primary, present agent, and yet at the same time suppose God to be such a present agent.

There are many who allow a present, continuing, immediate operation of God on the creation (and indeed such are the late discoveries and advances which have been made in natural philosophy, that all men of sense, who are also men of learning, are content to allow it), but yet, because so many of the constant changes and events in their continued form in the external world come to pass in a certain exact method, according to certain fixed, invariable laws, are averse to allow that God acts any otherwise than as limiting Himself by such invariable laws, fixed from the beginning of the creation (when He precisely marked out and determined the rules and paths of all His future operations), and that He ever departs since that from those paths. So that, though they allow an immediate divine operation in those days, yet they suppose it is [now] limited by what we call laws of nature, and seem averse to allow an arbitrary operation to be continued or even to be needed in these days.

But I desire it may be well considered whether there be any reason for this. For of the two kinds of divine operation, viz., that which is arbitrary and that which is limited by fixed laws, the former, viz., arbitrary, is the first and foundation of the other and that which all divine operation must finally be resolved into, and which all events and divine effects whatsoever primarily depend upon. Even the fixing of the method and rules of the other kind of operation is an instance of arbitrary operation. When I speak of arbitrary operation, I don't mean arbitrary in opposition to an operation directed by wisdom, but only in

[40] John Maclaurin (1693-1754). His book, posthumously published, was *Sermons and Essays,* 1755.

opposition to an operation confined to, and limited by, those fixed establishments and laws commonly called the laws of nature. The one of these I shall therefore, for want of better phrases, call 'a natural operation,' the other 'an arbitrary operation.' The latter of these, as I observed, is first and supreme, and to which the other is wholly subject and also wholly dependent, and without which there could be no divine operation at all, and no effect ever produced, and nothing besides God could ever exist. Arbitrary operation is that to which is owing the existence of the subjects of natural operation—the manner, measure, and all the circumstances of their existence. 'Tis arbitrary operation that fixes, determines, and limits the laws of natural operation.

Therefore arbitrary operation, being every way the highest, is that wherein God is most glorified. 'Tis the glory of God that He is an arbitrary being—that originally He, in all things, acts as being limited and directed in nothing but His own wisdom, tied to no other rules and laws but the directions of His own infinite understanding. So in those that are the highest order of God's creatures, viz., intelligent creatures, that are distinguished from other creatures in their being made in God's image, 'tis one thing wherein consists their highest natural dignity, that they have an image of this. They have a secondary and dependent arbitrariness. They are not limited in their operation to the laws of matter and motion, but that they can do what they please. The members of men's bodies obey the act of their wills without being directed merely by the impulse and attraction of other bodies in all their motions.

These things being observed, I would now take notice that the higher we ascend in the scale of created existence and the nearer we come to the Creator, the more and more arbitrary we should find the divine operations in the creature, or those communications and influences in which He maintains an intercourse with the creature. And it appears beautiful and every way fit [and] suitable that it should be so. See B. 1, tt.[41]

But before I proceed particularly to show this, I would observe how any divine operation may be said to be more or less arbitrary, or to come nearer to that which is absolutely arbitrary, in the sense I have spoken of it, in opposition to a being limited by that general rule called laws of nature. An operation is absolutely arbitrary when no use is made of any law of nature, and no respect had to any one such fixed rule or method.

There are these ways that the operations which are not absolutely and perfectly arbitrary may approach near to it:

1. One is, by arbitrary operations being mixed with those that are

[41] See p. 126, above. B. 1 refers to the first volume of *Miscellanies* in manuscript.

natural, i.e., when there is something in the operation that is arbitrary and tied to no fixed rule or law, and something else in the operation wherein the laws of nature are made use [of], and without which the designed effect could not take place. Instances will be given of this afterwards.

2. Another way is when, though some law or rule is observed, the rule is not general or very extensive, but some particular rule makes an exception to general laws of nature, and [is] a law that extends to comparatively few instances. This approaches to an arbitrary operation; for the less extensive the limitation of the operation or the smaller the number of instances or cases by which it is limited, 'tis manifest, the nearer the operation is to unlimited, or limited to no number of cases at all.

Thus supposing there were an exception to the general law of gravitation towards the center of the earth, and there were one kind of bodies that, on the contrary, had an inclination to fly from the center, and that in proportion to the quantity of matter, but that sort of bodies nowhere to be found but in some one certain island, and very rarely to be found there. This kind of operation would be nearer to arbitrary and miraculous than other divine operations—than those that are limited by the general laws of nature that obtain everywhere through the world.

3. Another way wherein a manner of operation approaches to arbitrary is when the limitation to a method is not absolute, even in the continued course of that sort of operations, so that the law fails of the nature of a fixed law—as all that are called laws of nature are. God generally keeps to that method but ties not Himself to it, sometimes departs from it according to His sovereign pleasure.

Having mentioned these things, I now proceed particularly to observe how, the higher we ascend in the scale or series of created existences and the nearer, in thus ascending, we come to the Creator, the more the manner of divine operation with respect to the creature approaches to arbitrary in these respects or in one or the other of them. Thus, in the first place, if we ascend with respect to time, and go back in the series of existences or events in the order of their succession to the beginning of the creation, and so till we come to the Creator, that after we have ascended beyond the limits and rise of the laws of nature, we shall come to arbitrary operation. The creation of the matter of the material world out of nothing, the creation even of every individual atom or primary particle, was by an operation perfectly arbitrary. And here, by the way, I would observe that creation out of nothing seems to be the only divine operation that is absolutely arbitrary, without any kind of use made of any antecedently fixed method of proceeding, such as is called a law of nature.

After the creation of the matter of the world out of nothing, the gradual bringing of the matter of the world into order was by an arbitrary operation. It was by arbitrary act divine that the primary particles of matter were put into motion, and had the direction and degree of their motion determined, and were brought into so beautiful and useful a situation, one with respect to another. But yet the operation by which these things were done was not so absolutely, purely, and unmixedly arbitrary as the first creation out of nothing. For in these secondary operations, or the works of what may be called secondary, some use was made of laws of nature before established, such, at least, as the laws of resistance and attraction or adhesion and *vis inertiae,* that are essential to the very being of matter, for the very solidity of the particles of matter itself consists in them; but the putting those particles into motion supposes 'em to exist in the moving, inert, resisting, and adhering matter. There is use made of the laws of resistance and adhesion. They are presupposed as the basis of this secondary operation of God in causing this resistance, *vis inertiae,* and adhesion to change place, and in causing the consequent impulses and mutual influences which is the end of those motions and dispositions of the situation of particles. So that the creation of particular natural bodies—as the creation of light, the creation of the sun, moon, and stars, of earth, air, and seas, flowers, rocks and minerals, the bodies of plants and animals—was by a mixed operation partly arbitrary and partly by stated laws. And thus [it is] as we descend from the first creation out of nothing through the rest of the operations of the six days.[42]

But it may be proper here to remark these following things: 1. Immediate creation seems not entirely to have ceased with this first work by which the world in general was brought out of nothing. But after that there was an immediate creation in making of the souls of Adam and Eve, and also with respect to the greater part of the body of Eve. 2. The mixing of arbitrary with natural operations was not only in arbitrarily making use of laws already established, as in putting material things in motion, variously compounding them, and the like, but also in establishing new, more particular laws of nature, with respect to particular creatures as they were made—as the laws of magnetism, many laws observable in plants, the laws of instinct in animals, and the law of the operation of the minds of men. 3. Most things in the visible

[42] Notwithstanding the obvious differences of idiom, the idea expressed here has a strong resemblance to C. S. Peirce's distinction between "firstness" and "secondness." See *Collected Papers of Charles Sanders Peirce,* vol. 1, paragraph 530.

world were brought into their present state so as to [be] of such a particular kind, or to complete their species of creatures by a secondary creation, which is a mixed operation, excepting the creation of the highest order of creatures, viz., intelligent minds, which were wholly created, complete in their kind, by an absolutely arbitrary operation. What may be said hereafter may lead us to the reason of this.

And if we proceed in the succession of existences till we come to the supreme being the other way, viz., to the end of the world (for though proceeding thus from preceding to future be, according to a more common way of speaking, descending, yet 'tis as truly ascending towards God as proceeding the other way, for God is the first and the last, the beginning and the end), now I say, if we ascend up to God this way, proceeding in the succession of events till we come to the end of time, this way of proceeding will again bring us to a disposition of the world by a divine arbitrary operation through the universe. For God will not leave the world to a gradual decay, languishing through millions of ages under a miserable decay till it be quite perished and utterly ruined according to a course of things, according to the laws of nature; but will Himself destroy the world, will roll the heavens together as a scroll, will change it as a man puts off an old garment and wears it not till it gradually drops to pieces, and will take it down as a machine is taken down when it has answered the workman's end. And this He will do by an arrest in the laws of nature everywhere, in all parts of the visible universe, and by an entire new disposition and mighty change of all things at once. For though all the laws of nature will not be abolished —those laws before mentioned in which is the being of the primary particles of matter will be continued—yet the arbitrary interposition, entirely beside and above those laws and in some respects contrary to 'em and interrupting their influence, may be said to be universal, as it will be in all parts of the material creation; and very many of the laws of nature will be utterly abolished, particularly many of the laws peculiarly respecting plants and animals and human bodies and man's animal life.

If we ascend towards God in the scale of existence according to the degrees of excellency and perfection, the nearer we come to God the nearer we shall come to arbitrary influence of the Most High on the creature, till at length, when we come to the highest rank, we shall come [to] an intercourse that is, in many respects, quite above those rules which we call the laws of nature. The lowest rank of material things are almost wholly under the government of the general laws of matter and motion. If we ascend from them to plants, which in many things are governed by more particular laws, distinct from the laws common to all material things, the laws of vegetation are doubtless, many of them, distinct from the general laws of matter and motion and therefore, by what was observed before, nearer akin to an arbitrary influence; if we ascend from the most imperfect to the most perfect kind of plants, we shall come to more particular laws still; and if from thence we rise to animals, we shall come to laws still more singular; and when we rise to the most perfect of them, we shall find particular laws or instincts yet nearer akin to an arbitrary influence. If we rise to mankind, and particularly the mind of man, by which especially he is above the inferior creatures, and consider the laws of the common operations of the mind, they are so high above such a kind of general laws of matter and are so singular that they are altogether untraceable. (The more particular laws are the harder to be investigated and traced.) And if we go from the common operations of the faculties of the mind and rise up to those that are spiritual (which are infinitely of the highest kind and are those by which the minds are most conversant with the Creator and have their very next union with Him), though these are not altogether without use made of means and some connection with antecedents (the connection, after the manner of the immutable laws of nature, never erring from the degree and exact measure, time, and precise state of the antecedent) and what we call, though improperly in this case, second causes, yet the operation may properly be said to be arbitrary and sovereign. And if we ascend from saints on earth to angels in Heaven, who always behold the face of the Father which is in Heaven, and constantly receive His command on every occasion, the will of God not being much known to them by any such methods as the laws of nature but immediately given on all emergencies, we shall come to greater degrees of an arbitrary intercourse. And if [we] rise to the highest step of all next to the supreme being Himself, even the mind of the man Christ Jesus who is united personally to the Godhead, doubtless there is a constant intercourse, as it were, infinitely above the laws of nature. N.B. When we come to the highest ranks of creatures, we come to them who themselves have the greatest image of God's arbitrary operation, who 'tis, therefore, most fit should be the subjects of such operations.

And if we ascend towards God conjunctly, proceeding in our ascent both according to the order of degrees and that order [i.e., of time], we shall find the rule hold still—the more arbitrary shall we find the divine influence and intercourse, and to a higher degree than by ascending in one way solely.

Thus if we ascend up to intelligent creatures, men and angels who are next to the Creator, and then go back to the beginning of the world, even to their creation, we shall find more of an arbitrary operation in their creation, and being brought to perfection in their kind, than in the creation of any other particular species of creatures. Thus it was not in the creation of angels as it was in the formation of sun, moon, and stars, minerals, plants, and animals—who were formed out of pre-existent principles by a secondary creation, as it is called, presupposing, making use of, and operating upon these principles or subsisting by certain general laws of nature already established; but the angels were immediately created and made perfect in their kind at once, by a primary creation, [an] operation absolutely arbitrary, as perfectly so as the creation of the primary particles of matter themselves. And so with respect to the creation of the soul of man.

And after these intelligent beings were created, at first the divine intercourse with them must be much more arbitrary than it is now. They could not be left to themselves and to the laws of nature to acquire that knowledge and exercise of their faculties by contracted habits and gradual association of ideas, as we do now, gradually rising from our first infancy. If man had been thus left, he must needs have soon perished. But we must suppose that there was an extraordinary influence and intercourse God had with man far above the law of nature, immediate instincts enlightening and conducting him, and arbitrarily fixing those habits in his mind which now are gradually established through a great length of time. So afterwards for some time, God continued a miraculous intercourse with our first parents; and we see that, for many of the first ages of the world, [there was] an arbitrary intercourse of God with mankind, not only some particular prophets of one nation or posterity but with eminent saints of all families. I say, such an arbitrary intercourse was much more common in those first ages than afterwards.

And if we proceed in the order of time the other way to the end of the world and till we come to Him who is the end as well as the beginning, 'tis true we shall find that an arbitrary influence will then be exerted everywhere throughout the creation, but more especially and many more ways towards intelligent being—for instance, towards mankind, in bringing souls departed from the other world, in raising the dead to life, in miraculously changing the living, in taking up the saints to meet the Lord, in gathering all, both good and bad, before the judgment seat, and in all the process of that day. The laws of nature must be in innumerable ways departed from, and an extraordinary operation found in the manifesting of the judge [and] in the manifestation of the judged one to another, in manifesting and declaring the actions of particular persons, and the secrets of their hearts, and the grounds of the sentence, and in all the process of that day. If the law of nature were not in numberless ways to be departed from, in these things, the day of judgment would take up more time by far than the world has stood. And in the execution of the sentence on both the righteous and the wicked, the glorious powers of God will be wonderfully and most extraordinarily manifested, in many respects, above all that ever was before in the arbitrary exertions of it. And if we look to the beginning and end, the birth and death of each individual person of mankind, we shall find the same rule hold, as concerning the beginning and end of the race of mankind in general. The soul of every man in his generation or birth must be immediately created and infused; or if we say that it is according to a fixed law of nature that the Creator forms and introduces the soul, it being determined by a law of nature what the precise state of the proper body shall be when the soul shall begin to exist in it, yet it must be a law of nature that is most peculiar and widely differing from all other laws of nature, and independent of them. And so, again, the Creator immediately and arbitrarily interposes when a man comes to die, in disposing of that soul that He infused in his birth.[43]

So if we consider the beginning or creation and end of each individual saint or member: thus in their beginning or creation (I mean their beginning as saints or their conversion), commonly at the time of that, God's sovereign arbitrary interposition and influence on their hearts is much more visible and remarkable than ordinarily they are the subjects of in the course of their lives. And when they come to die, the positive effects of God's arbitrary influence are immensely greater in the souls of the saints in their glorification than in the souls of the wicked in their damnation.

Thus let us proceed which way we will in the series of things in the creation, still the higher we ascend and the nearer we come to God in the gradation or succession of created things, the nearer it comes to this, that there is no other law than only the law of the infinite wisdom of the omniscient first cause and supreme disposer of all things, who in one simple, unchangeable, perpetual action comprehends all existence in its utmost compass and extent and infinite series.

'Tis fit that it should be so, as we proceed and go from step to step among the several parts and distinct existences and events of the universe, that which way soever we go, the nearer we come to God the less and less we should find that things are governed by general laws, and

[43] At this point in the manuscript a symbol directs the reader to a long digression, which might be called 'illustrations from the history of redemption,' in which Edwards cites numerous Biblical instances as evidence of God's arbitrary operations with men. I have omitted the digression because it adds little to the argument, and that little is to be found in *A History of the Work of Redemption, in extenso,* vol. 3, pp. 159-436.

that the arbitrariness of the supreme cause and governor should be more and more seen. For He is not seen to be the sovereign ruler of the universe, or God over all, any otherwise than He is seen to be arbitrary. He is not seen to be active in the government of the world any other way than it is seen He is arbitrary. It is not seen but that He Himself, in common with His creatures, is subject in His acting to the same laws with inferior beings, any other way than as it is seen that His arbitrary operation is every way and everywhere at the head of the universe and is the foundation and first spring of all.

Happiness

f. Spiritual happiness. As we have shown and demonstrated[44] (contrary to the opinion of Hobbes that nothing is substance but matter) that no matter is substance but only God who is a spirit, and that other spirits are more substantial than matter, so also it is true that no happiness is solid and substantial but spiritual happiness, although it may seem that sensual pleasure is most real and spiritual only imaginary, as it seems as if sensible matter were only real and spiritual substance only imaginery.

3. Happiness is the end of the creation as appears by this—because the creation had as good not be as not rejoice in its being. For certainly it was the goodness of the Creator that moved Him to create; and how can we conceive of another end proposed by goodness, than that He might delight in seeing the creatures He made rejoice in that being that He has given them? It appears also by this—because the end of the creation is that the creature might glorify Him. Now what is glorifying God but a rejoicing at that glory He has displayed? An understanding of the perfections of God, merely, cannot be the end of the creation, for he had as good not understand it as see it and not be at all moved with joy at the sight. Neither can the highest end of the creation be the declaring God's glory to others, for the declaring God's glory is good for nothing otherwise than to raise joy in ourselves and others at what is declared. Wherefore such happiness is the highest end of the creation of the Creator of the universe. And intelligent beings are the consciousness of the creation that is to be the immediate subject of this happiness. How happy, may we conclude, will be those intelligent beings that are to be made thus happy!

95. Happiness of Heaven. When the body enjoys the perfections of health and strength, the motion of the animal spirits are not only brisk

---

[44] Probably in the essay *Of Being*.

and free but also harmonious. There is a regular proportion in the motion from all parts of the body that begets delight in the inner soul and makes the body feel pleasantly all over. God has so excellently contrived the nerves and parts of the human body. But few men since the fall, especially since the flood, have health to so great a perfection as to have much of this harmonious motion. When it is enjoyed, one whose nature is not very much vitiated and depraved is very much assisted thereby in every exercise of body or mind. And it fits one for the contemplation of more exalted and spiritual excellencies and harmonies, as music does. But we need not doubt but that harmony will be in its perfection in the bodies of the saints after the resurrection, and that, as every part of the bodies of the wicked shall be excruciated with intolerable pain, so every part of the saints' refined bodies shall be as full of pleasure as they can hold, and that this will not take the mind off from but prompt and help it in spiritual delights, to which even the delights of their spiritual bodies shall be but a shadow.[45]

96. Trinity.[46] It appears that there must be more than a unity in infinite and eternal essence; otherwise the goodness of God can have no perfect exercise. To be perfectly good is to incline to and delight in making others happy in the same proportion as it is happy itself—that is, to delight as much in communicating happiness to another as enjoying of it himself and an inclination to communicate all his happiness. It appears that this is perfect goodness, because goodness and this delight are the same. But this delight is not perfect except it be equal to the highest delight of that being, that is, except his inclination to communicate happiness be equal to his inclination to be happy himself. Goodness is the exercise in communication of happiness; but if that communication be imperfect, that is, if it be not of all the happiness enjoyed by the being himself, the exercise of the goodness is imperfect, inasmuch as the communication of happiness and the exercise of goodness is the same. But to no finite being can God either incline to communicate goodness so much as He inclines to be happy Himself, for He cannot love a creature so much as He loves Himself; neither can He communicate all His goodness to a finite being. But no absolutely perfect being can be without absolutely perfect goodness, and no being can be perfectly happy which has not the exercise of that which he sincerely inclines to exercise. Wherefore, God must have a perfect exercise of His goodness, and therefore must have the fellowship of a person equal

[45] Nos. 95 and 198 are published in Dwight's edition, vol. 8, p. 532.

[46] A few sentences from no. 96 were published by E. C. Smyth in *Exercises Commemorating the Two-Hundredth Anniversary of the Birth of Jonathan Edwards,* Andover, 1904, Appendix 1, pp. 16-17.

with Himself. No reasonable creature can be happy, we find, without society and communion, not only because it finds something in others that is not in himself, but because he delights to communicate himself to another; this cannot be because of our imperfection but because we are made in the image of God. For the more perfect any creature is, the more strong this inclination; so that we may conclude that Jehovah's happiness consists in communion as well as the creature's.

97. Happiness. As was said in 96, that no being could be happy without the exercise of this inclination of communicating his happiness, now the happiness of society consists in this: in the mutual communications of each other's happiness. Neither does it satisfy, in society, only to receive the other's happiness without also communicating his own. Now it is necessary that to those whom we love most we should have the strongest desire of communicating happiness (to every [one] but one that be infinite, and cannot receive additions of happiness). And although God is the object of the creature's love (if a man be not depraved), yet God being infinitely happy, he cannot desire to communicate his happiness to Him—which is nothing to the happiness God enjoys. But in the Gospel God is come down to us, and the person of God may receive communications of happiness from us. The man Christ Jesus loves us so much that He is really the happier for our delight and happiness in Him.

198. Happiness. How soon do earthly lovers come to an end of their discoveries of each other's beauty! How soon do they see all that is to be seen, are they united as near as 'tis possible and have communion as intimate as possible! How soon do they come to the most endearing expressions of love that 'tis possible to come to, so that no new ways can be invented, given, or received! And how happy is that love in which there is an eternal progress in all these things, wherein new beauties are continally discovered, and more and more loveliness, and in which we shall forever increase in beauty ourselves. When we shall be made capable of finding out, and giving, and shall receive more and more endearing expressions of love forever, our union will become more close and communion more intimate.

Immortality of the Soul

1. The immortality of the soul may thus be argued: men, or intelligent beings, are the consciousness of the creation, whereby the universe is conscious of its own being, and of what is done in it, of the actions of the Creator and governor with respect to it. Now except the world had

such a consciousness of itself, it would be altogether in vain that it was. If the world is not conscious of its being, it had as good not be as be; as is very clear, for the creation was known as much in every respect from all eternity as it is now, to the Creator. Now it is as evident that the world is as much in being, if this consciousness lasts but a little while and then ceases, as it would be if there was no consciousness of it—that is, after the consciousness ceases, from that time forth forever it is in vain that there ever was such a consciousness. For instance, when the earth is destroyed, if its consciousness don't remain it is in vain that ever it has been.

20. Immortality of the soul. How doth it seem to grate upon one to think that an intelligent being, that consciousness, should be put out forever so as never to know that it ever did think or had a being! If it be put out as a punishment, it can never know that it is punished, never reflect on the justice of God or anything of that nature.

1006. Immortality of the soul. Some part of the world, viz., that which is the highest, the head and the end of the rest, must be of eternal duration—even the intelligent, reasonable creatures. For if those creatures, this head and end of all the rest of the creation, comes to an end and is annihilated, 'tis the same thing as if the whole were annihilated. If the world be of a temporal duration and then drops into nothing, 'tis in vain, i.e., no end is obtained worthy of God. There is nobody but what will own that, if God had created the world and then it had dropped into nothing the next minute, it would have been in vain; no end could be obained worthy of God, and the only reason is that the end would have been so small; by reason of the small continuance of the good obtained by it, it is infinitely little. And so it is still infinitely little if it stands a million of ages and then drops into nothing. That is as a moment in the sight of God. If the good obtained by the creation of the world be of so long continuance, 'tis equally small, when we compare it with God, as one moment. 'Tis in comparison of Him absolutely equivalent to nothing, and therefore an end not worthy of Him. No end is worthy of an infinite God but an infinite end. Therefore, the good that is obtained must be of infinite duration. If it be not so, who shall fix the bounds? Who shall say a million years is long enough? If it be, who shall say a good of a thousand years continuance does not become the wisdom of God? And if it does, how can one say but that less still would not answer the ends of wisdom? If it would, who can say that the sovereignty of God shall not fix on a good of a minute's continuance as sufficient—which is as great, in comparison with Him, as a million years?

The only reason why a good of a minute's continuance is not great enough to become the Creator of the world is that 'tis a good so little when compared with Him; and the same reason stands in equal force against a good of any limited duration whatsoever.

If there be nothing that ever began to be, or that ever God made worthy to exist, or whose existence was a thing valuable or worthy for the most high to value, then why did God ever cause it to have existence? But if otherwise, if it be valuable or worthy for the Most High to value, then why should its existence eternally cease after it has been a little while? If it be said, because, though it existed but a little while, its end was obtained, and so it may be thrown by as useless for the future, I ask, what end? On the supposition that nothing that ever began to be remains, then no end ever obtained remains. Nothing in any respect new or lately arrived at, or that was not from all eternity and before any creature was made, remains, if the whole creation ceases after it has been a little while or (which is tantamount) if the chief creatures that are the end of the inferior creatures cease forever after they have existed a little while.

Liberty of Conscience

8. Conscience. The dispute whether or no men may make laws to oblige the conscience. What nonsense it is for the world to be rent to pieces with a dispute whether men are obliged to do that which, at the same time, they are obliged in the same sense not to do! It is the same thing precisely, for the dispute is this: whether men are obliged in conscience to go contrary to their consciences when men command them so to do—which implies that men's consciences may sometimes tell them that some things are right and ought to be done, which at the same time, their consciences tell them, it is wrong and ought not to be done.

10. Pastors. This is certain and evident concerning its belonging to the people to choose their own pastor; that it is the people's part to choose with what food they will be fed, let what will be offered them. 'Tis their business to judge whether it be best for them to receive it in as their food. That they, in some cases, are to receive that as their food which they at the same time judge to be their poison, that is, they are to believe those things which, at the same time, they believe to be false, and even to think it best to do those things which they, at the same time, think it is best for them not to do, are contradictions. It's every man's business to choose that food which he thinks to be best for his eternal welfare, as certain as it is his business to get as much happiness as he can for himself in the other world, as all are fools that will not, and it is certainly the essence of folly to suffer men to hinder us from it, if we can help it. Wherefore it be the people's part to choose with what food they will be fed, and is also their business to choose with what feeders they will be fed. If I may choose my food, I may choose that feeder that will give the food that I choose, if I can obtain him, and I am a fool if I will be hindered by men, when I can help it, from being fed by such a feeder as I judge will be the means of my greatest eternal welfare.

11. Discipline. This is most certain, that, if men have no authority to make ecclesiastical laws, then I am not obliged to obey them because of their power and authority. I am not so obliged to obey them because of any power or authority they have, that is, I am not obliged to obey them any more than I should be obliged to obey the meanest, most obscure private person in the kingdom, if he should take on him to make laws. So that 'tis proved that I am not obliged to obey them because of their authority. But then, if it shall be said that we are obliged to obey for the sake of peace, I answer, 'tis most certain that, if those persons have no authority to make such laws, I am no more obliged to obey them merely for the sake of peace than the people of England would be obliged to obey the Grand Turk, who has no authority, if he should make laws for them. Supposing that a breach of his command would enrage all the people of Turkey, and that there should ensue every way as bad a breach of peace as the disobeying those who have no authority in England, now indeed I say, the people of England would be obliged, if so, to obey the Grand Turk if no worse thing would follow [from obeying] than the breach of peace [from disobeying] ; but it belongs to the people in England and not to the Grand Turk to judge whether there would or no ; so it belongs to me to judge whether it will be best for me to obey those who have no authority—to me, and not [to] the legislators.

14. Civil authority. The civil authorities having nothing to do with matters eccelesiastical, with those things which relate to conscience and eternal salvation or with any matter religious as religious, is reconcilable still with their having to do with some matters that, in some sense, concern religion. For although they have to do with nothing but civil affairs, and although their business extends no further than the civil interests of the people, yet by reason of the profession of religion and the difference that matters religious make in the state and circumstances of a people, many things become civil which otherwise would not. Now by the civil interests or advantages of a people (distinguished [from] those things which relate to conscience, the favor of God, and happiness

in the other world) I think is commonly meant their general interest or their interest as they are a people in this world, whether it [be] their general profit or pleasure or peace or honor. I say general interests or interests of a people, because the pleasure, profit, peace, or honor of a people in general or taken one with another may be advanced and thereby the interest or pleasure of a particular person may be depressed. And so also the interest of the whole, for a particular time, may be depressed, when yet taken one time with another it may be advanced. Now I say this interest of a people may be all that civil authority has to do with, and yet it may have to do with things in some sense religious for the before-mentioned reason—because many things, by reason of religion, become their civil advantage, that is, their advantage in this world which otherwise would not be so. Also many things become their civil disadvantage. Thus it is for the civil interest of a people not to be disturbed in their public assembling for divine worship, that is, it is for the general peace, profit, and pleasure of 'em in this world.

17. Confession of faith. With respect to declaring one's faith in Scripture expressions, this is certain, if there ought to be liberty of conscience: that every minister, every Christian, and every man upon earth is at liberty to declare or not to declare his consent to any man's being a minister, according as he does, internally in his mind, consent or not consent. 'Tis evident he has liberty of conscience to think about it, and if he has liberty of conscience [i.e., to think about it], he has liberty of declaring according to his thoughts. This liberty every minister has, that is required to give his consent to a man's being a minister. If so, 'tis also certain that, if a minister believes that no man can be fit but what believes such and such things to be true, he has liberty of conscience to declare his consent or dissent, according as he thinks this person believes or disbelieves those things. And if so, 'tis absolutely certain that he has power to insist upon those things which he shall think sufficient reasons—to make him state he does believe those things which he deems necessary before he gives his consent to his being a minister. And if he thinks that speaking in the words of the Scripture be not sufficient to make him think so, he has power to insist on more. So likewise every particular man and every congregation of men in the world have the same liberty to judge what man is fit to feed their souls. Not but that words and confessions of faith have been some of the chief engines that Satan has made use of to tear the church of God in pieces, not but that, if those were removed, the principal walls of separation would at the same time be removed, not that 'tis right for men to insist upon subscription to any creeds or confessions of faith, or any other particular ways of making known their faith. All that we plead for is that there be sufficient reasons to satisfy those, whose business it is to declare their consent to their being ministers, that the candidate does believe what is thought necessary by them to be believed, in order to their [his] fitness —not that they can demand any more than such satisfaction which way soever they come by it.

40. Ministers, relating to mm and gg.[47] 'Tis a thousand pities that the world's church office and power should so tear the world to pieces and raise such a fog and dust about apostolic office, power, and succession, pope's, bishop's, and presbyter's power. It is not such a desperately difficult thing to know what power belongs to each of these, if we will let drop those words that are without fixed meaning. The light of nature will lead us right along in a plain path. Without doubt, ministers are to administer the sacraments to Christians, and they are to administer them only to such as they think Christ would have them administer them. Without doubt, ministers are to teach men what Christ would have them to do, and to teach them who doth those things and who doth them not, who it is are Christians and who are not; and the people are to hear them as much in this as in other things. And that so far forth as the people are obliged to hear what I teach them, so great is my pastoral or ministerial or teaching power. And this is all the difference of power there is amongst ministers, whether apostles or whatever. Thus, if I in a right manner am chosen the teacher of a people, so far as they ought to hear what I teach them, so much power I have. Thus they are obliged to hear me only because they themselves have chosen me to guide them and therein declared that they thought me sufficiently instructed in the mind of Christ to teach them, and because I have the other requisites of being their teacher. Then I have power as other ministers have in these days. But if it were plain to them that I was under the infallible guidance of Christ, then I should have more power; and if it was plain to all the world of Christians that I was under the infallible guidance of Christ, and I was sent forth to teach the world the will of Christ, then I should have power in all the world. I should have power to teach them what they ought to do, and they would be obliged to hear me. I should have power to teach them who are Christians and who not: and, in this likewise, they would be obliged to hear me.

69. National church. This is evident by naked and natural reason, that those that live together do, if they have not overbalancing reasons on

---

[47] No. mm is not included in this text. It concerns the authority of the minister as different from that of the layman. It closes with the words, "How this distinction is known I leave to be yet discovered." For no. gg, see p. 236, below.

the other side, worship God together. By the word 'together' I don't mean as to place, for those that live within 100 rods may be further distant from me than he that lives five hundred. But I mean those who are joined together in the same interest, have dependence one on another, and whose welfare more especially depends on a communication with each other, and whom the providence of God have cast into such circumstances as that they subsist by communication, whatever those circumstances are, whether because they are under the same government, or live in the same place, or speak the same language, or whatever their families, positions, provinces, governments, kingdoms, nations, Christendom, world—and their obligation to worship together is in proportion to their nearness together. 'Tis evidently the duty of such to worship together because they are united in one common interest which they depend upon the object of their worship for, and because it is abundantly most convenient so to do.

70. *Vid.* 80[48] Conscience. To say that a man ought not to be guided wholly and entirely by his own private judgment in what he ought to believe is not only against the Gospel and the plainest reason, and most absurd; but the thing itself, the supposition that a man is not entirely guided by his own private judgment in what he believes, whether it ought to be or no, is a direct, flat, and immediate contradiction. And if it were never so much required, 'tis an utter impossibility, and is the same thing as to say that a man believes and yet believes not at the same time. For if he, in his own private judgment, sees no apparent reason, nor don't think that he sees any reason for the truth of such a thing, it is a contradiction to say that he believes, because not thinking in his own private judgment that he sees any reason for the truth is the same as not to believe it in his own private judgment. The papists really think that their church cannot teach anything but what is true, and so believe everything that the clergy teach 'em, guided entirely by their own private judgment, however dark and blind their judgment is. 'Tis because they think in their own private judgment that they see some reason why whatever their clergy teaches should be true, so believe that their clergy are infallible, let the reason of their believing so be their education or whatever 'tis, because that education, or the opinion of their fathers, appears to their dark minds as a reason. Or if their judgments are swayed by their interest, they depend nevertheless upon their private judgment. 'Tis because their interest has this influence on them as to make them think in their own private judgments that they see reason in things when, in reality, there is none. And if a man of a weak

[48] See p. 209, below.

capacity, and sensible of it, had never so great a mind to depend entirely upon the judgment of his superiors and truly to believe as they believed, he could not possibly do it except his own private judgment told him in the first place that there was reason why what those, his superiors, believed should be true. Yea, it is an absolute contradiction to suppose that he should believe what God declared to him for any other reason, viz., that his own private judgment told him that God was omniscent and could not lie, etc.

Love to God[49]

270. Glory of God. That no actions are good but what have the honor of God as their chief end proposed is not necessary. 'Tis very true that no actions are good any further than they have God for their ends, either the glorifying Him or the pleasing Him or enjoying Him; and love to God, or inclination towards Him, must be its spring and motive. Even glorifying God is not a good end, any further than our seeking His glory springs from love. And if a desire of enjoying God springs more from love than a desire [of] honoring him, it is a better principle.

530. Love to God. Self-love. Whether or no a man ought to love God more than himself. Self-love, taken in the most extensive sense, and love to God are not things properly capable of being compared one with another; for they are not opposites or things entirely distinct, but one enters into the nature of the other. Self-love is a man's love of his own pleasure and happiness and hatred of his own misery, or rather, 'tis only a capacity of enjoyment or suffering; for to say a man loves his own happiness or pleasure is only to say that he delights in what he delights; and to say that he hates his own misery is only to say that he is grieved or afflicted in his own affliction. So that self-love is only a capacity of enjoying or taking delight in anything. Now surely 'tis improper to say that our love to God is superior to our general capacity of delighting in anything. Proportionable to our love to God is our disposition to delight in His good. Now our delight in God's good can't be superior to our own general capacity of delighting in anything or, which is the same thing, our delight in God's good can't be superior to our love to delight in general; for proportionately as we delight in God's good, so shall we love that delight. A desire of and delight in God's good is love to God, and love to delight is self-love. Now the degree of delight in a particular thing and the degree of love to pleasure, or delight in general, ben't properly comparable one with another; for they are not entirely

[49] See *Original Sin,* part 1, ch. 1, sec. 5; see also *Nature of True Virtue,* ch. 4.

distinct, but one enters into the nature of the other. Delight in a particular thing includes a love to delight in general. A particular delight in anything can't be said to be superior to love to delight in general; for always in proportion to the degree of delight is the love a man hath to the delight, for he loves greater delight more or less, in proportion as it is greater. If he did not love it more, it would not be a greater delight to him. Love of benevolence to any person is an inclination to their good. But evermore equal to the inclination or desire anyone has of another's good is the delight he has in that other's good if it be obtained, and the uneasiness if it be not obtained. But equal to that delight is a person's love to that delight, and equal to that uneasiness is his hatred of that uneasiness. But love to our own delight or hatred of our own uneasiness is self-love, so that no love to another can be superior to self-love as most extensively taken.

Self-love is a man's love to his own good. But self-love may be taken in two senses, or any good may be said to be a man's own good in two senses. 1. Any good whatsoever that a man any way enjoys, or anything that he takes delight in—it makes it thereby his own good whether it be a man's own proper and separate pleasure or honor, or the pleasure or honor of another. Our delight in it renders it our own good in proportion as we delight in it. 'Tis impossible that a man should delight in any good that is not his own, for to say that would be to say that he delights in that in which he does not delight. Now take self-love for a man's love to his own good in this more general sense—and love to God can't be superior to it. But secondly, a person's good may be said to be his own good as 'tis his proper and separate good, which is his and what he has delight in directly and immediately. Love to good that is a man's own, in this sense, is what is ordinarily called self-love. And superior to this, love to God can and ought to be.

Self-love is either simple, mere self-love, which is a man's love to his own proper, single, and separate good, and is what arises simply and necessarily from the nature of a perceiving, willing being—it necessarily arises from that without the supposition of any other principle. I therefore call it simple self-love because it arises simply from that principle, viz., the nature of a perceiving, willing being. Self-love, taken in this sense, and love to God are entirely distinct and don't enter one into the nature of the other at all. 2. There is a compounded self-love which is exercised in the delight that a man has in the good of another—it is the value that he sets upon that delight. This I call compounded self-love because it arises from a compounded principle. It arises from the necessary nature of perceiving and willing being, whereby he takes his own pleasure or delight, but not from this alone; but it supposes also another principle that determines the exercise of this principle—a certain principle uniting this person with another that causes the good of another to be its good, and makes that to become delight which otherwise cannot. The first arises simply from his own being, whereby that which agrees immediately and directly with his own being is his good, though it arises also from a principle uniting him to another being, whereby the good of that other being does in a sort become his own. This second sort of self-love is not entirely distinct from love to God, but enters into its nature.

Corollary. Hence, 'tis impossible for any person to be willing to be perfectly and finally miserable for God's sake, for this supposes love to God is superior to self-love in the most general and extensive sense of self-love, which enters into the nature of love to God. It may be possible that a man may be willing to be deprived of all his own proper, separate good for God's sake. But then he is not perfectly miserable, but happy in the delight that he hath in God's good. For he takes greater delight in God's good, for the sake of which he parts with his own, than he did in his own. So that the man is not perfectly miserable; he is not deprived of all delight, but he is happy. He has greater delight in what is obtained for God than he had in what he has lost of his own, so that he has only exchanged a lesser joy for a greater. But if a man is willing to be perfectly miserable for God's sake, then he is willing to part with all his own separate good, but he must be willing also to be deprived of that which is indirectly his own, viz., God's good, which supposition is inconsistent with itself; for to be willing to be deprived of this latter sort of good is opposite to that principle of love to God itself, from whence such a willingness is supposed to arise. Love to God, if it be superior to any other principle, will make a man forever unwilling, utterly and finally, to be deprived of that part of his happiness which he has in God's being blessed and glorified, and the more he loves Him, the more unwilling he will be. So that this supposition, that a man can be willing to be perfectly and utterly miserable out of love to God, is inconsistent with itself.

Note. That love of God, which we have hitherto spoke of, is a love of benevolence only. But this is to be observed, that there necessarily accompanies a love of benevolence a love of appetite or complacence, which is a disposition to desire or delight in beholding the beauty of another, and a relation to or union with him. Self-love, in its most general extent, is very much concerned in this, and is not entirely distinct from it. The difference is only this: that self-love is a man's desire of, or delight in, his own happiness. This love of complacence is a placing of his happiness, which he thus desires and delights in, in a particular object. This sort of love, which is always in proportion to a love of benevolence, is also inconsistent with a willingness to be utterly miserable for God's sake; for if the man is utterly miserable, he is utterly excluded [from] the enjoyment of God. But how can man's love of complacence towards God be gratified in this? The more a man loves God, the more unwilling will he be to be deprived of this happiness.

567. Love to God. If a man has any true love to God, he must have a spirit to love God above all, because, without seeing something of the divine glory, there can be no true love to God. But if a man sees anything of divine glory, he'll see that He is more glorious than any other, for whereinsoever God is divine, therein He is above all others. If men are sensible only of some excellency in God that is common with Him to others, [they are] not sensible of anything of His divine glory. But so far as any man is sensible of excellency in God above others, so far must he love Him above others.

739. Love to God. Predominancy of grace. Though it be by many things most evident that there is but little grace in the hearts of the godly, in their present infant state, to what there is of corruption, yet 'tis also very evident by the Scripture that grace is the principle that reigns and predominates in the heart of a godly man in such a manner that it is the spirit that he is of, and so, that it denominates the man. Goodness or godliness prevails in him so that he is called a good man, a godly, righteous man, a saint or holy man; humility predominates, therefore all good men are called humble men; meekness predominates, so that all good men are denominated the meek; mercifulness prevails, so that all good men are called merciful men. So godly persons are represented as such as love God and not the world; for 'tis said, if any man love the world, the love of the Father is not in him. A true disciple of Christ is represented as one that loves Christ above father and mother, and wife and children, houses and lands, yea, [more] than his own life, that loves Him above all and therefore sells all for Him. Now, how can these things consist with his having so little grace and so much corruption, his having so little divine love and so much love to the world? Why can't it be so that a man may [have] some true love to God, and yet that love be so little and the love of the world so much that he may be said to love the world a great deal better than God?

I answer, 'tis from the nature of the object loved rather than from the degree of the principle in the lover. The object beloved is of supreme excellency, of a loveliness immensely above all, worthy to be chosen and pursued and cleaved to and delighted [in] far above all. And he that truly loves loves Him as seeing this superlative excellency, seeing it as superlative, and as being convinced that [it] is far above all. Though a man has but a faint discovery of the glory of God, yet if he has any true discovery of Him, so far as he sees this he is sensible that [God] is worthy to be loved far above all. The Spirit of God is a spirit of truth, and if he makes any true discovery of God, it must be a discovery of Him as lovely above all. If such an excellency is not discovered, there is no divine excellency discovered, for divine excellency is superlative, supreme excellency.

Now, that wherein a godly man may be said to love God above all seems to be built [on], and seems all to be no more than immediately follows: he that has God's supreme excellency thus discovered to him has a sense of heart of His being lovely above all. For spiritual knowledge and conviction consists in the sense of heart. And having such a sort of conviction and sense of heart, it follows that he doth in his heart esteem God above all, so that the love of God reigns in his practical judgment and esteem. And it will also follow, that God predominates in the stated established choice and election of his heart; for he that [has] a conviction and sense of heart of anything, as above all things eligible, must elect that above all. And therefore godly men are often in Scriptures represented as choosing God for their portion, or choosing the pearl of great price above all. From this it will follow that God and holiness predominates in his established purpose and resolution. He cleaves to the Lord with purpose of heart and so, in the sense of the Scriptures, with his whole heart.

Though there may be but little of the principle of love, yet the principle that is being built on such a conviction will be of that nature, viz., to prize God above all. There may be an endless variety of degrees of the principle; but the nature of the object is unalterable, and therefore, if there be a true discovery of the object, whether in a greater or lesser degree, yet if it be true or agreeable to the nature of the object discovered, the nature of that principle that is the effect of the discovery will answer the nature of the object; and so it will evermore be the nature of it to prize God above all, though there may be but little of such a principle.

And so may it be said of the man's love to, and choice of, holiness and of particular graces such as meekness, mercifulness, etc.—he sees the excellency of these things above all other qualifications, hence they predominate in the judgment and choice.

And then another way whereby grace predominates in the soul of a saint is by virtue of the covenant of grace and the promises of God on which Christian grace relies, and which engage God's strength and assistance to be on its side and to help it against its enemy when otherwise it would be overpowered. Where God infuses grace, He will give it a predominance by His upholding of it, and time after time giving it the victory when it seemed for a time to be overborn and ready to be swallowed. This is not owing to our strength, but to the strength of God who won't forsake the work of His hands, and will carry on His work where He has begun it, and always causeth us to triumph in Christ Jesus, who is the author and has undertaken to be the finisher of our faith.

Millenium

26. Millenium. How happy will that state be when neither divine nor human learning shall be confined and imprisoned within only two or three nations of Europe, but shall be diffused all over the world, and this lower world shall be all over covered with light, the various parts of it mutually lighting each other; when the most barbarous nations shall become as bright and polite as England, when ignorant heathen lands shall be packed with most-profound divines and most-learned philosophers; when we shall, from time to time, have the most-excellent books and wonderful performances brought from one end of the world and another to surprise us—sometimes new and wondrous discoveries from *rara Australis incognita,* admirable books of devotion, the most divine and angelic strains from among the Hottentots, and the press shall groan in wild Tartary; when we shall have the great advantage of the sentiments of men of the most-distant nations, different circumstances, customs, and tempers; [when] learning shall not be restricted to particular humans of a nation, or their singular way of making things; when the distant extremes of the world shall shake hands together and all nations shall be acquainted, and they shall all join the facets of their minds in exploring the glories of the Creator, their hearts in loving and adoring Him, their hands in serving Him, and their voices in making the welkin ring with His praise! What infinite advantages will they have for discourse of every kind! To what they know now, there will continually be something new and surprising discovered in one part of the world and another. The vast number of explorers, their different circumstances, their different paths to come at the truth—how many instructive and enlightening remains of antiquity will be discovered here and there now buried amongst ignorant nations!

262. Millenium. 'Tis probable that the world shall be more like Heaven in the millenium in this respect: that contemplation and spiritual employments, and those things that more directly concern

the mind and religion, will be more the saint's ordinary business than now. There will be so many contrivances and inventions to facilitate and expedite their necessary secular business that they shall have more time for more noble exercise, and that they will have better contrivances for assisting one another through the whole earth by more expedite, easy, and safe communication between distant regions than now. The invention of the mariner's compass is a thing discovered by God to the world to that end. And how exceedingly has that one thing enlarged and facilitated communication. And who can doubt but that yet God will make it more perfect, so that there need not be such a tedious voyage in order to hear from the other hemisphere? And so the country about the poles need no longer be hid to us, but the whole earth may be as one community, one body in Christ.

Morality

4. Morality. The controversy about the morality of the Sabbath, or the sanctity of the first day of the week, is founded on the great stress put upon the word 'morality,' and the arbitrary distinction that is made between moral duties and other duties. As much as if the morality of a duty were something given by God to us as a mark to know duties that are lasting from those that are but temporary, whereas morality is nothing but a mixed mode or idea, composed according to the will and pleasure of man, drawn only from a minute circumstance of a duty. If we consider actions without circumstances—and there is no action [that] is either moral or immoral but considers things with their circumstances—every duty whatsoever is a moral duty. A duty that the light of nature teaches is a duty of eternal reason, as much as any duty whatever. Thus the action of killing of a man is no wise a moral evil abstracted from its circumstances. And the action of circumcision is a moral good, and what the light of nature teaches us, and a duty of eternal reason, considered with its circumstances—considered with the circumstances that God has commanded it. For the light of nature teaches us as much that we ought to obey God as that we ought not to do the greatest injury ot our fellow creatures from revenge and malice. And there is as much natural reason for the one as for the other. Circumcision is nonetheless a duty of eternal reason because it is a duty at one time and not another, any more than brothers and sisters marrying together is not an immorality of eternal reason because it is a sin at one time and not another. There is no need to wonder why the command for the observation of the Sabbath is put into the decalogue, because [of which] men call it the moral law; neither is there any reason to question whether baptism and the Lord's Supper are to be observed because men say, "Nothing but what is moral is duty under the Gospel." O, how is the world darkened, clouded, distracted, and torn to pieces by those dreadful enemies of mankind called words!

80. Morality. *Vid.* 4. Only there is this difference, the morality of some duties is more immediate and direct than others; and even of those duties which are commonly called moral, there is a difference, so there are gradual steps from the most immediate to the most indirect.

1123. Moral virtue doth not primarily and summarily consist in truth; for if it were so, love could not properly be said to be the sum of all the moral commands of God and of all moral duties; all moral virtues could not be ultimately resolved into love as their common fountain and summary comprehension; particularly, the virtues of veracity and justice, and those commands of God that require us to speak the truth to our neighbors, and that require human judges to judge justly and according to truth, could not be properly resolved into the law of loving our neighbor as a general law that properly comprehends it, in the ground and reason of it; the virtue of love cannot [i.e., could not] be the comprehension and fountain and reason of those virtues; on the contrary, the love of truth is [i.e., would be] rather the sum and fountain and ground of the law of love. The great command of love don't stand in the place of the root and stock, and the law of truth in the place of branches from this general or common root; but, on the contrary, the law of truth is more general and original and stands in the place of the root, and the law of love is one of the branches from that root or common stock. Such is the case with moral virtues and duties, that general duties and rules contain the ground of particular duties that are, as it were, branches of the general. In particular, that general rule of doing justly implies the ground and reason of a great many particular duties and rules. As for instance, 'tis the duty of a man to pay his debts because that is to do justly; 'tis the duty of a judge to acquit the innocent and condemn him who is evidently guilty because that is to do justly, etc. And if this, therefore, were the case of all moral rules whatsoever with regard to truth—that all are summarily to be resolved into the law of truth as the most general law, comprehending all the rest—then this law or rule of acting according to truth would contain in it the reason of all other laws, and even the law of loving God and our neighbors. The reason why we ought to love God and our neighbors would be this, that we ought to act according to truth. And if so, the laws of speaking and acting according to truth, that forbid lying, etc., could not properly be represented as branches of the general law of love. And, this would not be the reason why we ought to speak and act according to truth—that we ought to speak and act according to love—but on the contrary, the reason why we ought to speak and act according to love would be this—that we ought to speak and act according to truth.

MYSTERIES

83. Theology. The things of Christianity are so spiritual, so refined, so high and abstracted, so much above the things we ordinarily converse with and our common affairs for which we adapt our words; and language not supplying of us with words completely adapted to these high and abstracted ideas, we are forced to use words which do no otherwise exhibit what we would than analogically—which words in their ordinary use do not in everything, but only in some part, exhibit what we intend they should when used in divinity. And therefore religion raises so many shadows and seeming contradictions. And it is for want of distinguishing that in the meaning of words in divinity from what is intended by them in their ordinary use that arise most of the jangles about religion in the world. And to one who is not much for elevated thought, many things, that are in themselves as easy and natural as the things we every day converse with, seem like impossibility and confusion. 'Tis so in every case—the more abstracted the science is, and by how much the higher the nature of those things are of which that science treats, and by so much the more our way of thinking and speaking of the things of that science be beside our way of thinking and speaking of ordinary things, by so much the more will that science abound in paradoxes and seeming contradictions.[50]

184. Union, spiritual. What insight I have of the nature of minds, I am convinced that there is no guessing what kind of unions and mixions by consciousness or otherwise there may be between them. So that all difficulty is removed in believing what the Scripture declares about spiritual unions of the persons of the Trinity, of the two natures of Christ, of Christ and the minds of saints.

583. Christian religion. Mysteries.[51] 'Tis very unreasonable to make it an objection against the Christian revelation that it contains some things that are very mysterious and difficult to our understandings, and that seem to us impossible. If God will give us a revelation from

[50] A similar passage is found in Dwight's edition, vol. 7, p. 268; see also vol. 7, p. 310.

[51] This item is printed in Dwight, vol. 7, p. 215.

Heaven of the very truth concerning His own nature, acts, counsels, and ways, and of the spiritual and invisible world, 'tis unreasonable to expect any other than that there should be many things in such a revelation that should be utterly beyond our understanding and seem impossible. For when was there ever a time when, if there had been a revelation from Heaven of the very truth in philosophical matters and concerning the nature of created things (which are of a vastly lower nature and must be supposed to be more proportioned to our understandings), there would not have been many things which would have appeared, not only to the vulgar but to the learned of that age, absurd and impossible? If those positions in philosophy, which are now received by the learned world as indubitable truths, had been revealed from Heaven to be truths in past ages, they would be looked upon as great mysteries and difficult, and would have seemed as impossible as the most mysterious Christian doctrines do now. I believe that even now, if there should come a revelation from Heaven of what is the very truth in these matters, without deviating at all to accommodate it to our received notions and principles, there would be many things in it that would seem to be absurd and contradictions. I do now receive principles as certain, which once, if they had been told me, I should have looked upon as difficult as any mystery in the Bible. Without doubt, much of the difficulty we have about the doctrines of Christianity arises from wrong principles that we receive. We find that those things that are received as principles in one age, and are never once questioned, concerning which it comes into nobody's thought that they possibly may not be true, are yet exploded in another age as light increases. If God makes a revelation to us, He must reveal to us the truth as it is, without accommodating Himself to our notions and principles, which would be indeed impossible. For those things which are our received notions in one age are contrary to what are so in another; and the word of God was not given for any particular age but for all ages. It surely becomes us to receive what God reveals to be truth, and to look upon His word as proof sufficient, whether what He reveals squares with our notions or not. I rather wonder that the Word of God contains no more mysteries in it. And I believe 'tis because God is tender of us and considers the weakness of our sight, and reveals only such things as He sees that man (though so weak a creature), if of an humble and honest mind, can well enough bear. Such a kind of tenderness we see in Christ towards His disciples, who had many things to say, but forebore because they could not bear 'em yet. God don't depart from truth to accommodate His revelation to our manner of thinking; yet, I believe, He accommodates Himself to our understanding in this manner of expressing and representing things, as we are wont to do when we are teaching little children.

986. Revealed religion. The only way, says Mr. Locke (as quoted by Mr. Shuckford[52] in the *Present State of the Republick of Letters,* vol. 5, p. 114), that reason can teach men to know God must be from considering His works; and if so, His works must be first known and considered before they can teach men to know the author of them. It seems to be but a wild fancy that man was at first raised up in this world and left entirely to himself, to find out by his own natural powers and faculties what was to be his duty and his business in it. If we could imagine the first men brought into the world in this manner, we must, with Diodorus Siculus, conceive them for many ages to be but very poor, sorry creatures. The invisible things of God are indeed to be understood by the things that are made. But men, in this state, would be for many generations considering the things of the world in lower views, in order to provide themselves the conveniences of life from them, before they would reflect upon them in such a manner as should awaken up in their minds any thoughts of a God. And when they should come to consider things in such a light as to discover by them that there was a God, yet how long must it be before they can be imagined to have arrived to such a thorough knowledge of the things of the world as to have just and true notions of Him? We see, in fact, that when men first began to speculate and reason about the things of the world, they reasoned and speculated very wrong. In Egypt, in Chaldea, in Persia, and in all other countries, false and ill-grounded notions of the things which God had made induced them to worship the creatures instead of the Creator, and that at times when other persons who had less philosophy were professors of a truer theology. The descendants of Abraham were worshipers of the God of Heaven when other nations, whose great and wise men pretended to reason about the works of the creation, did in no wise rightly apprehend or acknowledge the workmaster, but deemed either fire or the wind, or the swift air, or the circle of the stars, or the violent water, or the lights of heaven, to be the gods which govern the world. Being delighted with their beauty or astonished at their power, they took them for gods. In a word, if we look over all the accounts we have of the several nations of the earth, and consider everything that has been advanced by any or all the philosophers, we can meet with nothing to induce us to

[52] Samuel Shuckford (c. 1694-1754). *The Present State of the Republic of Letters* was a periodical published in London from 1728 to 1736. The editor, Andrew Reid, was especially interested in new scientific developments. Many New England clergymen had access to this periodical and gleaned from it much scientific and literary information.

think that the first religion of the world was introduced by the use and direction of mere natural reason. But on the other hand, all history, both sacred and profane, offers us various arguments to prove that God revealed to men in the first ages how He would be worshipped; but that when men, instead of adhering to what had been revealed, came to have their own understandings and to set up what they thought to be right in the room of what God Himself had directed, they lost and bewildered themselves in endless errors. This, I am sensible, is a subject that should be examined to the bottom, and I am persuaded, if it were, the result of the enquiry would be this: that he that thinks to prove that the world ever did, in fact, by wisdom know God, that any nation upon earth or any set of men ever did, from the principles of reason only without any assistance from revelation, find out the true nature and the true worship of the deity, must find out some history of the world entirely different from all the accounts which the present sacred and profane writers do give us, or his opinion must appear to be a mere guess and conjecture of what is barely possible, but what all history assures us never was really done in the world.

1100. Mysteries. 'Tis not necessary that persons should have clear ideas of the things that are the subject of a proposition, in order to being rationally convinced of the truth of the proposition. There are many truths of which mathematicians are convinced by strict demonstration, concerning many kinds of quantities, as surd quantities and fluxions, concerning which they have no clear ideas.[53]

1170. Christian religion. Necessity of a revelation. The slow progress the world makes in the investigation of truth, in things that seem pretty obvious, as in the instance of the roundness of the earth, may evince the necessity of a revelation to guide men into the knowledge of truth in divine things that are needful to be known in order to our being happy in the knowledge and favor and enjoyment of God.

1171. Mysteries. If things which fact and experience make certain, such as the miseries infants are sometimes the subjects of in this world, had been exhibited only in a revelation of things in an unseen state, they would be as much disputed as the Trinity and other mysteries revealed in the Bible.[54]

1233. There is nothing impossible or absurd in the doctrine of the incarnation of Christ. If God can join a body and a rational soul

[53] See vol. 7, p. 312.
[54] See vol. 7, p. 319.

together, which are of natures so heterogene and opposite that they cannot of themselves act one upon another, may He not be able to join two spirits together, which are of natures more similar? And if so, He may, for ought we know to the contrary, join the soul or spirit of a man to Himself. Had reason been so clear in it that a god cannot be incarnate, as many pretend, it could never have suffered such a notion to gain ground and possess the minds of so many nations; nay, and of Julian himself, who says that Jupiter begot Aesculapius out of his own proper substance and sent him down to Epidaurus to heal the distempers of mankind. Reason did not hinder Spinoza, Blount, and many other modern philosophers from asserting that God may have a body, or rather that the universe, or the matter of the universe, is God. Many nations believed the incarnation of Jupiter himself. Reason, instead of being utterly averse to the notion of a divine incarnation, both easily enough admitted that notion and suffered it to pass almost without contradiction among the most philosophical nations of the world.

1297. The necessity of revealed religion. Mankind need means of certainty, clearness, and satisfaction in things that concern their welfare, in proportion to the importance of those things; such as whether there be a future state of happiness and misery; what that state is; what the will of God is; what are the things which please Him; what those things which will displease Him and make us the objects of His anger and hatred; whether there be any reconciliation after we have offended, and how it may be obtained. We see that God takes care of mankind and all other creatures that usually they may not be without necessary means, by foresight or something equivalent, for their own preservation and comfortable existence, and that, in things of infinitely less importance.

But it is exceedingly apparent that without a revelation mankind must be forever in the most awful doubt with respect to those things. And not only those things—but if they are not led by revelation and direct teaching into a right way of using their reason, in arguing from effects to causes, etc., they would forever remain in the most woeful doubt and uncertainty concerning the nature and the very being of God.

This appears not only by the state of the heathen world, wise and unwise, learned and unlearned, polite nations and barbarous, ages after ages before the light of Christianity came abroad in the world, but also by what appears among those who in these late ages have renounced divine revelation, even the wisest and greatest of 'em, and such as are of the strongest and most acute abilities. By the account which Dr.

Leland[55] gives of the deistical writers of the last and present ages, Hobbes denied any distinction between soul and body; he denied a future state; he held that we are obliged to obey an infidel magistrate in matters of religion, that thought is free, but when it comes to public confession of faith, the private reason must submit to the public; he owned the being of a God, but says we know no more of Him but that He exists; held that God is corporeal; that by the law of nature all men have a right to all things, and over all persons, and that no way is so reasonable as for any man to anticipate, i.e., by force and wiles, to master all the persons of others that he can, so long as he sees no other power great enough to endanger him; that antecedent to civil laws, all actions are indifferent, nothing being good or evil in itself.

Toland was of opinion that there is no other god but the universe, therein agreeing with Spinoza.

The Earl of Shaftesbury casts reflections on the doctrine of future rewards and punishments, as if it were of disservice to the interests of virtue.

The author of *Christianity Not Founded in Argument*[56] represents even natural religion as not founded in argument any more than revealed, and pretends that all attempts to prove the principles of natural religion by reason, and even the being of a God, have done more harm than good; and takes a great deal of pains to destroy all certainty of reason. He represents it as perpetually fluctuating, and never capable of coming to any certainty in anything, as though truth and falsehood were equally to be proved by it. He absolutely declares against instructing children in religious or moral principles as a wicked attempt to prepossess their tender minds.

Chubb shows himself no friend to the doctrine of a particular providence. He plainly intimates that he looks upon God as having nothing now to do with the good or evil that is done among mankind, and that men's state and circumstances in the world are things which entirely depend on second causes, and in which providence doth not interpose at all. He endeavors to show that no proof can be brought for a future state from the present unequal distribution of things. He discardeth all hope of divine assistance in the practice of that which

---

[55] John Leland (1691-1766) published *A View of the Principal Deistical Writers, etc.* in 1754-1756. In the preface to the second volume and subsequent editions he says that, not long after the publication of the first volume, "I was put in mind of a considerable omission I had been guilty of in making no mention of Mr. Hume." It is in the second volume that he deals with Hume and Bolingbroke. What immediately follows in this item shows that Edwards used the work in which Leland had dealt with Hume, and therefore that this part of the manuscript was written as late as 1756.

[56] The book mentioned, by Henry Dodwell, the younger (c. 1700-1784), was published in 1742.

is good. He insists that prayer to God is no part of natural religion. He represents it as absolutely doubtful whether the soul be material or immaterial, or whether it be distinct from the body; and if it be, whether it be equally perishable with the body and shall die with it, or shall subsist after the dissolution of the body. These are points, he says, which he cannot possibly determine, because he has nothing to ground such determination upon; and at the same time declares that, if the soul be perishable with the body, there can surely be no place for argument with regard to a future state of existence to men or a future retribution. It is easy to see that he inclines most to think the soul is material. He absolutely discards the proof of a future state from the present unequal distributions of divine providence.

He signifies that, if there be a future retribution, 'tis most probable that only those shall be called to an account who have been greatly subservient to the public good or hurt of mankind. And as he supposes but few will be called to an account, so 'tis only for some particular actions—and that they will not be called to an account for foolishly using the names and terms by which the deity is characterized. The only offense against God is, he thinks, the want of a just sense of His kindness and the not making a public profession of gratitude to Him. And whether this will make a part of the grand inquest, he declares himself unable certainly to judge, but he plainly intimates that he thinks it will not, since among men it has been looked upon to be a mark of greatness of soul to despise and overlook such ingratitude rather than to show any resentment at it. The only thing, therefore, for which he supposes men will be accountable is their injuries and benefits one to another, and those only when done to the public. He afterwards sets himself to show that things would be as well ordered in the world without the expectation of a future judgment as with it, and that the belief of it is no great advantage to society.

Mr. Hume declares that the knowledge of the relation of cause and effect is of the highest importance and necessity, and that all our reasonings concerning matters of fact and experience, and concerning the existence of any being, are founded upon it; yet he sets himself to show that there is no real connection between cause and effect, and that there can be no certain nor even probable reasoning from the one to the other. He endeavors to subvert all proofs of a particular providence, of a future state, and of an intelligent cause of the universe. He speaks of the doctrine of the being of a God as uncertain and useless. He opposes the arguments from God's distributive justice for a future state, and denies that we have any evidence of any further degrees of justice in God than we see exercised in this present state.

Lord Bolingbroke insists that we must not ascribe to God any moral perfections distinct from His physical, especially holiness, justice, and goodness; that He has not those attributes according to the ideas we conceive of them, nor anything equivalent to those qualities as they are in us, and that to pretend to deduce moral obligations from those attributes, or to talk of imitating God in His moral attributes, is enthusiasm and blasphemy; that God made the world and established the laws of this system at the beginning, but that He doth not now concern Himself in the affairs of men, or if He doth, that His providence only extends to collective bodies but hath no regard to individuals, to their action or events that befall them; that the soul is not a distinct substance from the body; that the whole man is dissolved at death; that the doctrine of future rewards and punishments is a fiction that hath no real foundation in nature and reason, and that to pretend to argue for future retribution from the apprehended unequal distribution of this present state is absurd and blasphemous; that the sanctions of the law of nature and reason relate not to men individually, but collectively considered; that self-love is the only original spring from which our moral duties and affections flow; that polygamy is founded on the law of nature; that there is no such thing as natural shame or modesty. He intimates adultery not to be contrary to the law of nature, if it can be acted secretly. He seems to think that the law of nature forbids no incest but that of the highest kind, viz., the conjunction between fathers and daughters, sons and mothers. He insists that the ground of the obligation of the law of nature is not in being the work and appointment of God, but its being conducive to human happiness. He holds that the laws of nature in general, and the particulars of moral duty derived from them, are very uncertain, and in which men have always been very apt to mistake and make wrong conclusions.

These things from Dr. Leland's view of deistical writers.

I think a little sober reflection on those things which appear among the deists, in weighing them together with the nature of things, may convince us that a general renunciation of divine revelation, after nations have enjoyed it, would soon bring those nations to be more absurd, brutish, and monstrous in their notions and practices than the heathens were before the Gospel came among them.

For (1) these nations had many things among them derived originally from revelation, by tradition from their ancestors, the ancient founders of nations, or from the Jews, which led 'em to embrace many truths contained in the Scripture. And they valued such traditions. It was not in general their humor to despise such an original of doctrines or to contemn them, supposing they had their first foundation in divine revelation; but rather valued any doctrines highly on this account and had no notion of setting them aside in order to the drawing of everything from the fountain of their own reason. By this means, they had a great deal more of truth in matters of religion and morality than ever human reason would have discovered without those helps. But now the humor of the deists is to reject everything that they have had from supposed revelation, or any tradition whatsoever, and to receive nothing but what they can clearly see, and draw out the demonstrable evidence of, from the fountain of their own unassisted reason.

(2) The heathens, by tradition, received and believed many great truths of vast importance that were incomprehensible; and that was no objection with them against receiving them, that they were above their comprehension. But now, 'tis a maxim with the free thinkers that nothing is to be believed but what can be comprehended; and this leads 'em to reject all the principles of natural religion (as it is called), as well as revealed; for there is nothing pertaining to any doctrine of natural religion, not any perfection of God, nor His very existence from eternity, but what has many things incomprehensible.

(3) The heathens of old, in their reasoning, did not proceed in that exceeding haughtiness and dependence on their own mere singular understanding, disdaining all dependence on teaching, as our deists do, which tends to lead one to reject almost all important truth out of an affectation of thinking freely and independently and singularly. Some of the heathen protested their great need of teaching, and of divine teaching.

(4) The heathens did not proceed with that enmity against moral and divine truth, having not been so irritated by it. They were willing to pick up some scraps of this truth which comes from revelation, and which our deists reject all in a lump. (See a further reason under the next number, viz., No. 1298.)

1298. Necessity of revelation. If we suppose that God never speaks to or converses at all with mankind and has never from the beginning of the world said anything to 'em, but has perfectly let 'em alone as to any voluntary, immediate, and direct signification of His mind to them in any respect (teaching, commanding, promising, threatening, counseling, or answering them), such a notion, if established, would tend exceedingly to atheism. It would naturally tend to the supposition there is no being that made and governs the world. And if it should nevertheless be supposed that there is some being that is in some respect the original of all other beings, yet this notion would naturally lead to doubt of his being properly an intelligent, volitive being, and to doubt of all duties to him implying intercourse, such as prayer, praise, or any address to him, external or internal, or any respect to him at all analogous to that which we exercise towards rulers or friends or any intelligent beings we here see and know. And so it would tend to overthrow every doctrine and duty of natural religion.

Now in this respect deism has a tendency to a vastly greater degree of error and brutishness, with regard to matters of religion and morality, than the ancient heathens; for the heathens had no such notion that the deity never at all conversed with mankind in the ways above mentioned, but received many traditions, rules, and laws, as supposing they came from God, or the gods, by revelation.

1303. Planets, the uncertainty of their being inhabited. That some of the planets are such huge things, so vastly bigger than the globe of the earth, is no certain sign of their being inhabited. This planet we dwell upon may nevertheless be, as it were, elected to infinitely greater and more important purposes. Such an election there is with regard to the seed of plants and animals: whereas one is used for the purposes for which they are fitted—to produce a future plant and animal—vast multitudes are lost and thrown away in divine providence. Those seeds are as great a work of God's, perhaps, as the bodies of Saturn or Jupiter, notwithstanding their vast bulk—the greatness of the bulk is but a shadow of greatness or importance. Nevertheless they may, as it were, be rejected and neglected of God when a far lesser body may be chosen before them; as 'tis with divine election as exercised 'mongst mankind. A poor child may be infinitely more made of by God than some mighty potentate that rules over a large empire, though such a prince is like a vast huge body in comparison with the other; but truly his greatness is but the shadow of greatness.

1340. [57] Reason and revelation. Definition. By reason I mean that power or faculty an intelligent being has to judge of the truth of propositions, either immediately by only looking on the propositions, which is judging by intuition and self-evidence, or by putting together several propositions which are already evident by intuition, or at least whose evidence is originally derived from intuition. Great part of Tindal's arguing, in his *Christianity as Old as the Creation,*[58] proceeds on this ground, that, since reason is the judge whether there be any revelation or whether any pretended revelation be really such, therefore reason without revelation or undirected by revelation must be the judge concerning each doctrine and proposition contained in that

[57] A version of this item may be found in vol. 7, pp. 261ff., see also vol. 7, pp. 208ff.

[58] Published in 1730.

pretended revelation—which is an unreasonable way of arguing. 'Tis as much as to say that, seeing reason is to judge of the truth of any general proposition, therefore in all cases reason alone, without regard to that particular proposition, is to judge separately and independently of each particular proposition implied in or depending and consequent upon that general proposition. For whether any supposed or pretended divine revelation be indeed such is a general proposition, and the particular truths delivered in and by it are particular propositions implied in and consequent on that general. Tindal supposes each of these truths must be judged of by themselves, independently of our judging of that general truth, that the revelation that declares them is the word of God—evidently supposing that, if each of these propositions thus judged of particularly can't be said to be agreeable to reason, or if reason alone will not show the truth of them, then that general proposition that they depend on, viz., that the word that declares 'em is a divine revelation, is to be rejected, which is most unreasonable and contrary to all the rules of common sense and all rules of the proceeding of all mankind in their reasoning and judging of things in all affairs whatsoever. For this is true, that a proposition may be evidently true or we may have good reason to receive it as true, though the particular propositions that depend upon it and follow from it may be such that our reason independent on it can't see the truth, or can see it to be true by no other means than by first establishing that other truth that it depends upon. For otherwise there is an end of all use of our reasoning powers, an end of all arguing one proposition from another; and nothing is to be judged true but what appears true by looking on it directly and immediately without the help of another proposition first established, on which the evidence of it depends.

For therein consists all reason or argumentation whatsoever, viz., in discovering the truth of a proposition whose truth don't appear to our reason immediately or when we consider it alone, but by the help of some other proposition on which it depends. If this be not allowed, we must believe nothing at all but only self-evident propositions; and then we must have done with all such things as arguments. And all argumentations whatsoever and all Tindal's argumentations, in particular, are absurd. He himself, throughout his whole book, proceeds in that very method which this principle explodes. He argues and attempts to prove, or make evident, one proposition by another first established.

There are some general propositions, the truth of which can be known only by reason, from whence an infinite multitude of other propositions are inferred and reasonably and justly determined to be true, and rested in as such, on the ground of the truth of that general proposition from which they are inferred by the common consent of all mankind, being led thereto by the common and universal sense of the human mind. And yet not one of those propositions can be known to be true by reason, if reason considers them by themselves, independently on that general proposition.

Thus, for instance, what numberless truths are known only by consequence from that general proposition that the testimony of our senses may be depended on. Tindal says, p. 157, reason is to judge whether our senses are deceived. The truth of numberless particular propositions cannot be known by reason, considered independently of the testimony of our senses, and without an implicit trust in that testimony. So, that general truth that the testimony of our memories is worthy of credit can be proved only by reason. And yet what numberless truths are there which we know no other way, [which] cannot be known to be true by reason considering the truths in themselves or any otherwise than by the testimony of our memory and an implied faith in this testimony. So, that the agreed testimony of all we see and converse with continually is to be credited is a general proposition, the truth of which can be known only by reason. And yet how infinitely numerous propositions do men receive as truth that can't be known to be true by reason, viewing them separately from such testimony—even all occurrences and matters of fact, persons, things, and actions, works, events, and circumstances, and all other existence that we are told of in our neighborhood, in our country, or any part of the world that others tell us of, that we haven't seen ourselves. So, that the testimony of history and tradition is to be depended on, when attended with such and such credible circumstances, is a general proposition whose truth can be known only by reason. And yet how numberless are the particular truths concerning what has been before the present age that can't be known by reason, considered in themselves and separately from this testimony, which yet are truths of that sort and so circumstanced that all mankind do, ever did, and ever will rely on the truth of.

That the experience of mankind is to [be] depended on, or that those things which the world finds to be true by experience are worthy to be judged true, is a general proposition which none doubts. And by what the world finds true by experience can be meant nothing else than what is known to be true by one or the other of those forementioned kinds of testimony: viz., the testimony of history and tradition; the testimony of those we see and converse with; the testimony of our memories; and the testimony of our senses. I say, all that is known by the experience of mankind is known only by one or more of those testimonies, excepting only the existence of that idea or those few ideas which are this moment present in our minds, or the immediate objects of present consciousness. And yet how unreasonable would it be to say that we must first know these things to be true by reason before we give credit to our experience of the truth of 'em.

Not only are there innumerable truths that are reasonably received as following from such general propositions as have been mentioned, which can't be known by reason if they are considered by themselves, or otherwise than as inferred from these general propositions; but also many truths are reasonably received, and are received by the common consent of the reason of all rational persons as undoubted truths, whose truth not only would not otherwise be discoverable by reason but, when they are discovered by their consequence from that general proposition, appear in themselves not easy and reconcilable to reason, but difficult, incomprehensible, and their agreement with reason not understood. So that men, at least most men, are not able to explain or conceive of the manner in which they are agreeable to reason.

Thus, for instance, it is a truth which depends on that general proposition that credit is to be given to the testimony of our senses, that our souls and bodies are so united that they act on each other. But it is a truth that reason otherwise can't discover. And how it is revealed by the testimony of our senses, reason can't comprehend, or explain, or show, or conceive of any way that that which is immaterial and not solid nor extended can act upon matter which it cannot touch—only matter acts upon that. Or if any chooses to say that the soul is material, then other difficulties arise as great. For reason can't imagine any way that a solid mass of matter, whether at rest or in motion, should have perception, should understand, and should exert thought and volition, love, hatred, etc.

And if it be said that spirit acts on matter and matter on spirit by an established law of the Creator, which is no other than a fixed method of His own, producing effects—still the manner how 'tis possible to be will be inconceivable. We can have no conception of any way or manner in which God, who is a pure spirit, can act upon matter and impel it.

There are several things in mechanics and hydrostatics that, by the testimony of our senses, are true in fact, not only that reason never first discovered before the testimony of sense declared them but, now they are declared, they are very great paradoxes and, if proposed, would seem contrary to reason—at least to the reason of the generality of mankind, and such as are not either mathematicians or of more than common penetration—and what they cannot reconcile to their reason. But God has given reason to the common people to be as much their guide and rule as He has to mathematicians and philosophers.

Even the very existence of a sensible world, which we receive for certain from the testimony of our senses, is attended with difficulties and seeming inconsistences with reason, which are insuperable by the reason at least of most men. For if there be a sensible world, that world either exists in the mind only or out of the mind, and independent on its imagination or perception. If the latter, then that sensible world is some material substance, altogether diverse from all the ideas we have by any of our senses, [as that of] color or visible extension and figure (which is nothing but the quantity of color) and its various limitations (which are sensible qualities which we have by sight) ; and also diverse from any of the sensible qualities we have by other senses, as that [of] solidity (which is an idea we have by feeling), and that [of] extension and figure (which is only the quantity and limitation of those), and so of all other qualities. But that there should be any substance entirely distinct from any or all of those is utterly inconceivable. For if we exclude all color, solidity, or conceivable extension, dimensions, and figure, what is there left that we can conceive of? Is there not a removal in our minds of all existence and a perfect emptiness of everything? But if it be said that the sensible world has no existence but only in the mind, then the sensations themselves, or the organs of sense by which sensible ideas are let into the mind, have no existence but only in the mind. And those organs of sense have no existence but what is conveyed into the mind by themselves, for they are a part of the sensible world. And then it would follow that the organs of sense owe their existence to the organs of sense, and so are prior to them, being the causes or occasions of their own existence—which is a seeming inconsistence with reason, which, I imagine, the reason of all men cannot explain and remove.

There are innumerable propositions that we reasonably receive from the testimony of experience, all depending on the truth of that general proposition that experience is to be relied on (what is meant by experience has been already explained), that yet are altogether above reason and are paradoxes attended with such seeming inconsistencies with reason that reason can't clearly remove nor fully explain the mystery.

By experience we know there is such a thing as thought, love, hatred, etc. But yet this is attended with inexplicable difficulties. If there be such a thing as thought and affection, where be they? If they exist, they exist in some place or no place. That they should exist and exist in no place is above our comprehension. It seems a contradiction to say they exist and yet exist nowhere. And if they exist in some place, then they are not in other places or in all places, and therefore must be confined at one time to one place and that place must have certain limits; from whence it will follow that thought and love and hate have some figure, either round or square or triangular, which seems quite disagreeable to reason and utterly inconsonant to the nature of such things as thought and affection of mind.

'Tis evident, by experience, that something now is; but this proposition is attended with things that reason cannot comprehend, and which are paradoxes that seem contrary to reason, knots that reason cannot clearly untie. For if something now is, then either something was from all eternity or something began to be without any cause or reason of its existence. The last seems wholly inconsistent with natural sense and the other, viz., that something has been from all eternity, implies that there has been a duration which is without any beginning, which is an infinite duration, which is perfectly inconceivable and is attended with difficulties that seem contrary to reason. For we can't conceive how an infinite duration can be made greater any more than how a line of infinite length can be made longer. But yet we see that past duration is continually added to. If there were a duration past, without beginning, a thousand years ago, then that past infinite duration has now a thousand years added to it; and if so, it is greater than it was before by a thousand years because the whole is greater than a part. Now the past duration consists of two parts, viz., that which was before the last thousand years and that which is since. Thus there are seeming contradictions involved in this supposition of an infinite duration past. And moreover, if something has been from eternity, 'tis either an endless succession of causes and effects, as for instance an endless succession of fathers and sons or something equivalent; but this supposition is attended with manifold apparent contradictions (see my sermons on the existence of God), as there must have been some eternal, self-existent being, having the reason of his existence within himself—i.e., he must have existed from eternity without any reason of his existence—both which are inconceivable. That a being should exist from eternity, without any reason why it should be so rather than otherwise, is altogether inconceivable and seems quite repugnant to reason; and that a being should be self-existent or have the reason of his existence within himself seems also inconceivable and never, as I apprehend, has yet been explained.

If there has been anything from eternity, then that past eternity is either an endless duration of successive parts, as successive hours, minutes, etc., or it is an eternal duration without succession. The latter seems repugnant to reason and incompatible with any faculty of understanding that we have; and the other—an infinite number of successive parts—involves the very same contradictions with the supposition of an eternal succession of fathers and sons.

That the world has existed from eternity without a cause seems wholly inconsistent with reason. In the first place, 'tis inconsistent with reason that it should exist without a cause; for 'tis evident that it is not a thing the nature and manner of which is necessary in itself, and therefore it requires a cause or reason out of itself why it is so and not otherwise. And in the next place, if it exists from eternity, then succession has been from eternity, which involves the forementioned contradictions. But if it ben't without a cause, and don't exist from eternity, then it has been created out of nothing, which is altogether inconceivable and what reason cannot show to be possible; and many of the greatest philosophers have supposed it plainly inconsistent with reason. Many other difficulties might be mentioned, as following from that proposition, that something now is, that are insuperable by reason.

'Tis evident by experience that great evil, both moral and natural evil, abounds in the world. 'Tis manifest that great injustice, violence, treachery, perfidiousness, and extreme cruelty to the innocent abound in the world; as well as innumerable extreme sufferings, issuing finally in destruction and death, are general all over the world in all ages. But this could not otherwise have been known by reason, and now is attended with difficulties which the reason of many, yea most, of the learned men and greatest philosophers that have been in the world have not been able to surmount. That it should be so ordered or permitted, in a world absolutely and perfectly under the care and government of an infinitely holy and good God, has a seeming repugnancy to reason that few, if any, have been able fully to remove.

That men are to be blamed or commended for their good or evil voluntary actions is a general proposition received with good reason by the dictates of the natural, common, and universal moral sense of mankind in all nations and ages (which moral sense is commonly plainly included in what Tindal means by reason and the law of nature). And yet many things attend this truth that are difficulties and seeming repugnances to reason, that have proved altogether insuperable to the reason of most of the greatest and most learned men in the world.

I observe further that, when the difficulties which attend any general proposition which is recommended to us as true by any testimony or evidence that (considered by itself) seems sufficient, without contrary testimony or evidence to countervail it, and difficulties attend that proposition, if those difficulties are no greater and of no other sort than what might reasonably be expected to attend true propositions of that kind, then those difficulties are not only no valid or sufficient objection against that proposition, but they are no objection at all. Thus, there are many things that I am told concerning the effects of electricity, magnetism, etc., and many things that are recorded in the philosophical transactions of the Royal Society, which I have never seen and are very mysterious. But being well attested, their mysteriousness is no manner of objection against my belief of the accounts; because, from what I have observed and do know, such a mysteriousness is not other than is to be expected in a particular and exact observation of nature and a critical tracing of its operations. 'Tis to be expected that the further it is traced the more mysteries will appear.

To apply this to the case in hand; if the difficulties that attend that which is recommended, by good proof or testimony, to our reception as a divine revelation and this revelation is attended with difficulties, but yet with difficulties no greater nor of any other nature than such as (all things considered) might reasonably be expected to attend a revelation of such a sort of things of such a nature and given for such ends and purposes and under such circumstances—those difficulties not only are not of weight sufficient to balance the testimony or proof that recommends it, but they are of no weight at all as objections against the revelation. They are not reasonably to be looked upon as of the nature of arguments against it; but on the contrary they may, with good reason, be looked upon as confirmations and of the nature of arguments in its favor.

This is very evident and the reason of it very plain. For certainly whatever is reasonably expected to be found in truth, when we are seeking it, cannot be an objection against truth, when we have found it. If it be reasonably expected in truth beforehand, then reason unites it with truth as one property of that sort of truth. And if so, then reason unites it with the truth after it is found. Whatever reason determines to be a property of any kind of truth, that is properly looked upon, in some degree, as a mark of truth or of truths of that sort, or as belonging to the marks and evidences of it. For things are known by their properties. Reason determines truth by things which reason determines to be the properties of truth. And if we don't find such things belonging to supposed truth that were before reasonably expected in truth of that kind, this is an objection against it rather than the founding of it. The disappointment of reason is rather an objection with reason than something to induce its acceptance and acquiescence. If the expectation be reasonable, then the not answering of it must so far appear unreasonable, or against reason, and so an objection in the way of reason.

Thus, if anyone that is in search for persons or things of a certain kind reasonably expects beforehand that, if he be successful in finding the person or thing of the kind and quality that he is in search of, he shall find it possessed of certain properties—when he hath actually found something with all these properties and circumstances that he expected, he receives it and rests in it so much the more entirely as the very thing that he was in quest of. And surely it would be no argument with him that his invention is not right, that some things that he reasonably expected are wanting; but on the contrary this would rather be an objection with his reason.

In order to judge what sort of difficulties are to be expected in a revelation made to mankind by God, such as Christians suppose the Scriptures to be, we must remember that it is a revelation of what God knows to be the very truth concerning His own nature; of the acts and operations of His mind with respect to His creatures; of the grand scheme of infinite wisdom in His works, especially with respect to the intelligent and moral world; a revelation of the spiritual and invisible world; a revelation of that invisible world which men shall belong to after this life; a revelation of the greatest works of God, the manner of His creating the world and of His governing of it, especially with regard to the higher and more important parts of it; a revelation delivered in ancient languages.

Difficulties and incomprehensible mysteries are reasonably to be expected in a declaration from God of the precise truth as He knows it in matters of a spiritual nature. As we see, things that are invisible and not the objects of any of the external senses are very mysterious, involved much more in darkness, attended with more mystery and difficulty to the understanding than others—as many things concerning even the nature of our own souls themselves, that are the nearest to us, and the most intimately present with us, and so most in our view of any spiritual thing whatsoever.

The further things are from the nature of those things that language is chiefly formed to express—viz., things appertaining to the common business and vulgar affairs of life, things obvious to sense and men's direct view and most vulgar observation without speculation, reflection, and abstraction—the more difficult it is clearly to argue them in words. Our expressions concerning them, when words and language are applied to them, will be attended with greater abstractness, difficulty, and seeming inconsistence, language not being well fitted to express those things, words and phrases not being prepared for that end. Such a reference to sensible and vulgar things, from the original use and design of words and phrases, is unavoidably introduced, that naturally confounds and loses the mind and involves it in darkness. If God gives a revelation of things of religion, it must be mainly concerning those things that are spiritual, or the affairs of the moral and intelligent universe, which is the grand system of spirits. It must be chiefly about Himself and intelligent creatures. It may well be supposed that a revelation concerning another and an invisible world, a future state that we are to be in when separated from the body, should be attended with much mystery. It may well be supposed that things of such a world are of an exceeding different nature from the things of this world, the things of sense and all the objects and affairs which earthly language was made to express, and that they are not agreeable to such notions, imaginations, and ways of thinking that grow up with us and are connatural to us—as we are from our infancy formed to an agreeableness to the things which we are conversant with in this world. Moreover, we could not conceive of the things of sense if we had never had these external senses. And if we had had only some of those senses and not others, as for instance, if we had only a sense of feeling without the senses of seeing and hearing, how mysterious would a declaration of things of those last senses be! Or if we had feeling and hearing, but had been born without eyes or optic nerves, the things of light, being declared to us, would, many of them, be involved in mystery that would appear exceedingly strange to us.

I say, if we were born without eyes or optic nerves; for as to such as are born blind but yet born with optic nerves, I imagine they have some ideas by the state of the optic nerves, other than they could otherwise have, as an idea of darkness or blackness, and without that confused intermixture of specks or streaks of light with blackness, such as is in points in our . . .[59] which I suppose all have when they shut their eyes or when they are in darkness, and possibly such a kind of light, on some occasion, as we have by pressing our eyes with our fingers when they hurt, which confused light is perhaps from some motion of the animal spirits in the optic nerves, though not excited by rays, yet in some degree like that which is excited by a few weak rays.

Thus those that were in this manner without the sense of seeing, but had the other senses, might be informed by all about them that they can perceive things at a distance and perceive as plainly, and in some respects much more plainly, than by touching them, yea, that they could perceive things at so great a distance that it would take up many millions of ages to travel to them. They might be informed many things concerning colors that would all be perfectly incomprehensible, that yet might be believed, and it could not be said that nothing at all is proposed to their belief because they have no idea of color. They might be told that they perceive an extension, a length and breadth of color and termination and limits, and so a figure of this kind of exten-

[59] An illegible word.

sion, and yet that it is nothing that can be felt—which would be perfectly mysterious to them, and would seem to 'em an inconsistence, as they have no ideas of any such things as length, breadth, and line and figure of extension, but only certain ideas they have by touch.

They might be informed by them that they could perceive, at once, the extent and shape of a thing so great and multiform as a tree, which is a thing that it would take them up many days to perceive the extent and shape of by touch, which would seem very strange and impossible.

They might be told that, to them that see, some things appear a thousand times as great as some others that yet are made up of more visible parts, or less visible parts, than they—which would be very mysterious and seem quite inconsistent with reason.

These and many other things would be attended with unsearchable mysteries to 'em concerning objects of sight, and what they could never fully see how they can be reconciled with reason, at least without very long, particular, gradual, and elaborate instruction. And after all, they would not fully comprehend so as clearly to see how the ideas connected in those propositions do agree. And yet I suppose, in such a case the most rational persons would give full credit to things that they had, not by reason, but only by the revelation of the word of them that see. I suppose a person born blind, in the manner described, would nevertheless give full credit to the united testimony of the seeing world in things which they said about light and colors, and would entirely rest in their testimony.

If God gives us a revelation of the very truth, not only about spiritual beings and concerning them in an unexperienced and unseen state, but also concerning a spiritual being or beings of a superior kind and so of an unexperienced nature, entirely diverse from anything we do now experience in our present state and from anything that we can be conscious or immediately sensible of in any state whatsoever that our nature can be in, then especially may mysteries be expected in such a revelation.

The truth concerning any kind of perceiving being of a different nature from ours, though of a kind inferior, might well be supposed to be attended with difficulty, by reason of its diversity from what we are conscious of in ourselves, but much more so when the nature and kind is superior. For a superior perceptive nature may well be supposed in some respects to include and comprehend what belongs to an inferior, as the greater comprehends the less, and as the whole includes a part; and therefore the superior experiences may give him advantage to conceive of what belongs to the nature of the inferior. But on the contrary, an inferior nature don't include what belongs to a superior. When one of an inferior nature considers what belongs to a kind of beings of a nature entirely above his own, there is something belonging to it that is over and above all that the inferior nature is conscious of.

A very great superiority, even in beings of the same nature with ourselves, sets them so much above our reach that many of their affairs become incomprehensible and attended with inexplicable intricacies. Thus many of the affairs of adult persons are incomprehensible and appear inexplicably strange to the understandings of little children; and many of the affairs of learned men and great philosophers and mathematicians, things which they are conversant in and well acquainted with, are far above the reach of the vulgar and appear to them not only unintelligible but absurd and impossible and full of inconsistencies. But much more may this be expected when the superiority is not only in degree of improvement of the faculties and properties of the same kind of beings but also in the nature itself—as to its kind. So that, if there be a kind of created perceptive beings, in their nature vastly superior to the human nature (which none will deem to be impossible) and a revelation should be given us concerning the nature, acts, and operations of this kind of creatures, it would be no wonder if such a revelation should contain some things very much out of our reach, attended with great difficulty to our reason, being things of such a kind that no improvement of our minds, that we are capable of, will bring us to an experience of anything like them.

But above all, if a revelation be made us concerning that being that is uncreated and self-existent, who is infinitely diverse from and above all others in His nature, and so infinitely above all that no improvement or advancement of our nature can give us any consciousness of—in such a revelation it would be very strange indeed if there should not be some great mysteries quite beyond our comprehension, and attended with difficulties which it is impossible for us fully to solve and explain. It may well be expected that a revelation of truth concerning an infinite being should be attended with mystery. We find that the reasonings and conclusions of the best metaphysicians and mathematicians concerning infinities are attended with paradoxes and seeming inconsistencies. Thus it is concerning infinite lines, surfaces, and solids, which are things external. But much more may this be expected in infinite spiritual things such as infinite thought, idea, infinite apprehension, infinite reason, infinite will, love, and joy, infinite spiritual power, agency, etc. Nothing is more certain than that there must be an universal and unlimited being; and yet the very notion of such a being is all mystery, involving nothing but incomprehensibles, paradoxes, and seeming inconsistencies. It involves the notion of a being, self-existent and without any cause, which is utterly inconceivable and seems repugnant to all our ways of conception. An infinite spiritual being, or infinite understanding and will and spirtual power, must be omnipresent, without extension—which is nothing but mystery and seeming inconsistence.

The notion of an infinite eternal implies absolute immutability. That which is in all respects infinite and is so absolutely perfect, and to the utmost degree and at all times, can't be in any respect variable. And this immutability, being constant from eternity, implies duration without succession, and is wholly mystery and seeming inconsistence. It seems as much as to say, an infinitely great or long duration all at once or all in a moment—which seems to be saying an infinitely great in an infinitely little, or an infinitely long line in a point without any length.

Infinite understanding, which implies an understanding of all things, of all existence past, present, and future, and of all truth, and all reason and argument, implies infinite thought and reason. But how this can be absolutely without mutation or succession of acts seems mysterious and absurd. We can conceive of no such thing as thinking without successive acting of the mind about ideas. Perfect knowledge of all things, even of all the things of external sense, without any sensation or any reception of ideas from without is inconceivable mystery. Infinite knowledge implies a perfect comprehensive view of a whole future eternity, which seems utterly impossible. For how can there be any reaching of the whole of this, to comprehend it, without reaching to the utmost limits of it? But this can't be where there is no such thing as utmost limits. And again, if God perfectly views an eternal succession or chain of events, then He perfectly sees every individual part of that chain and there is no one link of it hid from His sight. And yet there is no one link that He sees but that there is a link, yea, innumerable links, beyond it. From which it would seem to follow that there is a link beyond all the links that He sees, and consequently that there is one link, yea, innumerable links, that He sees not, inasmuch as there are innumerable beyond every one that He sees. And many other like seeming contradictions might be mentioned which attend the supposition of God's ominscience. If there be an absolute immutability in God, then there never arises any new act in God or new exertion of Himself, and yet there arises new effects—which seems an utter inconsistence.

And so, innumerable other such like mysteries and paradoxes are involved in the notion of an infinite and eternal intelligent being. Insomuch that, if there had never been any revelation by which God had made known Himself by His word to mankind, the most speculative persons would, without doubt, have forever been exceedingly at a loss concerning the nature of the supreme being and first cause of the universe. And that the ancient philosophers and wiser heathen had so good notions of God as they had seems to be much more owing to tradition, which originated from divine revelation, than from their own invention; though human reason served to keep those traditions alive in the world and led the more considerate to embrace and retain the imperfect traditions which were to be found in any surrounding parts, they appearing, after once suggested and delivered, agreeable to reason.

If a revelation be made of the principal scheme of the wisdom of the supreme and infinitely wise ruler respecting His moral kingdom—wherein His all-sufficient wisdom is displayed in the case of its greatest trial; ordering and regulating the said moral kingdom to its great ends when in the most difficult circumstances; extricating it out of the most extreme calamities in which it had been involved by the malice and subtlety of the chief and most crafty of all God's enemies; it being the principal of all the effects of the wisdom of Him, the depth of whose wisdom is insearchable and absolutely infinite; His deepest scheme, by which mainly the grand design of the universal, incomprehensibly complicated system of all His operations and the infinite series of His administrations is most happily, completely, and gloriously attained; the scheme in which God's wisdom is mainly exercised and displayed—it may reasonably be expected that such a revelation will contain many mysteries.

We see that to be the case even as to many works of human wisdom or art. They appear strange, paradoxical, and incomprehensible [to] those that are vastly inferior in sagacity or entirely destitute of that skill or art. There are many of the effects of human art attended with many things that appear strange, altogether incomprehensible to children and many others, seeming to be beyond and against nature. And in many cases the effect produced not only seems to be beyond the power of any visible means but inconsistent with it. Being an effect contrary to what would be expected, the means seem inconsistent with the end.

If God reveals the exact truth in those things which, in the language of the heathen sages, are matters of philosophy, i.e., not the things of sense and of common life but matters of reflection and speculation—as especially things of morality and theology, things concerning the nature of the deity and the nature of man, so far as [he] is related to the deity, etc.—I say, if God reveals the real, precise truth concerning those things, it may most reasonably be expected that such a revelation should contain many mysteries and paradoxes—considering how many mysteries the doctrines of the greatest and best philosophers in all ages concerning those things have contained; or at least how very mysterious and seemingly repugnant they are to the reason of the vulgar and to persons of less understanding; and considering how mysterious the principles of philosophers, even concerning matters far inferior to those, would have appeared in any former age if they had been then revealed to be true, which, however, are now received as the most undoubted truths.

If God gives mankind His word in a large book, consisting of a vast variety of parts, many books, histories, prophecies, prayers, songs, parables, proverbs, doctrines, promises, sermons, epistles, and discourses of very many kinds, all connected together, all united in one grand drift and design, and one part having a various and manifold respect to others so as to become one great work of God and one grand system, as is the system of the universe with its vast variety of parts connected in one grand work of God—it may well be expected that there should be mysteries, things incomprehensible and exceeding difficult to our understanding, analogous to the mysteries that are found in all other works of God, as the works of creation and providence, and particularly such as are analogous to the mysteries that are observable in the system of the natural world, of the frame of man's own nature.

For such a system or Bible of the word of God is as much the work of God as any other of His works—the effect of the power, wisdom, and contrivance of a God whose wisdom is unsearchable, and whose nature and ways are past finding out. And as the system of nature and the system of revelation are both divine works, so both are in different senses a divine word, both are the voice of God to intelligent creatures, a manifestation and declaration of Himself to mankind. Man's reason was given him that he might know God and might be capable of discerning the manifestations He made of Himself in the effects and external expressions and emanations of the divine perfections.

If it be still objected that it is peculiarly unreasonable that mysteries should be supposed in a revelation given to mankind, because, if there be such a revelation, the direct and principal design of it must be to teach and instruct mankind and so to enlighten and inform their understandings, which is inconsistent with its delivering things to man which he can't understand, and so do not inform and enlighten but only puzzle and confound his understanding, I answer:

1. Men are capable of understanding as much as is revealed, and as much as is pretended to be revealed, though they can't understand everything that belongs to the things that are revealed, and although there are several things pertaining to the things revealed which God has not revealed; as for instance, God may reveal that there are three that have the same nature of the deity, whom it is most proper for us to look upon as three persons, though the particular manner of their distinction and how they differ may not be revealed, and we may there-

fore understand so much as is revealed concerning it. So He may reveal that the Godhead was united to man so as to be properly looked upon [as] the same person, but not reveal how it was effected.

2. No allowance is made in the objection for what may be understood of the word of God in future ages which is not now understood; and it is to be considered that divine revelation is not given only for the present and past ages.

3. The seeming force of this objection lies wholly in this, that we must suppose whatever God does tends to answer the end for which He does it; but that those parts of a revelation that we can't understand don't answer the end, inasmuch as informing our understandings is the very end of a revelation, if there be any such thing. But this objection is no other than just equivalent to an objection which may be made against many parts of the creation, particularly of this lower world. It is apparent the most direct and principal end of this lower world was to be for the habitation, use, and benefit of mankind, the head of this lower world. But here are some parts of it that seem to be of no use to man but rather for his inconvenience and prejudice, as the innumerable stones and rocks that overspread so great a part of the land, which, as to anything known, are altogether useless and of ten times greater inconvenience than benefit.

Thus it is reasonable to expect that in such a revelation there should be many things plain and easy to be understood; and that the revelation should be most intelligible wherever it is most necessary for us to understand it in order to our guidance and direction in the way to our happiness—but that there should also be many incomprehensible mysteries in it, yea, many things very difficult to our reason, in that degree which we have attained of the use of it; many things understood in part, but yet that room should be left for vast improvement in the knowledge of them; that the revelation should be of such a nature, containing such depths and hidden treasures of knowledge, that there should be room for improvement in understanding, and to find out more and more, to all the wisest and best of men, to the end of the world; and that the case, in this respect, should actually be the same as concerning the works of nature; that there should actually be a gradual improvement in the understanding of it; that many things that were formerly great difficulties and insuperable difficulties, unintelligible mysteries, should now by further study and improvement be well cleared and cease to remain any difficulty; and that other difficulties should be considerably diminished, though not yet fully cleared up.

It may be expected that, as in the system of nature, so in this system of revelation there should be many parts whose use is but little understood, and many that should seem wholly useless, yea, and some that should seem rather to do hurt than good.

So I might further observe that, if we have a revelation given in ancient languages used among a people whose custom and philosophy are but very imperfectly understood, many difficulties should arise from hence. And that in any short concise history, where only some particular facts and circumstances that concern the special purpose and design of that revelation are mentioned, and innumerable others are omitted that would be proper to be mentioned if the whole design were to give a clear, full account and clear idea [of] connected, continued history of such a people or such affairs as the history mentions, I say, in such a case, 'tis no wonder that many doubts and difficulties arise.

Nature and Grace

868. Signs of godliness. Sincerity. As the Scripture is plain concerning faith—that the operative or practical nature of it is the life and soul of it—so this is doubtless true concerning all other graces. The Scripture is as plain, that the operative nature of love (that sum of all grace) is the most peculiar criterion of the sincerity of it, and indeed that wherein the sincerity of it consists. That sense of divine things and those religious affections are true, sincere, and saving that reach the bottom of the heart, and that gain the heart. If the heart ben't gained and given to God, there is no sincerity and nothing is accepted; for the heart is what God requires and looks at. But then only is the heart gained when the will is gained, but when the will is gained the practice is gained; for the will commands the practice. Indeed practice, so far as the heart or the soul is concerned, consists in nothing else but the acts of the will. Indeed, there are external motions of the body, but these are no part of the man's practice than [as] those motions are the expressions of his will. We don't call the motions of the body in a convulsion any part of the man's practice.

Religion

w. Tone. A sad tone is to be avoided in public, either in prayer or preaching, because it generally is distasteful; and a whining tone that some use is truly very ridiculous. But a melancholy, musical tone doth really help in private, whether it is private prayer, reading, or soliloquy, not because religion is a melancholy thing, for it is far from it, but because it stills the animal spirits and calms the mind, and fits it for the most sedate thought, the clearest ideas, the brightest apprehension, and strongest reasonings, which are inconsistent with an unsteady motion of the animal spirits. Wherefore this may be a rational account why a melancholy air doth really help religious thoughts, because the mind is not fit for such high, refined, and exalted contemplation of religion, except it be first reduced to the utmost calmness.

x. Pleasantness of religion. It is no argument against true pleasantness of religion that it has no tendency to raise laughter, and rather to discourage [it], for that pleasure which is raised by laughter [is] never great. Everyone knows this by his own experience. And besides it is fleeting, external, and not lasting. The greater part of true pleasure don't raise laughter, as the joy of the light and enjoyment of most dear friends sincerely, but only raises a smile and not shaking laughter, which always rises from a mixture of pleasure and sorrow, and never from pure pleasure...[60] A thing is never ridiculous except there be something in it that is deformed and contrary to the universal law, therefore disagreeable to the soul. But that pleasure which is raised from the apprehension of something purely agreeable never laughs at it.[61] The pleasure of religion raises one clear above laughter, and rather tends to make the face to shine than to screw into a grimace; though, when it is at its height, it begets a sweet, inexpressibly joyful sense and we have only smiles, as so often by the great pleasure of a dear friend's society. The reason why the pleasures of religion be not always attended with such a smile is because we have so many sins and have so much offended God; and almost all our religious thoughts are unavoidably attended with repentance and a sense of our own misery. It is the pleasure of repentance alone that don't tend to a smile. The reason why religious thoughts will cause one to sigh sometimes is not from the melancholiness of religion, but because religious thoughts are of such an high moral and spiritual nature as very much abstracts the soul from the body, and so the operations of the body are deadened. Hence arises a sigh to renew it, as a sigh will arise from weariness of body, whether by sickness or labor, whether one is melancholy or no. 'Tis this abstraction of the soul as it might leave the body of men dead, and then the soul is in a trance.

gg. Religion. 'Tis certain that God did not create the world for nothing. 'Tis most certain that, if there were no intelligent beings in the world, all the world would be without any good at all; for senseless matter, in whatever excellent order it is placed, would be useless if there were

[60] Two or three words are illegible.
[61] See Descartes, *The Passions of the Soul,* art. cxxv.

no intelligent beings at all, neither God nor others. For what would it be good for? So, certainly, senseless matter would be altogether useless if there was no intelligent being but God, for God could neither receive good Himself nor communicate good. What could this vast universe of matter, placed in such excellent order and governed by such excellent law, be good for if there was no intelligence that could know anything of it? Wherefore, it necessarily follows that intelligent beings are the end of the creation, and that their end must be to behold and admire the doings of God and magnify Him for them, and to contemplate His glories in them. Wherefore, religion must be the end of the creation, the great end, the very end. If it were not for this, all those vast bodies we see ordered with such excellency, that are made in nicest rules of proportion, according to such laws of gravity and motion, would be all vanity or good for nothing and to no purpose at all. But religion is the very business, the noble business, of intelligent beings. And for this end God has placed us on this earth. If it were not for intelligence, it would be altogether in vain, with all the curious workmanship and accoutrements about it. It follows from this that we must be immortal. The world had as good have been without us as for us to be a few minutes and then be annihilated—if we are to own God's works, to His glory, and only glorify Him a few minutes and then be annihilated, and it shall after that be all one to eternity as if we never had been, and be in vain, after we are dead, that we have been once. And then, after the earth shall be destroyed, it shall be for the future entirely in vain that either the earth or mankind had ever been.

kk. Religion (corollary on the former on this subject). Since the world would be altogether good for nothing without intelligent beings, so intelligent beings would be altogether good for nothing except to contemplate the Creator. Hence we learn that devotion and not mutual love, charity, justice, beneficence, etc. is the highest end of man, and devotion is his principal holiness; for all justice, beneficence, etc. are good for nothing without it and to no purpose at all. For those duties are only for the advancement of the great business, and assist mutually each other to it.

ll. Religion. It may be said, if religion be really the very business of men for which God made them, it is a wonder 'tis no more natural to them. The world in general, learned and unlearned, say little about it. They are very awkward at it as if it were contrary to their natures. I answer, 'tis no wonder, because sin has brought them down nearer to the beast, a sort of animal incapable of religion at all.

42. Religion. . . .[62] the imagination and the blood would be chilled with the great idea, but this being . . .[62] the greatness, distance, and motion, etc. of this great universe has almost an omnipotent power upon the imagination; by it will man be chilled with the vast idea. But the greatness of vast expanse, immense distances, prodigious bulk, and rapid motion is but a little, trivial, and childish greatness in comparison of the noble, refined, exalted, divine, spiritual greatness. Yea, those are but the shadows of greatness and are worthless except as they conduce to true and real greatness and excellency, and manifest the power and wisdom of God. When we think of the sweet harmony of the parts of the corporeal world, it fills us with such astonishment that the soul is ready to break. Yet take all that infinite variety of sweet proportions, harmonious motions, and delightful correspondencies that are in this whole company of bodies, and they are all but shadows of excellency in comparison of those beauties and harmonies that may be in our finite spirits. That harmony of the world is indeed a very true picture and shadow of the real glories of religion. This great world contains many millions of millions of little worlds vastly greater than it. The glories of astronomy and natural philosophy consist in the harmony of the parts of the corporeal shadow of a world; the glories of religion consist in the sweet harmony of the greater and more-real world within themselves, with one another, and with the infinite fountain and original of them.

Self-Love

473. Natural man. Conversion. Self-love. Common work of the spirit. From a principle of self-love, that is to say, from a love of pleasure and a love of being loved, and a hatred of pain and an aversion to the being hated, many things may arise. First, there may arise the affection of gratitude, for as the soul necessarily loves pleasure or respect, so [it loves] that which the soul sees to be the cause of that pleasure or good, or to be the person that exercises that love and respect. A person may have a kind of benevolence and complacence in an immediate thing that has been the occasion of much delight and pleasure to him, by a certain kind of association of ideas and inclinations and acts of the mind. Ideas that are habitually associated together do partake of one another's love and complacence and benevolence, i.e., in the benevolence and delight the soul exercises towards them. But especially is it natural to the soul to exercise gratitude to persons that it conceives of as not only causes of pleasure but also, therein,

[62] Illegible words.

exercising respect—and that both as it loves the pleasure and the respect. As 'tis natural to the soul to exercise anger or malevolence to a person that it conceives of as hating him and doing him ill, so is there also a natural gratitude in the soul. Math. 5:46, "If ye love them that love you, what reward have ye, do not even the publicans the same?"

2. From self-love a person may come to love another person for good qualifications of mind. If a person conceives of another as having those qualifications of mind that would enable him to do him good and minister to his profit or pleasure, and [as being] disposed to respect and benevolence (which he will look upon as more or less valuable as he conceives of the person as greater or less, more or less considerable and honorable)—this may beget in his mind strong desire of a person's friendship, and of having a propriety in him and union with him, and may for the present cause a kind of benevolence from the person's imagination (whereby he imagines himself as being in friendship and union and enjoyment of him) and a complacence from that love of virtue which there may be from self-love, which we now are about to speak of.

3. There may be a love to many virtues that arises from self-love; so there may be a love of justice and a love of generosity because it conceives of such virtues as tending directly to man's good, and finds and knows that they tend to his own good whenever exercised towards him. And when the contrary vices are exercised, they are for his ill and excite his anger. And so a person may habitually hate it, yet desire it and make association with it. For the person is restrained from such acts himself, and therefore he is not an actor but only a sufferer by such vices, and so he has not benefit but only injury by 'em. For man may come to scorn some vices from pride, [if] it greatly affects his actions and his natural conscience suggests to him the relation between some vices and shame and contempt. A man may hate other vices from the things that usually attend them, as he may hate drunkards for their other vicious dispositions that attend it, as their boisterousness and ungoverned spite and scoffing, which he may hate for the reason aforesaid. A man may dislike men for some vices from envy; for he is restrained and he has not the pleasure of 'em, and his envy in such a case is without restraint, for he looks upon his zeal as good, and gives it the reins.

821. Self-love. Common grace. Saving grace. There are two affections that are natural to men, that do especially seem to imitate virtue. The one is gratitude, or a disposition to love others that love them. 'Tis as easy to account for such an affection's arising from self-love, as [to account for] anger and revenge, whereby men are disposed to hate those that hate them . . .[63]

2. 'Tis very plain, by experience, that pity is an affection natural to men. But this don't argue that men naturally have any true or proper love to others that don't arise from self-love; for men may pity those that they have no love to, provided they don't hate them, or if they do hate them, they may pity them if they see that their misery goes beyond their hatred. Pity is a painful sensation in us arising from the sight or sense of misery in others that is disproportionable to our disposition towards them. Whenever there is a disproportion between our disposition towards others and the state we see them in, it has a tendency to excite uneasiness in us, let that disposition be what it will. When we see those happy that we don't love, or when their happiness exceeds our love, or when their misery is less than our hatred—that excites our envy. And on the other hand, when we see those miserable that we don't hate, or when their misery exceeds our hatred, or when their happiness is less than our love, it excites our pity. This natural pity may excite in men hatred of many acts of sin. We have a remarkable instance in David, when he don't seem to have been much in the exercise of grace. 2 Sam. 12:5, 6, "And David's anger was greatly kindled against the man, and he said to Nathan, as the Lord liveth, the man that hath done this thing shall surely die, and he shall restore the lamb fourfold, because he did this thing, and because he had no pity."

And self-love may have influence to cause men to love virtue many more ways than one would be ready to imagine. The ways of the working of a man's heart are so mysterious that in many instances it may be difficult to give an account how such and such things should arise from self-love.

That natural men should love just, generous, meek, and benevolent persons, and persons possessed of such like virtues, with a love of appetition and complacence, though they have never received any benefit by those virtues in them and possibly have no expectation that ever they shall, is no more unaccountable than that they should love that sweet fruit and pleasant food, the sweetness of which they are sensible of or have an idea of, though they as yet receive no benefit of it, and don't know that ever they shall. Yet they love it, because they conceive of it as in itself tending to their pleasure, if there were opportunity and due application. So they conceive of those mentioned virtues as, in like manner, in their own nature tending to their good. Self-love makes them love the quality in general, in one case as in the other.

A natural [man] may love others, but 'tis some way or other as

[63] Biblical citations are omitted.

appendages and appurtenances to himself; but a spiritual man loves others as of God, or in God, or some way related to Him.

Sin

34. Original sin. There can be no question but that human nature, by some means or other, however it came about, is now, in these days, all over the world, in every man that comes into the world, very much vitiated. Now the rectitude of human nature and of rational beings most certainly is that they should be most highly affected with the highest excellencies, and less affected with lower excellencies; that the mind should have the sweetest taste and most perfect, exquisite delight of those things that are truly most delightful, and a lower delight and slower relish of those things that in themselves are less delightful; that the things that are most beautiful and amiable, as soon as ever they are seen, should most delight the eye, and those things which are less beautiful should less please the sight; that man should have the quickest and easiest sight and most-delightful perception of that which is best, and the slowest and dullest perception of that which is less good. This is the rectitude of human nature, and thus humans once were; or else most certainly human nature proceeded from God as an inconsistent, self-repugnant, and contradictory thing. But we know, as well as we know that we have being, that this rectitude is not the present state of human nature but the right contrary, in all universally, till human nature, by some means after we are born, is wrought up into this rectitude again. We are the highest species with the lowest excellencies. We have the easiest and greatest delight in things that in themselves are least delightful. Things that are less beautiful and amiable in themselves strike much quicker and deeper with the sense and proportion and constitution of the mind than things that have in themselves the highest excellence, most charming beauty, and exquisite sweetness. Yea, we can hardly bring ourselves to be in any measure pleased with the beauty, or to taste any sweetness at all, in things that are infinitely the greatest excellencies. How much soever one has been out of the way of ill examples or from the practice of vice, set before his eyes or represent to his mind the brightest and most amiable instances of virtue, and his mind responds but very heavily at the perception; but bring before [him] beauty of body, and some of the meanest perfections of mind, and the soul comes immediately alive and in a near rapture. And so in all other cases.

44. Eternal torments. Question. Seeing that the malicious or evil principle, which is the essence of the sin, is not infinite, though the God

against whom sin is committed be infinite, how can it be just to punish sin with an infinite punishment? I acknowledge, if man at the same time that he injured God had actually a full and complete idea of the infinite excellency and greatness of God whom he injured, he could not injure Him without an infinite pravity of soul; and then infinite punishment would undoubtedly be deserved. But all finite beings are uncapable of this full idea. Wherefore it is impossible for them to have this infinite restraint, nor of pravity of infinite strength to break through restraint. It seems that the pravity of an action is not to be measured by the real hidden excellency or greatness of the person offended, but by the understand[ing] the offender has of his greatness. That which was hidden is no aggravation, because he did not know it. If his idea be finite, then a finite pravity of mind is sufficient to conquer that idea.

Answer. Eternal punishment is just in the same respects infinite as the crime, and in no other; thus the crime or injury done, in itself considered, is really infinite, yet is finite in the idea or mind committing [it], that is, is in itself infinite but is not committed infinitely; so it is with the punishment. It is really in itself infinite but is never suffered infinitely. Indeed, if the soul was capable of having at once a full and complete idea of the eternity of misery, then it would properly be infinite suffering; but the soul is no more capable of having a full idea of that than of the infinite greatness and excellency of God, and we should have as full and as strong an idea of God's infinite perfection as the damned have of the eternity of their torment, if it were not for sin. Eternity is suffered as an infinite God is offended, that is, according to the comprehension of the mind. Then, if it were possible for a man eternally to be in pain, and all the while be deceived and think that he had suffered not above half an hour, and was assured that he was not to suffer above half an hour longer—though the misery in God's idea would be infinite, yet in the suffering it is finite, in the suffering it is no more than if one should partake of nothing, and suffer one hour, and drop into nothing again. Sin against God, in God's idea, is infinite, and the punishment is infinite no otherwise but in the idea of God; for all that is past and all that is to come, that is not comprehended in finite ideas, is not anywhere else but in the divine idea. See where we have proved that nothing has any existence but in ideas.[64]

301. Sin and original sin. The best philosophy that I have met with of original sin and all sinful inclinations, habits, and principles is that of Mr. Stoddard of this town of Northampton; this is that it is self-love, in conjunction with the absence of the image and love of God—that

[64] *Of Being.*

natural and necessary inclination that man has to his own benefit, together with the absence of original righteousness. Or in other words [it is] the absence of that influence of God's spirit, whereby love to God and to holiness is kept up to that degree that this other inclination is always kept in its due subordination; but this being gone, his self-love governs alone and, having not the superior principle to regulate it, breaks out into all manner of exorbitancies, and becomes in innumerable cases a vile and odious disposition and causes thousands of unlovely and hateful actions. There is nothing in the actions we call sin, but only the same self-love that necessarily belongs to that nature, working and influencing without regulation from that superior principle that particularly belongs to our nature and that is necessary in order to the harmonious exercise of it. This natural and necessary inclination to ourselves, without the governor and guide, will certainly, without anything else, produce or rather will become all those sinful inclinations which are in the corrupted nature of man . . .[65]

566. Law. Sin. Duty. It hardly seems to me true to say that the command of God is the prime ground of all the duty we owe to God. Obedience is but one part of the duty we owe to God. 'Tis our duty to love God, to honor Him, and have a supreme regard to Him, and submit to Him, and praise Him, and obey Him. These are distinct duties. To obey God is not a general, that under which the rest are properly included as particulars. That don't comprise the general nature and reason of all the rest. It is not the prime reason or ground of our obligation to love and honor God, that is, our duty to obey Him. I acknowledge that we are commanded to love and honor God, and that we ought to love and honor Him in obedience to that command, seeing God has commanded it; but our obligation to obedience is not the prime ground of our duty to love Him and honor Him; but, on the contrary, our obligation to love and honor God and to exercise a supreme regard to God is the very proper ground of our obligation to obey. That is the very reason that 'tis our duty to do as God bids us, because we have such a supreme regard, love, and honor to Him, as disobedience is quite contrary to. A command of any being can't be the prime foundation of obligation because there must be something prior, as a reason

[65] Solomon Stoddard, grandfather of Edwards and his predecessor and colleague in the Northampton pulpit, published a sermon, *Natural Men under the Government of Self-Love*, in 1717. See Dwight's edition, vol. 1, p. 662. I have included this paragraph from no. 301 because it records Edwards' acknowledgment of the debt to his grandfather and because the present tense used by Edwards probably indicates that it was written while Stoddard was still living. Stoddard died two years after Edwards went to Northampton. The remainder of 301 is omitted because it adds nothing Edwards' doctrine of original sin.

why a command is obligatory, and why obedience is due to it. If anyone should ask me why I am obliged to obey God more than the king of France, it would not be proper for me to answer, because God commands me to obey Him. There is something prior to God's command that is the ground of, and reason why, His command obliges.

676. All that a natural man doth is sin. *Vid.* Shephard's *Sincere Convert,* p. 105.[66] Let a woman seek to give all the content to her husband that may be, not out of any love to him but only out of love to another man; he abhors all that she doth.

Spiritual Knowledge

aa. Faith. There may undoubtedly be such a thing as is called the testimony of faith, that is, a sort of certainty of faith that is different from reason, that is, is different from discourse by a chain of arguments—a certainty that is given by the Holy Spirit. And yet such a belief may be altogether agreeable to reason, agreeable to the exactest rules of philosophy. Such ideas of religion may be in the mind, and a man may feel divinity in them and so may know they are from God, that our religion is of divine original; that is, it is divine truth. This faith may be to that degree of certainty, for he may certainly, intuitively see God and feel Him in those ideas; that is, he may certainly see that notion he has of God in them. This notion of God, or idea I have of Him, is that complex idea of such power, holiness, purity, majesty, excellency, beauty, loveliness, and ten thousand other things. Now when a man is certain he sees those things, he is certain he sees that which he calls divine. He is certain he feels those things to which he annexes the term 'God'; that is, he is certain that, when he sees and feels, he sees and feels. And he knows that what he thus sees and feels is the same thing he used to call God. There is such an idea of religion in his mind when he knows he sees and feels that power, that holiness, that purity, that majesty, that love, that excellency, that beauty and loveliness, that amounts to his idea of God. Now no man can say such a thing cannot be. A man may see a beauty, a charmingness, and feel a power that he can no way in the world describe. 'Tis so in corporeal beauties, in beautiful charming airs, etc., but even in those ideas that are very much abstracted from body. Then this is granted that he may feel such an excellency that may amount to his idea of God. But then you'll say, God and religion are the same. I say so much, that religion is tinged with a divine color, and of His air. And that is all the question, whether it has divine excellencies or no. That is, a certain property

[66] Thomas Shepard (1604-1649), *The Sincere Convert,* 1641.

is seen and felt in religious faith that is altogether ineffable and can't be called either powers of harmony or majesty, because neither of these half imply it, but rather divinity, which strongly certifies the mind that it is divine. Now no man can deny but that such an idea of religion may possibly be wrought by the Holy Spirit. 'Tis not unphilosophical to think so, and if there actually is such a thing, as we have shown may be, it may very significantly be called the testimony of the Spirit. This way of knowing or believing is very differing from all other kinds of knowledge or belief. 'Tis not by discourse, neither is it by intuition as other intuitions, neither can this kind of faith or this sort of knowledge be exercised in any common objects. For there are no such distinguishing, amiable properties of such a force as to draw the mind at such a rate as the divine properties.

123. Spiritual sight. When we explain spiritual things that consist in mental motions, energies, and operations, though we give the most accurate descriptions possible, we do not fully explain them, no, not so much as to give any manner of notion of them to one that never felt them, any more than we can fully explain the rainbow to one that never saw, though a rainbow is a very easy thing to give a definition of. Thus, for instance, there is a certain sweet motion of the mind that I call benevolence. 'Tis easily explained by general terms, circumstances, effects, and observations. But yet, the complex idea I have of benevolence consists chiefly of some simple ones that are got only by the internal feeling and sense of the mind. Yea, those spiritual ideas are of such a nature that, [even if] a person has once had them in the mind, having obtained them by actual sense, yet it may be impossible for him to bring the idea into his mind again distinctly, or indeed at all. We can't renew them when we please, as we can our idea of colors and figures, but [only] at some times when mind is particularly adapted to the reception of that idea. I can't have in my mind the idea of benevolence except the disposition of my mind is something benevolent or agreeable to that idea. At other times I have only a general idea of it by the effects of it, to wit, that 'tis an inclination to another's happiness, etc.; but those simple spiritual ideas that are most essential and considerable in it my mind is destitute of, and I have no more an idea of benevolence than a man has of a rainbow that has lost the idea of the colors. So it is in the more-complex spiritual ideas, such as holiness, humility, charity, which include many of those simple spirituals that are to the mind, as colors to the eye, not to be obtained by description. 'Tis thus in all virtues, so that 'tis no wonder the wicked man sees not the amiableness of holiness; for he has not that idea that is expressed by the holy by the name of holiness. 'Tis not because their minds are

not as apt to be delighted with harmony and proportion as others, but because they have not these ideas in which the sweet harmony consists. And it's impossible they should, because they never obtained them by internal sense and experience. The godly man's idea of God consists very much of these spiritual ideas, that are complicated of those simple ones [of] which the natural man is destitute. But as soon as ever he comes to have the disposition of his mind changed, and to feel some of those operations of mind by means of which he gets those simple ideas, [so] that he sees the beauty of them, so he gets the sight of the excellency of holiness and of God—though after this, when his mind is again indisposed, he will not be able to repeat those ideas. And at some times, according as God makes the internal disposition of his mind more or less agreeable thereto, will he have ideas more or less clear.

Corollary 1. Hence we have the reason why regeneration is so often in Scripture compared to opening the eyes of the mind, to calling out of darkness into marvelous light, enlightening the dark understanding, etc.

Corollary 2. Why the things of the Gospel seem all so tasteless and insipid to the natural men—they are a parcel of words to which they, in their own minds, have no correspondent ideas. 'Tis like a strange language or a dead letter, that is, sounds and letters without any signification. This is the reason they commonly account religion such a foolish thing, and the saints fools. This is the reason the Scripture is not sweet to them, and why the godly are called by the name of fanatics, and the like.

Corollary 3. Why spiritual knowledge is increased only by the practice of virtue and holiness—for we cannot have the idea without the adapted disposition of mind. And the more suitable the disposition, the more clear and intense the idea; but the more we practice the more is the disposition increased.

Corollary 4. From hence it necessarily follows that the best and most-able men in the world, with their greatest diligence and laboriousness, most-eloquent speaking, clearest illustrations, and convincing arguments, can do nothing towards causing the knowledge of the things of the Gospel. For the disposition, as we have shown, must necessarily be changed first.

201. Faith. There is such a thing as an appearing real, that is, [a] conviction of that quality of a thing that is incommunicable, that cannot be drawn out into formal arguments or be expressed in words, which is yet the strongest and most-certain conviction. We know how things appear that are real, with what an air. We know how those things appear which we behold with waking eyes. They appear real because we have a clear idea of them in all their various mutual relations and concurring circumstances, modes, and dispositions—the consent of the simple ideas among themselves, and with the congery of beings, and the whole train of ideas in our minds, and with the nature and constitution of our minds themselves, which consent and harmony consists in ten thousand little relations and mutual agreements that are ineffable. Such is the idea of religion (which is so exceedingly complex) in the minds of those who are taught by the Spirit of God. The idea appears so real to them and brings so many strong yet ineffable marks of truth, that 'tis a sort of intuitive evidence and an evidence that the nature of the soul will not allow it to reject. This is the testimony of the Spirit, and is a sort of seeing rather than reasoning the truth of religion, which the unlearned are as capable of as the learned, and which all the learning in the world can never overthrow.

238. Trinity. Those ideas which we call ideas of reflection, all ideas of the acts of the mind (as the ideas of thought, of choice, love, fear, etc.)—if we diligently attend to our own minds we shall find they are not properly representations but are, indeed, repetitions of these very things, either more fully or more faintly. They, therefore, are not properly ideas. Thus, 'tis impossible to have an idea of thought or of an idea, but it will [be] that same idea repeated. So if we think of love, either of our past love that is now vanished, or of the love of others which we have not, we either so frame things in our imagination that we have for a moment a love to that thing or to something we make represent it, or we excite for a moment that love which we have, and suppose it in another place; or we have only an idea of the antecedents, concomitants, and effects of loving and suppose something unseen, and govern our thoughts about [it] as we have learned how by experience and habit. Let anyone try himself in a particular instance and diligently observe. So if we have an idea of a judgment, not our own, we have the same ideas that are the terms of the proposition repeated in our own minds, and as being something in our own minds that is really our judgment, and suppose it there; that is, we govern our thought about it as if it were there, if we have a distinct idea of that judgment, or else we have only an idea of the attendants and effects of that judgment, and supply the name and our actions about it as we have habituated ourselves. And so, certainly, it is in all our spiritual ideas. They are the very same things repeated, perhaps very faintly and obscurely, and very quick and momentaneously, and with many new references, suppositions, and translations; but if the idea be perfect, it is only the same thing absolutely over again.

Now if this be certain, as it seems to me to be, then it's quite clear that, if God doth think of Himself and understand Himself with perfect clearness, fullness, and distinctness, that idea He hath of Himself is absolutely Himself again, and is God perfectly to all intents and purposes. That which God knowest of the divine nature and essence is really and fully the divine nature and essence again. So that, by God's thinking of Himself, the deity must certainly be generated. This seems exceeding clear to me. God doubtless understands Himself in the most perfect sense; for therein His infinite understanding chiefly consists. And He understands Himself at all times perfectly, without intermission or succession in His thought.

When we have the idea of another's love to a thing, if it be the love of a man to a woman that we are unconcerned about, we neither love in such cases nor have generally any proper idea at all of his love. We only have an idea of his actions that are the effects of love, as we have found by experience, and of those external things which belong to love and which appear in case of love. Or if we have any idea of it, it is either by forming our ideas so of persons and things, as we suppose they appear to them, that we have a faint vanishing notion of that affection; or if the thing be a thing that we so hate that this can't be, we have our love to something else faintly, at least, excited, and so in the mind, as it were, referred to that place. We think this is like that.

239. Spiritual knowledge. From what has been said under the foregoing head, we know wherein spiritual knowledge consists. For seeing, in order to the knowledge of spiritual things, there must be those things in the mind (at least in order to a knowledge anything clear and adequate), sinners must be destitute even of the ideas of many spiritual and heavenly things and of divine excellencies, because they don't experience them. 'Tis impossible for them so much as to have the idea of faith, trust in God, holy resignation, divine love, Christian charity, because his mind is not possessed of those things, and therefore can't have an idea of the excellencies and beauties of God and Christ, of which those things are the image. He knows not the things of the Spirit of God.

248. Spiritual knowledge. It need not be at all strange that sin should so blind the mind, seeing our particular natural temper oftentimes very much blinds us in similar affairs, as when our natural temper is melancholy, or jealous, cowardly, and the like.

256. Faith. One that is well acquainted with the Gospel and sees the beauties, the harmonies, the majesties, and the power, the glorious wisdom of it, and the like, may, only by viewing of it, be as certain that it is no human work as a man that is well acquainted with mankind and their works may, by contemplating the sun, know it is not a human work—or when he goes upon an island and sees the various trees, and the manner of their growing and blossoming and bearing fruit, may know that they are not the work of man.

397. Conversion. Spiritual knowledge. Hence we learn that the prime alteration that is made in conversion, that which is first and the foundation of all, is the alteration of the temper and disposition and spirit of the mind. For what is done in conversion is nothing but conferring the Spirit of God, which dwells in the soul and becomes there a principle of life and action. 'Tis this is the new nature, and the divine nature; and the nature of the soul being thus changed, it admits divine light. Divine things now appear excellent, beautiful, glorious, which did not when the soul was of another spirit. Indeed, the first act of the Spirit of God, or the first that this divine temper exerts itself in, is in spiritual understanding or in the sense of the mind, its perception of glory and excellency, etc.—in the ideas it has of divine things. And this is before any proper acts of the will. Indeed, the inclination of the soul, as immediately exercised in that sense of the mind which is called spiritual understanding or the intellect's love, is not only mere presence of ideas in the mind, but it is the mind's sense of their excellency, glory, and delightfulness. By this sense or taste of the mind, especially if it be lively, the mind distinguishes truth from falsehood.

408. Spiritual knowledge When the ideas themselves appear more lively and with greater strength and impression, as the ideas of spiritual things do [to] one that is spiritually enlightened, their circumstances and various relations and connections between themselves and with other ideas appear more; there are more of those habitudes and respects taken notice of, and they also are more clearly discerned. And therefore, hereby a man sees the harmony between spiritual things, and so comes to be convinced of their truth. Ratiocination, without this spiritual light, never will give one such an advantage to see things in their true relations and respects to other things, and to things in general. A mind, not spiritually enlightened, beholds spiritual things faintly, like fainting, fading shadows that make no lively impression on his mind—like a man that beholds the trees and things abroad in the night. The ideas ben't strong and lively and [are] very faint, and therefore he has but a little notion of the beauty of the face of the

earth. But when the light comes to shine upon them, then the ideas appear with strength and distinctness; and he has that sense of the beauty of the trees and fields given him in a moment which he would not have obtained, by going about amongst them in the dark, in a long time. A man that sets himself to reason without divine light is like a man that goes in the dark into a garden full of the most beautiful plants, and most artfully ordered, and compares things together by going from one thing to another to feel of them all, to perceive their beauty; but he that sees by divine light is like a man that views the garden when the sunlight shines upon it. There is, as it were, a light cast upon the ideas of spirtual things in the mind of the believer which makes them appear clear and real, which before were but faint, obscure representations.

489. Faith or spiritual knowledge. Preamble to the discourse on faith or spirit[ual] knowledge. There are these two ways in which the mind can be said to be sensible that anything is good or excellent:

1. When the mind judges that anything is such as, by the agreement of mankind, is called good or excellent, viz., that which is most to general advantage, and that between which and reward there is a suitableness, or that which is agreeable to the law of the country or law of God—'tis a being maturely convinced in judgment that a thing is according to the meaning of the word 'good,' as that word is generally applied.

2. The mind is sensible of good in another sense, when it is so sensible of the beauty and amiableness of the thing that 'tis sensible of pleasure and delight in the presence of the idea of it. This kind of sensibleness of good carries in it an act of the will or inclination, or spirit of the mind, as well as the understanding.

540. Spiritual understanding. Remember, when speaking of the creation of man and the state and nature with which he was created, to distinguish between mere speculative and rational understanding and that which it implies—a sense of heart—or [which] arises from it, wherein is exercised not merely the faculty of understanding but the other faculty of will or inclination in the heart. And to make a distinction between the speculative faculty and the heart, and then to show how many principles of heart God created man with, viz., natural and supernatural principles.

541. Spirit's operation. In the order of beings in the natural world, the more excellent and noble any being is, the more visible and immediate the hand of God is there in bringing them into being. And the most

noble of all, and that which is most akin to the nature of God, viz., the soul of man, is most immediately and directly from Him, so that here second causes have no causal influence at all. Second causes have something to do in bringing the body into being, but they have no influence here; but the soul is directly breathed from God. Heb. 12:9; Eccles. 12:7; Zach. 12:1. And so it is in this moral and spiritual world that the most noble and excellent gift and qualification (wherein is the glory and happiness of that most noble creature, the soul of man) is immediately from God. This is the excellency and dignity of this excellent and noble being, the soul, of which God is the immediate Father. All rational knowledge and outward virtue without this is but the body without the spirit. 'Tis the soul of all virtue and religious knowledge.

628. Spiritual knowledge. Faith. That spiritual light that is let into the soul by the Spirit of God discovering the excellency and glory of divine things. It not only directly evidences the truth of religion to the mind—as this divine glory is an evident stamp of divinity and truth—but it sanctifies the reasoning faculty and assists it to see the clear evidence there is of the truth of religion in rational arguments, and that two ways, viz., as it removes prejudices and so lays the mind more open to the force of arguments, and also secondly, as it positively enlightens and assists it to see the force of rational arguments, not only by removing prejudices but by adding greater light, clearness, and strength to the judgment in this matter. See how one way, No. 408.[67]

1090. Faith. Divine or a spiritual conviction of the truth of things of religion. Some have objected against a spiritual sight of divine things in their glorious, excellent, and divine form, as being the foundation of a conviction of the truth or real existence of 'em—because, say they, the existence of things is in the order of nature before forms or qualities of them, as excellent or odious. And so the knowledge of their existence must go before the sight of their form or quality. They must be known to be before they are seen to be excellent. I answer, it is true, things must be known to be before they are known to be excellent, if by this proposition this be understood: that things must be known really to exist before they can be known really to exist excellent[ly] or really to exist with such and such a beauty. And all the force of the objection depends on such a meaning of this assertion. But if thereby be intended that things must be known to have a real existence before the person has a clear understanding, idea, or appre-

[67] See p. 249, above.

hension of the thing proposed or objected to his view, as it is in its qualities either odious or beautiful, then the assertion is not true. For his having a clear idea of something proposed to his understanding or view as very beautiful or very odious, as it is proposed, does not suppose its reality; that is, it does not presuppose it, though its real existence may perhaps follow from it. But in our way of understanding things in general, of all kinds, we first have some understanding or view of the thing in its qualities before we know its existence. Thus it is in things that we know by our external senses, by our bodily sight for instance. We first see them, or have a clear idea of them by sight, before we know their existence by our sight. We first see the sun and have a strong, lively, and clear idea of it in its qualities, its shape, its brightness, etc., before we know there actual exists such a body.

Soul, Immaterial

361. Soul of man. Matter. Thought. *Vid.* Mind, p. [8] 40.[68]

Title to a Treatise

1168. Title to a treatise. The nature of true virtue, and the way in which it is obtained.[69]

Trinity

94. Trinity.[70] There has been much cry of late against saying one word, particularly about the Trinity, but what the Scripture has said.

[68] The "8" has been crossed out in the manuscript. It may have been a reference to no. 8 in the list of topics appended to *The Mind* (p. 70, above). The reference to "40" does not appear to be to the same series and it can hardly be taken to refer to that number in *The Mind* as given by Dwight (p. 42, above). It might be a reference to what Dwight numbers "21" (p. 34, above). It is of some interest that in the so-called index to *The Mind* (see p. xv, n. 31, an entry, "Matter's Thinking, p. 40," is strikingly like the writing, ink, and pen of *Miscellanies*, no. 361, and very unlike any other entry in the "index." It is tempting to think that, when Edwards wrote no. 361, he was then planning a reorganization and expansion of *The Mind*. No. 40 might then refer to what we know as no. 21 by the number assigned to it in some other arrangement, actual or proposed. There is reason to think that no. 361 was written after Edwards settled in Northampton. See my paper, "Jonathan Edwards's Later Interest in Nature," *New England Quarterly*, vol. 13, 1940, pp. 512ff.

[69] This note probably indicates that Edwards was preparing his *Dissertation concerning the Nature of True Virtue* when he wrote no. 1168.

[70] No. 94 was first published by E. C. Smyth in 1904 in *Exercises Commemorating the Two-Hundredth Anniversary of the Birth of Jonathan Edwards*, Appendix 1, pp. 8-16. The text there printed is that of the Dwight copy in the Andover-Newton Theological Library. The original manuscript is at present so faded and difficult to read that I have in a few instances supplied illegible words from Smyth's text.

judging it impossible but that, if we did, we should err in a question so much above us. But if they call that which rises and results from the joining of reason and Scripture, though it has not been said in Scripture in express words, I say, if they call this what is not said in Scripture, I am not afraid to say twenty things about the Trinity which the Scripture never said. There are deductions of reason from what has been said of the most mysterious matters, besides what has been said, and safe and certain from 'em too, as well as about the most obvious and easy matters.

I think that it is within the reach of naked reason to perceive certainly that there are three, distinct in God, the nature of which is one, and the three are manifestly distinct; and that there are not nor can be any more distinct, really and truly distinct, but three, either distinct persons or properties or anything else; and that of these three one is, more properly than anything else, begotten of the first, and that the other proceeds alike from both, and that the first neither is begotten nor proceeds. 'Tis often said that God is infinitely happy from all eternity in the enjoyment of Himself, in the reflection and infinite love of His own essence, that is, in the infinite idea He has of Himself, infinitely perfect. The Almighty's knowledge is not so different from ours, but that ours is the image of [it]. It is by an idea, as ours is, only 'tis infinitely perfect. If it were not by idea, it is in no respect like ours; 'tis not what we call knowledge nor anything whereof knowledge is the resemblance, for the whole of human knowledge, both in the beginning and end, arises by ideas. 'Tis also said that God's knowledge of Himself includes the knowledge of all things, and that He knows, and from eternity knew, all things by the looking on Himself and by the idea of Himself, because He is including all things—so that all God's knowledge is the idea of Himself. But yet it don't suppose imperfection in God to suppose that His idea of Himself is anything distinct from Himself. None will suppose that God has any such ideas as we, that are only, as it were, the shadows of things and not the very things. We cannot suppose that God reflects on Himself after the imperfect manner we reflect on things; for we can view nothing immediately. The immediate object of the mind's intuition is the idea always, and the soul perceives nothing but ideas. But God's intuition on Himself, without doubt, is immediate. But 'tis certain it can't be, except His idea be His essence. For His idea is the immediate object of His intuition. An absolutely perfect idea of a thing is the very thing; for it wants nothing that is in the thing, substance nor nothing else. That is the notion of the perfection of an idea, to want nothing; that is to say, whatsoever is perfect and absolutely like a thing is that thing. But

God's idea is absolutely perfect. I will form my reasoning thus: that nothing has any existence, any way at all, but in some consciousness or idea or other, and therefore that things that are in no created consciousness have no existence but in the divine idea—or, supposing the things in this room were in the idea of none but of God (they would have existence no other way as we have shown in natural philosophy)[71] and if the things in this room would nevertheless be real things, then God's idea, being a perfect idea, is really the thing itself and it (if so and all God's ideas are only His own ideas of Himself, as has been shown, must be His essence itself. It must be a substantial idea having all the perfection of the substance perfectly. So that by God's reflecting on Himself the being is begotten, that is, a substantial image of God begotten. I am satisfied that, though this word 'begotten' had never been used in Scripture, it would have been used in this case—that there is no other word that so properly expresses it. 'Tis this perfection of God's idea that makes all things truly and properly present to Him from all eternity, and is the reason why God has no succession; for everything that is, has been, or shall be, having been perfectly in God's idea from all eternity, and a perfect idea (which yet no finite being can have of anything) being the very thing, therefore all things from eternity were equally present with God, and there is no alteration made in idea by presence and absence, as there is in us.

Again, that which is the express and perfect image of God is God's idea of His own essence. There is nothing else can be an express and fully perfect image of God, but God's idea. Ideas are images of things and there are no other images of things in the most proper sense but ideas, because other things are only called images as they beget an idea in us of the thing of which they are the image—so that all other images of things are but images in a secondary sense. But we know that [the] Son of God is the express and perfect image of God, and His image in the primary and most proper sense. (2 Corinthians 4:4, "lest the light of the glorious gospel of Christ, who is the image of God, should shine unto them." Philippians 2:6, "who being in the form of God." Coloss. 1:15, "who is the image of the invisible God." Hebrews 1:3, "who being the brightness of his glory, and the express image of his person.")

Again, that image of God which God infinitely loves, and has His chief delight in, is the perfect idea of God. It has always been said that God's infinite delight consists in reflecting on Himself and viewing

---

[71] These words rather clearly indicate that, when Edwards wrote no. 94, he already distinguished his "natural philosophy" from his writings on *The Mind*. No. 94 was in all probability written before he settled in Northampton in 1727.

His own perfections or, which is the same thing, in His own perfect idea of Himself; so that 'tis acknowledged that God's infinite love is to, and His infinite delight [is] in, the perfect image of Himself. But the Scriptures tell us that the Son of God is that image of God which He infinitely loves. Nobody will deny this: that God infinitely loves His Son (John 3:35, "The Father loveth the Son;" 5:20). So it was declared from Heaven, by the Father at His baptism and transfiguration, "this is my beloved Son in whom I am well pleased." So the Father calls Him His elect, in which His soul delighteth (Isai. 42:1). He is called the beloved (Ephesians 1:6). The Son also declares that the Father's infinite happiness consisted in the enjoyment of Him; Proverbs 8:30, "I was daily His delight, rejoicing always before Him." Now none, I suppose, will say that God enjoys infinite happiness in two manners, one in the infinite delight He has in enjoying His Son, His image, and another in the view of Himself different from this. So if not, then these ways wherein God enjoys infinite happiness are both the same; that is, His infinite delight in the idea of Himself is the same with the infinite delight He has in His Son, and if so His Son and that idea He has of Himself are the same.

Again, that which is the express image of God, in which God enjoys infinite happiness, and is also the word of God is God's perfect idea of God. The word of God, in its most proper meaning, is a transcript of the divine perfections. This word is either the declared word of God or the essential. The one is the copy of the divine perfections given to us, the other is the perfect transcript thereof in God's own mind. But the perfect transcript of the perfections of God in the divine [mind] is the same with God's perfect idea of His own perfections. But I need tell none, how the Son of God is called the word of God.

Lastly, that which is the express image of God, in which He infinitely delights and which is His word and which is the reason or wisdom of God, is God's perfect idea of God. That God's knowledge or reason or wisdom is the same with God's idea, none will deny. And that all God's knowledge or wisdom consists in the knowledge or perfect idea of Himself is shown before and granted by all. But none needs to be told that the Son of God is often called in Scripture by the names of the wisdom and logos of God. Wherefore God Himself has put the matter beyond all debate, whether or no His Son is not the same with His idea of Himself; for it is most certain that His wisdom and knowledge is the very same with His idea of Himself. How much does the Son of God speak in proverbs under that name of wisdom!

There is very much of image of this in ourselves. Man is as if he were two, as some of the great wits of this age have observed. A sort of genie is with man, that accompanies him and attends wherever he goes, so that a man has conversation with himself. That is, he has a conversation with his own idea, so that, if his idea be excellent, he will take great delight and happiness in conferring and communing with it. He takes complacency in himself, he applauds himself. And wicked men accuse them[selves], and fight with themselves as if they were two. And man is truly happy then, and only then, when these two agree. And they delight in themselves and in their own idea and image as God delights in His.

The Holy Spirit is the act of God between the Father and the Son, infinitely loving and delighting in each other. Sure I am that, if the Father and the Son do infinitely delight in each other, there must be an infinitely pure and perfect act between them, an infinitely sweet energy which we call delight. This is certainly distinct from the other two. The delight and energy that is begotten in us by an idea is thus distinct from the idea, so it cannot be confounded in God, either with God begetting, or His idea and image—or Son. It is distinct from each of the other two, and yet it is God. The pure and perfect act of God is God, because God is a pure act. It appears that this is God, because that which acts perfectly is all act and nothing but act. There is image of this in created beings that approach to perfect action. How frequently do we say that the saints of Heaven are all transformed into love and dissolved into joy—become activity itself, changed into pure ecstasy! I acknowledge these are metaphorical in this case; but yet it is true that, the more perfect[72] the act is, the more it resembles those infinitely perfect acts of God in this respect. And I believe it will be plain to one that thinks intensely, that the perfect act of God must be a substantial act. We say that the perfect delights of reasonable creatures are substantial delights; but the delight of God is properly a substance, yea, an infinitely perfect substance, even the essence. It appears by the Holy Scriptures that the Holy Spirit is the perfect act of God. The name declares it, (1) the spirit of God denotes to us the activity, vivacity, and energy of God, and (2) it appears that the Holy Spirit is the pure act of God and energy of the deity, by His office, which is to activate us and quicken all things, and to beget energy and vivacity in the creature. And it also appears that the Holy Spirit is this act of the deity, even love and delight, because from eternity there was no other act in God but thus acting with respect to Himself, and delighting perfectly and infinitely in Himself as that infinite delight that is between the Father and the Son. For the object of God's perfect act must necessarily be Himself because there is no other. But

[72] Manuscript is torn.

we have shown that the object of the divine mind is God's Son and idea. And what other act can be thought of in God from eternity, but delighting in Himself, the act of love which God is (1 John 4:8, "he that loveth not, knoweth not God: for God is love")? And if God is love, and he that dwelleth in love dwelleth in God, and God in him, doubtless this intends principally that infinite love God has to Himself; so that the Scripture has told us that that love which is between the Father and Son is God. The Holy Spirit's name is the Comforter. But no doubt but 'tis the infinite delight God has in Himself is that Comforter, that is, the fountain of all delight and comfort.

It may be objected that at this rate one may prove an infinite number of persons in the Godhead; for each person has an idea of the other persons. Thus the Father may have an idea of His Son, but you will argue that His [i.e., the Son's] idea must be substantial. I answer, that the Son Himself is the Father's idea Himself, and, if He [i.e., the Son] has an idea of this idea, 'tis yet the same idea. A perfect idea of an idea is the same idea still to all intents and purposes. Thus, when I have a perfect idea of my idea of an equilateral triangle, it is an idea of the same equilateral triangle to all intents and purposes. So if you say that God the Father and Son may have an idea of their own delight in each other—but I say, a perfect idea or perception of one's own perfect delight cannot be different, at least in God, from that delight itself. You'll say, the Son has an idea of the Father. I answer, the Son Himself is the idea of the Father. And if you say, He has an idea of the Father, His idea is still an idea of the Father, and therefore the same with the Son. And if you say, the Holy Spirit has an idea of the Father, I answer, the Holy Ghost is Himself the delight and joyfulness of the Father in that idea, and of the idea in the Father. 'Tis still the idea of the Father. So that, if we turn in all the ways in the world, we shall never be able to make more than these three, God, the idea of God, and delight in God.

So I think it really evident from the light of reason that there are these three, distinct in God. If God has an idea of Himself, there is really a duplicity, because [if] there is no duplicity, it will follow that Jehovah thinks of Himself no more than a stone. And if God loves Himself and delight[s] in Himself, there is really a triplicity, three that cannot be confounded, each of which are the deity substantially. And this is the only distinction that can be found or thought of in God. If it shall be said that there are power, wisdom, goodness, and holiness in God, and that these may as well be proved to be distinct persons, because everything that is in God is God, [I answer], as to the power of God, power always consists in something—the power of the mind consists in its wisdom, the power of the body in plenty of animal spirits and toughness of limbs, etc.—and as it is distinct from those and other things, 'tis only a relation of adequateness and sufficiency of the essence to everything. But if we distinguish it from relation, 'tis nothing else but the essence of God. And if we take it for that which is that by which God exerts Himself, 'tis no other than the Father; for the perfect energy of God, with respect to Himself, is the most perfect exertion of Himself, of which the creation of the world is but a shadow. As to the wisdom of God, we have already observed that this wholly consists in God's idea of Himself, and is the same with the Son of God. And as to goodness, 'tis the perfect exertion of the essence of that attribute—it is nothing but infinite love which, the apostle John says, is God. And we have observed that all divine love may be resolved into God's infinite love to Himself. Therefore this attribute, as it was exerted from eternity, is nothing but the Holy Spirit, which is exactly agreeable to the notion some have had of the Trinity. And as to holiness, 'tis delight in excellency, 'tis God's sweet consent to Himself or, in other words, His perfect delight in Himself, which we have shown to be the Holy Spirit.

117. Trinity. Love is certainly the perfection as well as the happiness of a spirit. God doubtless, as He is infinitely perfect and happy, has infinite love. I cannot doubt but that God loves infinitely, properly speaking, and not only with that which some call self-love, whereby even the devils desire pleasure and are averse to pain, which is exceeding improperly called love and is nothing at all akin to that affection or delight which is [properly] called love. Then, there must have been an object from all eternity which God infinitely loves. But we have showed that all love arises from the perception, either of consent to being in general or a consent to that being that perceives.[73] Infinite loveliness to God, therefore, must consist either in infinite consent to entity in general or infinite consent to God. But we have shown that consent to entity and consent to God are the same, because God is the general and proper entity of all things. So that 'tis necessary that that object which God infinitely loves must be infinitely and perfectly consenting and agreeable to Him. But that which infinitely and perfectly agrees is the very same essence; for if it be different, it don't infinitely consent.

Again, we have shown that one alone cannot be excellent, inasmuch as, in such case, there can be no consent. Therefore, if God is excellent, there must be a plurality in God; otherwise there can be no consent in Him.

---

[73] See *The Mind*, no. 45, p. 47, above.

178. Spirit of God. 'Tis exceeding evident in natural philosophy that all the operations of the creatures are the immediate influence of the divine being; and that the method of influence is most simple, constant, and unvaried in the meanest and simplest beings, and more evident, compounded, and various and according to less simple rules in beings that are more perfect and compounded—and that in proportion as they are more or less perfect. 'Tis most simple in inanimate beings, less so in plants, more compounded still in the more-perfect plants, more evident in animals than in them, and most so in the most-perfect animal and most-compounded and least of all bound to constant laws—in man. And 'tis certainly beautiful that it should be so—that in the various ranks of beings those that are nearest to the first being should most evidently and variously partake of his influence; and 'tw'd be no more than just, to make out the proportion, if the soul of man be influenced by the operation of the Spirit of God, as the Scripture represents.

179. Logos. It the more confirms me in it (that the perfect idea God has of Himself is truly and properly God) that the existence of all corporeal things is only ideas.[74]

259. Trinity. 'Tis evident that there are no more than these three, really distinct in God—God, and His idea, and His love and delight. We can't conceive of any further real distinctions. If you say there is the power of God, I answer, the power of a being, even in creatures, is nothing distinct from the being itself besides a mere relation to an effect. If you say there is the infiniteness, eternity of God, and immutability of God—they are mere modes or manners of existence. If you say there is the wisdom of God—that is the idea of God. If you say there is the holiness of God—that is not different from His love, as we have shown, and is the Holy Spirit. If you say there is the goodness and mercy of God—they are included in His love, they are His love with a relation. We can find no more in God that (even in creatures) are distinct from the very being; or there is no more than these three in God but what (even in creatures) are nothing but the same with the very being, or only some mere modes or relations. Duration, expansion, changeableness or unchangeableness, so far as attributed to creatures, are only mere modes and relations of existence. There are no more than those three that are distinct in God, even in our way of conceiving. There is, in resemblance to this threefold distinction in God, a threefold distinction in a created spirit—namely, the spirit itself, and

---

[74] *Ibid.*

its understanding, and its will or inclination or love. And this indeed is all the real distinction there is in created spirits.

293. Spirit creation. It was made especially the Holy Spirit's work to bring the world to its beauty and perfection out of the chaos; for the beauty of the world is a communication of God's beauty. The Holy Spirit is the harmony and excellency and beauty of the deity, as we have shown. Therefore, 'twas His work to communicate beauty and harmony to the world, and so we read that it was He that moved upon the face of the waters.

308. Trinity. With respect to that objection against this explication of the Trinity that, according to this [sort] of reasoning, there would not only be three persons but an infinite number—for we must suppose that the Son understands the Father as well as the Father the Son, and consequently the Son has an idea of the Father, and so that idea will be another person, and so [it] may be said of the Holy Ghost—this objection is but a color without substance, and arises from a confusion of thought and a misunderstanding of what we say. In the first place, we don't suppose that the Father and the Son and the Holy Ghost are three distinct beings that have three distinct understandings. It is the divine essence that understands, and it is the divine essence that is understood. 'Tis the divine being that loves, and it is the divine being that is loved. The Father understands, the Son understands, and the Holy Ghost understands because every one is the same understanding divine essence, and not that each of them have a distinct understanding of their own. 2. We never supposed that [the] Father generated the Son by understanding the Son, but that God generated the Son by understanding His own essence, and therefore the Son is that idea itself or understanding of the essence. The Father understands the Son no otherwise than as He understands the essence—that is, the essence of the Son. The Father understands the idea He has merely in His having that idea, without any other act. Thus a man understands his own partial idea merely by his having that idea in mind. So the Son understands the Father, in that the essence of the Son understands the essence of the Father as, in Himself, the understanding of the essence. And so of the Holy Ghost. After you have in your imagination multiplied understandings and loves never so often, it will be the understanding and loving of the very same essence, and can never make more than these three, God, and the idea of God, and the love of God. I would not be understood to pretend to give a full explication of the Trinity; for I think it still remains an incomprehensible mystery, the greatest and the most glorious of all mysteries.

309. Trinity. The name of the second person in the Trinity, Λόγος, evidences that He is God's idea, whether we translate the word 'the reason of God' or 'the word of God.' If the reason or the understanding of God, the matter is past dispute; for everyone will own that the reason or understanding of God is His idea. And if we translate it 'the word of God,' 'tis either the outward word of God or His inward. None will say He is His outward. Now the outward word is speech, but the inward word, which is the original of it, is thought, the Scripture being its own interpreter. For how often [is] thinking in Scripture called speaking, when applied to God and men! So that 'tis the idea, if we take Scripture for our guide, that is the inward word.

Unity of the Godhead

651. One God. Unity of the Godhead. It appears that there is but one Creator and governor of the world by considering how the world is created and governed. The world is evidently so created and governed as to answer but one design in all the different parts of it and in all ages, and therefore we may justly argue that 'tis but one design that orders the world. This appears, first, by the mutual subserviency of all the various parts of the world. This great body is as much one, and all the members of it mutually dependent and subservient, as in the body of man one part is so and acts so and is in every respect ordered so as constantly to promote the design that others are made for. All the parts help one another and mutually forward each other's ends. In all the immense variety of things that there are in the world, every one has such a nature and is so ordered in every respect and circumstance as to comply with the rest of the universe, and to fall in with and subserve to the purposes of the other parts. This argues that 'tis the same design and contrivance or the same designing, contriving being that makes and orders one part as doth the other. It appears also, 2. by this: that the same laws of nature obtain throughout the universe; every part of matter, everywhere, is governed by exactly the same laws, which laws are only the appointment of the governors. This argues, therefore, that they are all governed by one appointment or will. 3. The same laws obtain in all ages, without any alteration. There is no alteration seen in any one instance, in all those numberless and infinitely various effects that are the result of those laws in different circumstances. This argues that 'tis not several that have the government by turns, but that 'tis one being that has the management of the same things in all ages of the world—one design and contrivance. [Not] only the identity of law in inanimate beings, but in the same sort of animals, especially in

the nature of man, in all men, in all ages of the world, shows that all men in all ages are in the hand of the same being. Another thing that argues that the world has but one Creator and governor is the great analogy that is in the works of creation and providence; the analogy there is in the bodies of all animals and in all plants and in the different parts of the inanimate creation; and the analogy there is, likewise, between the corporeal and spiritual parts of the creation; and the analogy in the constitution and government of different orders of being—this argues that the whole is the fruit of but one wisdom and design.

697. Unity of the Godhead. The unity of the Godhead will necessarily follow from God's being infinite; for to be infinite is to be all, and it would be a contradiction to suppose two alls, because, if there be two or more, one alone is not all but the sum of them put together are all. Infinity and omneity, if I may so speak, must go together, because, if any being falls short of omneity, then it is not infinite. Therein it is limited. Therein there is something that it don't extend to or that it don't comprehend. If there be something more, then there is something beyond. And wherein this being don't reach and include that which is beyond, therein it is limited—its bounds stop short of this that is not comprehended. An infinite being, therefore, must be an all-comprehending being. He must comprehend in himself all being. That there should be another being underived and independent, and so no way comprehended, will argue him not to be infinite, because then there is something more, there is more entity. There is some entity beside what is in this being, and therefore his entity can't be infinite. Those two beings put together are more than one; for they taken together are a sum total, and one taken alone is but a part of that sum total and therefore is finite. For whatsoever is a part is finite. God, as He is infinite and the being whence all are derived and from whom everything is given, does comprehend the entity of all His creatures; and their entity is not to be added to His, as not comprehended in it, for they are but communications from Him. Communications of being ben't additions of being. The reflections of the sun's light don't add at all to the sum total of the light. 'Tis true mathematicians conceive of greater than infinite, in some respects, and of several infinites being added one to another; but 'tis because they are in some respect finite, as a thing conceived infinitely long may not be infinitely thick, and so its thickness may be added to. Or if it be conceived infinitely long one way, yet it may be conceived having bounds or an end another. But God is in no respect limited, and therefore can in no respect be added to.

Vanity of the World

725. Vanity of the world. After the fall, the place of paradise was altered. It was changed from earth to Heaven, and God ordered it so that nothing paradisiacal should be any more here. And though sometimes there be great appearances of it and men are ready to flatter themselves that they shall obtain it, yet it is found that paradise is not here, and there is nothing but the shadow of it. Those things that look most paradisiacal will have some sting to spoil them.

Wisdom of the Creation

192. Wisdom of the creation. The contrivance of the organs of speech are peculiarly wonderful. In the first place, no other way in the world can be thought of so convenient for the communicating our minds as by sounds. But one would think that it would be impossible that it should be done by sounds, or that organs should be contrived that should quickly and easily give so many clearly distinguishable sounds and yet short ones, as there are innumerable different sentiments of mind to be expressed. For we see nothing else in the world by which such a distinction can be made, or anything like. We can make but few distinct sounds by anything else we can find or make—but with the organs of speech an infinite number, by the various ordering of the throat and tongue. And these distinctions are very clear and plain, and yet all reducible to a very few simple ones, so that almost every sound may be, by rule, easily reduced to four and twenty letters,[75] and at the same time these organs shall be excellently adapted to innumerable other uses.

World Will Come to an End

867. Christian religion. Immortality of the soul. A future state. That this world will come to an end. The natural world, which is in such continual labor, as is described in the first chapter of Ecclesiastes, constantly going round in such revolutions, will doubtless come to an end. These revolutions are not for nothing. There is some great event and issue of things that this labor is for, some grand period aimed at. Does God make the world restless, to move and revolve in all its parts, to make no progress, to labor with motions so mighty and vast, only to come to the same place again, to be just where it was before? Doubtless some end is nearer approached to by these revolutions. Some great end is nearer to an accomplishment after a thousand revolutions

---

[75] *Ibid.*

are finished than when there was only one finished or before the first revolution began. The sun don't go round day after day and year after year for no other end but only to come to the same place again from whence it first set out, and to bring the world to the same state again that it was in before. The waters of the sea are not so restless, continually, to ascend into the heavens, and then descend on the earth, and then return to the sea again, only that things may be as they were before. One generation of men don't come, another go, and so continually from age to age, only that at last there may be what there was at first, viz., mankind upon earth. The wheels of God's chariot, after they have gone round a thousand times, don't remain just in the same place that they were in at first, without having carried the chariot nearer to a journey's end. We see it is not so in the lesser parts of the creation that are systems by themselves, as the world is a great system, and where the revolutions very much resemble those in the great system, as in the body of men and other animals. The reciprocation of the heart and lungs, and the circulation of the blood, and the continual circular labors of all parts of the system are not to last always. They tend to a journey's end. See No. 990. See No. 547.[76]

Corollary 1. This is a confirmation of a future state; for if these revolutions have not something in another state that is to succeed this that they are subservient to, then they are in vain. If anything of this world is to remain after the revolutions of this world are at an end, doubtless it will be that part of this world that is the end of all the rest, or that creature for which all the rest is made. And that is man. For if he wholly ceases, and is extinct, it is as if the whole were totally extinct, because he is the end of all. He is that creature to serve whom the labors and revolutions of this world are, and whom they affect. And therefore, if he don't remain after the revolutions have ceased, then no end is obtained by all those revolutions. Because nothing abides as the fruit of 'em after they are finished but all comes to no more than just what was before any of those revolutions, or before this world itself began, viz., an universal nonexistence. All is extinct, and all is as if the world never had been, and therefore all has been in vain; for nothing remains as the fruit. He that is carried in the chariot don't remain after he is brought, with so much labor and vast ado, to the end of his journey, but ceases to be, as the chariot itself does.

Corollary 2. This confirms the divinity of the Christian revelation, which gives this account of things: that this world is to come to an end; it is to be destroyed; that the revolutions of the world have an appointed period; and that man, the end of this lower world, is to

[76] No. 990, p. 265; no. 547, p. 134.

remain in being afterwards; and gives a most rational account of the good period, design, and issue of all things worthy of the infinite wisdom and majesty of God.

990. That the world will come to an end. See No. 867. As it is with the body of man—its meat and its clothing perishes and is continually renewed, and at last the body itself perishes; the food that is taken down quickly perishes and is cast forth to the dunghill, and there is a constant succession of new food; and its garments are worn out and new garments are put on, one after another; at last the body itself, that is thus fed and clothed, wears out—so there is all reason to think it will be with the world, it that needs nourishment. The face of the earth continually needs a new supply of rain, and also of nitrous parts by the snow and frost or by other means gradually drawn in from the atmosphere that it is encompassed with, and of nourishment by falling leaves or rotting plants or otherwise to feed it. The sea is constantly fed by rain and rivers to maintain it. The earth, in all parts, has constant new supplies of water to maintain its fountains and streams that are, as it were, its arteries and veins. The sun itself, that nourishes the whole planetary system, is nourished by comets,[77] by new supplies from time to time communicated from them. And so the world is continually changing its garments, as it were. The face of the earth is annually clothed, as it were, with new garments, and is stripped naked in the winter. The successive generations of inhabitants and successive kingdoms and empires and new states of things in the world are, as it were, new garments; and as these wear out, one after another, so there is reason to think the world itself, whose meat and clothing thus perishes, will itself perish at last. The body of man often lies down and sleeps and rises up again, but at last will lie down and rise no more. So the world every year, as it were, perishes in the winter or sinks into an image of death, as sleep is in the body of man, but it is renewed again in the spring. But at last it will perish and rise no more.

1038. Those kind of heavenly bodies called comets give great evidence that the world is not from eternity and will come to an end, and that this is true not only of this globe of the earth but also of the whole visible creation, for:

1. Those celestial bodies are very considerable parts of the frame of the universe. They are large bodies, and there is a great number of

[77] Newton expressed this view in a private conversation late in life, but it was first reported long after his death. The memorandum was found among the Conduitt papers and first published by Edmond Turnor in 1806. See Sir David Brewster, *The Life of Sir Isaac Newton*, 1831, p. 320, Appendix III; see also L. T. More, *Isaac Newton, a Biography*, 1934, p. 662.

them, much greater than of planets, and they have ever appeared from age to age, as far as any history reaches back. It would, therefore, be unreasonable to suppose any other than that they are coeval with the frame of the universe. But these bodies cannot have been from eternity; for nothing is more manifest than [that] they are constantly spending themselves, sending forth, in vast and continual streams, parts of themselves clear off from their own bodies, and at most places to a vast distance into the immense etherial expanse. And there is nothing appears of any continual reflux or constant stream of matter to them to answer it. Yea, 'tis very manifest there is no such thing—these bodies moving nowhere but to and fro in the empty etherial spaces where are no bodies with which they have communication to repay their expenses and restore their loss. Therefore, it must be that they suffer a constant diminution, and therefore cannot have been from eternity, and will in length of time, if the frame of the universe continue long enough, be totally spent. And it being so, 'tis so manifest that a very considerable part of the frame of the universe that has hitherto stood through all past ages will come to an end. It is a great argument that the whole is to be dissolved.

2. What must be naturally, and almost necessarily, supposed to be the use of those bodies argues that the whole universe is corruptible and must come to an end. For seeing they are constantly expending and wasting themselves, and sending forth their own substance, and that substance that they emit is not annihilated, it must necessarily be that other parts of the frame of the universe must receive what they expend. And since the etherial spaces are not replete with what they emit but still remain empty spaces, and since also there is no part of these spaces but where the attraction of the heavenly bodies reaches, as the sun and planets, it must necessarily follow that this matter gradually gathers to them. And since the attraction of the sun through all parts of these etherial spaces, excepting what is very near the bodies of the planets, is vastly greater than of all other bodies, it will follow that most of this matter is drawn to the sun; hence we may argue that the use of it is continually to repair the sun's expense by its constant immense profusion of beams of light. Whence we may suppose that, when those comets are all spent and wasted, as they can't last always, the sun will want this nourishment and, having no new supplies, must be gradually spent and so the solar system be destroyed. The same may doubtless be said of the fixed stars, those bodies shining by their own light; their expense of beams must gradually destroy them as necessarily as the sun, and hence all must in time come to an end. See further, 1041.

1041. Add this to 1038. The world is not from eternity and will come to an end.

3. What now appears in the motions of these comets is an evidence that the world is not from eternity. For these bodies, some of them at least, are so long in performing their revolutions, and have their course through the system of the planets and athwart their courses, whereby they are in the way of having their motions disturbed by their attractions, and come so very near the sun in some part of their orbit, and are at so vast a distance from it in other parts, at which time they are more within the reach of the attraction of other fixed stars, and so little a variation of their motions being sufficient to destroy them by causing them to strike the body of the sun, as particularly that noted comet that appeared *anno* 1680—I say, considering all these things, 'tis impossible that in a course of nature their motions should be continued from eternity, an infinitely less than an eternal duration being sufficient quite to destroy their motions that are so in the way of disturbance. Indeed, the disturbance of their motions may be such as to bring their orbits nearer to circles, and to cause them to keep at a greater distance from the sun, as well as to make the ellipses in which they move narrower, so as to bring them nearer to the sun, and at length to strike its body. But in either, we must suppose a gradual variation which can't fail at length of coming to a destruction of their motions, unless we suppose an infinitely exact adjustment of accidents that disturb their motion, so as exactly to rectify at one time what is disordered at another, and so maintain the revolution throughout eternity—which supposition would equally militate against the scheme of those that hold the eternity of the world, and so its independence on a Creator.

And as their motion must needs be something disturbed by the planets, so the motion of the planets must mutually be disturbed by them, and so the whole system must gradually be destroyed. The motion of the comets must be something disturbed and retarded by the stream of the sun's beams which they pass through; for as these beams are corporeal, and the motion of the comets being athwart the course of the stream of rays, [they] must be retarded by them, nothing the less for the swift motion of those rays. It is all one whether those particles of matter are at rest or in motion, as to impeding the motions of the comets, provided that motion be neither their motion nor against it but at right angles with it—as the motion of comets, take one time with another, is. However subtle the matter of the sun beams is, yet the quantity of matter is something, especially very near the sun's body where some of the comets come.

4. Without the exact care of a wise Creator and disposer, these comets must needs have had their motion destroyed, and have destroyed the motions of some of the planets by clashing with them, or by coming from time to time very near to them. There being so great a number of them, and their motion being every way, in all manner of directions through the expanse of the heavens, some of them athwart or very near the course of some of the planets and the course of other comets, as particularly it has been observed that the course of that comet that appeared in the year 1680 was very near the orbit of the earth—therefore it could not but have come to pass before now that they should have clashed or crossed one another so often as to have destroyed the motion one of another, so that at least the regular and almost equable and circular motion of the earth, on which its welfare depends, should long ago have been destroyed.

If any one says that perhaps there was once a vastly greater number of planets and comets, and all whose directions and courses were such as to cross one another have clashed long ago, and have destroyed each other, and fallen down into the sun, and none are now left but such as can move freely without mutual disturbance—to this I answer two things:

1. This is not true in fact, as has been observed of the courses of the earth and the comet that appeared in 1680 that still remain across one another, or coming very near one to another.

2. If this supposition should be allowed, it would [not] help the matter. If that ever was the case, that there [was] a vastly greater number of planets and comets, many of which crossed one another in their motions and in process of time crashed and destroyed one another, if this ever was, it was at some certain season. And if it was at a certain season, it was a certain number of years or ages ago. And if so, then it was infinitely later than from eternity, and so the same difficulty returns, viz., why didn't these heavenly bodies clash sooner, when they had been in motion an eternity before that? How came it to pass they maintained their motions without destroying one another through an infinite duration?

Numerical Index to Selections from the *Miscellanies*